ADVANCED DUNGEONS & DRAGONS®

SPECIAL REFERENCE WORK

PLAYERS HANDBOOK

A COMPILED VOLUME OF INFORMATION FOR PLAYERS OF
ADVANCED DUNGEONS & DRAGONS, INCLUDING: CHARACTER RACES,
CLASSES, AND LEVEL ABILITIES; SPELL TABLES AND DESCRIPTIONS;
EQUIPMENT COSTS; WEAPONS DATA; AND INFORMATION ON ADVENTURING.

by Gary Gygax
© **1978 — TSR Games**
All rights reserved
Illustrations by David C. Sutherland III
D. A. Trampier
Cover by D. A. Trampier

Printed in U.S.A.
6th Printing, January, 1980
ISBN 0-935696-01-6

FOREWORD

Players, players, and more players — that's what comprises the **D&D** phenomenon. And phenomenal is what it is, as the audience for this, the granddaddy of all role-playing games, continues to expand.

D&D players, happily, come in all shapes and sizes, and even a fair number of women are counted among those who regularly play the game — making **DUNGEONS & DRAGONS** somewhat special in this regard. This widespread appeal cuts across many boundaries of interest and background, which means that **D&D** players are marked by a wide range of diversity. In fact, one could easily use the analogy that there are as many *types* of **D&D** players as there are **D&D** monsters (after that, draw your own conclusions!). There are unquestionably fast players, slow players, clever players, foolish players, cautious players, reckless players, generous players, greedy players, friendly players, and obnoxious players...

As diverse as this melange of enthusiasts is, they all seem to share one commonality: a real love for **DUNGEONS & DRAGONS** and a devotion that few other games can claim. This remarkable loyalty is a great factor in the game's explosion of popularity, and **DUNGEONS & DRAGONS** has become a gaming cult, as avid **D&Der's** have ceaselessly "spread the gospel", enrolling new players in expanding groups which just seem to grow and grow.

If you're reading this, then you're a **D&D** player — and this book is for you! This is the second release of the **ADVANCED DUNGEONS & DRAGONS** series, and is designed to be a player's book in every respect — giving you all the background you require on the game system, as well as the information you'll need to go adventuring. Although this book does not stand alone in terms of supplying all information needed to undertake a campaign, it will complement the other two parts of the whole (the previously released **MONSTER MANUAL** and the upcoming **DUNGEON MASTERS GUIDE**) to provide the entirety of what will be **ADVANCED DUNGEONS & DRAGONS** (along with a greatly expanded version of **GODS, DEMI-GODS & HEROES** which will follow).

The sheer bulk of this book may seem considerable (and it is, of course), but there are many things *not* included. These things (such as the details of the combat tables, for instance) are those parts of the game that rightly fall outside the realm of player reference, and thus are included instead in the more voluminous **DUNGEON MASTERS GUIDE**. As the author points out, this bit of the "unknown" outside of the players' normal reach will make the game much more interesting and challenging.

ADVANCED DUNGEONS & DRAGONS is a game that is demanding for players and Dungeon Masters alike, but the rewards in terms of enjoyment are vast. There is nothing quite like a successful **D&D** campaign, and its success is based upon the efforts of all participants. The Dungeon Master is pivotal, of course, but the players are just as important, for they are the primary actors and actresses in the fascinating drama which unfolds before them. For that reason, their outlook and their conduct will greatly affect the flavor and tempo of the campaign. Accordingly, they should do their best to further the success of the entire undertaking. This is often no more than a matter of simple etiquette, and following a few simple guidelines will suffice to make the game experience more fun for everyone concerned, to wit:

1) Be an organized player; have the necessary information on your character readily at hand and available to the Dungeon Master.

2) Cooperate with the Dungeon Master and respect his decisions; if you disagree, present your viewpoint with deference to his position as game moderator. Be prepared to accept his decision as final and remember that not everything in the game will always go your way!

3) Cooperate with the other players and respect their right to participate. Encourage new and novice players by making suggestions and allowing them to make decisions on courses of action rather than dictating their responses.

4) If you are unable to participate in an adventure, give the other players and the DM some concrete guidelines if your character is going to be included in the adventuring group; be prepared to accept the consequences, good or bad, in any case.

5) Get in the spirit of the game, and use your persona to play with a special personality all its own. Interact with the other player characters and non-player characters to give the game campaign a unique flavor and "life". Above all, let yourself go, and enjoy!

Enough of the preliminaries — let's get on with the game! Let's see now, where did I stash away all those material components?...

Mike Carr
TSR Games & Rules Editor

2 June 1978

CONTENTS

APPENDICES

TABLES AND CHARTS

PREFACE

The whole of **ADVANCED DUNGEONS & DRAGONS** was a project which involved varying degrees of my thought, imagination, and actual working time over a period of more than a year and one-half. Because of other demands, the project was perforce set aside for a day or a week or even longer, making it hard to get back to. Knowing that this would be the case when I began, the **MONSTER MANUAL** was selected as the first of the three volumes in the advanced game to work on — hundreds of different creatures lend themselves to segmental treatment. Only after that book was finished did I begin to put the sheaved reams of notes for the Players and Dungeon Masters books into order, and that only as the bones — tables, charts and matrices — for rough typing and careful rechecking before a final manuscript was built around them.

This latter part of the **ADVANCED DUNGEONS & DRAGONS** project I approached with no small amount of trepidation. After all, the game's major appeal is to those persons with unusually active imagination and superior, active intellect — a very demanding audience indeed. Furthermore, a great majority of readers master their own dungeons and are necessarily creative — the most critical audience of all! Authoring these works means that, in a way, I have set myself up as final arbiter of fantasy role playing in the minds of the majority of **D&D** adventurers. Well, so be it, I rationalized. Who better than the individual responsible for it all as creator of the "Fantasy Supplement" in **CHAINMAIL**, the progenitor of **D&D**; and as the first proponent of fantasy gaming and a principal in TSR, the company one thinks of when fantasy games are mentioned, the credit and blame rests ultimately here. Some last authority must be established for a very good reason.

There is a need for a certain amount of uniformity from campaign to campaign in **D&D**. This is not to say that *conformity* or sameness is desirable. Nobody wishes to have stale campaigns where dungeons, monsters, traps, tricks, and goals are much the same as those encountered in any one of a score of other campaigns. Uniformity means that classes are relatively the same in abilities and approach to solving the problems with which the campaign confronts them. Uniformity means that treasure and experience are near a reasonable mean. Uniformity means that the campaign is neither a give-away show nor a killer — that rewards are just that, and great risk will produce commensurate rewards, that intelligent play will give characters a fighting chance of survival.

No individual can actually dictate the actual operations of a campaign, however, for that is the prerogative of the Dungeon Master, first and foremost, and to the players in the individual campaign thereafter. In like manner, players greatly influence the events of each particular campaign, and they must accept a large portion of blame if it is a poor game, and if the campaign is outstanding, they deserve high praise for helping to shape the game and playing well. So at best I give you parameters here, and the rest is up to the individuals who are the stuff **D&D** is made of.

Naturally, every attempt has been made to provide all of the truly essential information necessary for the game: the skeleton and muscle which each DM will flesh out to create the unique campaign. You will find no pretentious dictums herein, no baseless limits arbitrarily placed on female strength or male charisma, no ponderous combat systems for greater ''realism'', there isn't a hint of a spell point system whose record keeping would warm the heart of a monomaniacal statistics lover, or anything else of the sort. You will find material which enables the Dungeon Master to conduct a campaign which is challenging, where the unexpected is the order of the day, and much of what takes place has meaning and reason within the framework of the game ''world''.

It is important to keep in mind that, after all is said and done, **ADVANCED DUNGEONS & DRAGONS** is a game. Because it is a game, certain things which seem ''unrealistic'' or simply unnecessary are integral to the system. Classes have restrictions in order to give a varied and unique approach to each class when they play, as well as to provide play balance. Races are given advantages or limits mainly because the whole character of the game would be drastically altered if it were otherwise. Everything in the **ADVANCED DUNGEONS & DRAGONS** system has purpose; most of what is found herein is essential to the campaign, and those sections which are not — such as sub-classes of characters, psionics, and similar material — are clearly labeled as optional for inclusion.

What is here is, hopefully, presented in as logical a sequence as possible, clearly, understandably, and with as few ambiguities as could be managed. Many readers will want more material. There is a wealth of commercial and fan material available for fulfilling such needs. Similarly, even the most important material herein can be altered and bent to suit the needs of individual campaigns. Where possible, true *guidelines* have been laid down to provide the barest of frameworks for those areas of the campaign which should be the most unusual and unique. Read the work (or both works if you are a DM) through and assess for yourself what **ADVANCED D&D** really is. I am convinced that it does for the old **D&D** + supplements what **GREYHAWK** did for **D&D** when it first appeared, and then some. I have put into these works what should be the important parts of a superior **D&D** campaign, cutting out material which actually adds little or nothing to the game, revising the old, and adding and expanding in the essential areas.

Special thanks are due to the following persons who contributed to the original game or have been so kind as to give their comments, criticism, and contributions to this game: Dave Arneson, Peter Aronson, Brian Blume, Joe Fischer, Ernie Gygax, Tom Holsinger, Timothy Jones, Tim Kask, Jeff Key, Rob Kuntz, Len Lakofka, Alan Lucion, Steve Marsh, Mike Mornard, Doug Schwegman, Dennis Sustare, Dave Sutherland, Dave Trampier, Jim Ward, Tom Wham, Skip Williams, and all of the good players and kindly Dungeon Masters who have taken the time to talk with me at conventions or drop me a line in order to pass on their experiences, suggestions and ideas. Also thanks to Judges Guild, whose suggestions have helped with this work, and whose products have helped **D&D**.

INTRODUCTION

Even if you are not familiar with fantasy role playing games in general, and **DUNGEONS & DRAGONS** in particular, you will find this work (with its companion volumes, **MONSTER MANUAL** and **DUNGEON MASTERS GUIDE**) is a complete game system in itself. It will stand alone, and it has been written and edited in order to make the whole as easily understood as possible without taking anything away from its complexity and completeness. If, on the other hand, you are a veteran adventurer of many swords & sorcery campaign games, **ADVANCED DUNGEONS & DRAGONS** will prove to be superior to any past offerings in the fantasy role playing game field. You will find it easy to integrate your existing character or characters into the new system, and at the same time the game will be both familiar and different. There are nuances not found in previous efforts. All the necessary information is presented in clear and concise terms, in a format which logically follows the flow of play.

The characters and races from which the players select are carefully thought out and balanced to give each a distinct and different approach to the challenges posed by the game. Advantages and disadvantages, advancement in level, characteristics and abilities are all detailed and explained so that selection of a player-character type — or the integration of an existing character — can be done with foreknowledge and projection. In a similar vein, the individuals running the campaign games, the *Dungeon Masters*, will have available more data and guidelines upon which to build more interesting and detailed milieux.

Clerics and fighters have been strengthened in relation to magic-users, although not overly so. Clerics have more and improved spell capability. Fighters are more effective in combat and have other new advantages as well. Still, magic-users are powerful indeed, and they have many new spells. None of these over-shadow thieves. All recommended sub-classes — druids, paladins, rangers, illusionists, and assassins — as well as the special *monk* class of character, are included in order to assure as much variety of approach as possible. Non-human races — dwarven, elven, gnome, half-elven, half-orcish, and halfling — are likewise included. Each offers some advantage and difference, yet has distinct disadvantages, just as human characters do. But some readers might still be wondering what fantasy role playing games are all about, so enough about contents and on to explanations.

ADVANCED DUNGEONS & DRAGONS is a world. Of course, this world is not complete. It needs organizers and adventurers to order and explore it. It needs you! A fantasy role playing game is an exercise in imagination and personal creativity. The organizer of the campaign, the Dungeon Master, must use the system to devise an individual and unique world. Into this world of weird monsters, strange peoples, multitudinous states, and fabulous treasures of precious items and powerful magic stride fearless adventurers — you and your fellow players. Inexperienced and of but small power at first, by dint of hard fighting and clever deeds, these adventurers advance in ability to become forces to be reckoned with — high priests or priestesses, lords, wizards and arch-magi, master thieves. The abilities of each adventurer are fixed, but even such characteristics as strength, intelligence, and wisdom are mutable in a fantasy world. By means of group co-operation and individual achievement, an adventurer can become ever more powerful. Even death loses much of its sting, for often the character can be resurrected, or reincarnated. And should that fail there is always the option to begin again with a new character. Thus **ADVANCED DUNGEONS & DRAGONS** is, as are most role playing games, open-ended. There is no "winner", no final objective, and the campaign grows and changes as it matures.

This new system provides the Dungeon Master with more and better material from which to devise the campaign milieu, and that in turn means a more interesting and imaginative game for the players. A word of advice is in order here regarding this new system:

Considerable enjoyment and excitement in early play stems from not knowing exactly what is going on. Being uncertain of how a given situation will turn out, not knowing every magic item available, and so forth, adds spice to the game. Later, this knowledge simulates actual experience, for the seasoned campaigner will have learned through game play. Under the circumstances, it is strongly urged that players do not purchase or read the **DUNGEON MASTERS GUIDE**. Leave discovery of the information therein to actual adventuring, and you will find that the game is even more fun! Some of the details of the campaign milieu — worldly knowledge common to a typical adventurer — will be given to you by your Dungeon Master. Exploration, travel, and adventure in the "world" will eventually reveal the secrets heretofore hidden, and the joy of actually earning them will be well worth the wait.

Enjoy the game, and always bear in mind that it is fantasy. Magical worlds have a strange way of differing, but while yours may not be quite the same as the one described here, it is ripe for adventure and plunder. Cleverness and imagination, along with a bit of luck, will always prevail — won't they?

THE GAME

Swords & sorcery best describes what this game is all about, for those are the two key fantasy ingredients. **ADVANCED DUNGEONS & DRAGONS** is a fantasy game of role playing which relies upon the imagination of participants, for it is certainly make-believe, yet it is so interesting, so challenging, so mind-unleashing that it comes near reality.

As a role player, *you become* Falstaff the fighter. You know how strong, intelligent, wise, healthy, dexterous and, relatively speaking, how commanding a personality you have. Details as to your appearance, your body proportions, and your history can be produced by you or the Dungeon Master. You act out the game as this character, staying within your "god-given abilities", and as molded by your philosophical and moral ethics (called alignment). You interact with your fellow role players, not as Jim and Bob and Mary who work at the office together, but as Falstaff the fighter, Angore the cleric, and Filmar, the mistress of magic! The Dungeon Master will act the parts of "everyone else", and will present to you a variety of new characters to talk with, drink with, gamble with, adventure with, and often fight with! Each of you will become an artful thespian as time goes by — and you will acquire gold, magic items, and great renown as you become Falstaff the Invincible!

This game lets all of your fantasies come true. This is a world where monsters, dragons, good and evil high priests, fierce demons, and even the gods themselves may enter your character's life. Enjoy, for this game is what dreams are made of!!

The game is ideally for three or more adult players: one player must serve as the *Dungeon Master*, the shaper of the fantasy milieu, the "world" in which all action will take place. The other participants become *adventurers* by creating characters to explore the fantastic world and face all of its challenges — monsters, magic, and unnamed menaces. As is typical for most of us in real life, each character begins at the bottom of his or her chosen class (or profession). By successfully meeting the challenges posed, they gain *experience* and move upwards in power, just as actual playing experience really increases playing skill. Imagination, intelligence, problem solving ability, and memory are all continually exercised by participants in the game.

Although the masculine form of appellation is typically used when listing the level titles of the various types of characters, these names can easily be changed to the feminine if desired. This is fantasy — what's in a name? In all but a few cases sex makes no difference to ability!

As with most other role playing games, this one is not just a single-experience contest. It is an ongoing campaign, with each playing session related to the next by results and participant characters who go from episode to episode. As players build the experience level of their characters and go forth seeking ever greater challenges, they must face stronger monsters and more difficult problems of other sorts (and here the Dungeon Master must likewise increase his or her ability and inventiveness). While initial adventuring usually takes place in an underworld dungeon setting, play gradually expands to encompass other such dungeons, town and city activities, wilderness explorations, and journeys into other dimensions, planes, times, worlds, and so forth. Players will add characters to their initial adventurer as the milieu expands so that each might actually have several characters, each involved in some separate and distinct adventure form, busily engaged in the game at the same moment of "Game Time". This allows participation by many players in games which are substantially different from game to game as dungeon, metropolitan, and outdoor settings are rotated from playing to playing. And perhaps a war between players will be going on (with battles actually fought out on the tabletop with minature figures) one night, while on the next, characters of these two contending players are helping each other to survive somewhere in a wilderness.

Each individual campaign has its own distinct properties and "flavor". A good Dungeon Master will most certainly make each game a surpassing challenge for his or her players. Treasure and experience gained must be taken at great risk or by means of utmost cleverness only. If the game is not challenging, if advancement is too speedy, then it becomes staid and boring. Conversely, a game can be too deadly and become just as boring, for who enjoys endlessly developing new characters to march off into oblivion in a single night of dungeon adventuring?!

Sometimes, however, because of close interaction (or whatever other reason) two or more Dungeon Masters will find that their games are compatible to the extent that participants in these individual campaigns can use the characters created in one to adventure in the others. In such cases the Dungeon Masters have created a very interesting ''world'' indeed, for their milieux will offer interesting differences and subtle shifts which will pose highly challenging problems to these players.

Ultimately, despite the fact that this is a game system created by someone else, the game's viability rests principally with the referee. The Dungeon Master must design and map out the dungeon, town, city, and world maps. He or she must populate the whole world, create its past history, and even devise some rationale for what transpired (and will probably happen). As players, you help immeasurably by participating, by letting the referee know that you appreciate his or her efforts, and by playing well and in a sportsmanly fashion. Good play inspires better creations to challenge that play.

Skilled players always make a point of knowing what they are doing, i.e. they have an objective. They co-operate — particularly at lower levels or at higher ones when they must face some particularly stiff challenge — in order to gain their ends. Superior players will not fight everything they meet, for they realize that wit is as good a weapon as the sword or the spell. When weakened by wounds, or nearly out of spells and vital equipment, a clever party will seek to leave the dungeons in order to re-arm themselves. (He who runs away lives to fight another day.) When faced with a difficult situation, skilled players will not attempt endless variations on the same theme; when they find the method of problem solving fails to work, they begin to devise other possible solutions. Finally, good players will refrain from pointless argument and needless harassment of the Dungeon Master when such bog the play of the game down into useless talking. Mistakes are possible, but they are better righted through reason and logic, usually at the finish of play for the day.

This game is unlike chess in that the rules are not cut and dried. In many places they are guidelines and suggested methods only. This is part of the attraction of **ADVANCED DUNGEONS & DRAGONS**, and it is integral to the game. Rules not understood should have appropriate questions directed to the publisher; disputes with the Dungeon Master are another matter entirely. THE REFEREE IS THE FINAL ARBITER OF ALL AFFAIRS OF HIS OR HER CAMPAIGN. Participants in a campaign have no recourse to the publisher, but they do have ultimate recourse — since the most effective protest is withdrawal from the offending campaign. Each campaign is a specially tailored affair. While it is drawn by the referee upon the outlines of the three books which comprise **ADVANCED DUNGEONS & DRAGONS**, the players add the color and details, so the campaign must ultimately please all participants. It is *their* unique world. You, the reader, as a member of the campaign community, do not belong if the game seems wrong in any major aspect. Withdraw and begin your own campaign by creating a milieu which suits you and the group which you must form to enjoy the creation. (And perhaps you will find that preparation of your own milieu creates a bit more sympathy for the efforts of the offending referee . . .)

One of the most important items you must have to play the game is a *character record*. This can be a specially printed sheet done by TSR and available in pads, or you can simply use a note pad and design your own record sheet for your character if your Dungeon Master is agreeable, for he or she will usually retain at least a copy of all such records.

As information is developed for your character — his or her *abilities, race, class, alignment* — it must be accurately recorded. All details of the capabilities and possessions of the character must be noted. Where equipment and weapons are carried must be listed. Spells known and spells memorized for an adventure have to be kept track of. A running total of experience points must be maintained. All of these subjects are discussed herein. Ask your DM how records of your character should be kept, read the rules and commentary, and record the data you develop according to the rules (and your campaign referee's instructions) in a form suitable to your DM.

All in all, this is a game for enjoyment. We are certain that it will provide endless hours of entertainment and excitement. That is the sole purpose for its creation. So enjoy, and may the dice be good to you!

CREATING THE PLAYER CHARACTER

Each participant in the campaign created by the referee must create one or more game *personas*. The game persona of each participant is called the *player character* in order to differentiate it from personas created by the referee, called *non-player characters*. The Dungeon Master is advised to limit player characters to one per participant at commencement of the campaign, though as play progresses, additional player characters may be added in a judicious manner. Each player develops the abilities of his or her character through random number generation (by means of dice rolling) to determine the basic characteristics of the persona, the *abilities*. The player then decides what race the character is, what the character's class is, the alignment of the character, and what the character's name is to be. The character will speak certain languages determined by race, class, and alignment. He or she will have a certain amount of gold pieces to begin with, and these funds will be used to purchase equipment needed for adventuring. Finally, each character begins with a certain number of *hit points*, as determined by the roll of the die (or dice) commensurate with the character's class. Class determines the type of die (or dice) rolled. All characters begin at 1st level. All of this is completely explained in the following paragraphs.

An Explanation of the Usages of the Term ''Level'': The term *level* has multiple meanings in this game system. Although substitute terminology could have been used in **ADVANCED DUNGEONS & DRAGONS**, common usage of the term *level* to include multiple meanings is prevalent amongst existing players, so the term has been retained herein. The usages for level are:

1. *Level as an indication of character power:* A player character begins the game at 1st level, i.e. the lowest possible level for a player character. The higher the level number, the more powerful the character is.

2. *Level as used to indicate the depth of the dungeon complex beneath the ground:* The 1st level of a dungeon is the first layer of the underground complex of tunnels, passages, rooms, chambers, and so forth. It is the 1st level beneath the ground. Beneath the 1st level is the 2nd, below that is the 3rd, 4th, 5th, etc. The higher the number, the lower the dungeon level (and the more hazardous its perils).

3. *Level as a measure of magic spell difficulty:* The magic spells available to some classes of characters are graded by difficulty factor — which, incidentally, reflects the spells' effectiveness to some extent. 1st level spells are the basic ones available to beginning characters. They are generally the least powerful spells. Next come 2nd level spells, then come 3rd level spells, and so on. The highest level of any type of magic spell is 9th level, spells usable only by 18th level magic-users — lesser magic-users can possibly employ such spells under certain circumstances which are explained hereafter, but only at considerable risk.

4. *Level as a gauge of a ''monster's'' potential threat:* Relatively weak creatures, monsters with few hit points, limited or non-existent magical abilities, those which do little damage when attacking, and those which have weak, or totally lack, venom are grouped together and called 1st level monsters. Slightly more powerful creatures are ordered into 2nd level, then comes 3rd, 4th, 5th, and so on all the way up to 10th level (the highest, which includes the greatest monsters, demon princes, etc.).

It was initially contemplated to term character power as *rank*, spell complexity was to be termed *power*, and monster strength was to be termed as *order*. Thus, instead of a 9th level character encountering a 7th level monster on the 8th dungeon level and attacking it with a 4th level spell, the terminology would have been: A 9th rank character encountered a 7th order monster on the 8th (dungeon) level and attacked it with a 4th power spell. However, because of existing usage, level is retained throughout with all four meanings, and it is not as confusing as it may now seem.

CHARACTER ABILITIES

Each and every character has six principal characteristics, the character's abilities. These abilities are *strength, intelligence, wisdom, dexterity, constitution,* and *charisma.* (See also APPENDIX I, Psionic Ability.) The range of these abilities is between 3 and 18. The premise of the game is that each player character is above average — at least in some respects — and has superior potential. Furthermore, it is usually essential to the character's survival to be exceptional (with a rating of 15 or above) in no fewer than two ability characteristics. Each ability score is determined by random number generation. The referee has several methods of how this random number generation should be accomplished suggested to him or her in the **DUNGEON MASTERS GUIDE.** The Dungeon Master will inform you as to which method you may use to determine your character's abilities. The principal abilities are detailed as follows:

Strength: Strength is a measure of muscle, endurance, and stamina combined. For purposes of relating this ability to some reality, assume that a character with a strength of 3 is able to lift a maximum of 30 pounds weight above his or her head in a military press, while a character with 18 strength will be able to press 180 pounds in the same manner. Strength is the forte of fighters, for they must be physically powerful in order to wear armor and wield heavy weapons. Therefore, strength is the major characteristic (or *prime requisite*) of *fighters,* and those fighters with strength of 16 or more gain a bonus of 10% of earned experience (explained later). Furthermore, fighters with an 18 strength are entitled to roll percentile dice in order to generate a random number between 01 and 00 (100) to determine *exceptional strength;* exceptional strength increases hit probability and damage done when attacking, and it also increases the weight the character is able to carry without penalty for encumbrance, as well as increasing the character's ability to force open doors and similar portals. The tables below give complete information regarding the effects of strength. Note that only fighters are permitted to roll on the exceptional strength section of STRENGTH TABLE II: ABILITY ADJUSTMENTS.

STRENGTH TABLE I.

Ability Score	General Information
3	
4	
5	Here or lower the character can only be a magic-user
6	Minimum strength for a gnome, half-orc or halfling character
7	
8	Minimum strength for a dwarf character
9	Minimum strength for a fighter character
10	
11	
12	Minimum strength for an assassin or paladin character
13	Minimum strength for a ranger character
14	Maximum strength possible for a female halfling character
15	Maximum strength possible for a female gnome character, minimum strength for a monk character
16	Maximum strength possible for a female elf character
17	Maximum strength possible for a female dwarf or female half-elf or male halfling character
18	Maximum strength possible for all non-fighter characters
18/01-50	Maximum strength possible for a female human or male gnome character
18/51-75	Maximum strength possible for a male elf or female half-orc character
18/76-90	Maximum strength possible for a male half-elf character
18/91-99	Maximum strength possible for a male dwarf or male half-orc character
18/00	Maximum human strength

STRENGTH TABLE II.: ABILITY ADJUSTMENTS

Ability Score	Hit Probability	Damage Adjustment	Weight Allowance	Open Doors On A	Bend Bars/ Lift Gates
3	-3	-1	-350	1	0%
4-5	-2	-1	-250	1	0%
6-7	-1	none	-150	1	0%
8-9	normal	none	normal	1-2	1%
10-11	normal	none	normal	1-2	2%
12-13	normal	none	+100	1-2	4%
14-15	normal	none	+200	1-2	7%
16	normal	+1	+350	1-3	10%
17	+1	+1	+500	1-3	13%
18	+1	+2	+750	1-3	16%
18/01-50	+1	+3	+1,000	1-3	20%
18/51-75	+2	+3	+1,250	1-4	25%
18/76-90	+2	+4	+1,500	1-4	30%
18/91-99	+2	+5	+2,000	1-4 (1)*	35%
18/00	+3	+6	+3,000	1-5 (2)*	40%

*The number in parentheses is the number of chances out of six for the fighter to be able to force open a locked, barred, magically held, or wizard locked door, but only one attempt ever (per door) may be made, and if it fails no further attempts can succeed.

Notes Regarding Strength Table II:

Hit Probability adjustments refer to the score generated by dice roll in melee combat. Subtraction from or addition to the number rolled is made according to the table as applicable. (A full listing of combat tables appears in the **DUNGEON MASTERS GUIDE.**)

Damage Adjustment likewise applies to melee combat. The damage done by scoring a successful hit on an opponent is adjusted downwards or upwards as applicable. Thus, if a hit would normally score 1-6 points of damage upon the opponent, and the character's strength was only 3, the actual damage done would be reduced by 1 point; but, on the other hand, if the attacker had strength of 18/00, the actual damage done would be adjusted upwards by 6 hit points, and possible damage would jump from 1-6 to 7-12.

Weight Allowance is given in number of *gold pieces* over and above the maximum normally stated for unencumbered movement. (See **MOVEMENT.**) The conversion ratio of gold pieces to pounds of weight is 10 to 1. If a character could normally carry 500 gold pieces without encumbrance, but the character had strength of 17 instead of the normal 8-11 range, 1,000 gold pieces could be carried without incurring movement penalty.

Open Doors indicates the number of chances out of 6 which the character has of opening a stuck or heavy door on *that* try. Successive attempts may be made at no penalty with regard to damage to the character attempting to force the door open, but each such attempt requires time and makes considerable noise.

Bend Bars/Lift Gates states the percentage chance the character has of bending normal soft iron bars or of lifting a vertically moving gate (such as a small portcullis barring a passage). The attempt may be made but once, and if the score required is not made, the character will *never* succeed in the task. Example: A character with 16 strength is trapped in a dead end passage by a set of iron bars which drop down from the ceiling when a stone slab is stepped on and triggers the release of the gate. The character first attempts to lift the gate, a roll of 01-10 indicating success, but the percentile dice come up 74, so failure is indicated. The character next attempts to bend the bars in order to squeeze between them, the percentage chance of success is the same as for lifting the gate, and this time a 07 is rolled, so the character slips out and is free.

Intelligence: Intelligence is quite similar to what is currently known as intelligence quotient, but it also includes mnemonic ability, reasoning, and learning ability outside those measured by the written word. Intelligence dictates the number of languages in which the character is able to converse.* Moreover, intelligence is the forte of magic-users, for they must be perspicacious in order to correctly understand magic and memorize spells. Therefore, intelligence is the major characteristic of *magic-users*, and those with intelligence of 16 or more gain a bonus of 10% of earned experience. Spells above 4th level cannot be learned by magic-users with minimal intelligence, and intelligence similarly dictates how many spells may be known and what level spells may be known, for only the highest intelligence is able to comprehend the mighty magics contained in 9th level spells. The tables below allow ready assimilation of the effects of intelligence on all characters — and with regard to magic-users in particular.

*Non-human characters typically are able to speak more languages than are human characters, but intelligence likewise affects the upper limit of their abilities as well, and there are racial limitations. (See **CHARACTER RACES.**)*

INTELLIGENCE TABLE I.

Ability Score	General Information	Possible Number of Additional Languages
3		0
4	Minimum intelligence for a half-elf character	0
5	Here or lower the character can only be a fighter	0
6	Minimum intelligence for a halfling character	0
7	Minimum intelligence for a gnome character	0
8	Minimum intelligence for an elf character	1
9	Minimum intelligence for a paladin or magic-user character	1
10	Minimum intelligence for use of 5th level magic spells	2
11	Minimum intelligence for an assassin character	2
12	Minimum intelligence for use of 6th level magic spells	3
13	Minimum intelligence for a ranger character	3
14	Minimum intelligence for use of 7th level magic spells	4
15	Minimum intelligence for an illusionist character	4
16	Minimum intelligence for use of 8th level magic spells	5
17	Maximum intelligence for a half-orc character	6
18	Minimum intelligence for use of 9th level magic spells	7

INTELLIGENCE TABLE II.: ABILITY FOR MAGIC-USERS

Ability Score	Chance to Know Each Listed Spell	Minimum Number of Spells/Level	Maximum Number of Spells/Level
9	35%	4	6
10-12	45%	5	7
13-14	55%	6	9
15-16	65%	7	11
17	75%	8	14
18	85%	9	18
19 or more	95%	10	All

Notes Regarding Intelligence Table II:

Each and every magic-user character must employ the Table in order to determine which and how many of each group of spells (by level) he or she can learn. At first, only the 1st level group of spells are checked. Successive level groups are checked only when the character reaches a level at which the appropriate group of spells is usable by him or her.

Chance to Know Each Listed Spell pertains to the percentage chance the character has by reason of his or her intelligence to learn any given spell in the level group. The character may select spells desired in any order he or she wishes. Each spell may be checked only once. Percentile dice are rolled, and if the number generated is equal to or less than the percentage chance shown, then the character can learn and thus know that spell (it may be in his or her spell books — explained hereafter). Example: A character with an intelligence of 12 desires to know a *charm person* spell that he finds in a book or scroll, percentile dice are rolled, but the number generated is 52, so that spell is not understood and can not be used by the character (see, however, the paragraph below regarding the minimum number of spells knowable).

Minimum Number of Spells/Level states the fewest number of spells by level group a magic-user can learn. If one complete check through the entire group fails to generate the minimum number applicable according to intelligence score, the character may selectively go back through the group, checking each spell not able to be learned once again. This process continues until the minimum number requirement has been fulfilled. This means, then, that certain spells, when located, can be learned — while certain other spells can never be learned and the dice rolls indicate which ones are in each category. Example: The magic-user mentioned above who was unable to learn a *charm person* spell also fails to meet the minimum number of spells he or she can learn. The character then begins again on the list of 1st level spells, opts to see if this time *charm person* is able to be learned, rolls 04, and has acquired the ability to learn the spell. If and when the character locates such a spell, he or she will be capable of learning it.

Maximum Number of Spells/Level is the obverse of the minimum number which can be known. According to the character's intelligence, this maximum number which the magic-user can possibly know (have in his or her spell books) varies from 6 to an unlimited number. As soon as this maximum is reached, the character may not check any further in the level group.

Change in Intelligence: If intelligence goes down or up for any reason, and such change is relatively permanent, the magic-user must check again as explained above for known spells by level group.

Acquisition of Heretofore Unknown Spells: Although the magic-user must immediately cease checking to determine if spells are known after the first complete check of each spell in the level group, or immediately thereafter during successive checks when the minimum number of spells which can be known is reached, it is possible to acquire knowledge of additional spells previously unknown as long as this does not violate the maximum number of spells which can be known. New spells can be gained from captured or otherwise acquired spell books or from scrolls of magic spells. In the latter event the scroll is destroyed in learning and knowing the new spell or spells. (This subject is detailed more fully in the section explaining magic-users as characters.)

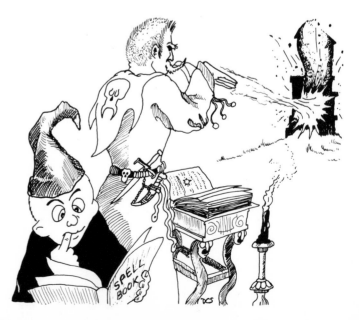

Wisdom: Wisdom is a composite term for the character's enlightenment, judgement, wile, will power, and (to a certain extent) intuitiveness. It has a certain effect on saving throws against some magical attack modes. It is of utmost importance to *clerics*, their major characteristic, and those with wisdom of 16 or greater add 10% to earned experience. Furthermore, clerics with exceptional wisdom (16 or greater) also gain bonus spells over and above the number they are normally able to use. The two tables which follow detail the information pertaining to the effects of wisdom.

WISDOM TABLE I.

Ability Score	General Information	Magical Attack Adjustment*
3		-3
4		-2
5	Here or lower the character can only be a thief	-1
6		-1
7		-1
8		none
9	Minimum wisdom for a cleric character	none
10		none
11		none
12	Minimum wisdom for a druid character	none
13	Minimum wisdom for a paladin or multi-classed half-elven cleric character	none
14	Maximum wisdom for a half-orc character	
	Minimum wisdom for a ranger character	none
15	Minimum wisdom for a monk character	+1
16		+2
17	Maximum wisdom for a halfling character	
	Minimum wisdom for use of 6th level spells	+3
18	Minimum wisdom for use of 7th level spells	+4

This adjustment applies to the saving throw of the character in question, the penalty for low wisdom, or the bonus for high wisdom, being used to alter the result of the die roll accordingly. The adjustment applies only to mental attack forms involving will force, i.e. beguiling, charming, fear, hypnosis, illusion, magic jarring, mass charming, phantasmal forces, possession, rulership, suggestion, telepathic attack, etc.

WISDOM TABLE II.: ADJUSTMENTS FOR CLERICS

Ability Score	Spell Bonus	Chance of Spell Failure
9	none	20%
10	none	15%
11	none	10%
12	none	05%
13	One 1st level	0%
14	One 1st level	0%
15	One 2nd level	0%
16	One 2nd level	0%
17	One 3rd level*	0%
18	One 4th level**	0%

Minimum wisdom for use of 6th level spells
**Minimum wisdom for use of 7th level spells*

Notes Regarding Wisdom Table II:

Spell Bonus indicates the number of additional spells the cleric is entitled to according to wisdom ability score. Note that these spells are only available when the cleric is entitled to spells of the applicable level. Bonus spells are cumulative, so a cleric with 14 wisdom is entitled to two 1st level bonus spells, one with 15 wisdom has two 1st and one 2nd level bonus spells, etc.

Chance of Spell Failure states the percentage chance of failure clerics with low wisdom risk when casting spells. To determine if a spell fails, percentile dice are rolled, and if the number generated is equal to or less than the number shown for failure, the spell is expended and has absolutely no effect whatsoever.

For additional information regarding clerics, see the section pertaining to clerics as characters given hereafter (**CHARACTER CLASSES**).

Dexterity: Dexterity encompasses a number of physical attributes including hand-eye coordination, agility, reflexes, precision, balance, and speed of movement. A high dexterity indicates superiority in all of the above attributes, while a low dexterity might well indicate that one of these attributes is actually superior, but that the others are very poor. Dexterity affects all characters with regard to initiative in attack, the projection of missiles from hand or other means, and in defensive measures. Dexterity is the major characteristic of the *thief* class of character, and it affects their professional activities (such as picking pockets, opening locks, and so forth) accordingly. Thieves with a dexterity ability score of 16 or more gain a bonus of 10% of earned experience. The two tables which follow outline the effects of dexterity on characters.

DEXTERITY TABLE I.

Ability Score	General Information	Reaction/ Attacking Adjustment	Defensive Adjustment
3		-3	+4
4		-2	+3
5	Here or lower the character can only be a cleric	-1	+2
6	Minimum dexterity for a half-elf or magic-user character	0	+1
7	Minimum dexterity for an elf character	0	0
8	Minimum dexterity for a halfling character	0	0
9	Minimum dexterity for a thief character	0	0
10		0	0
11		0	0
12	Minimum dexterity for an assassin character	0	0
13		0	0
14	Maximum dexterity for a half-orc character	0	0
15	Minimum dexterity for a monk character	0	-1
16	Minimum dexterity for an illusionist character	+1	-2
17	Maximum dexterity for a dwarf character	+2	-3
18		+3	-4

Notes Regarding Dexterity Table I:

Reaction/Attacking Adjustment is the penalty or bonus for both *surprise* (q.v.) situations and missile combat attacks.

Defensive Adjustment refers to the penalty or bonus applicable to a character's saving throws against certain forms of attack (such as fire ball, lightning bolts, etc.) due to dodging ability. It also applies to the character's parrying and/or dodging ability in missile or melee combat; in this case the penalty subtracts from the armor class (q.v.) of the character, making him or her easier to hit, while the bonus adds to the defensive value of the character's armor class, making him or her harder to hit. For example, a character with plate mail and shield is normally treated as armor class 2; if the character has 3 dexterity, there is a +4 penalty, so the armor class changes to 6 (2 + 4). However, if the same character has a dexterity of 18, there is a bonus of -4, so armor class changes from 2 to a -2 (2 + -4 = 1, 0, -1, -2).

DEXTERITY TABLE II.: ADJUSTMENTS FOR THIEVES

			Penalty or Bonus for:		
Ability Score	Picking Pockets	Opening Locks	Locating/ Removing Traps	Moving Silently	Hiding in Shadows
9	-15%	-10%	-10%	-20%	-10%
10	-10%	-05%	-10%	-15%	-05%
11	-05%	0	-05%	-10%	0
12	0	0	0	-05%	0
13	0	0	0	0	0
14	0	0	0	0	0
15	0	0	0	0	0
16	0	+05%	0	0	0
17	+05%	+10%	0	+05%	+05%
18	+10%	+15%	+05%	+10%	+10%

Notes Regarding Dexterity Table II:

All "Penalty or Bonus for" categories are fully detailed under **CHARACTER CLASSES**, *Thieves*. The penalties and bonuses are applied to the base chances of success for each named category. Racial adjustments for dwarves, elves, etc. are additional pluses.

Constitution: Constitution is a term which encompasses the character's physique, fitness, health, and resistance. Since constitution affects the character's hit dice and chances of surviving such great system shocks as being changed by magic spell or resurrected from the dead, it is of considerable importance to all classes. Constitution scores of above a certain number are necessary for becoming certain sub-classes of characters. Effects of constitution are given on the table below.

It is of utmost importance to understand that a character's *initial* constitution score is also the maximum number of times the character can be raised from the dead/resurrected, and that each such revivification reduces the character's constitution score by 1. Although a character's constitution can be restored to its former score, or even raised above this number, by magical means, this in no way alters the initial score limitation, nor does such magical change in constitution restore to the character additional chances for revivification. Thus, if a character has an initial constitution of 15, he or she can never be brought back to life by a raise dead or resurrection spell more often than 15 times. Note that a rod of resurrection is considered the same as a spell of the same sort. The 16th death is final and irrevocable without use of some other magical means such as a wish.

CONSTITUTION TABLE

Ability Score	General Information	Hit Point Adjustment	System Shock Survival	Resurrection Survival
3		-2	35%	40%
4		-1	40%	45%
5	Here or lower the character can only be an illusionist	-1	45%	50%
6	Minimum constitution for an elf or half-elf character	-1	50%	55%
7	Minimum constitution for a fighter character	0	55%	60%
8	Minimum constitution for a gnome character	0	60%	65%
9	Minimum constitution for a paladin character	0	65%	70%
10	Minimum constitution for a halfling character	0	70%	75%
11	Minimum constitution for a monk character	0	75%	80%
12	Minimum constitution for a dwarf character	0	80%	85%
13	Minimum constitution for a half-orc character	0	85%	90%
14	Minimum constitution for a ranger character	0	88%	92%
15		+1	91%	94%
16		+2	95%	96%
17		+2 (+3)*	97%	98%
18		+2 (+4)*	99%	100%

Bonus applies only to fighters; all other classes may be given a maximum hit point bonus adjustment for constitution of +2.

Notes Regarding Constitution Table:

Hit Point Adjustment indicates the subtraction from or addition to each hit die for a character. (Hit dice are explained fully under the appropriate heading.) Note that subtraction can never reduce any hit die below 1, i.e. if a die is rolled and a 1 comes up, or if a 2 is rolled and the penalty due to constitution is -2, the die is read as 1 (hit point) regardless of subtractions. Note also that the only class of characters which is entitled to bonuses above +2 per hit die is *fighters* (including the fighter sub-classes *paladins* and *rangers*). Thus, even though a cleric, magic-user, or thief has a constitution of 17 or 18, the additional hit points for each hit die due to superior constitution is +2.

System Shock Survival states the percentage chance the character has of surviving the following forms of magical attacks (or simple application of the magic): aging, petrification (including flesh to stone spell), polymorph any object, polymorph others. Example: The wicked necromancer polymorphs (others) his hireling into a giant roc, with the rather foolish agreement of the changee; the hireling must make a saving throw based on his constitution score using the table above. Assuming he survives, a further saving throw would have to be made if he was again polymorphed or dispelled back to original form. The saving throw must be equal to or less than the percentage shown.

Resurrection Survival shows the percentage chance the character has of being successfully raised from the dead or resurrected by a cleric. The score of the percentile dice must be equal to or less than the number shown on the table, or the character fails to be revivified and is completely and totally dead forever. Remember that a character can never be raised from the dead/resurrected a total number of times in excess of the character's initial constitution score.

Charisma: Charisma is the measure of the character's combined physical attractiveness, persuasiveness, and personal magnetism. A generally non-beautiful character can have a very high charisma due to strong measures of the other two aspects of charisma. It is important to all characters, as it has an effect on dealings with others, principally non-player characters, mercenary hirelings, prospective retainers, and monsters. It absolutely dictates the total number of henchmen a character is able to retain. It affects loyalty of all hirelings and retainers. It is the key to leadership. The following table expresses the facts regarding charisma scores.

CHARISMA TABLE

Ability Score	General Information	Maximum No. of Henchmen	Loyalty Base	Reaction Adjustment
3		1	-30%	-25%
4		1	-25%	-20%
5	Here or lower the character can only be an assassin	2	-20%	-15%
6		2	-15%	-10%
7		3	-10%	-05%
8	Minimum charisma for an elf character	3	-05%	normal
9		4	normal	normal
10		4	normal	normal
11		4	normal	normal
12	Maximum charisma for a half-orc character*	5	normal	normal
13		5	normal	+05%
14		6	+05%	+10%
15	Minimum charisma for a druid character	7	+15%	+15%
16	Maximum charisma for a dwarf character**	8	+20%	+25%
17	Minimum charisma for a paladin character	10	+30%	+30%
18		15	+40%	+35%

*Charisma maximum applies only with respect to non-orcs and non-half-orcs (see **CHARACTER RACES**, Half-Orcs).

Charisma maximum applies only with respect to non-dwarves (see **CHARACTER RACES, Dwarves).

Notes Regarding Charisma Table:

Maximum Number of Henchmen states the number of non-player characters who will serve as permanent retainers of the player character. It does not affect the number of mercenary soldiers, men-at-arms, servitors, and similar persons in the pay of the character.

Loyalty Base simply shows the subtraction from or addition to the henchmen's and other servitors' loyalty (q.v.) scores.

Reaction Adjustment indicates the penalty or bonus due to the character because of charisma in meeting and dealing with persons and creatures encountered. For example, the character might encounter a basically neutral intelligent creature and seek to converse in order to gain some advantage. If the charisma of the character is low, he or she will be working under a handicap which will have to be overcome by generous offers and gifts if a chance of success is hoped for. On the other hand, if the character's charisma score is high, he or she will begin negotiations from a strong starting position due to charm and magnetism.

CHARACTER RACES

After a player has determined the abilities of his or her character, it is then time to decide of what racial stock the character is to be. For purposes of the game the racial stocks are limited to the following: *dwarven, elven, gnome, half-elven, halfling, half-orc,* and *human.* Each racial stock has advantages and disadvantages, although in general human is superior to the others for reasons you will discover as you read on. The Dungeon Master may have restrictions as to which races are allowed in the campaign due to the circumstances of the milieu.

Two tables for easy reference are given below in order that you can select the racial stock of your character based on abilities generated and with an eye towards what *class* (q.v.) of adventurer the character will be. Most non-human races are able to work in two or more classes at the same time, and some gain ability score bonuses as well, but most are limited as to how great a level they may attain in a given class, except in the case of a thief.

CHARACTER RACE TABLE I.: CHARACTER CLASS LIMITATIONS

	Racial Stock of Character						
Character Class	Dwarven	Elven	Gnome	Half-Elven	Halfling	Half-Orc	Human
CLERIC (A)*	no	no	no	yes	no	yes	yes
Druid (N)	no	no	no	yes	no	no	yes
FIGHTER (A)	yes	yes	yes	yes	yes	yes	yes
Paladin (LG)	no	no	no	no	no	no	yes
Ranger (G)	no	no	no	yes	no	no	yes
MAGIC-USER (A)	no	yes	no	yes	no	no	yes
Illusionist (A)	no	no	yes	no	no	no	yes
THIEF (N to E)	yes	yes	yes	yes	yes	yes	yes
Assassin (E)	yes	yes	yes	yes	no	yes	yes
MONK (L)	no	no	no	no	no	no	yes

Notes Regarding Character Race Table I:

Character Class names are shown in capital letters if the class is major, sub-classes are shown with the first letter capitalized only. The letter or letters appearing after each class indicate the *alignment* (q.v.) possibilities of each character class: **(A)** means *any,* **(N)** means *neutral only,* **(LG)** means *lawful good only,* **(G)** means *good only,* **(N to E)** means any *neutral* to any *evil* alignment, **(E)** means *evil only,* and **(L)** means *lawful only.* **(A)*** a cleric cannot be *true neutral* unless of the *druid* subclass.

Racial Stock of Characters shows the seven races of player characters, and reading down each heading gives quick reference as to what classes each race is able to become in regard to their player character role.

A ''no'' indicates that the race cannot become the character class in question.

A ''yes'' indicates that the race is able to become the character class in question.

CHARACTER RACE TABLE II.: CLASS LEVEL LIMITATIONS

Character Class	Racial Stock of Character						
	Dwarven	Elven	Gnome	Half-Elven	Halfling	Half-Orc	Human
CLERIC	(8)	(7)	(7)	5	no	4	U
Druid	no	no	no	U	(6)	no	U
FIGHTER	9[1]	7[2]	6[3]	8[4]	6[5]	10	U
Paladin	no	no	no	no	no	no	U
Ranger	no	no	no	8[4]	no	no	U
MAGIC-USER	no	11[6]	no	8[7]	no	no	U
Illusionist	no	no	7[8]	no	no	no	U
THIEF	U	U	U	U	U	8[9]	U
Assassin	9	10	8	11	no	U	U
MONK	no	no	no	no	no	no	U

[1]*Dwarven fighters with less than 17 strength are limited to 7th level; those with 17 strength are limited to 8th level.*

[2]*Elven fighters with less than 17 strength are limited to 5th level; those with 17 strength are limited to 6th level.*

[3]*Gnome fighters of less than 18 strength are limited to 5th level.*

[4]*Half-elven fighters of less than 17 strength are limited to 6th level; those of 17 strength are limited to 7th level.*

[5]*Halfling fighters of **Hairfeet** sub-race, as well as all other types of sub-races with strength of under 17, are limited to 4th level. **Tallfellows** of 17 strength and **Stouts** of 18 strength can work up to 5th level. **Tallfellows** that somehow obtain 18 strength can work up to 6th level.*

[6]*Elven magic-users with intelligence of less than 17 are limited to 9th level; those with intelligence of 17 are limited to 10th level.*

[7]*Half-elven magic-users with intelligence of less than 17 are limited to 6th level; those with intelligence of 17 are limited to 7th level.*

[8]*Gnome illusionists with intelligence or dexterity under 17 are limited to 5th level; those with both intelligence and dexterity of 17 are limited to 6th level.*

[9]*Half-Orc thieves with dexterity of less than 17 are limited to 6th level; those with dexterity of 17 are limited to 7th level.*

Notes Regarding Character Race Table II:

Numbers in Parentheses () indicate that this class exists only as non-player characters in the race in question.

Numbers — not in *parenthesis* — indicate the maximum level attainable by a character of the race in question.

U appearing in a race column indicates that a character of the race in question has no limitation as to how high the character can go with regard to level in the appropriate class.

Penalties and Bonuses for Race:

Certain racial stocks excel in certain ability areas and have shortcomings in others. These penalties and bonuses are applied to the initial ability scores generated by a player for his or her character as soon as the racial stock of the character is selected, and the modified ability scores then are considered as if they were the actual ability scores generated for all game purposes. These penalties and bonuses are shown below:

Race	Penalty or Bonus
Dwarf	Constitution +1; Charisma -1
Elf	Dexterity +1; Constitution -1
Half-Orc	Strength +1; Constitution +1; Charisma -2
Halfling	Strength -1; Dexterity +1

There are certain other disadvantages and advantages to characters of various races; these are described in the paragraphs pertaining to each race which follow.

Character Ability Scores by Racial Type:

As noted previously in the section pertaining to character abilities, the non- and part-human races must meet certain minimum ability scores, and some races have lower maximum possible scores as well. In order for your character to be of one of these races, these minimums and maximums must be met. The minimum scores must have been generated in the initial abilities rolls, or if bonuses are given for the race, then the minimums must be met considering such bonuses. Maximums applicable are easily met, for the ability score is simply lowered to conform to the maximum.

The table below shows these minimum and maximum figures at a glance.

CHARACTER RACE TABLE III: ABILITY SCORE MINIMUMS & MAXIMUMS

Character Ability Scores	CHARACTER'S RACE					
	Dwarven	Elven	Gnome	Half-Elven	Halfling	Half-Orc
STRENGTH*	M/F	M/F	M/F	M/F	M/F	M/F
Min.	8/8	3/3	6/6	3/3	6/6	6/6
Max.	18/17	18/16	18/15	18/17	17/14	18/18
INTELLIGENCE						
Min.	3/3	8/8	7/7	4/4	6/6	3/3
Max.	18/18	18/18	18/18	18/18	18/18	17/17
WISDOM						
Min.	3/3	3/3	3/3	3/3	3/3	3/3
Max.	18/18	18/18	18/18	18/18	17/17	14/14
DEXTERITY						
Min.	3/3	7/7	3/3	6/6	8/8	3/3
Max.	17/17	19/19	18/18	18/18	18/18	14/14
CONSTITUTION						
Min.	12/12	6/6	8/8	6/6	10/10	13/13
Max.	19/19	18/18	18/18	18/18	19/19	19/19
CHARISMA						
Min.	3/3	8/8	3/3	3/3	3/3	3/3
Max.	16/16	18/18	18/18	18/18	18/18	12/12

*As noted previously, fighters of all races might be entitled to an exceptional strength bonus, see **CHARACTER ABILITIES, Strength**.

Notes Regarding Character Race Table III:

Minimum Scores indicate the lowest possible roll for consideration of a character to be of the racial type indicated. Scores below the minimum indicated are not allowable, so any character with less than the minimum shown can not be of the appropriate race.

Maximum Scores include racial penalties and bonuses; thus, some races can exceed the 18 total possible in the initial generation of abilities with three six-sided dice. Penalties and bonuses for race are taken before adjusting for maximum score.

The Slash (/) separates the minimums and maximums possible for *males*, shown first, and *females*, shown after the slash, thus: males/females, minimum and maximum as applicable. A male dwarf needs a minimum strength of 8, as does a female of that race; a male dwarf can have a maximum strength of 18, but a female dwarf can have a maximum strength of 17; this reads as 8/8, 18/17.

CHARACTER RACE DESCRIPTIONS

All of the non-human or part-human races closely resemble humans in many aspects. It is assumed that similarities are sufficiently apparent so as to warrant no further comment, and only special racial characteristics which are dissimilar to humans will be dealt with. Characters differ slightly within their respective races as a whole.

Dwarves:

The race of dwarves typically dwells in hilly or mountainous regions. For details of the race in general the reader is referred to **ADVANCED DUNGEONS & DRAGONS, MONSTER MANUAL**. As player characters, both dwarves and their cousins the "mountain dwarves" can be considered.

A character of the dwarven race can be a fighter (maximum of 9th level), a thief, or an assassin (maximum of 9th level). It is also possible for a

dwarven character to opt to work simultaneously in the fighter and thief classes; in the latter event the dwarf will be limited to the armor permitted a thief when performing any functions of that class. Experience will always be divided between the two classes also, even though the dwarf may no longer advance upwards in fighting ability level. (Complete information regarding this subject is given hereunder in the section dealing with **CHARACTER CLASSES**.)

Because of their very nature, dwarves are non-magical and do not ever use magical spells. However, this nature gives them a bonus with regard to their saving throws (see **COMBAT, Saving Throws**) against attacks by magic wands, staves, rods and spells. This bonus is +1 for every 3½ points of constitution ability. Thus, if a dwarf had a constitution of 7 he or she would gain a +2 on dice rolls made as saving throws, at 14 constitution the bonus would be +4, and at 18 constitution the bonus would be the maximum normally possible, +5.

Similarly, dwarves have exceptional constitutional strength with regard to toxic substances, ingested or injected. Therefore, all dwarven characters make saving throws against poison in the same manner and with the same bonuses as they do against magical attacks from wands, staves, rods, and spells.

All dwarves are able to speak the following languages (q.v.): dwarven, gnome, goblin, kobold, and orcish; in addition, dwarven characters are able to speak the "common tongue" of all humankind. However, except for their alignment language (see **ALIGNMENT**), they are unable to learn more than two additional languages regardless of their intelligence ability.

Dwarves are able to see radiation in the infra-red spectrum, so they can see up to 60' in the dark noting varying degrees of heat radiation. This ability is known as "infravision".

Dwarves are miners of great skill. They are able to detect the following facts when within 10' or less of the particular phenomenon (except determination of approximate depth, which can be done at any distance):

Detect grade or slope in passage, upwards or downwards	75% probability (d4, score 1-3)
Detect new construction or passage/tunnel	75% probability
Detect sliding or shifting walls or rooms	66 2/3% probability (d6, score 1-4)
Detect traps involving pits, falling blocks and other stonework	50% probability (d4, score 1-2 or d6, score 1-3)
Determine approximate depth underground	50% probability

Note that the dwarven character must be actively seeking to determine the phenomenon in question in order to be able to determine the answer; the information does not simply spring to mind unbidden.

In melee combat (see **COMBAT**), dwarves add 1 to their dice rolls to hit opponents who are half-orcs, goblins, hobgoblins, or orcs. When being attacked by ogres, trolls, ogre magi, giants, and/or titans, dwarves subtract 4 from their opponents' "to hit" dice rolls because of the dwarves' small size and combat ability against these much bigger creatures.

As has already been noted, dwarven characters get a bonus of 1 added to their initial constitution ability, and a penalty of 1 on their charisma score due to racial characteristics. It is very important to note the actual charisma score prior to racial adjustment, however, for dwarven characters do not suffer charisma penalties, nor are they limited to a 16 charisma maximum with regard to their own race. For example, let us suppose a player who has rolled a charisma score of 18 decides to have a dwarven character, thus reducing charisma score by 1 due to racial characteristics. However, the highest score possible for a dwarf is 16 (see **CHARACTER ABILITIES, CHARISMA TABLE**), so the character's charisma score is recorded as 16 (18), the parenthetical number being the actual score rolled. With regard to non-dwarven henchmen, the character is limited to a maximum of 8, but with regard to dwarves the character has a score of 18 charisma, so up to 15 henchmen would serve the character if the additional servitors (over and above 8) were themselves dwarves.

Elves:

There are many sorts of elves, and descriptions of the differing types are found in **ADVANCED DUNGEONS & DRAGONS, MONSTER MANUAL**. Elven player characters are always considered to be high elves, the most common sort of elf.

A character of elven stock can opt to be a fighter (maximum of 7th level), a magic-user (maximum of 11th level), a thief, or an assassin (maximum of 10th level). An elven character can also be multi-classed, i.e. a fighter/magic-user, a fighter/thief, a magic-user/thief, or a fighter/magic-user/thief. If the character is multi-classed, the following restrictions and strictures apply: Although able to operate freely with the benefits of armor, weapons, and magical items available to the classes the character is operating in, any thieving is restricted to the armor and weaponry usable by the thief class. All earned experience is always divided equally among the classes of the character, even though the character is no longer able to gain levels in one or more of the classes. (More detailed information is given in the **CHARACTER CLASSES** section hereafter.)

Elven characters have a 90% resistance to *sleep* and *charm* spells (if these spells are cast upon them a percentile dice roll of 91% or better is required to allow the magic any chance of having an effect, and even then the saving throw against spells is allowed versus the *charm* spell).

When employing either a bow of any sort other than a crossbow, or a short or long sword, elven characters gain a bonus of +1 on their die rolls "to hit".

All elven characters are able to speak the following languages in addition to that of their chosen alignment: elvish, gnome, halfling, goblin, hobgoblin, orcish, gnoll, and the "common tongue" of mankind. Elven

characters of above 15 intelligence are able to learn one additional language for every point of intelligence over 15, i.e. a character with an 18 intelligence score could learn three additional languages (q.v.).

Elves have the ability to see into the infra-red spectrum, so they are able to see up to 60' in darkness, noting varying degrees of heat radiation.

Secret or concealed doors are difficult to hide from elves. Merely passing within 10' of the latter makes an elven character 16 2/3% (1 in 6) likely to notice it. If actively searching for such doors, elven characters are 33 1/3% (2 in 6) likely to find a secret door and 50% likely (3 in 6) to discover a concealed portal.

As has been shown previously, elven characters add a bonus of +1 to their initial dexterity score. Likewise, as elves are not as sturdy as humans, they deduct 1 from their initial constitution score.

If alone and not in metal armor (or if well in advance — 90' or more — of a party which does not consist entirely of elves and/or halflings) an elven character moves so silently that he or she will *surprise* (q.v.) monsters 66 2/3% (d6, 1 through 4) of the time unless some portal must be opened in order to confront the monster. In the latter case the chance for surprise drops to 33 1/3% (d6, 1-2).

Gnomes:

A gnome's preferred habitation is an area of rolling, rocky hills, well-wooded and uninhabited by humans. Details of the race are found in **ADVANCED DUNGEONS & DRAGONS, MONSTER MANUAL**.

A character of the gnome race can select to be a fighter (maximum of 6th level), an illusionist (maximum of 7th level), a thief, or an assassin (maximum of 8th level). It is also possible for a gnome character to be two classes at the same time (a fighter/illusionist, a fighter/thief, or an illusionist/thief, for example). In the latter case, the character is restricted to the wearing of leather armor, regardless of which class combination he or she has chosen, unless only fighting is performed by the character. As with any such multi-class character, gnomes with two character classes must always divide earned experience equally between levels, even though it might no longer be possible to advance upwards in level in one of the classes. (See **CHARACTER CLASSES** for more information regarding this subject.)

Similar to their cousins, the dwarves, gnomes are highly magic resistant. A gnome player character gains a bonus of +1 for every 3½ points of constitution ability score, just as dwarven characters do. A constitution of 4 gains a +1, 7 gains a +2, 11 gains a +3, 14 gains a +4, and 18 gains a +5 bonus to saving throws versus magic wands, staves, rods, and spells.

Gnome characters are able to speak the following languages in addition to their alignment language (q.v.) and the "common tongue" of humanity: dwarvish, gnome, halfling, goblin, kobold, and they can also communicate with any burrowing mammal (such as moles, badgers, ground squirrels, etc.). Gnomes are unable to learn more than two languages in addition to those noted above, regardless of how high their intelligence score is.

Gnomes have infravision, the ability to see into the infra-red spectrum, so a gnome character is able to see up to 60' in the dark, noting varying heat radiation.

Being miners of exceptional merit, gnomes are able to detect the following facts when within 10' of the area to be examined, or at any time with respect to determination of their approximate depth underground:

Detect grade or slope in passage upwards or downwards	80% probability (d10, score 1-8)
Detect unsafe walls, ceilings, or floors	70% probability (d10, score 1-7)
Determine approximate depth underground	60% probability (d10, score 1-6)
Determine direction of travel underground	50% probability (dANY, score any half)

It is important to note that the gnome must be actively seeking to determine the matter in question. The phenomenon does not otherwise become apparent to the character, for he or she must concentrate on the subject to get some form of answer.

In melee combat, gnome characters add 1 to their dice rolls to hit opponents who are kobolds or goblins. When being attacked by gnolls, bugbears, ogres, trolls, ogre magi, giants, and/or titans, gnome characters subtract 4 from their opponents' "to hit" dice rolls because of the gnomes' small size and their combat skill against these much bigger creatures.

Half-Elves:

Half-elves do not form a race unto themselves, but rather they can be found amongst both elvenkind and men. For details of the typical half-elf see **ADVANCED DUNGEONS & DRAGONS, MONSTER MANUAL** under the heading *Elf.*

A character of half-elven race can play as a cleric (maximum of 5th level), druid, fighter (maximum of 8th level), ranger (maximum of 8th level), magic-user (maximum of 8th level), thief, or assassin (maximum of 11th level). A character of half-elven race can also opt to become a multi-classed individual, i.e. cleric/fighter, cleric/ranger, cleric/magic-user, fighter/magic-user, fighter/thief, magic-user/thief, cleric/fighter/magic-user, or a fighter/magic-user/thief. Half-elven characters who choose the cleric as one of their multi-classes aren't limited by that class' proscriptions upon weapons usable, but they are quite restricted in level. Half-elven characters who choose the thief class as one of their multi-roles are limited to the weaponry and armor of that class when operating as a thief. All earned experience is always divided evenly between the classes of the multi-classed character, even though the character is no longer able to gain levels in one or more of the classes. (See **CHARACTER CLASSES**, and consult the various classes for more detailed information pertaining to half-elven characters operating within the stated classes.)

Half-elven characters have a 30% resistance to *sleep* and *charm* spells (if the spells are cast upon them, a percentile dice roll of 31% or better is required to allow the magic any chance of having an effect, and even then the saving throw against spells is allowed versus the *charm* spell).

All half-elven characters are able to speak the "common tongue" of men, their alignment language (q.v.), and the following: elvish, gnome, halfling, goblin, hobgoblin, orcish, and gnoll. Half-elven characters of above 16 intelligence are able to learn one additional language for every point of intelligence above 16, so that a 17 intelligence indicates the character can learn one additional language, and an 18 intelligence indicates two languages can be learned in addition to those listed above.

Half-elves have the ability to see into the infra-red spectrum, so they are able to see up to 60' in darkness, noting varying degrees of heat radiation.

Secret or concealed doors are difficult to hide from half-elves, just as they are noticeable by elves. Merely passing within 10' of a concealed door gives the half-elven character a 1 in 6 chance (16 2/3%) chance of spotting it. If the character is actively seeking to discover such doors, he or she has a 2 in 6 chance (33 1/3%) of spotting a secret door and a 3 in 6 chance (50%) of locating a concealed door.

Halflings:

Halflings are very much like small humans, thus their name. As player characters, it is assumed that any of the sub-races of the race of halflings can be considered as that of the halfling character in question. Complete information on halflings is found in **ADVANCED DUNGEONS & DRAGONS, MONSTER MANUAL.**

A character of the halfling race can be a fighter, a thief, or a fighter/thief. As halflings are unable to work beyond 6th level as fighters, it is most probable that the character will be a thief or a multi-classed fighter/thief. In the latter case the character is limited to the armor and weaponry of a thief whenever any such functions are to be performed during the course of an adventure. Furthermore, earned experience is always divided evenly between the two classes, even though the character may no longer be able to gain additional levels as a fighter.

All halfling characters have a high resistance to magic spells, so for every 3½ points of constitution ability the character possesses, he or she gains a +1 on saving throws versus wands, staves, rods, and spells. This converts

to the following bonuses for constitution: 4-6 = +1, 7-10 = +2, 11-13 = +3, 14-17 = +4, and 18 = +5.

As halflings also have a similar resistance to poisons of all sorts, they gain a constitution bonus identical to that for saving throws versus magical attacks when they make saving throws versus poison, i.e. +1 to +5 depending on constitution score.

All halfling characters are able to speak the following languages in addition to mankind's "common tongue" and the alignment language: dwarven, elven, gnome, goblin, halfling, and orcish. Halflings with intelligence above 16 can learn one additional language for every point of intelligence they possess above the 16 minimum, so at 17 intelligence the character can learn one additional language, and at 18 intelligence two can be learned.

Certain halfling characters have infravision. Those with mixed blood are assumed to have infravision which functions up to 30' distant, while those of pure Stoutish blood are able to see heat radiation variation at up to 60' (normal infravision).

Similarly, halflings of mixed type and those of pure Stoutish blood are able to note if a passage is an up or down grade 75% (d4, 1-3) of the time, and they can determine direction 50% of the time. Note that these abilities function only when the character is concentrating on the desired information to the exclusion of all other thought and activity.

If alone (or well in advance — 90' or more — of a party which does not consist entirely of halflings or elves not in metal armor) and not in metal armor, halfling characters are able to move very silently; thus, if they do not have to open some form of door or other screen, they will *surprise* (q.v.) a monster 66 2/3% (d6, 1-4) of the time. If a door must be opened, chance for surprise drops to 33 1/3% (d6, 1-2).

Halfling characters must accept a penalty of -1 from their initially generated strength ability score, and they gain a bonus of +1 on dexterity.

Half-Orcs:

Orcs are fecund and create many cross-breeds, most of the offspring of such being typically orcish. However, some one-tenth of orc-human mongrels are sufficiently non-orcish to pass for human. Complete details of orcs and cross-breeds will be found under the heading *Orc* in **ADVANCED DUNGEONS & DRAGONS, MONSTER MANUAL.**

As it is assumed that player characters which are of half-orc race are within the superior 10%, they have certain advantages. A half-orc character can become a cleric (maximum of 4th level), a fighter (maximum of 10th level), a thief (maximum of 8th level), or an assassin. It is also possible for a half-orc character to operate in two classes at the same time: cleric/fighter, cleric/thief, cleric/assassin, fighter/thief, or fighter/assassin. When playing a multi-classed character, the half-orc must abide by the restrictions of the least favorable class with regard only to armor. All earned experience is always divided equally between the player's two classes, even though the character might no longer be able to progress upwards in level in one of the two classes. (See **CHARACTER CLASSES** for more information regarding this subject.)

Half-orc characters are able to speak the "common tongue" of humanity, their alignment language, and orcish as well. These characters are able to learn a maximum of two additional languages.

Half-orcs have infravision, so that they can detect varying degrees of heat radiation up to 60' distant in the dark.

As has been shown before, half-orc characters have bonuses of +1 to both their strength and constitution scores initially rolled, but they must subtract a charisma penalty of -2. Note that this penalty is in regard to those non-player character henchmen who are not themselves of half-orc race, so the initial, unaltered, charisma ability score should be recorded (cf. *Dwarves*).

Humans:

Human characters are neither given penalties nor bonuses, as they are established as the norm upon which these subtractions or additions for racial stock are based. Human characters are not limited as to what class of character they can become, nor do they have any maximum limit — other than that intrinsic to the class — of level they can attain within a class. As they are the rule rather than the exception, the basic information given always applies to humans, and racial changes are noted for differences as applicable for non-human or part-human stocks.

RACIAL REFERENCES

In addition to the various attributes of the races of characters already mentioned, there are also certain likes and dislikes which must be considered in selecting a racial type for your character. The dealings which a character has with various races will be affected by racial preferences to some extent. Similarly, the acquisition of hirelings by racial type might prove difficult for some characters if they go outside a narrow field. Your Dungeon Master will certainly take racial preferences into account during interaction between your character and the various races which he or she will encounter. The following table will serve as a guide in determining which races your character will like, be rather indifferent to, or dislike.

RACIAL PREFERENCES TABLE

Basic Acceptability of Racial Type

Race	Dwarves	Elves	Gnomes	Half-Elves	Halflings	Half-Orcs	Humans
DWARVEN	P	A	G	N	G[1]	H	N
ELVEN	A	P	T	G	T	A	N
GNOME	G	T	P	T	G	A	N
HALF-ELVEN	N	P	T	P	N	A	T
HALFLING	G[2]	G[3]	T	N	P	N	T
HALF-ORC	H	A	H	A	N	P	T
HUMAN	N	N	N	T	N	N	P

[1] Only with regard to Tallfellows and Stouts, other halflings are regarded with tolerance (T).

[2] Only Stouts regard dwarves as acceptable, other halflings tolerate them (T).

[3] Only Tallfellows regard elves as good company, other halflings are tolerant (T).

Notes on the Racial Preferences Table:

P: P indicates that the race is generally *preferred*, and dealings with the members of the race will be reflected accordingly.

G: G means that considerable *goodwill* exists towards the race.

T: T indicates that the race is viewed with *tolerance* and generally acceptable, if not loved.

N: N shows that the race is thought of *neutrally*, although some suspicion will be evidenced.

A: A means that the race is greeted with *antipathy*.

H: H tokens a strong *hatred* for the race in question.

CHARACTER CLASSES (Descriptions, Functions, Levels)

Character class refers to the profession of the player character. The approach you wish to take to the game, how you believe you can most successfully meet the challenges which it poses, and which role you desire to play are dictated by character class (or multi-class). *Clerics* principally function as supportive, although they have some offensive spell power and are able to use armor and weapons effectively. *Druids* are a sub-class of cleric who operate much as do other clerics, but they are less able in combat and more effective in wilderness situations. *Fighters* generally seek to engage in hand-to-hand combat, for they have more hit points and better weaponry in general than do other classes. *Paladins* are fighters who are lawful good (see **ALIGNMENT**). At higher levels they gain limited clerical powers as well. *Rangers* are another sub-class of fighter. They are quite powerful in combat, and at upper levels gain druidic and magic spell usage of a limited sort. *Magic-users* cannot expect to do well in hand-to-hand combat, but they have a great number of magic spells of offensive, defensive, and informational nature. They use magic almost exclusively to solve problems posed by the game. *Illusionists* are a sub-class of magic-user, and they are different primarily because of the kinds of spells they use. *Thieves* use cunning, nimbleness, and stealth. *Assassins*, a sub-class of thief, are quiet killers of evil nature. *Monks* are aesthetic disciples of bodily training and combat with bare hands. Each class is detailed fully in succeeding paragraphs. It is up to you to select what class you desire your character to be. Selection must be modified by abilities generated and possibly by the race of your character.

The following tables will enable you to determine the major differences between character classes at a glance. Specific comparisons must be done in light of the detailed information given in the sections which discuss the individual classes in question. Note that non-human and semi-human race characters who are multi-classed are typically bound by the limitations of the thief class only. That is, a fighter/magic-user can benefit from both armor, weaponry and spells; a fighter/thief is limited by the constraints of the thief class.

CHARACTER CLASSES TABLE I: HIT DICE, SPELL ABILITY, AND CLASS LEVEL LIMIT

Class of Character	Hit Die Type	Maximum Number of Hit Dice	Spell Ability	Class Level Limit
CLERIC	d8	9	yes	none
Druid	d8	14	yes	14 (The Great Druid)
FIGHTER	d10	9	no	none
Paladin	d10	9	yes*	none
Ranger	d8 (+d8)**	10 (+1)**	yes***	none
MAGIC-USER	d4	11	yes	none
Illusionist	d4	10	yes	none
THIEF	d6	10	no****	none
Assassin	d6	15	no****	14 (Master of Assassins)
MONK	d4 (+d4)**	17 (+1)**	no	17 (Grand Master of Flowers)

*Clerical spell ability up to 4th level spells, first gained at 9th level.

**The ranger beings with two eight-sided hit dice (2d8), but thereafter goes up one die per level, to the indicated maximum, as do all other classes. The monk begins with two four-sided dice (2d4), and goes up thereafter as do rangers, at one die per level.

***Druidic spell ability up to 3rd level spells, first gained at 8th level; and magic-user spell ability up to 2nd level, first gained at 9th level.

****At 10th level (12th level with regard to assassins) thieves gain the ability to read magic-users' (and illusionists') spells from scrolls.

Notes Regarding Character Classes Table I.:

Class of Character is self-explanatory. Multi-classes have been omitted, but certain facts pertaining to them are given hereafter.

Hit Dice Type shows the type of die to be rolled by a character of the appropriate class at each level of experience (q.v.) he or she has gained so as to determine how many hit points (q.v.) the character has. Multi-classed characters determine their hit points as follows:

1. Roll the hit die (or dice) appropriate to each class the character is professing.

2. Total the sum of all dice so rolled, and adjust for *constitution* (q.v.).

3. Divide the total by the character's classes (two or three), dropping fractions under ½, rounding fractions of ½ or greater upwards to the next whole number.

4. The number derived (quotient) is the number of hit points the multi-classed character gains with the rise in that experience level.

Note that when multi-classed characters are no longer able to progress in any given class, they no longer gain the hit dice for that class. (See **CHARACTER HIT POINTS**).

Maximum Number of Hit Dice assumes that the character has no racial limitation to prevent rise commensurate with the number of hit dice. Note that additional *hit points* are still gained with increase in level, even though no additional *hit dice* can be, in those cases where there is no class (or race) level limit. (See **CHARACTER HIT POINTS.**)

Spell Ability simply indicates whether or not the class of character is able to employ spells. (For details of spells see **CHARACTER SPELLS.**)

Class Level Limit tells how high in levels the character can progress in the class in question. As shown, most character classes do not have any upper limit, although racial limitations might affect non-human or semi-human characters.

CHARACTER CLASSES TABLE II.: ARMOR AND WEAPONS PERMITTED

Class of Character	Armor	Shield	Weapons*	Oil	Poison
CLERIC	any	any	club, flail, hammer, mace, staff	yes	never**
Druid	leather	wooden	club, dagger, dart, hammer, scimitar, sling, spear, staff	yes	?
FIGHTER	any	any	any***	yes	?
Paladin	any	any	any***	yes	never
Ranger	any	any	any***	yes	?
MAGIC-USER	none	none	dagger, dart, staff	yes	?
Illusionist	none	none	dagger, dart, staff	yes	?
THIEF	leather	none	club, dagger, dart, sling, sword****	yes	?
Assassin	leather	any	any***	yes	yes
MONK	none	none	bo sticks, club, crossbow, dagger, hand axe, javelin, jo stick, pole arm, spear, staff	no	?

*This heading includes any magical weapons of the type named unless use by the class in question is specifically proscribed in the description of the magic weapon.

**This prohibition is strictly for clerics who are not of *evil* alignment; the latter may use poison if permitted in the campaign by the referee.

***Characters under 5' height cannot employ the longbow or any weapon over 12' in length. Those under 100 pounds of body weight cannot use the heavy crossbow or pole arms in excess of 200 gold piece weight equivalent, including two-handed swords.

****A thief may use a short sword, broad sword, or long sword but not a bastard sword or a two-handed sword.

Note Regarding Poison: The question mark indicates that the use of poisons is possible providing the referee so allows. Uses and limitations are determined by the referee with suggestions from the **DUNGEON MASTERS GUIDE.**

The Cleric

As has been stated previously in the section detailing **CHARACTER ABILITIES**, the principal attribute of a cleric is *wisdom*. A character must have a minimum wisdom ability score of 9 (13 if a multi-classed half-elven cleric but 9 if a multi-classed half-orc cleric). If wisdom ability is greater than 15, the character adds 10% to *experience* (q.v.) awarded to him or her by the referee. Example: A cleric character gains an award of 975 experience points from the DM after a successful adventure. Because the character has a wisdom ability score in excess of 15, he or she then adds 98 experience points (975 × .10 = 97.5, or 98 E.P.) to the 975, for a total of 1,073 E.P. Of course, a cleric will benefit in other ways by having a high wisdom score. He or she gains bonus spells from high wisdom, as well as a better chance to avoid the effects of certain magical attacks.

High ability scores in strength and constitution are also desirable for a character of this class, and good dexterity is likewise of benefit.

This class of character bears a certain resemblance to religious orders of knighthood of medieval times. The cleric has an eight-sided die (d8) per level to determine how many *hit points* (q.v.) he or she has. The cleric is dedicated to a deity, or deities, and at the same time a skilled combatant at arms. The cleric can be of any *alignment* (q.v.) save (true) neutral (see *Druid* hereafter) alignment, depending upon that of the deity the cleric serves. All clerics have certain holy symbols which aid them and give power to their spells. All are likewise forbidden to use edged and/or pointed weapons which shed blood. All clerics have their own *spells*, bestowed upon them by their deity for correct and diligent prayers and deeds.

A study of the spells usable by clerics (see **CHARACTER SPELLS**) will convey the main purpose of the cleric. That is, the cleric serves to fortify, protect, and revitalize. The cleric also has a limited number of attack spells, some of which are simply the reverse form of curative incantations. Note that all spells must be spoken or read aloud. In addition, the cleric has the ability to wear armor, carry effective weaponry, and engage in hand-to-hand (melee) combat with a reasonable chance of success. Another important attribute of the cleric is the ability to turn away (or actually command into service) the *undead* and less powerful *demons* and *devils*.

The undead are: ghasts, ghosts, ghouls, liches, mummies, shadows, skeletons, spectres, wights, wraiths, vampires, and zombies. These creatures, as well as demons and devils, are detailed in **ADVANCED DUNGEONS & DRAGONS, MONSTER MANUAL**. The matrix showing what effect clerics of various levels have upon such creatures is for use by the Dungeon Master only. As a rule of thumb, a cleric is effective against any undead monster whose hit dice are not greater than those of the cleric. Only high level clerics have any hope of driving away or influencing demons or devils.

Only humans will normally have clericism as their sole class; thus they are the only clerics with unlimited advancement in level.

Clerics have nearly as good a prospect of success in melee combat as fighters (the best in such situations). They move upwards in combat ability in steps consisting of three ability levels. Similarly, they make *saving throws* (q.v.) against magical and poison attacks in like steps.

Clerics can employ a fair number of magic items including most potions; clerical and "protection" scrolls; most rings; some wands, rods, and staves; many other magical items; and all of the non-edged, non-pointed magical weaponry. As they are able to wear armor, clerics can employ all forms of magic armor and magic shields, too.

When a cleric achieves 8th level (Patriarch or Matriarch) he or she automatically attracts followers if the cleric establishes a place of worship — a building of not less than 2,000 square feet in floor area with an altar, shrine, chapel, etc. These followers are fanatically loyal and serve without pay so long as the cleric does not change deities and/or alignment. These followers number between 20 and 200 (2d10, totaled, and multiplied by 10). In addition, there will be followers who are *men-at-arms* (q.v.), and your referee will relay the types and numbers at the appropriate time.

Upon reaching 9th level (High Priest or High Priestess), the cleric has the option of constructing a religious stronghold. This fortified place must contain a large temple, cathedral, or church of not less than 2500 square feet on the ground floor. It can be a castle, a monastery, an abbey or the like. It must be dedicated to the cleric's deity (or deities). The cost of construction will be only one-half the usual for such a place because of religious help. If the cleric then clears the surrounding territory and humans dwell in this area, there will be a monthly revenue of 9 silver pieces per inhabitant from trade, taxation, and tithes.

CLERICS TABLE I

Experience Points	Experience Level	8-Sided Dice for Accumulated Hit Points	Level Title
0—1,500	1	1	Acolyte
1,501—3,000	2	2	Adept
3,001—6,000	3	3	Priest
6,001—13,000	4	4	Curate
13,001—27,500	5	5	Perfect
27,501—55,000	6	6	Canon
55,001—110,000	7	7	Lama
110,001—225,000	8	8	Patriarch
225,001—450,000	9	9	High Priest
450,001—675,000	10	9+2	High Priest (10th level)
675,001—900,000	11	9+4	High Priest (11th level)

225,000 experience points per level for each additional level beyond the 11th.

Clerics gain 2 h.p. per level after the 9th.

SPELLS USABLE BY CLASS AND LEVEL — CLERICS

Cleric Level	Spell Level						
	1	2	3	4	5	6	7
1	1	-	-	-	-	-	-
2	2	-	-	-	-	-	-
3	2	1	-	-	-	-	-
4	3	2	-	-	-	-	-
5	3	3	1	-	-	-	-
6	3	3	2	-	-	-	-
7	3	3	2	1	-	-	-
8	3	3	3	2	-	-	-
9	4	4	3	2	1	-	-
10	4	4	3	3	2	-	-
11	5	4	4	3	2	1*	-
12	6	5	5	3	2	2	-
13	6	6	6	4	2	2	-
14	6	6	6	5	3	2	-
15	7	7	7	5	4	2	-
16	7	7	7	6	5	3	1**
17	8	8	8	6	5	3	1
18	8	8	8	7	6	4	1
19	9	9	9	7	6	4	2
20	9	9	9	8	7	5	2
21	9	9	9	9	8	6	2
22	9	9	9	9	9	6	3
23	9	9	9	9	9	7	3
24	9	9	9	9	9	8	3
25	9	9	9	9	9	8	4
26	9	9	9	9	9	9	4
27	9	9	9	9	9	9	5
28	9	9	9	9	9	9	6
29	9	9	9	9	9	9	7

*Usable only by clerics of 17 or greater wisdom
**Usable only by clerics of 18 or greater wisdom

The Druid

The druid is a sub-class of clerics. They are the only absolute neutrals (see **ALIGNMENT**), viewing good and evil, law and chaos, as balancing forces of nature which are necessary for the continuation of all things. As priests of nature, they must have a minimum wisdom of 12 and a charisma of 15. Both of these major attributes must exceed 15 if a druid is to gain a 10% bonus to earned experience.

It will be noted that the spells usable by druids are more attuned to nature and the outdoors than are the spells of other clerics or magic-users.

Nonetheless, druids serve to strengthen, protect, and revitalize as the usual cleric does. The more powerful druidic spells, as well as their wider range of weaponry, make up for the fact that druids are unable to use any armor or shields other than leather armor and wooden shields (metallic armor spoils their magical powers). They must speak or read spells aloud. Due to their involvement with living, growing things, druids have no power to turn or control undead, demons, or devils.

Druids can be visualized as medieval cousins of what the ancient Celtic sect of Druids would have become had it survived the Roman conquest. They hold trees (particularly oak and ash), the sun, and the moon as deities. Mistletoe is the holy symbol of druids, and it gives power to their spells. They have an obligation to protect trees and wild plants, crops, and to a lesser extent, their human followers and animals. Thus, druids will never destroy woodlands or crops no matter what the circumstances. Even though a woods, for example, were evilly hostile, druids would not destroy it, although nothing would prevent them from changing the nature of the place if the desire and wherewithal existed. In similar fashion, they avoid slaying wild animals or even domestic ones except as necessary for self-preservation and sustenance.

If druids observe any creature destroying their charges, the druids are unlikely to risk their lives to prevent the destruction. Rather, it is probable that the druids will seek retribution and revenge at a later date as opportunity presents itself.

In connection with their nature worship, druids have certain innate powers which are gained at higher level. At 3rd level (Initiate of the 1st Circle), a druid gains the following abilities:

1. Identification of plant type

2. Identification of animal type

3. Identification of pure water

4. Power to pass through overgrown areas (undergrowth of tangled thorns, briar patches, etc.) without leaving a discernible trail and at normal *movement rate* (q.v.)

At 7th level (Initiate of the 5th Circle), the following additional powers are gained:

1. Immunity from *charm* spells cast by any creature basically associated with the woodlands, i.e. dryads, nixies, sylphs, etc.

2. Ability to change form up to three times per day, actually becoming, in all respects save the mind, a reptile, bird or mammal.

    A. Each type of creature form can be assumed but once per day.

    B. The size of creature form assumed can vary from as small as a bullfrog, bluejay, or bat to as large as a large snake, an eagle, or a black bear (about double the weight of the druid).

    C. Each assumption of a new form removes from 10% to 60% (d6, multiply by 10) of the hit points of damage, if any, the druid has sustained prior to changing form.

Druids have their own secret language, and all speak it in addition to their other tongues (alignment, common, and others known). Upon becoming a 3rd level druid (Initiate of the 1st Circle), and with each level increase thereafter, a druid gains a language of his choice: centaur, dryad, elvish, faun, gnome, green dragon, hill giant, lizardman, manticore, nixie, pixie, sprite, treantish.

In melee combat, druids fight as clerics, but they do suffer somewhat from their inability to wear protective armor of metal. They likewise make *saving throws* (q.v.) as clerics, but against fire and lightning (electrical) attacks they get a bonus of +2 on their dice rolls.

Druids can use those magic items not otherwise proscribed which are for all classes and those for regular clerics which are not written, i.e. books and scrolls.

At the upper levels there are only a limited number of characters. At 12th level (Druid) there can be but nine of these nature priests. Each such 12th

level druid is the leader of a body of lesser druids and will have an entourage of three of their underlings, i.e. the lowest (in experience) Druid (12th level) will have three Aspirants (1st level) to serve him or her, while the highest (in experience) will have three Initiates of the 7th Circle (9th level). Initiates of the 8th and 9th Circles are under direct supervision of the three Archdruids and The Great Druid respectively.

Above all other druids is a lone figure, The Great Druid. The supreme druid is always attended by nine Initiates of the 9th Circle.

(Note: It is possible that other henchmen and hirelings, as well as worshippers, will be found with any particular druid. All servitors of upper-level druids are faithful protectors. They are not otherwise considered *henchmen* (q.v.) *per se.*)

At such time as a druid class player character attains experience points sufficient to advance him or her to Druid (12th level), the corresponding powers are gained only:

1. If there are currently fewer than nine other characters of Druid level, or

2. The player character bests one of the nine Druid level characters in spell or hand-to-hand combat. If the combat is not mortal, the losing combatant drops the exact number of experience points necessary to place him or her in the beginning of the next lower level.

If the player character succeeds, he or she becomes a Druid, with full powers, and the former Druid (assuming case 2, above) becomes an Initiate of the 9th Circle. If the player character loses, he or she remains at lower level and actually has fewer experience points in the bargain.

This process is repeated with respect to a Druid becoming an Archdruid and for an Archdruid becoming the Great Druid. Multiple attempts to move upwards are possible as long as the character survives.

DRUIDS (CLERICS) TABLE I.

Experience Points	Experience Level	8-Sided Dice for Accumulated Hit Points	Level Title
0 — 2,000	1	1	Aspirant
2,001 — 4,000	2	2	Ovate
4,001 — 7,500	3	3	Initiate of the 1st Circle
7,501 — 12,500	4	4	Initiate of the 2nd Circle
12,501 — 20,000	5	5	Initiate of the 3rd Circle
20,001 — 35,000	6	6	Initiate of the 4th Circle
35,001 — 60,000	7	7	Initiate of the 5th Circle
60,001 — 90,000	8	8	Initiate of the 6th Circle
90,001 — 125,000	9	9	Initiate of the 7th Circle
125,001 — 200,000	10	10	Initiate of the 8th Circle
201,001 — 300,000	11	11	Initiate of the 9th Circle
300,001 — 750,000	12	12	Druid
750,001 — 1,500,000	13	13	Archdruid
1,500,001	14	14	The Great Druid

SPELLS USABLE BY CLASS AND LEVEL — DRUIDS (CLERICS)

Druidic Level	Spell Level						
	1	2	3	4	5	6	7
1	2	-	-	-	-	-	-
2	2	1	-	-	-	-	-
3	3	2	1	-	-	-	-
4	4	2	2	-	-	-	-
5	4	3	2	-	-	-	-
6	4	3	2	1	-	-	-
7	4	4	3	1	-	-	-
8	4	4	3	2	-	-	-
9	5	4	3	2	1	-	-
10	5	4	3	3	2	-	-
11	5	5	3	3	2	1	-
12	5	5	4	4	3	2	1
13	6	5	5	5	4	3	2
14	6	6	6	6	5	4	3

Druids as a class do not dwell permanently in castles, or even in cities or towns. All druids prefer to live in sacred groves, dwelling in sod, log, or stone buildings of smallish size. When attaining levels above the 11th, characters will generally inhabit building complexes set in woodlands and similar natural surroundings.

The Fighter

The principal attribute of a fighter is *strength*. To become a fighter, a character must have a minimum strength of 9 and a constitution of 7 or greater. A good dexterity rating is also highly desirable. If a fighter has strength above 15, he or she adds 10% to experience points awarded by the Dungeon Master. Also, high strength gives the fighter a better chance to hit an opponent and causes an increased amount of damage.

Fighters have a ten-sided die (d10) for determination of their hit points per level. No other class of character (save the *paladin* and *ranger* (qq.v.) subclasses of fighters) is so strong in this regard. Fighters are the strongest of characters in regards to sheer physical strength, and they are the best at hand-to-hand combat. Any sort of armor or weapon is usable by fighters. Fighters may be of any alignment — good or evil, lawful or chaotic, or neutral.

Although fighters do not have magic spells to use, their armor and weapons can compensate. They have the most advantageous combat table and generally have good saving throw (q.v.) possibilities as well.

Fighters can employ many magical items, including potions; "protection" scrolls; many rings; a few wands; one rod; many other magic items; and all forms of armor, shields and weapons.

When a fighter attains 9th level (Lord), he or she may opt to establish a *freehold*. This is done by building some type of castle and clearing the area in a radius of 20 to 50 miles around the stronghold, making it free from all sorts of hostile creatures. Whenever such a freehold is established and cleared, the fighter will:

1. Automatically attract a body of men-at-arms led by an above-average fighter. These men will serve as mercenaries so long as the fighter maintains his or her freehold and pays the men-at-arms; and

2. Collect a monthly revenue of 7 silver pieces for each and every inhabitant of the freehold due to trade, tariffs, and taxes.

FIGHTERS TABLE

Experience Points	Experience Level	10-Sided Dice for Accumulated Hit Points	Level Title
0—2,000	1	1	Veteran
2,001—4,000	2	2	Warrior
4,001—8,000	3	3	Swordsman
8,001—18,000	4	4	Hero
18,001—35,000	5	5	Swashbuckler
35,001—70,000	6	6	Myrmidon
70,001—125,000	7	7	Champion
125,001—250,000	8	8	Superhero
250,001—500,000	9	9	Lord
500,001—750,000	10	9+3	Lord (10th Level)
750,001—1,000,000	11	9+6	Lord (11th Level)

250,000 experience points per level for each additional level beyond the 11th.

Fighters gain 3 h.p. per level after the 9th.

The Paladin

A paladin character is a fighter sub-class, but unlike normal fighters, all paladins must begin as lawful good in alignment (q.v.) and always remain lawful good or absolutely lose all of the special powers which are given to them. They have both fighting abilities and limited spell powers (at high level). To become a paladin a character must be human, have a strength of not less than 12, a minimum intelligence of 9, a wisdom of 13 or more, a minimum constitution of 9, and not less than 17 charisma. If a paladin has both *strength* and *wisdom* in excess of 15, he or she gains the benefit of adding 10% to the experience points awarded by the Dungeon Master.

Law and good deeds are the meat and drink of paladins. If they ever knowingly perform an act which is chaotic in nature, they must seek a high level (7th or above) cleric of lawful good alignment, confess their sin, and do penance as prescribed by the cleric. If a paladin should ever knowingly and willingly perform an evil act, he or she loses the status of paladinhood immediately and irrevocably. All benefits are then lost, and no deed or magic can restore the character to paladinhood; he or she is everafter a fighter.

The benefits of a paladin are:

1. Detect evil at up to 60' distance, as often as desired, but only when the paladin is concentrating on determining the presence of evil and seeking to detect it in the right general direction.

2. Make all *saving throws* (q.v.) at +2 on the dice.

3. Immunity to all forms of disease.

4. The ability to "lay on hands", either on others, or on his or her own person, to cure wounds; this heals 2 hit points of damage per level of experience the paladin has attained, but laying on hands can be performed but once per day.

5. The ability to cure disease of any sort; this can be done once per week for each five levels of experience the paladin has attained, i.e. at levels 1 through 5 one disease per week, at levels 6 through 10 two diseases, at levels 11 through 15 three diseases, etc.

6. The continuing emanation of a *protection from evil* (see **CHARACTER SPELLS**) in a 1" radius round the paladin.

Furthermore:

7. At 3rd level, the paladin gains the power to affect undead and devils and demons as if he or she were a 1st level cleric, and this power goes upwards with each level of experience the paladin gains; so at 4th level the effect is that of a 2nd level cleric, at 5th it is that of a 3rd level cleric, etc. (See *The Cleric* above.)

8. At 4th level — or at any time thereafter — the paladin may call for his warhorse; this creature is an intelligent heavy warhorse, with 5 +5 hit dice (5d8 plus 5 hit points), AC 5, and the speed of a medium warhorse (18"); it will magically appear, but only one such animal is available every ten years, so that if the first is lost the paladin must wait until the end of the period for another.

9. If a paladin has a "Holy Sword" (a special Magic Sword which your referee is aware of and will explain to you if the need arises), he or she projects a circle of power 1" in diameter when the Holy Sword is unsheathed and held; and this power dispels magic (see **CHARACTER SPELLS**, *dispel magic*) at the level of magic use equal to the experience level of the paladin.

10. At 9th level (through 20th level) of experience, paladins gain the ability to employ cleric *spells* (q.v.). They may never use scrolls of spells, however, except those normally usable by fighters.

The following strictures apply to paladins:

1. They may never retain more than ten magic items; these may never exceed:

   armor, 1 (suit)
   shield, 1
   weapons*, 4
   any other magic items, 4

   *these include daggers, swords, etc.; and such items as magic bows and magic arrows are considered as but 1 weapon

2. They will never retain wealth, keeping only sufficient treasures to support themselves in a modest manner, pay henchmen, men-at-arms, and servitors, and to construct or maintain a small castle. (Your DM will give details of this as necessary.) Excess is given away, as is the *tithe* (see 3. below).

3. An immediate tithe (10%) of all income — be it treasure, wages, or whatever — must be given to whatever charitable religious *institution* (not a clerical player character) of lawful good alignment the paladin selects.

4. Paladins will have henchmen of lawful good alignment and none other; they will associate only with characters and creatures of good alignment; paladins can join a company of adventurers which contains non-evil neutrals only on a single-expedition basis, and only if some end which will further the cause of lawful good is purposed.

5. If possible, paladins will take service or form an alliance with lawful good characters, whether players or not, who are clerics or fighters (of noble status).

Paladins do not attract a body of men-at-arms to service as do regular fighters.

PALADINS (FIGHTERS) TABLE I.

Experience Points	Experience Level	10-Sided Dice for Accumulated Hit Points	Level Title
0—2,750	1	1	Gallant
2,751—5,500	2	2	Keeper
5,501—12,000	3	3	Protector
12,001—24,000	4	4	Defender
24,001—45,000	5	5	Warder
45,001—95,000	6	6	Guardian
95,001—175,000	7	7	Chevalier
175,001—350,000	8	8	Justiciar
350,001—700,000	9	9	Paladin
700,001—1,050,000	10	9+3	Paladin (10th level)
1,050,001—1,400,000	11	9+6	Paladin (11th level, etc.)

350,000 experience points per level for each additional level above the 11th.

Paladins gain 3 h.p. per level after the 9th.

SPELLS USABLE BY CLASS AND LEVEL — PALADINS (FIGHTERS)

Paladin Level	Clerical Spell Level			
	1	2	3	4
9	1	-	-	-
10	2	-	-	-
11	2	1	-	-
12	2	2	-	-
13	2	2	1	-
14	3	2	1	-
15	3	2	1	1
16	3	3	1	1
17	3	3	2	1
18	3	3	3	1
19	3	3	3	2
20*	3	3	3	3

*Maximum spell ability

The Ranger

Rangers are a sub-class of fighter who are adept at woodcraft, tracking, scouting, and infiltration and spying. All rangers must be of good *alignment* (q.v.), although they can be lawful, chaotic, or neutral otherwise. A ranger must have strength of not less than 13, intelligence of not less than 13, wisdom of not less than 14, and a 14 or greater constitution. If the ranger has ability scores of greater than 15 in strength, intelligence *and* wisdom, he or she gains the benefit of adding 10% to experience points awarded by the referee.

Unlike other fighter-types, rangers have eight-sided hit dice (d8) but at first level they get *two*, rather than but one, hit dice. It should also be noted that rangers get 11 hit dice rather than the 9 of other fighter-types. In addition to considerable prowess as fighters, rangers have druidic and magical spell capabilities when they attain high level; thus, they are very formidable opponents, for they have other abilities and benefits as well:

1. When fighting humanoid-type creatures of the "giant class", listed hereafter, rangers add 1 hit point for each level of experience they have attained to the points of damage scored when they hit in melee combat. Giant class creatures are: bugbears, ettins, giants, gnolls, goblins, hobgoblins, kobolds, ogres, ogre magi, orcs, and trolls. Example: a 5th level ranger hits a bugbear in melee combat, and the damage done to the opponent will be according to the ranger's weapon type, modified by strength, and +5 (for his or her experience level) because the opponent is a bugbear — a "giant class" humanoid.

2. Rangers *surprise* (q.v.) opponents 50% of the time (d6, score 1 through 3) and are themselves surprised only 16⅔% of the time (d6, score 1).

3. Tracking is possible both outdoors and underground in dungeons and like settings:

   a. Underground the ranger must have observed the creature to be tracked within 3 turns (30 minutes) of the commencement of tracking, and the ranger must begin tracking at a place where the creature was observed:

Creature's Action	Chance to Track
going along normal passage or room	65%
passes through normal door or uses stairs	55%
goes through a trap door	45%
goes up or down a chimney or through concealed door	35%
passes through a secret door	25%

   b. Outdoors there is a base 90% chance of a ranger being able to follow a creature, modified as follows:

—for each creature above 1 in the party being tracked	+02%
—for every 24 hours which have elapsed between making the track and tracking	-10%
—for each hour of precipitation	-25%

4. At 8th level, rangers gain limited druidic spell ability, and additional spells are added through 17th level.

5. At 9th level rangers gain limited magic-user spell ability, as with druidic spell ability. Rangers cannot read druid or magic-user spells from magic scrolls in any event.

6. At 10th level (Ranger Lord), rangers are able to employ all non-written magic items which pertain to clairaudience, clairvoyance, ESP, and telepathy.

7. Also at 10th level, each ranger attracts a body of 2-24 followers. Note that these henchmen once lost, can never be replaced, although mercenaries can be hired, of course. These followers are determined by the DM who then informs the ranger.

The following restrictions and strictures apply to rangers:

1. Any change to non-good alignment immediately strips the ranger of all benefits, and the character becomes a fighter, with eight-sided hit dice, everafter, and can never regain ranger status.

2. Rangers may not hire men-at-arms, servants, aides, or henchmen until they attain 8th or higher level.

3. No more than three rangers may ever operate together at any time.

4.   Rangers may own only those goods and treasure which they can carry on their person and/or place upon their mount; all excess must be donated to a worthy communal or institutional cause (but never to another player character). (cf. *Paladin* above.)

Although rangers do not attract a body of mercenaries to serve them when, and if, rangers construct strongholds, they conform to the fighter class in other respects.

RANGERS (FIGHTERS) TABLE I.

Experience Points	Experience Level	8-Sided Dice for Accumulated Hit Points	Level Title
0 — 2,250	1	2	Runner
2,251 — 4,500	2	3	Strider
4,501 — 10,000	3	4	Scout
10,001 — 20,000	4	5	Courser
20,001 — 40,000	5	6	Tracker
40,001 — 90,000	6	7	Guide
90,001 — 150,000	7	8	Pathfinder
150,001 — 225,000	8	9	Ranger
225,001 — 325,000	9	10	Ranger Knight
325,001 — 650,000	10	11	Ranger Lord
650,001 — 975,000	11	11 + 2	Ranger Lord (11th level)
975,001 — 1,300,000	12	11 + 4	Ranger Lord (12th level)

325,000 experience points per level for each additional level above the 12th.

Rangers gain 2 h.p. per level after the 10th.

SPELLS USABLE BY CLASS AND LEVEL — RANGERS (FIGHTERS)

Ranger Level	Druidic 1	2	3	Magic-User** 1	2
8	1	-	-	-	-
9	1	-	-	1	-
10	2	-	-	1	-
11	2	-	-	2	-
12	2	1	-	2	-
13	2	1	-	2	1
14	2	2	-	2	1
15	2	2	-	2	2
16	2	2	1	2	2
17*	2	2	2	2	2

*maximum spell ability
**The ranger must check as to which spells he or she can learn, just as if he or she were a magic-user.

FIGHTERS', PALADINS', & RANGERS' ATTACKS PER MELEE ROUND TABLE

Level	Attacks per Melee Round*
Fighter 1-6	1/1 round
Paladin 1-6	1/1 round
Ranger 1-7	1/1 round
Fighter 7-12	3/2 rounds
Paladin 7-12	3/2 rounds
Ranger 8-14	3/2 rounds
Fighter 13 & up	2/1 round
Paladin 13 & up	2/1 round
Ranger 15 & up	2/1 round

*With any thrusting or striking weapon

Note: This excludes melee combat with monsters (q.v.) of less than one hit die (d8) and non-exceptional (0 level) humans and semi-humans, i.e. all creatures with less than one eight-sided hit die. All of these creatures entitle a fighter to attack once for each of his or her experience levels (See **COMBAT**).

The Magic-User

It is absolutely essential to have high *intelligence* for a character who is a magic-user — especially if a broad selection of spells is to be had, as well as the use of the highest level spells. A magic-user must have an intelligence of no less than 9 and a minimum dexterity of 6. For details of the effects of intelligence on spell use, see **CHARACTER ABILITIES**. A magic-user with intelligence of 16 or more also gains the benefit of adding 10% to experience points awarded to him or her by the Dungeon Master.

Magic-users draw upon arcane powers in order to exercise their profession. While they have mighty spells of offensive, defensive, and informational nature, magic-users are very weak in combat. They have but four-sided dice (d4) to determine how many hit points of damage they can withstand, and magic-users have the least favorable table and progression as regards missile and melee combat. Furthermore, they can wear no armor and have few weapons they can use, for martial training is so foreign to magic-use as to make the two almost mutually exclusive. Magic-users can be of any *alignment* (explained hereafter).

When a magic-user begins his or her profession, the character is usually assumed to possess a strange tome in which he or she has scribed the formulae for some of the spells known to the character. This *spell book*, and each book later added (as the magic-user advances in levels of ability, a book of spells for each higher level of spells which become usable will have to have been prepared through study and research), must be maintained by the magic-user. He or she must memorize and prepare for the use of each spell, and its casting makes it necessary to reabsorb the incantation by consulting the proper book of spells before it can again be cast. (See **CHARACTER SPELLS** for more details.) As with all other types of spells, those of magic-users must be spoken or read aloud.

There are many powerful items of magic which only this class of character can employ. Most magic scrolls, wands, staves, and many of the miscellaneous items of magic are usable only by this class. Thus, while magic-users are not strong in combat with weapons, they are possibly the most fearsome of all character classes when high levels of ability are finally attained. Survival to that point can be a problem, however, as low-level magic-users are quite weak.

When a magic-user attains 11th level (Wizard) or higher, he or she may enchant items or scribe magic scrolls. This process requires the undivided attention of the magic-user for quite long periods of time — weeks to months — and it is also costly. As the Dungeon Master is carefully instructed to keep exact record of game time spent in such activity, the magic-user will effectively remove himself or herself from a number of adventures while enchanting items or inscribing scrolls of magic spells. As this relative inactivity means that the character will not get experience points and treasure (monetary or magical) gained from adventures which take place during the inactive period, it is not usual for a Wizard to manufacture many items or scrolls. However, as occasional enchantment of items or penning of magic scrolls will take place, your referee has complete information on the process, including probabilities, time required, materials needed, and costs.

It is possible for a magic-user of 11th or higher level to construct a stronghold and clear the countryside in a 10 or 20 mile radius of all monsters, thus ruling an area much as a noble. If this is accomplished, a revenue of 5 silver pieces per inhabitant per month is generated in the territory ruled.

MAGIC-USERS TABLE I.

Experience Points	4-Sided Dice for Experience Accumulated Level Hit Points		Level Title
0 — 2,500	1	1	Prestidigitator
2,501 — 5,000	2	2	Evoker
5,001 — 10,000	3	3	Conjurer
10,001 — 22,500	4	4	Theurgist
22,501 — 40,000	5	5	Thaumaturgist
40,001 — 60,000	6	6	Magician
60,001 — 90,000	7	7	Enchanter
90,001 — 135,000	8	8	Warlock
135,001 — 250,000	9	9	Sorcerer
250,001 — 375,000	10	10	Necromancer
375,001 — 750,000	11	11	Wizard
750,001 — 1,125,000	12	11 + 1	Wizard (12th level)

1,125,001 — 1,500,000	13	11+2	Wizard (13th level)
1,500,001 — 1,875,000	14	11+3	Wizard (14th level)
1,875,001 — 2,250,000	15	11+4	Wizard (15th level)
2,250,001 — 2,625,000	16	11+5	Wizard (16th level, or Mage)
2,625,001 — 3,000,000	17	11+6	Wizard (17th level)
3,000,001 — 3,375,000	18	11+7	Wizard (18th level or Arch-Mage)

375,000 experience points per level for each additional level beyond the 18th.

Magic-Users gain 1 h.p. per level after the 11th.

SPELLS USABLE BY CLASS AND LEVEL — MAGIC-USERS

Magic-Users Level	1	2	3	4	5	6	7	8	9
1	1	-	-	-	-	-	-	-	-
2	2	-	-	-	-	-	-	-	-
3	2	1	-	-	-	-	-	-	-
4	3	2	-	-	-	-	-	-	-
5	4	2	1	-	-	-	-	-	-
6	4	2	2	-	-	-	-	-	-
7	4	3	2	1	-	-	-	-	-
8	4	3	3	2	-	-	-	-	-
9	4	3	3	2	1	-	-	-	-
10	4	4	3	2	2	-	-	-	-
11	4	4	4	3	3	-	-	-	-
12	4	4	4	4	4	1	-	-	-
13	5	5	5	4	4	2	-	-	-
14	5	5	5	4	4	2	1	-	-
15	5	5	5	5	5	2	1	-	-
16	5	5	5	5	5	3	2	1	-
17	5	5	5	5	5	3	3	2	-
18	5	5	5	5	5	3	3	2	1
19	5	5	5	5	5	3	3	3	1
20	5	5	5	5	5	4	3	3	2
21	5	5	5	5	5	4	4	4	2
22	5	5	5	5	5	5	4	4	3
23	5	5	5	5	5	5	5	5	3
24	5	5	5	5	5	5	5	5	4
25	5	5	5	5	5	5	5	5	5
26	6	6	6	6	5	5	5	5	5
27	6	6	6	6	6	6	6	5	5
28	6	6	6	6	6	6	6	6	6
29	7	7	7	7	6	6	6	6	6

The Illusionist

Illusionists form a sub-class of magic-users, and in most respects they conform to the characteristics of the latter. To be an illusionist, a character must have a minimum intelligence of 15 and a minimum dexterity of 16 (a high manual dexterity is required in casting of the spells used by this class). An important difference between illusionists and magic-users is that the former do not gain any experience bonus for having high scores in their required abilities of intelligence and dexterity.

While being equal, or even slightly inferior, to normal magic-users in most respects, illusionists have different and highly effective spells to employ. A perusal of the number and types of spells usable by illusionists (see **CHARACTER SPELLS**) will reveal that they are at least as powerful as normal magic-users and possibly slightly more potent at very high levels. The power of illusionists due to their spells is offset, however, by the limitations placed upon the magic items they can use. The magical items usable by illusionist class characters are enumerated below:

— all potions not restricted to fighters only

— illusionist scrolls and magic-user scrolls which contain spells usable by illusionists

— all rings

— rod of cancellation, staff of striking, and wands of enemy detection, fear, illusion, magic detection, metal & mineral detection, secret door & trap detection, wonder

— miscellaneous magic items usable by every class of characters, crystal balls (but not with any added powers), all robes (excluding robe of the arch-magi), and books and similar written works readable by magic-users

— artifacts which are not proscribed items with respect to illusionists (such as armor, swords, axes, etc.)

— magic daggers

Illusionists are capable of manufacturing those magical items which create or sustain illusion. They may do so at 10th level (Illusionist) and above; this is done in much the same manner in which regular magic-users create magic items.

ILLUSIONISTS (MAGIC-USERS) TABLE I.

Experience Points	Experience Level	4-Sided Dice for Accumulated Hit Points	Level Title
0—2,250	1	1	Prestidigitator
2,251—4,500	2	2	Minor Trickster
4,501—9,000	3	3	Trickster
9,001—18,000	4	4	Master Trickster
18,001—35,000	5	5	Cabalist
35,001—60,000	6	6	Visionist
60,001—95,000	7	7	Phantasmist
95,001—145,000	8	8	Apparitionist
145,001—220,000	9	9	Spellbinder
220,001—440,000	10	10	Illusionist
440,001—660,000	11	10+1	Illusionist (11th level)
660,001—880,000	12	10+2	Illusionist (12th level)

220,000 experience points per level of experience beyond the 12th.

Illusionists gain 1 h.p. per level after the 10th.

SPELLS USABLE BY CLASS AND LEVEL — ILLUSIONISTS (MAGIC-USERS)

Illusionists Level	1	2	3	4	5	6	7
1	1	-	-	-	-	-	-
2	2	-	-	-	-	-	-
3	2	1	-	-	-	-	-
4	3	2	-	-	-	-	-
5	4	2	1	-	-	-	-
6	4	3	1	-	-	-	-
7	4	3	2	-	-	-	-
8	4	3	2	1	-	-	-
9	5	3	3	2	-	-	-
10	5	4	3	2	1	-	-
11	5	4	3	3	2	-	-
12	5	5	4	3	2	1	-
13	5	5	4	3	2	2	-
14	5	5	4	3	2	2	1
15	5	5	4	4	2	2	2
16	5	5	5	4	3	2	2
17	5	5	5	4	3	2	2
18	5	5	5	5	3	3	2
19	5	5	5	5	4	3	2
20	5	5	5	5	4	3	3
21	5	5	5	5	5	4	3
22	5	5	5	5	5	5	4
23	5	5	5	5	5	5	5
24	6	6	6	6	5	5	5
25	6	6	6	6	6	6	6
26	7	7	7	7	6	6	6

The Thief

The profession of thief is not dishonorable, albeit is neither honorable nor highly respected in some quarters. The major ability for a thief is dexterity, and a character must have not less than a 9 to become a thief. High intelligence is also desirable. Any thief character with a dexterity greater than 15 gains the benefit of being able to add a bonus of 10% to experience points awarded to him or her by the referee. A glance at the **CHARACTER ABILITY** section preceding this will reveal that high dexterity also benefits thieves in the performance of their class functions. These functions are detailed a bit later.

All thieves are neutral or evil, although they can be neutral good (rarely), and of lawful or chaotic nature. Most thieves tend towards evil.

Thieves are principally meant to take by cunning and stealth. Thieves have six-sided hit dice (d6). They are, however, able to wear light (leather) armor and use a fair number of weapons. Although they fight only slightly more effectively than do magic-users, they are able to use stealth in combat most effectively by *back stabbing*. This ability is explained hereafter.

The primary functions of a thief are: 1) *picking pockets*, 2) *opening locks*, 3) *finding/removing traps*, 4) *moving silently*, and 5) *hiding in shadows*. These functions are basically self-explanatory. The chance for success of any performance is based on the ability level of the thief performing it. This is modified with respect to picking pockets by the experience level of his or her victim and by the powers of the observer with respect to hiding in shadows.

These functions are detailed as follows:

1. Picking pockets (or folds of a garment or a girdle) also includes such activities as pilfering and filching small items. It is done by light touch and sleight of hand.

2. Opening locks includes figuring out how to open sliding puzzle locks and foiling magical closures. It is done by picking with tools and by cleverness, plus knowledge and study of such items.

3. Finding/removing traps pertains to relatively small mechanical devices such as poisoned needles, spring blades, and the like. Finding is accomplished by inspection, and they are nullified by mechanical removal or by being rendered harmless.

4. Moving silently is the ability to move with little sound and disturbance, even across a squeaky wooden floor, for instance. It is an ability which improves with experience.

5. Hiding in shadows is the ability to blend into dark areas, to flatten oneself, and by remaining motionless when in sight, to remain unobserved. It is a function of dress and practice.

Secondary functions of a thief are: 1) *listening at doors* to detect sounds behind them, 2) *ascending and descending vertical surfaces* such as walls, and 3) *back stabbing* those who happen upon the thief in the performance of his or her profession.

These functions are described as follows:

1. Listening at doors includes like activity at other portals such as windows. It is accomplished by moving silently to the door and pressing an ear against it to detect sound.

2. Ascending and descending vertical surfaces is the ability of the thief to climb up and down walls. It assumes that the surface is coarse and offers ledges and cracks for toe and hand holds.

3. Back stabbing is the striking of a blow from behind, be it with club, dagger, or sword. The damage done per hit is twice normal for the weapon used per four experience levels of the thief, i.e. double damage at levels 1-4, triple at 5-8, quadruple at levels 9-12, and quintuple at levels 13-16. Note that striking by surprise from behind also increases the hit probability by 20% (+4 on the thief's "to hit" die roll).

Additional abilities which accrue to thieves are:

1. All thieves, regardless of alignment, have their own language, the "Thieves' Cant". This language is known in *addition* to others which may be learned because of race and/or intelligence.

2. At 4th level (Burglar), thieves are able to read 20% of languages, and this ability increases by 5% with each additional level of experience until an 80% probability is attained. This enables the possible reading of instructions and treasure maps without having to resort to a magic item or spell.

3. At 10th Level (Master Thief), thieves are able to decipher magical writings and utilize scrolls of all sorts, excluding those of clerical, but not druidic, nature. However, the fact that thieves do not fully comprehend magic means that there is a 25% chance that writings will be misunderstood. Furthermore, magic spells from scrolls can be mispronounced when uttered, so that there is an increasing chance per level of the spell that it will be the *reverse* of its intent.

These primary, secondary, and tertiary functions are displayed on a table hereafter.

Thieves cannot build strongholds as some other classes of characters do. They can, however, build a tower or fortified building of the small castle type (q.v.) for their own safety; but this construction must be within, or not more than a mile distant from, a town or city.

Any thief character of 10th or greater level may use his small castle type building to set up a headquarters for a gang of thieves, and he or she will accordingly attract from 4-24 other thieves. However, this will bring the enmity of the local Thieves Guild, and they will struggle to do away with the rival organization. Once begun, warfare will end only when and if all the Master Thieves on either or both sides are dead, or if the thief character removes to another locale.

THIEVES TABLE I

Experience Points	Experience Level	6-Sided Dice for Accumulated Hit Points	Level Title
0 — 1,250	1	1	Rogue (Apprentice)
1,251 — 2,500	2	2	Footpad
2,501 — 5,000	3	3	Cutpurse
5,001 — 10,000	4	4	Robber
10,001 — 20,000	5	5	Burglar
20,001 — 42,500	6	6	Filcher
42,501 — 70,000	7	7	Sharper
70,001 — 110,000	8	8	Magsman
110,001 — 160,000	9	9	Thief
160,001 — 220,000	10	10	Master Thief
220,001 — 440,000	11	10+2	Master Thief (11th level)
440,001 — 660,000	12	10+4	Master Thief (12th level)

220,000 experience points per level for each additional level beyond the 12th.

Thieves gain 2 h.p. per level after the 10th.

THIEF FUNCTION TABLE (PLUS RACIAL ADJUSTMENTS)

Level of the Thief	Pick Pockets	Open Locks	Find/ Remove Traps	Move Silently	Hide in Shadows	Hear Noise	Climb Walls	Read Languages
1	30%	25%	20%	15%	10%	10%	85%	-
2	35%	29%	25%	21%	15%	10%	86%	-
3	40%	33%	30%	27%	20%	15%	87%	-
4	45%	37%	35%	33%	25%	15%	88%	20%
5	50%	42%	40%	40%	31%	20%	90%	25%
6	55%	47%	45%	47%	37%	20%	92%	30%
7	60%	52%	50%	55%	43%	25%	94%	35%
8	65%	57%	55%	62%	49%	25%	96%	40%
9	70%	62%	60%	70%	56%	30%	98%	45%
10	80%	67%	65%	78%	63%	30%	99%	50%
11	90%	72%	70%	86%	70%	35%	99.1%	55%
12	100%	77%	75%	94%	77%	35%	99.2%	60%
13	105%	82%	80%	99%	85%	40%	99.3%	65%
14	110%	87%	85%	99%	93%	40%	99.4%	70%
15	115%	92%	90%	99%	99%	50%	99.5%	75%
16	125%	97%	95%	99%	99%	50%	99.6%	80%
17	125%	99%	99%	99%	99%	55%	99.7%	80%

Race of the Thief								
Dwarf	-	+10%	+15%	-	-	-	-10%	-5%
Elf	+5%	-5%	-	+5%	+10%	+5%	-	-
Gnome	-	+5%	+10%	+5%	+5%	+10%	-15%	-
Half-Elf	+10%	-	-	-	+5%	-	-	-
Halfling	+5%	+5%	+5%	+10%	+15%	+5%	-15%	-5%
Half-Orc	-5%	+5%	+5%	-	-	+5%	+5%	-10%

Notes Regarding Thief Function Table:

Percentile dice are rolled to determine whether the thief is successful or not. Any score equal to or less than the percentage shown for the appropriate level of thief performing the designated function will indicate success.

Picking Pockets fails if a score above the percentage shown for the level of thief attempting the function is generated. If the score is 21% or more above the number shown, the victim notices the thief's attempt. The potential victim reduces the thief's chances for success by 5% for every level of experience he or she is above the 3rd, i.e. -5% at 4th level, etc. For example, a high level thief (Master Thief, 12th level) is planning to pick the pockets of a magic-user he has noticed nearby. The base chance for success is 100%, the thief is a half-elf and adds 10% for racial ability; the thief also has 18 dexterity ability score, so another 10% is added. This totals a nice, safe 120% — can't fail! However, the victim happens to be 12th level also, so the subtraction is $9 \times -5\% = -45\%$. This brings the chance for success down to 75%. A good chance, but if 96% or higher is rolled, the thief will be *noticed*, and . . . Success gains an item from the victim; the item is determined at random from a list of possessions unless the exact location of a particular item is known by the thief.

Opening Locks may be attempted by any given thief but once per lock. If the score generated exceeds the adjusted (for *ability* and *race*) base score, the thief has failed; and no amount of trying will ever enable him or her to succeed with that lock, although the thief may try again when he or she has risen to a higher level of experience. Success opens the lock.

Finding/Removing Traps is accomplished in exactly the same manner as opening locks. Roll for each function separately (a trap must be located before removal can be attempted). One try only per thief is allowed. Success deactivates the trap.

Moving Silently can be attempted each time the thief moves. It can be used to approach an area where some creature is expected, thus increasing chances for *surprise* (q.v.), or to approach to back stab, or simply done to pass some guard or watchman. Failure (a dice score in excess of the adjusted base chance) means that movement was not silent (see **SURPRISE**). Success means movement was silent.

Hiding in Shadows cannot be accomplished under direct observation. It can be accomplished with respect to creatures with *infravision* (q.v.) only if some heat producing light source is near to the creature or to the thief

attempting to so hide. Success makes the thief virtually invisible until he or she moves. Note that spells such as *detect invisibility* or *true seeing* will reveal a thief hiding in shadows if such sight is directed towards him or her.

Hearing Noise is simply listening intently. The thief and his or her accomplices must themselves be quiet (but not silent as in moving). This function can be repeated as often as desired. It requires a full minute to listen, i.e. one-tenth of a normal turn, or time equal to a melee round. Note that sleeping creatures, undead, and many other creatures do not make sounds discernible through a portal. Success informs the hearer that someone or something awaits beyond the portal.

Climbing Walls is attempted whenever needed and desired. It is assumed that the thief is successful until the mid point of the climb. At that point the dice are rolled to determine continued success. A score in excess of the adjusted base chance indicates the thief has slipped and fallen. (Your referee will inform you of what amount of damage has been done from the fall.) Success indicates that safe ascent or descent has been accomplished. Note that in some cases a third d10 will have to be rolled to determine the success or failure.

Reading Languages can be attempted but once. Failure — a score greater than the percentage chance shown for the experience level of the thief — means that the language is not understood and no amount of reading will make it comprehensible. However, the thief can try again with each new experience level he or she gains.

The Assassin

Assassins are a sub-class of the thieves, and they have the functions of the latter as well as their own. Thus, to be an assassin, a character must have a minimum *strength* of 12, an *intelligence* of 11 or more, and a *dexterity* score of not less than 12. Assassins do not gain any experience bonuses for having high ability scores.

Just as do thieves, assassins have six-sided dice (d6) for determining the number of *hit points* (q.v.) they can sustain. Assassins are evil in alignment (perforce, as the killing of humans and other intelligent life forms for the purpose of profit is basically held to be the antithesis of weal). They can, of course, be neutral as regards lawful and chaotic evil. As mentioned above, assassins have thieving capabilities and their own ability functions. Because they can use any sort of shield and weapon, they are generally superior to thieves in combat.

An assassin character need not be a member of the Assassins Guild of the town or city he or she dwells in, but all non-player assassin characters are members of such guilds. There is one such guild in most towns and cities, and each controls an area of from 10 to 100 miles radius around the headquarters town or city. Any assassin discovered in a guild area who is not a member of the local Assassins Guild will be invited to join, thus coming under the authority and command of the Guildmaster Assassin. The assassin character need not join, but he or she will be under sentence of death if the character performs an assassination while not a guild member. Further discussion of Assassins' Guilds is given later.

The primary function of assassins is killing. They may use poison — ingested or insinuated by weapon. Poison ingested must be put into the food or drink, and the character performing this action must detail exactly when, where, and how the poisoning will be done. The DM will then adjudicate the action. Poisoned weapons (see **POISON**) used run the risk of being noticed by others. All non-assassins within 10' of the bared weapon have a 10% cumulative chance each per *melee round* (q.v.) of noting the poison and attacking the poison-using assassin and/or calling for the city watch. (There is a 20% chance for attacking the assassin, a 50% chance for calling for the watch, and a 30% chance for shouting for the watch and then attacking the assassin.)

Example: An assassin draws a dagger with a poisoned blade. The first melee round it can be seen by two persons. The percentile dice are rolled for each, but unless 10 or less is rolled, they do not notice the venom. The next melee round the two first seeing the weapon have a 20% chance of noticing the poison, and any others seeing it for the first time have but a 10% chance. If any onlooker *does* see the poison, percentile dice are rolled: a score of 01 to 20 indicates attack, 21 to 70 indicates a hue and cry for the watch, and 71-00 indicates both.

Assassins attack on the same combat tables as thieves do, including *back stabbing*. However, if they *surprise* (q.v.) a victim, they may attack on the ASSASSINATION TABLE. This gives a roughly 50% chance of immediately killing the victim; and if this fails, normal damage according to weapon type and strength ability modifiers still accrues to the victim. Thus, if a poisoned weapon is used, the victim must also make the saving throw versus poison or die. The assassin decides which attack mode he or she will use: assassination, back stabbing, or normal melee combat.

Primary abilities of assassins which enhance their function are those of being able to speak *alignment languages* and being able to *disguise*, as follows:

1. Assassins with intelligence of 15 or more are able to learn an alignment tongue (even those special languages of druids and thieves). This ability is gained at 9th level (Assassin) and with each advance in experience level thereafter. The maximum number of alignment languages which can be spoken by an assassin is *four* — one for each point of intelligence above 14, i.e. one at 15, two at 16, three at 17, and four at 18 intelligence. Note: An assassin would have to be of 12th level (Chief Assassin) and have 18 intelligence to be able to speak four alignment languages. The assassin may select from the following languages:

CHAOTIC EVIL	NEUTRAL EVIL
CHAOTIC GOOD	NEUTRAL GOOD
CHAOTIC NEUTRALITY	NEUTRALITY
LAWFUL EVIL	DRUIDIC
LAWFUL GOOD	THIEVES' CANT
LAWFUL NEUTRALITY	

2. Disguise can be donned in order to gain the opportunity to poison or surprise a victim — or for other reasons. The assassin can disguise himself or herself so as to appear to be a human, semi-human, or humanoid creature of either sex. Disguise can lower height by two or three inches, or raise it by up to four or five inches. It can make the assassin look slimmer or appear much heavier. Disguise can make the assassin appear to be virtually any class of character, a simple pilgrim, a merchant, etc. There is a chance, however, that the victim, or one of his or her henchmen or guards, will notice the disguise. There is a base chance of 2% per day of a disguised assassin being spotted. This chance goes upwards by 2% if the assassin is posing as another class, another race, and/or the opposite sex (maximum of 8% chance). Each concerned party (victim, henchmen, bodyguards) in proximity to the assassin will be checked for, immediately upon meeting the disguised assassin and each 24 hour period thereafter. The chance for spotting a disguised assassin goes downward by 1% for each point below 24 of combined intelligence and wisdom of the observer concerned, i.e. a victim with an intelligence and wisdom combined total of 20 has reduced his or her chances of spotting the disguised assassin by 4%. The reverse is also true; intelligence and wisdom above a combined total of 30 increase the chance of detection by 1% per point. Note: *True seeing* or a *wand of enemy detection* will discover an assassin, as will *detect evil*, or *know alignment* in some cases.

The secondary function of the assassin is spying. This mission can be coupled with the stealing of some item.

Tertiary functions of assassins are the same as thieves. They have all abilities and functions of thieves; but, except for back stabbing, assassins perform thieving at two levels below their assassin level, i.e. a 3rd level assassin has the thieving abilities of a 1st level thief, a 4th level assassin the abilities of a 2nd level thief, etc.

Performing an assassination will gain experience points for the character — awarded for both the fee paid and the level of the victim. These awards are determined by the referee on the basis of a formula given in **ADVANCED DUNGEONS & DRAGONS, DUNGEON MASTERS GUIDE**.

Typical fees paid (in gold pieces) for assassination are:

MINIMUM FEES FOR ASSASSINATION

Level of Assassin	Level of Victim							
	0	1-2	3-4	5-6	7-9	10-12	13-15	16+
1	50	100	150	200	250	-	-	-
2	60	120	175	250	300	350	-	-
3	75	150	225	300	400	500	-	-
4	100	200	300	450	600	750	1000	-
5	150	300	450	700	900	1100	1300	1500
6	250	500	750	1000	1300	1600	2000	2500
7	400	800	1200	1600	2000	2500	3500	4500
8	600	1200	1800	2400	3000	3750	5000	7500
9	850	1700	2600	3500	4400	6000	7500	10000
10	1200	2400	3600	4800	6000	8000	10000	15000
11	1700	3500	5100	7000	9000	12000	15000	20000
12	2500	5000	7500	10000	13000	17500	20000	25000
13	3500	7000	11000	15000	19000	25000	32500	40000
14	5000	10000	15000	20000	27500	35000	45000	60000
15	10000	20000	35000	50000	75000	100000	150000	250000

Important, popular, and/or noble victims will be considered as being above their actual level with respect to fee. For example, an elder of a town who is generous and just (thus popular) might be only 4th level, but for purposes of payment for assassination the character would be considered at three times actual level.

An assassin character cannot have any hirelings until he or she attains 4th level; at that time lower level assassins may be taken into service. Upon attaining 8th level, the character may also include thieves amongst his or her hirelings. Upon attaining 12th level, the character may hire any class desired. Of course, only neutral or evil characters will serve an assassin. The total number of henchmen is that dictated by the character's charisma score. "Followers" are also possible, but these come only at the two uppermost levels of the assassin class.

In order for an assassin character to gain experience levels above the 13th (Prime Assassin), he or she must have the requisite experience points and then either assassinate the local Guildmaster Assassin (14th level) or challenge him or her to a duel to the death. Likewise, a 14th level player character assassin can journey to the place where the Grandfather of Assassins (15th level) has his or her headquarters and slay him or her by assassination or in a duel. Note that duplicity, trickery, ambush, and all forms of treachery are considered as fair by assassins. A higher level character can accept a challenge and then have the challenger slain by archers, for instance.

As Guildmaster (or Guildmistress) Assassin, a character will have a body of guild members which numbers between 7-28. Upon change of leadership it is 75% likely that each guild member will leave the area. Thus, it will be necessary for the new Guildmaster to allow new members into the guild. These new assassins will all be 1st level and must be worked up in experience levels. The maximum number of such "followers" of the local guild will be set by your referee. They are in addition to normal henchmen. Note that guild members are loyal only to strength, power, and profit.

The headquarters of a guild is always within a large town or big city. It must not be a noticeable fortress or an ostentatious place. It is typically a warehouse or other nondescript structure, with safeguards and traps added. This avoids attention and unwanted notoriety. All expenses of maintaining the guild and its members — excluding the Guildmaster — are assumed to be fully paid for by normal guild activities. Any improvements, changes, the expenses of the leader, and all other special costs must be borne by the Guildmaster Assassin.

The headquarters of the Grandfather of Assassins can be virtually anywhere and of any form — cavern, castle, monastery, palace, temple, you name it. However, if it is a large and obvious place, the headquarters must be located well away from all communities — such as in the midst of a murky woods, a dismal marsh or fen, a lonely moor, a deserted island, a remote coast, or far into forsaken hills or atop a mountain. Upon attaining the headship of all assassins, the new Grandfather or Grandmother must pay all remaining followers of the former head 1000 gold pieces for each of their experience levels, destroy the old headquarters, and construct a new one somewhere else.

ASSASSINS (THIEVES) TABLE

Experience Points	Experience Level	6-Sided Dice for Accumulated Hit Points	Level Title
0—1,500	1	1	Bravo (Apprentice)
1,501—3,000	2	2	Rutterkin
3,001—6,000	3	3	Waghalter
6,000—12,000	4	4	Murderer
12,001—25,000	5	5	Thug
25,001—50,000	6	6	Killer
50,001—100,000	7	7	Cutthroat
100,001—200,000	8	8	Executioner
200,001—300,000	9	9	Assassin
300,001—425,000	10	10	Expert Assassin
425,001—575,000	11	11	Senior Assassin
575,001—750,000	12	12	Chief Assassin
750,001—1,000,000	13	13	Prime Assassin
1,000,001—1,500,000	14	14	Guildmaster Assassin
1,500,001 and Over	15	15	Grandfather of Assassins

The Monk

The monk is the most unusual of all characters, the hardest to qualify for, and perhaps, the most deadly. That is why the class is given out of alphabetical order at the end of the section pertaining to character classes.

To be a monk a character must have the following *minimum* ability scores: *strength* 15, *wisdom* 15, *dexterity* 15, and *constitution* 11. Monks never gain any experience points bonuses. Dexterity gives them no armor class adjustment.

Monks are monastic aesthetics who practice rigorous mental and physical training and discipline in order to become superior. Therefore they must always be *lawful* in alignment, although they can be evil, good, or neutral with respect to their approach to lawfulness. A monk who for any reason loses this lawful alignment loses all monk abilities and must begin again as a first level character. Non-player character monks will be aligned as follows: 50% lawful good, 35% lawful neutral, 15% lawful evil.

A brief study of CHARACTER CLASSES TABLES I and II will reveal that the monk appears to be quite weak, even considering that at the topmost level a monk can have 18, albeit four-sided, hit dice (an average of 45 hit points without constitution score additions, if any) and has a good selection of weapons to choose from. Monks have no spell ability, cannot wear armor or use a shield, and not even flaming oil is usable by them. This seems to make a weak character class indeed. But this impression is false, for monks have their own special attack and defense capabilities, certain other powers, and most of the abilities of the thief class and some clerical-type capabilities as well. So, while the class has drawbacks, it is very strong.

With respect to combat, monks attack on the same table as thieves. However, they add one-half of a hit point per level of experience to the amount of damage they score when they successfully attack an opponent with a weapon. This simulates their study and knowledge of weapons and anatomy. A 1st level monk scores x + ½ HP of damage, where x equals the damage done by the weapon used and HP equals the number of hit points of damage. A 2nd level monk does x + 1 when he or she scores a hit, a 3rd level x + 1½, and so on all the way to Grand Master of Flowers who scores x + 8½ HP damage. Monks of median level and above actually fight better without weapons, using their open hands, despite the weapon damage bonus they receive.

Open hand combat damage is shown on MONKS TABLE II below. In addition, the monk has a chance to *stun*, or even kill, an opponent. An opponent is stunned by a monk for 1-6 (d6) melee rounds if the score of the monk's "to hit" die score exceeds the minimum number required for a hit by 5 or more, i.e. if 15 is required, a score of 20 would indicate a *stun*. The "to hit" scores rolled by the monk are never modified by any strength ability bonuses. The chance to kill is a percentage which equals the armor class (AC) of the opponent, modified by the number of experience levels above seven which the monk has attained. AC -1 is a negative chance for killing, as an example, but a monk of 9th level (two above 7th) would allow a 1% chance of killing. Note that 1) the monk must score a hit, and 2) the hit must stun the opponent, and 3) the percentile dice score must be equal to or less than the armor class of the stunned opponent, modified by the monk's levels over 7th, in order to score a kill.

Open hand fighting also allows the monk multiple attacks at such time as the monk has attained the 4th or higher experience level.

Monks make saving throws on the table used by thieves, but they gain certain advantages: Non-magical missiles (arrows, bolts, bullets, thrown daggers, thrown javelins, thrown spears, etc.) which would normally hit can be dodged or knocked aside if the monk is able to make his or her saving throw against *petrification* for each such potential hit. In other respects, if a monk makes his or her saving throw against an attack form, the monk will sustain *no* damage from the attack, even if the attack form was a *fireball*, for instance. At 9th level (Master of the North Wind) or higher, a monk who fails to make his or her saving throw will still sustain but one-half the total potential damage which the attack form could deliver, if possible. That is, a fireball would do 50% of total damage, but the gaze of a basilisk would still petrify the monk.

At 1st level of experience, a monk is as likely to be surprised as any other character, i.e. 33 1/3%. This chance goes down to 32% at 2nd level, and it thereafter goes down 2% per level, so there is only a 30% chance of surprising a 3rd level monk, 28% chance at 4th level, 26% chance at 5th level, etc.

Monks have the following thief abilities which they perform at identical level of experience to that of a thief, i.e. a 1st level monk performs as a 1st level thief, a 2nd level monk as a 2nd level thief, etc. The abilities are:

1. Open Locks

2. Find/Remove Traps
3. Move Silently
4. Hide in Shadows
5. Hear Noise
6. Climb Walls

Although the chance of falling while climbing walls is the same as that of a thief of equal level, monks can escape taking damage as follows:

— At 4th level (Disciple), a monk can fall up to 20' if he or she is within 1' of a wall.

— At 6th level (Master), a monk can fall up to 30' if he or she is within 4' of a wall.

— At 13th level (Master of Winter), a monk can fall any distance if he or she is within 8' of a wall.

The monk must have an opportunity to periodically make contact with the wall during the descent. The wall is used by the monk to slow the fall so that no hit points of damage are sustained from the fall. Note that when reference to a wall is made, any similar surface, such as a tree trunk, cliff face, and the like, are equally useful to the monk.

The other abilities of monks are shown on the MONKS ABILITY TABLE below.

MONKS TABLE I: EXPERIENCE POINTS AND LEVELS

Experience Points	Experience Level	4-Sided Dice for Accumulated Hit Points	Level Title
0 — 2,250	1	2	Novice
2,251 — 4,750	2	3	Initiate
4,751 — 10,000	3	4	Brother
10,001 — 22,500	4	5	Disciple
22,501 — 47,500	5	6	Immaculate
47,501 — 98,000	6	7	Master
98,001 — 200,000	7	8	Superior Master
200,001 — 350,000	8	9	Master of Dragons
350,001 — 500,000	9	10	Master of the North Wind
500,001 — 700,000	10	11	Master of the West Wind
700,001 — 950,000	11	12	Master of the South Wind
950,001 — 1,250,000	12	13	Master of the East Wind
1,250,001 — 1,750,000	13	14	Master of Winter
1,750,001 — 2,250,000	14	15	Master of Autumn
2,250,001 — 2,750,000	15	16	Master of Summer
2,750,001 — 3,250,000	16	17	Master of Spring
3,250,001 & +	17	18	Grand Master of Flowers

MONKS TABLE II: MONKS ABILITY TABLE

Level Title	Level	Effective Armor Class	Move	Open Hand Attacks per Melee Round*	Open Hand Damage	Special Abilities
Novice	1	10	15"	1	1-3	-
Initiate	2	9	16"	1	1-4	-
Brother	3	8	17"	1	1-6	A
Disciple	4	7	18"	5/4	1-6	B
Immaculate	5	7	19"	5/4	2-7	C
Master	6	6	20"	3/2	2-8	D
Superior Master	7	5	21"	3/2	3-9	E
Master of Dragons	8	4	22"	3/2	2-12	F
Master of the North Wind	9	3	23"	2	3-12	G
Master of the West Wind	10	3	24"	2	3-13	H
Master of the South Wind	11	2	25"	5/2	4-13	I
Master of the East Wind	12	1	26"	5/2	4-16	J
Master of Winter	13	0	27"	5/2	5-17	K
Master of Autumn	14	-1	28"	3	5-20	-
Master of Summer	15	-1	29"	3	6-24	-
Master of Spring	16	-2	30"	4	5-30	-
Grand Master of Flowers	17	-3	32"	4	8-32	-

*Listings with a slash indicate extra attacks after the appropriate number of rounds, i.e. 5/4 means 5 attacks per 4 rounds, with the additional attack coming at the end of the round sequence.

Notes Regarding Special Abilities:

Each special ability is designated by a capital letter.

A. The ability to *speak with animals* as druids do which begins at 3rd level of experience.

B. The ability to mask the mind so that *ESP* has only a 30% chance of success. This power begins at 4th level, and with each level of experience which the monk gains thereafter, the chance for success of ESPing the monk's thoughts drops by 2%, i.e. 28% chance of success on a 5th level monk, 26% on a 6th level, etc.

C. At 5th experience level a monk is not subject to diseases of any sort, nor is he ever affected by *haste* or *slow* spells.

D. The ability to use self-induced catalepsy to appear dead. This can be done perfectly, as the 6th (or higher) level monk is able to lower his or her body temperature and heart rate. The monk is able to maintain this state for twice the number of turns (10 minute periods) which equal his level, i.e. 12 turns at 6th level, 14 at 7th, etc.

E. At 7th level the monk gains the ability to heal damage on his or her body. The amount of damage which can be healed is 2-5 hit points (d4 + 1), and this amount increases by 1 hit point with each experience level gained thereafter, i.e. 3-6 HP at 8th level, 4-7 at 9th, etc. This may be done once per day.

F. The ability to *speak with plants* as druids do. This power is attained at 8th level.

G. *Beguiling, charms, hypnosis,* and *suggestion* spells have only a 50% chance of affecting a monk of the 9th level of experience. That is, the monk is 50% resistant to such magic. This resistance increases 5% per level thereafter, so that at 10th level such spells have but a 45% chance of affecting the monk, 40% at 11th level, and so on. Saving throws apply if resistance fails.

H. *Telepathic* and *mind blast* attacks (see **ADVANCED DUNGEONS & DRAGONS, MONSTER MANUAL,** *Mind Flayer*) upon a monk of 10th or higher level are made as if the character had an 18 intelligence, due to the monk's mental discipline.

I. At 11th and higher levels of experience monks are not affected by poison of any type.

J. Geas and quest spells have no effect upon monks of 12th or higher level.

K. The last ability gained, and perhaps the most terrible power, is that fabled attack which enables the monk to set up vibrations in the body of the victim, and the monk can then control such vibrations so as to cause death to occur when the monk stops them. Known as the "quivering palm", the monk merely touches his victim to set up the deadly vibrations. The victim can be virtually any creature. This power is limited as follows:

1. It can be attempted but once per week, and the monk must touch the intended victim within 3 melee rounds or the power is drained for one week.

2. It has no affect on the undead or creatures which can be hit only by magical weaponry.

3. The victim cannot have more hit dice than the monk using the power, and in any event, the total hit points of the victim cannot exceed those of the monk by more than 200%, or the power has no effect.

4. The command to die (the control of the vibrations) must be given by the monk within a set time limit, or else the vibrations simply cease of their own accord and do no damage whatsoever. The time limit of death command is one day per level of experience the monk has gained at the time the power is used.

There are a number of strictures which monk characters must abide by. These restrictions apply to 1) armor and weapons, 2) treasure, 3) magic items usable, 4) strength ability adjustments, 5) henchmen, and 6) advancement in level, as follows:

1. Armor, as previously stated, cannot be worn. Weapons usable by monk characters are shown on **CHARACTER CLASSES TABLE II**; weapons not listed cannot be used.

2. Monks, much like paladins (q.v.), may not retain more than a small fraction of whatever treasure they gain. A monk may possess no more than two magic weapons and three other magic items (see 3 below) at any time. While monks may retain money sufficient for their modest needs, and to support their henchmen (see 5 below), all other treasure and excess magic items must be bestowed upon (non player) religious institutions. (See also Followers hereafter.)

3. Magic items usable by monks include all magical varieties of weapons listed (unless proscribed), rings, and those miscellaneous magic items which are usable by thieves. No other magic items of any sort may be employed by monks.

4. Monks do not gain any bonuses, either with respect to increasing "to hit" probability or to increase hit points of damage, for strength ability.

5. Until attaining the rank of Master, monks may not have any hirelings or henchmen at all. At 6th level of experience, monks may hire persons on a short-duration basis — for the duration of a single adventure only. At this level, they may also acquire up to two henchmen. Henchmen may be fighters (but not paladins nor rangers), thieves, or assassins. With each level of experience above the 6th which the monk attains, he or she may add one additional henchman, until the maximum number established by the monk's charisma score is reached. Monks will gain followers upon attaining 8th level; this is discussed hereafter.

6. There can be only a limited number of monks above 7th level (Superior or Master). There are three 8th level (Master of Dragons) and but one of each higher level. When a player character monk gains sufficient experience points to qualify him or her for 8th level, the commensurate abilities are attained only temporarily. The monk must find and defeat in single combat, hand-to-hand, without weapons or magic items, one of the 8th level monks — the White, the Green, or the Red. The same must be done at the ninth and higher levels. The

loser of these combats loses enough experience points to place him or her at the lowest number possible to attain the level just beneath the new level. The monk character will know where to locate the higher level monks; and he or she must proceed immediately to do combat or else lose experience points equal to the number which will place him or her at the lowest number possible to have attained the level just beneath that of the monk he or she should have sought out but did not. That is, the player character drops to 7th level in the above case and must then work upwards once again.

Followers: When a monk player character attains the 8th level of experience, he or she will gain a number of monks as followers upon defeating the monk which held the 8th level position that the player character has now gotten. He or she will attract from 2-5 1st level monks if the player character has a monastery or monastery-like building to use as a headquarters. These followers may be worked upwards in levels of experience. The player character will attract 1 or 2 additional monks of 1st level for each additional level of experience the player gains.

While followers of a monk are as loyal as his or her other henchmen, they automatically leave service when they attain the level of Superior Master (7th).

All followers will be of the exact same alignment as the monk player character. If he or she changes alignment, the current followers will desert, but new ones can still be gained by advancement in level.

The monastery or monastery-like headquarters of the monk can be that of the character he or she defeated to attain 8th or higher level, or it can be a building specially constructed by the monk player character after attaining 8th or higher level. In the latter case, the monk may retain up to 250,000 gold pieces value in treasure in order to finance construction of the place. He or she may also retain sufficient funds thereafter to maintain such a place.

Note that monk followers require no support, upkeep, or pay of any sort.

The Multi-Classed Character

The game assumes that only non- or semi-human characters can be multi-classed, and only certain class combinations are possible, depending on the race of the character. Although these are listed in the section dealing with each race of character, multi-class character possibilities are also shown below in order to aid in selection of your character's class or multi-class. Cleric combinations (with fighter types) may use edged weapons.

Cleric/Fighter: This combination is strong in defensive and revitalization capabilities, plus the offensive missile and melee combat power of the fighter. Hit points average will be good. Half-elves and half-orcs may be cleric/fighters.

Cleric/Fighter/Magic-user: One of the best of the multi-class options, this gives good offensive and defensive spell capability plus the fighter's melee combat strength. Half-elves may be cleric/fighter/magic-users.

Cleric/Ranger: See cleric/fighter above. This combination is potent in outdoor situations as well. Half-elves may be cleric/rangers.

Cleric/Magic-user: This combination gives the character a great variety and selection of spells, as well as the use of armor and more weapons. Hit points are somewhat better than those of the magic-user class alone. Half-elves may be cleric/magic-users.

Cleric/Thief: This is a combination of classes which gives both defensive and stealth potential. Hit points are improved with regard to the thief class only. As with all thief class combinations, however, any functions as a thief are under the restrictions of that class with regard to armor, i.e. only leather armor and no shield. Half-orcs may be cleric/thieves.

Cleric/Assassin: Seemingly strange, this combination is quite understandable when the race which can operate in these two classes at the same time is noted. The combination gives great potential in defensive and stealth situations and very powerful assassination attack capabilities. Hit points are good because of clerical hit dice. Half-orcs may be clerical assassins.

Fighter/Magic-user: Obviously, this combination allows excellent armor protection, the use of weaponry, and spells. Hit points are good on the average (5½ + 2½ = 8 ÷ 2 = 4 hit points per double-classed level). *Elves* and *half-elves* may be fighter/magic-users.

Fighter/Illusionist: See Fighter/Magic-user above. *Gnomes* may be fighter/illusionists.

Fighter/Thief: By combining these two classes — the armor, weapons, and combat capabilities of the fighter with the stealth and other abilities of the thief — a very effective character is created, even though thieving functions restrict the character to leather armor and no shield. Hit points are good. *Dwarves, elves, gnomes, half-elves, halflings,* and *half-orcs* may be fighter/thieves.

Fighter/Assassin: This combination gives excellent missile and melee combat ability, plus assassination and stealth potential. Hit points are good. *Half-orcs* may be fighter/assassins.

Fighter/Magic-user/Thief: Combat, spell, and stealth capabilities are given to the character who opts this multi-class combination. This is a very powerful mix. Hit points are good (5½ + 2½ + 3½ = 11½ ÷ 3 = 4) on the average. *Elves* and *half-elves* may be fighter/magic-user/thieves.

Magic-user/Thief: This combination does not offer all of the options open to a fighter/magic-user/thief, but advancement is usually more rapid. Average hit points are fair, i.e. 3 per level. *Elves* and *half-elves* may be magic-user/thieves.

Illusionist/Thief: See Magic-User/Thief above. *Gnomes* may be illusionist/thieves.

The Character With Two Classes

Unlike multi-classed characters who are of non- or semi-human race, the character with two classes must be human. To attain the second class, the character must switch his or her profession at some point. Thereafter no progression in the original class is possible.

In order to switch from one class to another, the character must have an ability score of 15 or more in the principal attribute(s) ability of the original class and a 17 or 18 in the principal attribute(s) of the class changed to. Note that nearly any combination of classes is thus possible, i.e. cleric & fighter, cleric & paladin, cleric & ranger, etc. Alignment will preclude some combinations.

When the character opts to cease his or her old profession and become a new class, the character retains the number of hit dice (and the commensurate hit points) due to a character of the level of his or her class. However, all other functions of the character are at 1st level of experience, for that is his or her ability in the newly espoused class. Furthermore, if, during the course of any adventure, the character resorts to the use of any of the capabilities of functions of his or her former class, the character gains *no* experience for the adventure. Having switched classes, the character must perform strictly within the parameters of his or her new profession. Reversion to the former class negates all experience potential for the new class with respect to the course of recent activities, i.e. the adventure during which original profession functions were resorted to.

At such time as the character has attained a level of experience in his or her new class which exceeds the character's former class level, the following benefits are gained:

1. A hit die appropriate to the new class is gained for each increase in level of experience, up to the maximum normal for the class in question (and thereafter hit points are likewise gained), and

2. The character may mix functions freely and still gain experience, although restrictions regarding armor, shield, and/or weapon apply with regard to operations particular to one or both classes.

Example: A character with ability scores of 15 strength, 17 intelligence, 12 wisdom, 10 dexterity, 16 constitution, and 7 charisma is begun as a fighter. After attaining 6th level, the player switches the character to magic-user. This allows the character to retain six ten-sided hit dice, but in all other respects he or she must be a 1st level magic-user, wearing no armor, carrying those weapons usable by his or her new class, and using spells to combat opponents. When 7th level of experience is gained, however, the

character gets a four-sided hit die for additional hit points he or she can sustain at the new level. Furthermore, the character can now carry (but not wear) armor and weapons not normally usable by magic-users, and resort to their use if the need arises and not be penalized in respect to experience as a magic-user, for he or she has already surpassed in the new class the disciplines of the former. Thus, no harm accrues to his or her experience as a magic-user. Note that this does *not* allow spell use while armor clad, such as an elven fighter/magic user is able to do.

ALIGNMENT

After generating the *abilities* of your character, selecting his or her *race*, and deciding upon a *class*, it is necessary to determine the *alignment* of the character. It is possible that the selection of the class your character will profess has predetermined alignment: a druid is neutral, a paladin is lawful good, a thief can be neutral or evil, an assassin is always evil. Yet, except for druids and paladins, such restrictions still leave latitude — the thief can be lawful neutral, lawful evil, neutral evil, chaotic evil, chaotic neutral, neutral, or even neutral good; and the assassin has nearly as many choices. The alignments possible for characters are described below.

Chaotic Evil: The major precepts of this alignment are freedom, randomness, and woe. Laws and order, kindness, and good deeds are disdained. Life has no value. By promoting chaos and evil, those of this alignment hope to bring themselves to positions of power, glory, and prestige in a system ruled by individual caprice and their own whims.

Chaotic Good: While creatures of this alignment view freedom and the randomness of action as ultimate truths, they likewise place value on life and the welfare of each individual. Respect for individualism is also great. By promoting the gods of chaotic good, characters of this alignment seek to spread their values throughout the world.

Chaotic Neutral: Above respect for life and good, or disregard for life and promotion of evil, the chaotic neutral places randomness and disorder. Good and evil are complimentary balance arms. Neither are preferred, nor must either prevail, for ultimate chaos would then suffer.

Lawful Evil: Creatures of this alignment are great respecters of laws and strict order, but life, beauty, truth, freedom and the like are held as valueless, or at least scorned. By adhering to stringent discipline, those of lawful evil alignment hope to impose their yoke upon the world.

Lawful Good: While as strict in their prosecution of law and order, characters of lawful good alignment follow these precepts to improve the common weal. Certain freedoms must, of course, be sacrificed to bring order; but truth is of highest value, and life and beauty of great importance. The benefits of this society are to be brought to all.

Lawful Neutral: Those of this alignment view regulation as all-important, taking a middle road betwixt evil and good. This is because the ultimate harmony of the world — and the whole of the universe — is considered by lawful neutral creatures to have its sole hope rest upon law and order. Evil or good are immaterial beside the determined purpose of bringing all to predictability and regulation.

Neutral Evil: The neutral evil creature views law and chaos as unnecessary considerations, for pure evil is all-in-all. Either might be used, but both are disdained as foolish clutter useless in eventually bringing maximum evilness to the world.

Neutral Good: Unlike those directly opposite them (neutral evil) in alignment, creatures of neutral good believe that there must be some regulation in combination with freedoms if the best is to be brought to the world — the most beneficial conditions for living things in general and intelligent creatures in particular.

True Neutral: The "true" neutral looks upon all other alignments as facets of the system of things. Thus, each aspect — evil and good, chaos and law — of things must be retained in balance to maintain the status quo; for things as they are cannot be improved upon except temporarily, and even then but superficially. Nature will prevail and keep things as they were meant to be, provided the "wheel" surrounding the hub of nature does not become unbalanced due to the work of unnatural forces — such as human and other intelligent creatures interfering with what is meant to be.

Naturally, there are all variations and shades of tendencies within each alignment. The descriptions are generalizations only. A character can be basically *good* in its "true" neutrality, or tend towards *evil*. It is probable that your campaign referee will keep a graph of the drift of your character on the alignment chart. This is affected by the actions (and desires) of your character during the course of each adventure, and will be reflected on the graph. You may find that these actions are such as to cause the declared alignment to be shifted towards, or actually to, some other.

Changing Alignment:

While involuntary change of alignment is quite possible, it is very difficult for a character to voluntarily switch from one to another, except within limited areas. Evil alignment can be varied along the like axis. The neutral character can opt for some more specific alignment. Your referee will probably require certain stringent sacrifices and appropriate acts — possibly a quest, as well — for any other voluntary alignment change. In fact, even axial change within evil or good, or radial movement from neutrality may require strong proofs of various sorts.

Further voluntary change will be even more difficult. Changing back to a forsaken alignment is next to impossible on a voluntary basis. Even involuntary drift will bring the necessity of great penance.

CHARACTER HIT POINTS

Each character has a varying number of hit points, just as monsters do. These hit points represent how much damage (actual or potential) the character can withstand before being killed. A certain amount of these hit points represent the actual physical punishment which can be sustained. The remainder, a significant portion of hit points at higher levels, stands for skill, luck, and/or magical factors. A typical man-at-arms can take about 5 hit points of damage before being killed. Let us suppose that a 10th level fighter has 55 hit points, plus a bonus of 30 hit points for his constitution, for a total of 85 hit points. This is the equivalent of about 18 hit dice for creatures, about what it would take to kill four huge warhorses. It is ridiculous to assume that even a fantastic fighter can take that much punishment. The same holds true to a lesser extent for clerics, thieves, and the other classes. Thus, the majority of hit points are symbolic of combat skill, luck (bestowed by supernatural powers), and magical forces.

Hit points are determined by *hit dice*. At 1st level a character has but one hit die *(exception: rangers and monks begin with two dice each)*. At each successive level another hit die is gained, i.e. the die is rolled to determine how many additional hit points the character gets. Hit points can be magically restored by *healing* potions, *cure wounds* spells, rings of regeneration, or even by *wish* spells. However, a character's hit points can never exceed the total initially set by hit dice, constitution bonus (or penalty) and magical devices. For example, if a character has 26 hit points at the beginning of an adventure, he or she cannot drink a potion or be enchanted to above that number, 26 in this case.

As an example, let us assume that the character with 26 hit points mentioned above is engaged in an adventure. Early in the course of exploring the dungeon, he or she falls into a 10' deep pit taking one six-sided die (1d6) of damage — 4 hit points of damage, so the character drops to 22 hit points. Next, he or she takes 15 hit points of damage in combat, so the character drops to 7 hit points. A cleric in the party uses a *cure serious wounds* spell on the character, and this restores 10 (for example, depending upon the die roll) of his or her lost hit points, so the character has a total of 17. Later activities reduce the character to 3 hit points, but the party uses a *wish* spell to restore all members to full hit points, so at that time the character goes up to 26 once more.

Rest also restores hit points, for it gives the body a chance to heal itself and regain the stamina or force which adds the skill, luck, and magical hit points.

Your character's class will determine which sort of die you will roll to determine hit points. In some campaigns the referee will keep this total secret, informing players only that they feel "strong", "fatigued" or "very weak", thus indicating waning hit points. In other campaigns the Dungeon Master will have players record their character's hit points and keep track of all changes. Both methods are acceptable, and it is up to your DM as to which will be used in the campaign you participate in.

ESTABLISHING THE CHARACTER

By determining abilities, race, class, alignment, and hit points you have

created your character. Next you must name him or her, and possibly give some family background (and name a next of kin as heir to the possessions of the character if he or she should meet an untimely death) to *personify* the character. Having done all that, your Dungeon Master will introduce your character to the campaign setting. In all likelihood, whether the locale is a village, town, or city, your character will have to acquaint himself or herself with the territory.

The first step will often be getting into the place, i.e. a gate guard demanding to know what business you have in the town or city. Thereafter it will be necessary to locate a safe and reasonably priced place in which to lodge — typically an inn of some sort, but perhaps a rented cot, a loft or even chambers at a hostel. Since the location selected will have to serve as base and depot, it must be relatively safe from intrusion or burglary. Once a headquarters has been found, your character can set about learning the lay of the land, and attempt to find the trade establishments needed to supply the desired equipment for adventuring. Perhaps it will also be necessary to locate where other player characters reside in order to engage in joint expeditions.

In any event, your character created, personified, and established will be ready to adventure once equipment is purchased and relations with other player characters are settled. If player characters are not immediately available, or if they are not co-operative, it is advisable that men-at-arms be hired. Hirelings of this sort, as well as *henchmen* (q.v.), are detailed in the sections entitled **HIRELINGS** and **HENCHMEN.**

CHARACTER LANGUAGES

All humans, as well as those semi-humans and non-humans in close contact with people, speak the "common tongue". This language is spoken by all states in the central campaign area, but your referee may well have areas in which the common tongue is different from that which your character speaks.

In addition to the common tongue, all intelligent creatures able to converse in speech use special languages particular to their alignment. These *alignment languages* are: Chaotic Evil, Chaotic Good, Chaotic Neutral, Lawful Evil, Lawful Good, Lawful Neutral, Neutral Evil, Neutral Good, and Neutrality. The alignment of your character will dictate which language he or she speaks, for *only one alignment dialect can be used by a character* (cf. **CHARACTER CLASSES**, *The Assassin*). If a character changes alignment, the previously known language is no longer able to be spoken by him or her.

In addition to the above, *druids* (q.v.) have their own special tongue, and *thieves* have their secret speech, the Thieves' Cant.

Therefore, a character will speak at least two languages — common and alignment. He or she might also be able to converse in the special patois of druids or thieves. Semi-human and non-human characters are able to speak racial tongues as well. (See **CHARACTER RACES**.) In most campaigns, it is likely that open alignment speech will be frowned upon as a serious breach of social etiquette.

A character can learn additional languages. Even the rather slow (80 I.Q.) can learn one additional language. However, his vocabulary, usage, and ability to translate must, perforce, be limited. The very bright can learn five, six, or even seven. (For details of the number of tongues which can be learned see **CHARACTER ABILITIES**, *Intelligence*.) Here is how a new language is learned:

The character must find a person (human, semi-human, or non-human) or talking creature who speaks the language which is to be learned. The character must then be in close proximity to his or her instructor for up to one year, and prior to that period the language can be learned one month early for each point of intelligence above 12. Thus, a character with 13 intelligence learns the new language in 11 months, 14 intelligence learns in 10 months, all the way to 18 intelligence which requires but six months to learn. Only one new language can be studied at any given time.

Which languages are knowable in a campaign is strictly up to the DM who runs it. The following list gives some of the languages typically used:

Dwarvish	Halfling	Lizardman
Elvish	Hobgoblin	Ogrish
Goblin	Kobold	Orcish

All of the above may not normally be available due to campaign circumstances, and languages not listed might be common. Consult your Dungeon Master. Note that if, for example, you capture a centaur or talking dragon of some sort, it is possible to learn the appropriate creature tongue.

MONEY

Starting Money

Your character is unusual, exceptional as compared to the norm. This applies to abilities and funds as well. Thus, he or she will have a large supply of coins with which to purchase equipment and supplies to begin adventuring. The possible number of gold pieces with which a player begins depends upon the character class:

Cleric	30-180 g.p. (3d6)
Fighter	50-200 g.p. (5d4)
Magic-user	20- 80 g.p. (2d4)
Thief	20-120 g.p. (2d6)
Monk	5- 20 g.p. (5d4)

To determine the number of gold pieces your character has at the start, simply roll the appropriate dice and total the sum (adding a decimal place if necessary).

Most of these funds will quickly be spent on the costs of staying in the adventuring area and acquiring the equipment which will be used for adventuring. (See BASIC EQUIPMENT AND SUPPLIES COSTS table hereafter.)

The Monetary System

The basic unit of exchange is the *gold piece* (g.p. hereafter). There are coins of lesser and greater value, and these are shown on the table below. It is also common to use gems of various sorts and values as coin.

10 copper pieces (c.p.)	= 1 silver piece
20 silver pieces (s.p.)	= 1 g.p.
2 electrum pieces (e.p.)	= 1 g.p.
1 platinum piece (p.p.)	= 5 g.p.

Thus:

$$200 \text{ c.p.} = 20 \text{ s.p.} = 2 \text{ e.p.} = 1 \text{ g.p.} = 1/5 \text{ p.p.}$$

It is assumed that the size and weight of each coin is relatively equal to each other coin, regardless of type.

Your character will most probably be adventuring in an area where money is plentiful. Think of the situation as similar to Alaskan boom towns during the gold rush days, when eggs sold for one dollar each and mining tools sold for $20, $50, and $100 or more! Costs in the adventuring area are distorted because of the law of supply and demand — the supply of coin is high, while supplies of equipment for adventurers are in great demand.

Money Changing, Banks, Loans & Jewelers

Large sums of lower value coins can be changed to a smaller number of larger value coins, and vice versa, at a relatively small cost — typically 3% of the transaction. This is done at the *money changer's*. The money changer will also score as a banker, keeping funds and giving a marker to vouch for the amount. Note that bankers will *not* usually give any interest.

Bankers will give loans according to the reliability, reknown, status, and material possessions of the individual. An unknown and low-level character is unlikely to get a loan without giving security for the value of the amount borrowed. Furthermore, the interest rate will be high — typically 10% per month or even 5% per week. A well-known and propertied character can typically get large loans at relatively low interest — 1% per week or thereabouts.

Jewelers, and gem merchants, will buy and sell jewelry and gems. The buying price will usually be 20% under the actual value of the piece or stone.

Characters should carefully shop around whenever possible to determine which establishment offers them the best value.

EQUIPPING THE CHARACTER

Careful selection of equipment and supplies for characters is very important. Often there will not be sufficient funds to purchase everything desired, so intelligent choices will have to be made. Also, the choice of equipment should always be done with respect to encumbrance (see **MOVEMENT**) restrictions.

In many campaigns it is necessary for the characters to shop in a number of places in order to obtain everything they desire. A few games will have a trader's establishment in which everything, or nearly everything, can be found, but the average costs will be higher because these traders are middle-men.

As in most dealings, the buyer should always beware. Things may be as they appear or they might be otherwise . . .

A list of goods typically desired by characters follows.

BASIC EQUIPMENT AND SUPPLIES COSTS

Armor

Banded	90 g.p.	Ring	30 g.p.
Chain	75 g.p.	Scale	45 g.p.
Helmet, great	15 g.p.	Shield, large	15 g.p.
Helmet, small	10 g.p.	Shield, small	10 g.p.
Leather	5 g.p.	Shield, small, wooden	1 g.p.
Padded	4 g.p.	Splinted	80 g.p.
Plate	400 g.p.	Studded	15 g.p.

Arms

Arrow, normal, single	2 s.p.	Javelin	10 s.p.
Arrow, normal, dozen	1 g.p.	Lance	6 g.p.
Arrow, silver, single	1 g.p.	Mace, footman's	8 g.p.
Axe, battle	5 g.p.	Mace, horseman's	4 g.p.
Axe, hand or throwing	1 g.p.	Morning Star	5 g.p.
Bardiche	7 g.p.	Partisan	10 g.p.
Bec de corbin	6 g.p.	Pick, Military, footman's	8 g.p.
Bill-Guisarme	6 g.p.	Pick, Military, horseman's	5 g.p.
Bow, composite short	75 g.p.	Pike, awl	3 g.p.
Bow, composite, long	100 g.p.	Quarrel (or Bolt), light, single	1 s.p.
Bow, long	60 g.p.	Quarrel (or Bolt), heavy, score	2 g.p.
Bow, short	15 g.p.		
Crossbow, heavy	20 g.p.	Ranseur	4 g.p.
Crossbow, light	12 g.p.	Scimitar	15 g.p.
Dagger and scabbard	2 g.p.	Sling & Bullets, dozen	15 s.p.
Dart	5 s.p.	Sling Bullets, score	10 s.p.
Fauchard	3 g.p.	Spear	1 g.p.
Fauchard — Fork	8 g.p.	Spetum	3 g.p.
Flail, footman's	3 g.p.	Sword, bastard, & scabbard	25 g.p.
Flail, horseman's	8 g.p.		
Fork, Military	4 g.p.	Sword, broad, & scabbard	10 g.p.
Glaive	6 g.p.	Sword, long & scabbard	15 g.p.
Glaive-Guisarme	10 g.p.	Sword, short & scabbard	8 g.p.
Guisarme	5 g.p.	Sword, two-handed	30 g.p.
Guisarme — Voulge	7 g.p.	Trident	4 g.p.
Halberd	9 g.p.	Voulge	2 g.p.
Hammer, Lucern	7 g.p.		
Hammer	1 g.p.		

Clothing

Belt	3 s.p.	Cloak	5 s.p.
Boots, high, hard	2 g.p.	Girdle, broad	2 g.p.
Boots, high, soft	1 g.p.	Girdle, normal	10 s.p.
Boots, low, hard	1 g.p.	Hat	7 s.p.
Boots, low, soft	8 s.p.	Robe	6 s.p.
Cap	1 s.p.		

Herbs

Belladona, sprig	4 s.p.	Wolvesbane, sprig	10 s.p.
Garlic, bud	5 c.p.		

Livestock

Chicken	3 c.p.	Horse, medium war	225 g.p.
Cow	10 g.p.	Horse, riding (light)	25 g.p.
Dog, guard	25 g.p.	Mule	20 g.p.
Dog, hunting	17 g.p.	Ox	15 g.p.
Donkey	8 g.p.	Pigeon	2 c.p.
Goat	1 g.p.	Piglet	1 g.p.
Hawk, large	40 g.p.	Pig	3 g.p.
Hawk, small	18 g.p.	Pony	15 g.p.
Horse, draft	30 g.p.	Sheep	2 s.p.
Horse, heavy war	300 g.p.	Songbird	4 c.p.
Horse, light war	150 g.p.		

Miscellaneous Equipment & Items

Backpack, leather	2 g.p.	Pouch, belt, large	1 g.p.
Box, iron, large	28 g.p.	Pouch, belt, small	15 s.p.
Box, iron, small	9 g.p.	Quiver, 1 doz. arrows cap.	8 s.p.
Candle, tallow	1 c.p.	Quiver, 1 score arrows cap.	12 s.p.
Candle, wax	1 s.p.	Quiver, 1 score bolts cap.	15 s.p.
Case, bone, map or scroll	5 g.p.	Quiver, 2 score bolts cap.	1 g.p.
Case, leather, map or scroll	15 s.p.	Rope, 50'	4 s.p.
Chest, wooden, large	17 s.p.	Sack, large	16 c.p.
Chest, wooden, small	8 s.p.	Sack, small	10 c.p.
Lantern, bullseye	12 g.p.	Skin for water or wine	15 s.p.
Lantern, hooded	7 g.p.	Spike, iron, large	1 c.p.
Mirror, large metal	10 g.p.	Thieves' picks & tools	30 g.p.
Mirror, small, silver	20 g.p.	Tinder Box, with flint & steel	1 g.p.
Oil, flask of	1 g.p.	Torch	1 c.p.
Pole, 10'	3 c.p.		

Provisions

Ale, pint	1 s.p.	Mead, pint	5 s.p.
Beer, small, pint	5 c.p.	Rations, iron, 1 week	5 g.p.
Food, merchant's meal	1 s.p.	Rations, standard, 1 week	3 g.p.
Food, rich meal	1 g.p.	Wine, pint, good	10 s.p.
Grain, horse meal, 1 day	1 s.p.	Wine, pint, watered	5 s.p.

Religious Items

Beads, Prayer	1 g.p.	Symbol, Holy*, wooden	7 s.p.
Incense, stick	1 g.p.	Water, Holy*, vial	25 g.p.
Symbol, Holy*, iron	2 g.p.	* or Unholy	
Symbol, Holy*, silver	50 g.p.		

Tack and Harness

Barding, chain	250 g.p.	Saddle	10 g.p.
Barding, leather	100 g.p.	Saddle Bags, large	4 g.p.
Barding, plate	500 g.p.	Saddle Bags, small	3 g.p.
Bit and Bridle	15 s.p.	Saddle Blanket	3 s.p.
Harness	12 s.p.		

Transport

Barge (or Raft), small	50 g.p.	Galley, small	10,000 g.p.
Boat, small	75 g.p.	Ship, merchant, large	15,000 g.p.
Boat, long	150 g.p.	Ship, merchant, small	5,000 g.p.
Cart	50 g.p.	Ship, war	20,000 g.p.
Galley, large	25,000 g.p.	Wagon	150 g.p.

ARMOR

Armor, along with the use of a shield, is the basis for determination of how easily a character can be struck by an opponent's weapon. Other factors modify this, of course. Dexterity and magical effects are the two principal modifiers.

Do not confuse armor which is worn with the armor class (AC) rating of a monster. Although a creature might be given a very high armor class because of its exceptionally thick hide, armor plating, chitinous exoskeleton, or the like, other factors are considered in such ratings. For example, the size of the creature, its speed, its agility, and perhaps its supernatural (extra-dimensional or multi-planed existence) aspects are considered in the armor class of all non-human type monsters. Therefore, a monster with an armor class of 2 will not be carrying a shield.

Armor types are given on the table below. Note that the inclusion of a shield raises armor class (AC) by a factor of 1 (5%), but that assumes attack from the front where the character can interpose it between himself and a blow.

— A *small shield* can be counted against only one attack per melee round.

— A *normal-sized shield* can effectively be counted against two attacks per melee round.

— A *large shield* is counted against up to three attacks per melee round.

Attacks from the right flank and rear always negate the advantage of the shield.

The cost of armor and shield varies. Generally speaking, the better the protection, the greater the expense.

Note: Magic armor negates weight, so that movement does not consider any encumbrance from magic armor. There are otherwise various types of magic armor.

ARMOR CLASS TABLE

Type of Armor	Armor Class Rating
None	10
Shield only	9
Leather or padded armor	8
Leather or padded armor + shield/ studded leather/ring mail	7
Studded leather or ring mail + shield/ scale mail	6
Scale mail + shield/chain mail	5
Chain mail + shield/splint mail/ banded mail	4
Splint or banded mail + shield/ plate mail	3
Plate mail + shield	2

For each +1 of magic armor or magic shield, a decrease in armor class of 1 is given. For example, a non-armored character with a +1 shield is AC 8, a +2 shield AC7, etc. The same is true with regard to pluses of magic armor of any type. A +1 converts to a 5% probability. Thus +2 equals a 10% lesser likelihood of being hit. Magic plate mail +3 and magic shield +5 are equal to AC -6, or can be treated as AC 2 with a subtraction of 8 from attackers' "to hit" dice rolls.

WEAPONS

The choice of weapons used by your character might be circumscribed by the class of your character, but selection is otherwise a matter of your preferences based on various factors presented hereafter. Of course, the initial cost of the weapon might affect your selection at the beginning. Beyond this consideration, there are factors of size and weight. The damage inflicted by the weapon is important, as is the amount of space required to wield it. These details are given hereafter.

Weapon Proficiency

At the start, your character will be able to employ but a limited number of weapons. The number is determined by class. When the character moves up in levels of experience to the next higher combat melee table, he or she is assumed to have acquired proficiency in an additional weapon. The new weapon is of his or her choice. Note that proficiency with a normal weapon is subsumed in using a magical weapon of the same type. If proficiency with any given weapon is not held by the character, it is used at a penalty as shown on the table which follows.

WEAPON PROFICIENCY TABLE

Class of Character	Initial Number of Weapons	Non-proficiency Penalty	Added Proficiency in Weapons Per Level
CLERIC	2	-3	1/4 levels
Druid	2	-4	1/5 levels
FIGHTER	4	-2	1/3 levels
Paladin	3	-2	1/3 levels
Ranger	3	-2	1/3 levels
MAGIC-USER	1	-5	1/6 levels
Illusionist	1	-5	1/6 levels
THIEF	2	-3	1/4 levels
Assassin	3	-2	1/4 levels
MONK	1	-3	1/2 levels

Notes Regarding Weapon Proficiency Table:

Initial Number of Weapons shows the number which the character may select to be proficient with, i.e. a cleric could select a flail and staff, club and mace, or any combination of two permitted weapons.

Non-proficiency Penalty indicates the subtraction from the character's "to hit" dice which applies to attacks by the character using such a weapon in missile or melee combat. (See **COMBAT**.)

Added Proficiency in Weapons gives the number of additional weapons the character can use with proficiency upon attaining the indicated number of levels above the 1st. Thus, at 1st level a cleric can use two weapons with proficiency, at 5th level the cleric selects another for a total of three, at 9th level the total is four, at 13th five, etc.

WEIGHT AND DAMAGE BY WEAPON TYPE

Weapon Type	Approximate Weight in Gold Pieces	Damage vs. Opponent Size S or M	Size L	NOTES
Arrow	2	1-6	1-6	
Axe, Battle	75	1-8	1-8	
Axe, Hand or throwing	50	1-6	1-4	
Bardiche	125	2-8	3-12	
Bec de corbin	100	1-8	1-6	
Bill-Guisarme	150	2-8	1-10	includes Scorpion
Bo Stick	15	1-6	1-3	
Club	30	1-6	1-3	
Dagger	10	1-4	1-3	
Dart	5	1-3	1-2	
Fauchard	60	1-6	1-8	
Fauchard-Fork	80	1-8	1-10	
Flail, footman's	150	2-7	2-8	
Flail, horseman's	35	2-5	2-5	
Fork, Military	75	1-8	2-8	
Glaive	75	1-6	1-10	includes Couteaux de Breche
Glaive — Guisarme	100	2-8	2-12	
Guisarme	80	2-8	1-8	includes Bill/Bill Hook
Guisarme-Voulge	150	2-8	2-8	includes Lochaber Axe
Halberd	175	1-10	2-12	
Hammer, Lucern	150	2-8	1-6	
Hammer	50	2-5	1-4	
Javelin	20	1-6	1-6	
Jo Stick	40	1-6	1-4	
Lance* (light horse)	50	1-6	1-8	
Lance* (medium horse)	100	2-7	2-12	
Lance* (heavy horse)	150	3-9	3-18	
Mace, footman's	100	2-7	1-6	
Mace, horseman's	50	1-6	1-4	
Morning Star	125	2-8	2-7	includes Godentag and Holy Water Sprinkler
Partisan	80	1-6	2-7	includes Bohemian Ear-Spoon
Pick, Military, footman's	60	2-7	2-8	
Pick, Military, horseman's	40	2-5	1-4	
Pike, Awl	80	1-6	1-12	
Quarrel (or Bolt), light	1	1-4	1-4	
Quarrel (or Bolt), heavy	2	2-5	2-7	
Ranseur	50	2-8	2-8	includes Chauves Souris, Ransom, Rhonca, Roncie, Runka
Scimitar	40	1-8	1-8	includes Cutlass, Sabre, Sickle-sword, Tulwar, etc.
Sling bullet	2	2-5	2-7	
Sling stone	1	1-4	1-4	
*Spear**	40-60	1-6	1-8	
Spetum	50	2-7	2-12	includes Corseque, Korseke
Staff, Quarter	50	1-6	1-6	
Sword, Bastard	100	2-8	2-16	
Sword, Broad	75	2-8	2-7	
Sword, Long	60	1-8	1-12	
Sword, Short	35	1-6	1-8	includes all pointed cutting & thrusting weapons with blade length between 15" and 24".
Sword, Two-handed	250	1-10	3-18	
Trident	50	2-7	3-12	
Voulge	125	2-8	2-8	

Italics: Indicates weapon does twice the damage indicated by the die (dice) roll to larger than man-sized creatures (L) when it is set (firmly grounded) to receive a charging opponent.

* This weapon does twice indicated damage against creatures of any size when it is employed by an attacker riding a charging mount.

** This weapon also does twice the damage indicated to *any* opponent when the weapon is set to receive their charge.

WEAPON TYPES, GENERAL DATA, AND "TO HIT" ADJUSTMENTS

Hand Held Weapon Type	Length	Space Required	Speed Factor	2	3	4	5	6	7	8	9	10
				Armor Class Adjustment								
Axe, Battle	c. 4'	4'	7	-3	-2	-1	-1	0	0	+1	+1	+2
Axe, Hand	c. 1½'	1'	4	-3	-2	-2	-1	0	0	+1	+1	+1
Bardiche	c. 5'	5'	9	-2	-1	0	0	+1	+1	+2	+2	+3
Bec de Corbin	c. 6'	6'	9	+2	+2	+2	0	0	0	0	0	-1
Bill-Guisarme	8'+	2'	10	0	0	0	0	0	0	+1	0	0
Bo Stick	c. 5'	3'	3	-9	-7	-5	-3	-1	0	+1	0	+3
Club	c. 3'	1'-3'	4	-5	-4	-3	-2	-1	-1	0	0	+1
Dagger	c. 15"	1'	2	-3	-3	-2	-2	0	0	+1	+1	+3
Fauchard	8'+	2'	8	-2	-2	-1	-1	0	0	0	-1	-1
Fauchard-Fork	8'	2'	8	-1	-1	-1	0	0	0	+1	0	+1
Fist or Open Hand	2'+	-	1	-7	-5	-3	-1	0	0	+2	0	+4
Flail, Footman's	c. 4'	6'	7	+2	+2	+1	+2	+1	+1	+1	+1	-1
Flail, Horseman's	c. 2'	4'	6	0	0	0	0	0	+1	+1	+1	0
Fork, Military	7'+	1'	7	-2	-2	-1	0	0	+1	+1	0	+1
Glaive	8'+	1'	8	-1	-1	0	0	0	0	0	0	0
Glaive-Guisarme	8'+	1'	9	-1	-1	0	0	0	0	0	0	0
Guisarme	6'+	2'	8	-2	-2	-1	-1	0	0	0	-1	-1
Guisarme-Voulge	7'+	2'	10	-1	-1	0	+1	+1	+1	0	0	0
Halberd	5'+	5'	9	+1	+1	+1	+2	+2	+2	+1	+1	0
Hammer, Lucern	5'+	5'	9	+1	+1	+2	+2	+2	+1	+1	0	0
Hammer	c. 1½'	2'	4	0	+1	0	+1	0	0	0	0	0
Jo Stick	c. 3'	2'	2	-8	-6	-4	-2	-1	0	+1	0	+2
Lance (heavy horse)	c. 14'	1'	8	+3	+3	+2	+2	+2	+1	+1	0	0
Lance (light horse)	10'	1'	7	-2	-2	-1	0	0	0	0	0	0
Lance (medium horse)	12'	1'	6	0	+1	+1	+1	+1	0	0	0	0
Mace, Footman's	c. 2½'	4'	7	+1	+1	0	0	0	0	0	+1	-1
Mace, Horseman's	c. 1½'	2'	6	+1	+1	0	0	0	0	0	0	0
Morning Star	c. 4'	5'	7	0	+1	+1	+1	+1	+1	+1	+2	+2
Partisan	7'+	3'	9	0	0	0	0	0	0	0	0	0
Pick, Military, Footman's	c. 4'	4'	7	+2	+2	+1	+1	0	-1	-1	-1	-2
Pick, Military, Horseman's	c. 2'	2'	5	+1	+1	+1	+1	0	0	-1	-1	-1
Pike, awl	18'+	1'	13	-1	0	0	0	0	0	0	-1	-2
*Ranseur**	8'+	1'	8	-2	-1	-1	0	0	0	0	0	+1
Scimitar	c. 3'	2'	4	-3	-2	-2	-1	0	0	+1	+1	+3
Spear	5'-13'+	1'	6-8	-2	-1	-1	-1	0	0	0	0	0
*Spetum**	8'+	1'	8	-2	-1	0	0	0	0	0	+1	+2
Staff, quarter	6'-8'	3'	4	-7	-5	-3	-1	0	0	+1	+1	+1
Sword, bastard**	c. 4½'	4'+	6	0	0	+1	+1	+1	+1	+1	+1	0
Sword, broad	c. 3½'	4'	5	-3	-2	-1	0	0	+1	+1	+1	+2
Sword, long	c. 3½'	3'	5	-2	-1	0	0	0	0	0	+1	+2
Sword, short	c. 2'	1'	3	-3	-2	-1	0	0	0	+1	0	+2
Sword, two-handed	c. 6'	6'	10	+2	+2	+2	+2	+3	+3	+3	+1	0
Trident	4'-8'+	1'	6-8	-3	-2	-1	-1	0	0	+1	0	+1
Voulge	8'+	2'	10	-1	-1	0	+1	+1	+1	0	0	0

Italics indicate weapon capable of dismounting a rider on a score equal to or greater than the "to hit" score.

  *Weapon capable of disarming opponent on a score required to hit AC 8.
**Treat as long sword if used one-handed.

Any weapon strikes at +2 against an opponent's back (or similarly unseen); against stunned, prone, and motionless opponents, any weapon strikes at +4.

Hurled Weapons and Missiles	Fire Rate	S	M	L	2	3	4	5	6	7	8	9	10
		Range			Armor Class Adjustment								
Axe, hand	1	1	2	3	-4	-3	-2	-1	-1	0	0	0	+1
Bow, composite, long	2	6	12	21	-2	-1	0	0	+1	+2	+2	+3	+3
Bow, composite, short	2	5	10	18	-3	-3	-1	0	+1	+2	+2	+2	+3
Bow, long	2	7	14	21	-1	0	0	+1	+2	+3	+3	+3	+3
Bow, short	2	5	10	15	-5	-4	-1	0	0	+1	+2	+2	+2
Club	1	1	2	3	-7	-5	-3	-2	-1	-1	-1	0	0
Crossbow, heavy	½	8	16	24	-1	0	+1	+2	+3	+3	+4	+4	+4
Crossbow, light	1	6	12	18	-2	-1	0	0	+1	+2	+3	+3	+3
Dagger	2	1	2	3	-5	-4	-3	-2	-1	-1	0	0	+1
Dart	3	1½	3	4½	-5	-4	-3	-2	-1	0	+1	0	+1
Hammer	1	1	2	3	-2	-1	0	0	0	0	0	0	+1
Javelin	1	2	4	6	-5	-4	-3	-2	-1	0	+1	0	+1
Sling (bullet)	1	5	10	20	-2	-2	-1	0	0	0	+2	+1	+3
Sling (stone)	1	4	8	16	-5	-4	-2	-1	0	0	+2	+1	+3
Spear	1	1	2	3	-3	-3	-2	-2	-1	0	0	0	0

Rate of fire is based on the turn (for table-top miniatures) or the melee round. Ranges are: S = *Short*, M = *Medium*, L = *Long*.

Armor Class Adjustment is based on the weapon or missile being discharged at short range. Adjust by -1 at all medium ranges, -2 at all long ranges.

HIRELINGS

At any time, a character may attempt to hire various different sorts of workers, servants, or guards. The success of such hiring is entirely dependent upon availability of the type desired, wage and bonus offers, and to some extent the character's charisma. Typical hirelings are:

Alchemist	Blacksmith	Linkboy	Teamster
Armorer	Crossbowman	Man-at-arms	Valet
Bearer	Engineer	Steward	

Your character will have to locate the whereabouts of whatever type of hirelings he or she desires to take into service, and it will be up to your character to determine wages and salaries in the area he or she is in.

Employment can be by the hour, day, week, month, or year according to the desires of the character and agreeability of the persons to be hired. Your referee will handle all such matters as they occur.

Note that the number of hirelings is in no way limited by charisma, and hirelings differ considerably from *henchmen* who are discussed immediately hereafter. The loyalty of hirelings is quite similar to that of henchmen, though, and the discussion of the loyalty of henchmen can be applied to hirelings of all sorts. (See **HENCHMEN** hereafter.)

HENCHMEN

As discussed in the preceding section regarding **CHARACTER ABILITIES,** charisma has a great effect on the number of henchmen a character is able to attract.

A henchman is a more or less devoted follower of a character. In return for the use of his or her abilities and talents, the henchman receives support, lodging, and a share of his or her master's or mistress' earnings — in the form of stipends or as a share of treasure taken. Henchmen are always of a character race and character class, but are never player characters.

The alignment of a henchman should be compatible with that of the player character whom he or she serves. Difference in alignment will certainly affect the loyalty of all henchmen, if alignment is radically different.

It will usually be necessary for your character to visit various inns and drinking establishments in search of henchmen. It is also possible that a number of notices will have to be posted, perhaps in conjunction with the employment of a crier to announce the employment offered. The cost of such is often high — in rounds of drinks, food, tips, gratuities, bribes, fees and so forth. These costs are in addition to actual sums paid to the henchman eventually employed. Locating non-human characters such as dwarves, elves, and the like might be even more protracted, difficult, and costly than the hiring of human and semi-human henchmen. This depends on campaign circumstances — such as whether or not non-humans are common in the area and whether or not non-humans tend to associate with humans and frequent the inns and taverns.

Once a henchman is brought into your character's service, it will be necessary to pay a wage plus support and upkeep. Your referee will inform you as to such costs. When a henchman accompanies your character on adventures, he or she must be given a portion of treasure, both money and magic, just as a player character would. However, the share can be lesser, for all of the henchman's expenses are paid for by his or her master or mistress. Naturally, it is a good idea to give a henchman as much treasure as possible, for in that way the henchman gains experience points.

Experience awarded to henchmen is usually much less than that which would be given to a player character. This is because the henchmen are acting under the direction of their master or mistress. So you should expect that your character's henchmen will get about 50% of the experience points which their share in the slaying of opponents and garnered treasure actually totals — possibly even less if your character bore the brunt of the action and closely directed the henchmen. The loyalty of henchmen is based on many factors. Charisma of the player character is very important. Remuneration — support, upkeep, wages, bonuses, and sharing of treasure — plays a big part also. The involvement of henchmen in adventuring is important, as are the activities of the character (and what he requires of the henchmen) during the course of adventuring. For example:

Assuming the character has above average charisma, he or she could be somewhat less than generous in remuneration and still have henchmen with about average loyalty. If remuneration or activity were above the minimum required, loyalty would be correspondingly higher. If both remuneration and activity were exceptional, the loyalty base of henchmen would be likewise exceptional. Actions to protect the lives and welfare of henchmen, or saving the life of or resurrecting henchmen, give loyalty above average.

Disloyalty will come into play in combat and other stress situations. Disloyal henchmen will betray or desert their master or mistress. (See **MORALE.**)

TIME

Time in the campaign is very important. Your referee will keep strict account of the time consumed by various characters, for it is likely to separate them, since not all participants are likely to play at the same actual time. Time costs characters money in support, upkeep, and wage payments. It takes time to adventure, to heal wounds, to memorize spells, to learn languages, to build strongholds, to create magic items — a very long time in the last given case.

In adventuring below ground, a *turn* in the dungeon lasts 10 minutes (see also **MOVEMENT**). In combat, the turn is further divided into 10 *melee rounds*, or simply *rounds*. Rounds are subdivided into 10 *segments*, for purposes of determining initiative (q.v.) and order of attacks. Thus a *turn* is 10 minutes, a *round* 1 minute, and a *segment* 6 seconds.

Outdoors, time is measured in *days*, usually subdivided into daylight (movement) and night (rest) periods. Thus, while actual time playing is about the same for a dungeon adventure, the *game* time spent is much greater in the case of outdoor adventures.

DISTANCE

For purposes of the game distances are basically one-third with respect to spell and missile range from outdoors to indoors/underground situations. Thus most ranges are shown as *inches* by means of the symbol ", i.e. 1", etc. Outdoors, 1" equals 10 yards. Indoors 1" equals 10 feet. Such a ratio is justifiable, to some extent, regardless of game considerations.

Actual effective range of an arrow shot from a longbow is around 210 yards maximum, in clear light and open terrain. Underground, with little light and low ceilings overhead, a bowshot of 210 feet is about maximum. Archery implies arching arrows. Slings are in this category as are hurled darts and javelins, all arching in flight to achieve distance. Crossbows are a notable exception, but under the visibility conditions of a dungeon setting, a yards to feet conversion is not unreasonable.

Magic and spells are, most certainly, devices of the game. In order to make them fit the constrictions of the underground labyrinth, a one for three reduction is necessary. It would be folly, after all, to try to have such as effective attack modes if feet were not converted to yards outdoors, where visibility, movement, and conventional weapons attack ranges are based on actual fact. (See **MOVEMENT.**)

Distance scale and areas of effect for spells (and missiles) are designed to fit the game. The tripling of range outdoors is reasonable, as it allows for recreation of actual ranges for hurled javelins, arrows fired from longbows, or whatever. In order to keep magic spells on a par, their range is also tripled. IT IS IMPERATIVE THAT OUTDOOR SCALE BE USED FOR RANGE ONLY, NEVER FOR SPELL AREA OF EFFECT (which is kept at 1" = 10') UNLESS A FIGURE RATIO OF 1:10 OR 1:20 (1 casting equals 10 or 20 actual creatures or things in most cases) IS USED, AND CONSTRUCTIONS SUCH AS BUILDINGS, CASTLES, WALLS, ETC. ARE SCALED TO FIGURES RATHER THAN TO GROUND SCALE. Note that the foregoing assumes that a ground scale of 1" to 10 yards is used.

Movement scale is kept as flexible as possible in order to deal with the multitude of applications it has, i.e. dungeon movement (exploring and otherwise), city travel, treks through the outdoors, and combat situations arising during the course of any such movements. Your referee will have information which will enable him or her to adjust the movement rate to the applicable time scale for any situation.

MONSTER, THE TERM

It is necessary to stress that the usage of the term "monster" is generic for any creature encountered during the course of adventuring. A monster can be exactly what the name implies, or it can be a relatively harmless animal, a friendly intelligent beast, a crazed human, a band of dwarves, a thief — virtually anything or anyone potentially threatening or hostile.

When your referee indicates your character has encountered a monster, that simply indicates a confrontation between your character and some type of creature is about to take place. The results of such a meeting will depend on many factors, including the nature of the monster and your character's actions. All *monsters* are not bad...

CHARACTER SPELLS

The casting of spells, clerical and magical, is a very important aspect of play. Most spells have a *verbal* component, and so must be uttered. Most spells also have a *somatic* (movement of the caster's body, such as gesturing) component. Some spells have a third component, that of *material*.

Clerical spells, including the druidic, are bestowed by the gods, so that the cleric need but pray for a few hours and the desired verbal and somatic spell components will be placed properly in his or her mind. First, second, third, and even fourth level spells are granted to the cleric through meditation and devout prayer. This spell giving is accomplished by the lesser servants of the cleric's deity. Fifth, sixth, and seventh level spells can be given to the cleric ONLY by the cleric's deity directly, not through some intermediary source. Note that the cleric might well be judged by his or her deity at such time, as the cleric must supplicate the deity for the granting of these spells. While the deity may grant such spells full willingly, a deed, or sacrifice, atonement or abasement may be required. The deity might also ignore a specific spell request and give the cleric some other spell (or none at all). Your Dungeon Master will handle this considering a cleric's alignment and faithfulness to it and his or her deity. Note that some cleric spells (and all druid spells) also require material ingredients in order for the desired effect to take place. Such components must be supplied by the cleric (or druid), as material is not bestowed.

Magical spells, those of the magic-user and illusionist, are not bestowed by any supernatural force. Rather, the magic-user (or illusionist) must memorize each spell, verbal and somatic components, and supply himself or herself with any required materials as well. Such memorization requires the character to consult his or her spell books in order to impress the potent, mystical spell formulae upon the mind. Additional items for the material component must then be acquired, if necessary.

Spells of any sort must therefore be selected prior to setting out on an adventure, for memorization requires considerable time. (Your Dungeon Master will inform you fully as to what state of refreshment the mind of a spell caster must be in, as well as the time required to memorize a given spell.) As a rule of thumb, allow 15 minutes of game time for memorization of one spell level, i.e. a 1st level spell or half of a 2nd level spell. Such activity requires a mind rested by a good sleep and nourished by the body.

Once cast, a spell is totally forgotten. Gone. The mystical symbols impressed upon the brain carry power, and speaking the spell discharges this power, draining all memory of the spell used. This does not preclude multiple memorization of the same spell, but it does preclude multiple use of a single spell memorized but once. When a spell caster shoots his or her spell-bolt, so to speak, it is gone.

As previously shown in the **CHARACTER CLASSES** section, the number of spells usable by a character depend upon class and level. Details of spell casting are given later in the section on *combat* (q.v.).

The nature and components of the various spells are given in the section immediately after the spell tables. These spell descriptions also contain such information as is pertinent, i.e. range, duration, effect, etc. Your Dungeon Master may add to or delete from a spell(s) and may even add or delete entire spells. He will inform you of these changes prior to selecting spells or when new spells become available to your character.

Material components for spells are assumed to be kept in little pockets, stored in the folds and small pockets of the spell caster's garb. Of course, some materials are too bulky, and in these cases the materials must be accounted for carefully. Also, some materials are rare, and these must be found and acquired by the spell user.

Special cases which pertain to each class of spell-using character type will be noted before each set of spell explanations.

SPELL TABLES

CLERICS

Number	1st Level	2nd Level	3rd Level
1	Bless	Augury	Animate Dead
2	Command	Chant	Continual Light
3	Create Water	Detect Charm	Create Food & Water
4	Cure Light Wounds	Find Traps	Cure Blindness
5	Detect Evil	Hold Person	Cure Disease
6	Detect Magic	Know Alignment	Dispel Magic
7	Light	Resist Fire	Feign Death
8	Protection From Evil	Silence 15' Radius	Glyph Of Warding
9	Purify Food & Drink	Slow Poison	Locate Object
10	Remove Fear	Snake Charm	Prayer
11	Resist Cold	Speak With Animals	Remove Curse
12	Sanctuary	Spiritual Hammer	Speak With Dead

Number	4th Level	5th Level	6th Level	7th Level
1	Cure Serious Wounds	Atonement	Aerial Servant	Astral Spell
2	Detect Lie	Commune	Animate Object	Control Weather
3	Divination	Cure Critical Wounds	Blade Barrier	Earthquake
4	Exorcise	Dispel Evil	Conjure Animals	Gate
5	Lower Water	Flame Strike	Find The Path	Holy (Unholy) Word
6	Neutralize Poison	Insect Plague	Heal	Regenerate
7	Protection from Evil 10' Radius	Plane Shift	Part Water	Restoration
8	Speak With Plants	Quest	Speak With Monsters	Resurrection
9	Sticks to Snakes	Raise Dead	Stone Tell	Symbol
10	Tongues	True Seeing	Word Of Recall	Wind Walk

DRUIDS (Clerics)

Number	1st Level	2nd Level	3rd Level	4th Level
1	Animal Friendship	Barkskin	Call Lightning	Animal Summoning I
2	Detect Magic	Charm Person Or Mammal	Cure Disease	Call Woodland Beings
3	Detect Snares & Pits	Create Water	Hold Animal	Control Temperature 10' Radius
4	Entangle	Cure Light Wounds	Neutralize Poison	Cure Serious Wounds
5	Faerie Fire	Feign Death	Plant Growth	Dispel Magic
6	Invisibility To Animals	Fire Trap	Protection From Fire	Hallucinatory Forest
7	Locate Animals	Heat Metal	Pyrotechnics	Hold Plant
8	Pass Without Trace	Locate Plants	Snare	Plant Door
9	Predict Weather	Obscurement	Stone Shape	Produce Fire
10	Purify Water	Produce Flame	Summon Insects	Protection From Lightning
11	Shillelagh	Trip	Tree	Repel Insects
12	Speak With Animals	Warp Wood	Water Breathing	Speak With Plants

Number	5th Level	6th Level	7th Level
1	Animal Growth	Animal Summoning III	Animate Rock
2	Animal Summoning II	Anti-Animal Shell	Chariot Of Sustarre
3	Anti-Plant Shell	Conjure Fire Elemental	Confusion
4	Commune With Nature	Cure Critical Wounds	Conjure Earth Elemental
5	Control Winds	Feeblemind	Control Weather
6	Insect Plague	Fire Seeds	Creeping Doom
7	Pass Plant	Transport Via Plants	Finger Of Death
8	Sticks To Snakes	Turn Wood	Fire Storm
9	Transmute Rock To Mud	Wall Of Thorns	Reincarnate
10	Wall Of Fire	Weather Summoning	Transmute Metal To Wood

MAGIC-USERS

Number	1st Level	2nd Level	3rd Level	4th Level	5th Level
1	Affect Normal Fires	Audible Glamer	Blink	Charm Monster	Airy Water
2	Burning Hands	Continual Light	Clairaudience	Confusion	Animal Growth
3	Charm Person	Darkness 15' Radius	Clairvoyance	Dig	Animate Dead
4	Comprehend Languages	Detect Evil	Dispel Magic	Dimension Door	Bigby's Interposing Hand
5	Dancing Lights	Detect Invisibility	Explosive Runes	Enchanted Weapon	Cloudkill
6	Detect Magic	ESP	Feign Death	Extension I	Conjure Elemental
7	Enlarge	Fools Gold	Fireball	Fear	Cone Of Cold
8	Erase	Forget	Flame Arrow	Fire Charm	Contact Other Plane
9	Feather Fall	Invisibility	Fly	Fire Shield	Distance Distortion
10	Find Familiar	Knock	Gust Of Wind	Fire Trap	Extension II
11	Friends	Leomund's Trap	Haste	Fumble	Feeblemind
12	Hold Portal	Levitate	Hold Person	Hallucinatory Terrain	Hold Monster
13	Identify	Locate Object	Infravision	Ice Storm	Leomund's Secret Chest
14	Jump	Magic Mouth	Invisibility 10' Radius	Massmorph	Magic Jar
15	Light	Mirror Image	Leomund's Tiny Hut	Minor Globe of Invulnerability	Monster Summoning III
16	Magic Missile	Pyrotechnics	Lightning Bolt	Monster Summoning II	Mordenkainen's Faithful Hound
17	Mending	Ray Of Enfeeblement	Monster Summoning I	Plant Growth	Passwall
18	Message	Rope Trick	Phantasmal Force	Polymorph Other	Stone Shape
19	Nystul's Magic Aura	Scare	Protection From Evil 10' Radius	Polymorph Self	Telekinesis
20	Protection From Evil	Shatter	Protection From Normal Missiles	Rary's Mnemonic Enhancer	Teleport
21	Push	Stinking Cloud	Slow	Remove Curse	Transmute Rock To Mud
22	Read Magic	Strength	Suggestion	Wall Of Fire	Wall Of Force
23	Shield	Web	Tongues	Wall Of Ice	Wall Of Iron
24	Shocking Grasp	Wizard Lock	Water Breathing	Wizard Eye	Wall Of Stone
25	Sleep				
26	Spider Climb				
27	Tenser's Floating Disc				
28	Unseen Servant				
29	Ventriloquism				
30	Write				

41

Number	6th Level	7th Level	8th Level	9th Level
1	Anti-Magic Shell	Bigby's Grasping Hand	Antipathy/Sympathy	Astral Spell
2	Bigby's Forceful Hand	Cacodemon	Bigby's Clenched Fist	Bigby's Crushing Hand
3	Control Weather	Charm Plants	Clone	Gate
4	Death Spell	Delayed Blast Fireball	Glassteel	Imprisonment
5	Disintegrate	Drawmij's Instant Summons	Incendiary Cloud	Meteor Swarm
6	Enchant An Item	Duo-Dimension	Mass Charm	Monster Summoning VII
7	Extension III	Limited Wish	Maze	Power Word, Kill
8	Geas	Mass Invisibility	Mind Blank	Prismatic Sphere
9	Glassee	Monster Summoning V	Monster Summoning VI	Shape Change
10	Globe Of Invulnerability	Mordenkainen's Sword	Otto's Irresistible Dance	Temporal Stasis
11	Guards And Wards	Phase Door	Permanency	Time Stop
12	Invisible Stalker	Power Word, Stun	Polymorph Any Object	Wish
13	Legend Lore	Reverse Gravity	Power Word, Blind	
14	Lower Water	Simulacrum	Serten's Spell Immunity	
15	Monster Summoning IV	Statue	Symbol	
16	Move Earth	Vanish	Trap The Soul	
17	Otiluke's Freezing Sphere			
18	Part Water			
19	Project Image			
20	Reincarnation			
21	Repulsion			
22	Spiritwrack			
23	Stone To Flesh			
24	Tenser's Transformation			

ILLUSIONISTS (Magic-Users)

Number	1st Level	2nd Level	3rd Level
1	Audible Glamer	Blindness	Continual Darkness
2	Change Self	Blur	Continual Light
3	Color Spray	Deafness	Dispel Illusion
4	Dancing Lights	Detect Magic	Fear
5	Darkness	Fog Cloud	Hallucinatory Terrain
6	Detect Illusion	Hypnotic Pattern	Illusionary Script
7	Detect Invisibility	Improved Phantasmal Force	Invisibility 10' Radius
8	Gaze Reflection	Invisibility	Non-detection
9	Hypnotism	Magic Mouth	Paralyzation
10	Light	Mirror Image	Rope Trick
11	Phantasmal Force	Misdirection	Spectral Force
12	Wall Of Fog	Ventriloquism	Suggestion

Number	4th Level	5th Level	6th Level	7th Level
1	Confusion	Chaos	Conjure Animals	Alter Reality
2	Dispel Exhaustion	Demi-Shadow Monsters	Demi-Shadow Magic	Astral Spell
3	Emotion	Major Creation	Mass Suggestion	Prismatic Spray
4	Improved Invisibility	Maze	Permanent Illusion	Prismatic Wall
5	Massmorph	Projected Image	Programmed Illusion	Vision
6	Minor Creation	Shadow Door	Shades	First Level Magic-User Spells
7	Phantasmal Killer	Shadow Magic	True Sight	
8	Shadow Monsters	Summon Shadow	Veil	

SPELL EXPLANATIONS

Each spell is presented here in exactly the same format. The spell is first identified by name and type of magic it involves. Thereafter its level, range (distance it can be cast), duration, area of effect, components, casting time, and saving throw are shown. Finally, an explanation of the spell and a description of its effects are given in some detail.

Range is shown in inches (See **DISTANCE**) or as "touch", which indicates the caster must physically contact the recipient of the spell with his or her hand.

Duration is given as number of turns, rounds, or simply "instantaneous", as in the case of a lightning bolt which lasts only a brief moment. (See **TIME.**)

Area of Effect shows how large an area the spell covers, or how many persons or creatures it will affect.

Components, as previously mentioned, are verbal (V), somatic (S), and/or material (M). This indicates which are part of the spell.

Casting Time shows the number of melee rounds, or segments of a melee round, required to cast the spell. Remember that there are 10 segments to a melee round, 10 melee rounds to a turn. Some spells require additional time and preparation.

Saving Throw tells whether a saving throw is possible, and if it is possible, whether success negates (*neg.*) the spell or reduces its effects by 50% (½).

CLERIC SPELLS

Notes Regarding Cleric Spells:

All material components required for the various spells are used by completion of the spell in question with the notable exceptions of standard religious items, i.e. religious symbols and prayer beads or similar devices.

The reversal of some spells might well place the cleric in a questionable position with respect to alignment. The use of spells which promote weal must be shunned by evil clerics in many cases. Likewise, spells which are baneful may be used only at peril by clerics of good alignment. Incautious use of spells will change the cleric's alignment, if such usage continues unchecked, and it is up to the player to guard his or her character's alignment with care. In any event, the cleric must decide which application of a reversible spell will be used prior to learning it, i.e. it is not possible to have one spell both ways. In like manner, the mere *request* for a spell (or its opposite) through prayer will *not* guarantee that the spell will be given to the cleric. As the spell level becomes higher, confidence will decrease that that deity will concur.

Your Dungeon Master might alter the material components of spells, require only religious adjuncts as material, or just do away with them. Consult your referee in this regard and ask his ruling and reasoning.

First Level Spells:

Bless (Conjuration/Summoning) Reversible

Level: *1*	Components: *V, S, M*
Range: *6"*	Casting Time: *1 round*
Duration: *6 melee rounds*	Saving Throw: *None*
Area of Effect: *5" × 5"*	

Explanation/Description: Upon uttering the *bless* spell, the caster raises the morale of friendly creatures by +1. Furthermore, it raises their "to hit" dice rolls by +1. A blessing, however, will affect only those not already engaged in melee combat. This spell can be reversed by the cleric to a *curse* upon enemies which lowers morale and "to hit" by -1. The caster determines at what range (up to 6") he or she will cast the spell, and it then affects all creatures in an area 5" square centered on the point the spell was cast upon. In addition to the verbal and somatic gesture components, the *bless* requires holy water, while the *curse* requires the sprinkling of specially polluted water.

Command (Enchantment/Charm)

Level: *1*	Components: *V*
Range: *1"*	Casting Time: *1 segment*
Duration: *1 round*	Saving Throw: *Special*
Area of Effect: *One creature*	

Explanation/Description: This spell enables the cleric to issue a *command* of a single word. The *command* must be uttered in a language which the spell recipient is able to understand. The individual will obey to the best of his/her/its ability only so long as the *command* is absolutely clear and unequivocal, i.e. "Suicide!" could be a noun, so the creature would ignore the *command*. A *command* to "Die!" would cause the recipient to fall in a faint or cataleptic state for 1 round, but thereafter the creature would be alive and well. Typical *command* words are: back, halt, flee, run, stop, fall, fly, go, leave, surrender, sleep, rest, etc. Undead are not affected by a *command*. Creatures with intelligence of 13 or more, and creatures with 6 or more hit dice (or experience levels) are entitled to a saving throw versus magic. (Creatures with 13 or higher intelligence *and* 6 hit dice/levels do not get 2 saving throws!)

Create Water (Alteration) Reversible

Level: *1*	Components: *V, S, M*
Range: *1"*	Casting Time: *1 round*
Duration: *Permanent*	Saving Throw: *None*
Area of Effect: *Up to 27 cubic feet*	

Explanation/Description: When the cleric casts a *create water* spell, four gallons of water are generated for every level of experience of the caster, i.e. a 2nd level cleric creates eight gallons of water, a 3rd level twelve gallons, a 4th level sixteen gallons, etc. The water is clean and drinkable (it is just like rain water). Reversing the spell, *destroy water*, obliterates without trace (such as vapor, mist, fog or steam) a like quantity of water. Created water will last until normally used or evaporated, spilled, etc. Water can be created or destroyed in an area as small as will actually contain the liquid or in an area as large as 27 cubic feet (one cubic yard). The spell requires at least a drop of water to create, or a pinch of dust to destroy, water. Note that water cannot be created within a living thing.

Cure Light Wounds (Necromantic) Reversible

Level: *1*	Components: *V, S*
Range: *Touch*	Casting Time: *5 segments*
Duration: *Permanent*	Saving Throw: *None*
Area of Effect: *Character touched*	

Explanation/Description: Upon laying his or her hand upon a creature, the cleric causes from 1 to 8 hit points of wound or other injury damage to the creature's body to be healed. This healing will not affect creatures without corporeal bodies, nor will it cure wounds of creatures not living or those which can be harmed only by iron, silver, and/or magical weapons. Its reverse, *cause light wounds*, operates in the same manner; and if a person is avoiding this touch, a melee combat "to hit" die is rolled to determine if the cleric's hand strikes the opponent and causes such a wound. Note that *cured* wounds are permanent only insofar as the creature does not sustain further damage, and that caused wounds will heal — or can be cured — just as any normal injury will. Caused light wounds are 1 to 8 hit points of damage.

Detect Evil (Divination) Reversible

Level: *1*
Range: *12''*
Duration: *1 turn + ½ turn/level*
Area of Effect: *1'' path*

Components: *V, S, M*
Casting Time: *1 round*
Saving Throw: *None*

Explanation/Description: This is a spell which discovers emanations of evil, or of good in the case of the reverse spell, from any creature or object. For example, evil alignment or an evilly cursed object will radiate evil, but a hidden trap or an unintelligent viper will not. The duration of a *detect evil* (or *detect good*) spell is 1 turn + ½ turn (5 rounds, or 5 minutes) per level of the cleric. Thus a cleric of 1st level of experience can cast a spell with a 1½ turn duration, at 2nd level a 2 turn duration, 2½ at 3rd, etc. The spell has a path of detection 1'' wide in the direction in which the cleric is facing. It requires the use of the cleric's holy (or unholy) symbol as its material component, with the cleric holding it before him or her.

Detect Magic (Divination)

Level: *1*
Range: *3''*
Duration: *1 turn*
Area of Effect: *1'' path, 3'' long*

Components: *V, S, M*
Casting Time: *1 round*
Saving Throw: *None*

Explanation/Description: When the *detect magic* spell is cast, the cleric detects magical radiations in a path 1'' wide, and up to 3'' long, in the direction he or she is facing. The caster can turn 60° per round. Note that stone walls of 1' or more thickness, solid metal of but 1/12' thickness, or 3' or more of solid wood will block the spell. The spell requires the use of the cleric's holy (or unholy) symbol.

Light (Alteration) Reversible

Level: *1*
Range: *12''*
Duration: *6 turns + 1 turn/level*
Area of Effect: *2'' radius globe*

Components: *V, S*
Casting Time: *4 segments*
Saving Throw: *None*

Explanation/Description: This spell causes excitation of molecules so as to make them brightly luminous. The *light* thus caused is equal to torch light in brightness, but its sphere is limited to 4'' in diameter. It lasts for the duration indicated (7 turns at 1st experience level, 8 at 2nd, 9 at 3rd, etc.) or until the caster utters a word to extinguish the light. The light spell is reversible, causing *darkness* in the same area and under the same conditions, except the blackness persists for only one-half the duration that light would last. If this spell is cast upon a creature, the applicable magic resistance and saving throw dice rolls must be made. Success indicates that the spell affects the area immediately behind the creature, rather than the creature itself. In all other cases, the spell takes effect where the caster directs as long as he or she has a line of sight or unobstructed path for the spell; *light* can spring from air, rock, metal, wood, or almost any similar substance.

Protection From Evil (Abjuration) Reversible

Level: *1*
Range: *Touch*
Duration: *3 rounds/level*
Area of Effect: *Creature touched*

Components: *V, S, M*
Casting Time: *4 segments*
Saving Throw: *None*

Explanation/Description: When this spell is cast, it acts as if it were a magical armor upon the recipient. The protection encircles the recipient at a one foot distance, thus preventing bodily contact by creatures of an enchanted or conjured nature such as aerial servants, demons, devils, djinn, efreet, elementals, imps, invisible stalkers, night hags, quasits, salamanders, water weirds, wind walkers, and xorn. Summoned animals or monsters are similarly hedged from the protected creature. Furthermore, any and all attacks launched by evil creatures incur a penalty of -2 from dice rolls "to hit" the protected creature, and any saving throws caused by such attacks are made at +2 on the protected creature's dice. This spell can be reversed to become *protection from good*, although it still keeps out enchanted evil creatures as well. To complete this spell, the cleric must trace a 3' diameter circle upon the floor (or ground) with holy water for protection from evil, with blood for protection from good — or in the air using burning incense or smoldering dung with respect to evil/good.

Purify Food & Drink (Alteration) Reversible

Level: *1*
Range: *3''*
Duration: *Permanent*
Area of Effect: *1 cubic foot/level, 1'' square area*

Components: *V, S*
Casting Time: *1 round*
Saving Throw: *None*

Explanation/Description: When cast, the spell will make spoiled, rotten, poisonous or otherwise contaminated food and/or water pure and suitable for eating and/or drinking. Up to 1 cubic foot of food and/or drink can be thus made suitable for consumption. The reverse of the spell *putrefies food and drink*, even spoiling holy water. Unholy water is spoiled by *purify water*.

Remove Fear (Abjuration) Reversible

Level: *1*
Range: *Touch*
Duration: *Special*
Area of Effect: *Creature touched*

Components: *V, S*
Casting Time: *4 segments*
Saving Throw: *None*

Explanation/Description: By touch, the cleric instills courage in the spell recipient, raising the creature's saving throw against magical *fear* attacks by +4 on dice rolls for 1 turn. If the recipient has already been affected by fear, and failed the appropriate saving throw, the touch allows another saving throw to be made, with a bonus of +1 on the dice for every level of experience of the caster, i.e. a 2nd level cleric gives a +2 bonus, a 3rd level +3, etc. A "to hit" dice roll must be made to touch an unwilling recipient. The reverse of the spell, *cause fear*, causes the victim to flee in panic at maximum movement speed away from the caster for 1 round per level of the cleric causing such fear. Of course, *cause fear* can be countered by *remove fear* and vice versa.

Resist Cold (Alteration)

Level: *1*
Range: *Touch*
Duration: *1 turn/level*
Area of Effect: *Creature touched*

Components: *V, S, M*
Casting Time: *1 round*
Saving Throw: *None*

Explanation/Description: When this spell is placed on a creature by a cleric, the creature's body is inured to cold. The recipient can stand zero degrees Fahrenheit without discomfort, even totally nude. Greater cold, such as that produced by a sword of cold, *ice storm*, cold wand, or white dragon's breath, must be saved against. All saving throws against cold are made with a bonus of +3, and damage sustained is one-half (if the saving throw is not made) or one-quarter (if the saving throw is made) of damage normal from that attack form. The resistance lasts for 1 turn per level of experience of the caster. A pinch of sulphur is necessary to complete this spell.

Sanctuary (Abjuration)

Level: *1*
Range: *Touch*
Duration: *2 rounds + 1 round/level*
Area of Effect: *One creature*

Components: *V, S, M*
Casting Time: *4 segments*
Saving Throw: *None*

Explanation/Description: When the cleric casts a *sanctuary* spell, any opponent must make a saving throw versus magic in order to strike or otherwise attack him or her. If the saving throw is not made, the creature will attack another and totally ignore the cleric protected by the spell. If the saving throw is made, the cleric is subject to normal attack process including dicing for weapons to hit, saving throws, damage. Note that this spell does not prevent the operation of area attacks (*fireball, ice storm*, etc.). During the period of protection afforded by this spell, the cleric cannot take offensive action, but he or she may use non-attack spells or otherwise act in any way which does not violate the prohibition against offensive action. This allows the cleric to heal wounds, for example, or to *bless*, perform an *augury, chant*, cast a *light* in the area (not upon an opponent!), and so on. The components of the spell include the cleric's holy/unholy symbol and a small silver mirror.

Second Level Spells:

Augury (Divination)

Level: *2*	Components: *V, S, M*
Range: *0*	Casting Time: *2 rounds*
Duration: *Special*	Saving Throw: *None*

Explanation/Description: The cleric casting an *augury* spell seeks to divine whether an action in the immediate future (within 3 turns) will be for the benefit of, or harmful to, the party. The base chance for correctly divining the *augury* is 70%, plus 1% for each level of the cleric casting the spell, i.e. 71% at 1st level, 72% at 2nd, etc. Your referee will determine any adjustments due for the particular conditions of each *augury*. For example, assume that a party is considering the destruction of a weird seal which closes a portal. *Augury* is used to find if weal or woe will be the ultimate result to the party. The material component for *augury* is a set of gem-inlaid sticks, dragon bones, or similar tokens, or the wet leaves of an infusion which remain in the container after the infused brew is consumed. If the last method is used, a crushed pearl of at least 100 g.p. value must be added to the concoction before it is consumed.

Chant (Conjuration/Summoning)

Level: *2*	Components: *V, S*
Range: *0*	Casting Time: *1 turn*
Duration: *Time of chanting*	Saving Throw: *None*
Area of Effect: *3'' radius*	

Explanation/Description: By means of the *chant*, the cleric brings into being a special favor upon himself or herself and his or her party, and causes harm to his or her enemies. Once the *chant* spell is completed, all attacks, damage and saving throws made by those in the area of effect who are friendly to the cleric are at +1, while those of the cleric's enemies are at -1. This bonus/penalty continues as long as the cleric continues to chant the mystic syllables and is stationary. An interruption, however, such as an attack which succeeds and causes damage, grappling the chanter, or a magical *silence*, will break the spell.

Detect Charm (Divination) Reversible

Level: *2*	Components: *V, S*
Range: *3''*	Casting Time: *1 round*
Duration: *1 turn*	Saving Throw: *None*
Area of Effect: *One creature*	

Explanation/Description: When used by a cleric, this spell will detect whether or not a person or monster is under the influence of a *charm* spell. Up to 10 creatures can be thus checked before the spell wanes. The reverse of the spell protects from such detection, but only a single creature can be so shielded.

Find Traps (Divination)

Level: *2*	Components: *V, S*
Range: *3''*	Casting Time: *5 segments*
Duration: *3 turns*	Saving Throw: *None*
Area of Effect: *1'' path*	

Explanation/Description: When a cleric casts a *find traps* spell, all traps — concealed normally or magically — of magical or mechanical nature become visible to him or her. Note that this spell is directional, and the caster must face the desired direction in order to determine if a trap is laid in that particular direction.

Hold Person (Enchantment/Charm)

Level: *2*	Components: *V, S, M*
Range: *6''*	Casting Time: *5 segments*
Duration: *4 rounds + 1 round/level*	Saving Throw: *Neg.*
Area of Effect: *One to three creatures*	

Explanation/Description: This spell holds immobile, and freezes in places, from 1-3 humans or humanoid creatures (see below) for 5 or more melee rounds. The level of the cleric casting the *hold person* spell dictates the length of time the effect will last. The basic duration is 5 melee rounds at 1st level, 6 rounds at 2nd level, 7 rounds at 3rd level, etc. If the spell is cast at three persons, each gets a saving throw at the normal score; if only two persons are being enspelled, each makes their saving throw at -1 on their die; if the spell is cast at but one person, the saving throw die is at -2. Persons making their saving throws are totally unaffected by the spell. Creatures affected by a *hold person* spell are: brownies, dryads, dwarves, elves, gnolls, gnomes, goblins, half-elves, halflings, half-orcs, hobgoblins, humans, kobolds, lizard men, nixies, orcs, pixies, sprites, and troglodytes. The spell caster needs a small, straight piece of iron as the material component of this spell.

Know Alignment (Divination) Reversible

Level: *2*	Components: *V, S*
Range: *1''*	Casting Time: *1 round*
Duration: *1 turn*	Saving Throw: *None*
Area of Effect: *One creature/round*	

Explanation/Description: A *know alignment* spell enables the cleric to exactly read the aura of a *person* — human, semi-human, or non-human. This will reveal the exact alignment of the person. Up to 10 persons can be examined with this spell. The reverse totally obscures alignment, even from this spell, of a single person for 1 turn, two persons for 5 rounds, etc. Certain magical devices will negate the ability to *know alignment*.

Resist Fire (Alteration)

Level: *2*	Components: *V, S, M*
Range: *Touch*	Casting Time: *5 segments*
Duration: *1 turn/level*	Saving Throw: *None*
Area of Effect: *Creature touched*	

Explanation/Description: When this spell is placed upon a creature by a cleric, the creature's body is toughened to withstand heat, and boiling temperature is comfortable. The recipient of the *resist fire* spell can even stand in the midst of very hot or magical fires such as those produced by red-hot charcoal, a large amount of burning oil, flaming swords, *fire storms*, *fire balls*, *meteor swarms*, or red dragon's breath — but these will affect the creature, to some extent. The recipient of the spell gains a bonus of +3 on saving throws against such attack forms, and all damage sustained is reduced by 50%; therefore, if the saving throw is not made, the creature sustains one-half damage, and if the saving throw is made only one-quarter damage is sustained. Resistance to fire lasts for 1 turn for each level of experience of the cleric placing the spell. The caster needs a drop of mercury as the material component of this spell.

Silence, 15' Radius (Alteration)

Level: *2*	Components: *V, S*
Range: *12''*	Casting Time: *5 segments*
Duration: *2 rounds/level*	Saving Throw: *None*
Area of Effect: *30' diameter sphere*	

Explanation/Description: Upon casting this spell, complete silence prevails in the area of its effect. All sound is stopped, so all conversation is impossible, spells cannot be cast, and no noise whatsoever issues forth. The spell can be cast into the air or upon an object. The spell of *silence* lasts for 2 rounds for each level of experience of the cleric, i.e. 2 rounds at 1st level, 4 at 2nd, 6 at 3rd, 8 at 4th and so forth. The spell can be cast upon a creature, and the effect will then radiate from the creature and move as it moves. If the creature is unwilling, it saves against the spell, and if the saving throw is made, the spell effect locates about one foot behind the target creature.

Slow Poison (Necromantic)

Level: *2*	Components: *V, S, M*
Range: *Touch*	Casting Time: *1 segment*
Duration: *1 hour/level*	Saving Throw: *None*
Area of Effect: *Creature touched*	

Explanation/Description: When this spell is placed upon a poisoned individual it greatly slows the effects of any venom, even causing a supposedly dead individual to have life restored if it is cast upon the victim within a number of turns less than or equal to the level of experience of the cleric after the poisoning was suffered, i.e. a victim poisoned up to 10 turns previously could be temporarily saved by a 10th or higher level cleric who cast *slow poison* upon the victim. While this spell does not neutralize the venom, it does prevent it from substantially harming the individual for the duration of its magic, but each turn the poisoned creature will lose 1 hit point from the effect of the venom (although the victim will never go below 1 hit point while the *slow poison* spell's duration lasts). Thus, in the example above, the victim poisoned 10 turns previously has only 10 hit points, so when the 10th level cleric casts the spell, the victim remains with 1 hit point until the spell duration expires, and hopefully during that period a full cure can be accomplished. The material components of this spell are the cleric's holy/unholy symbol and a bud of garlic which must be crushed and smeared on the victim's bare feet.

Snake Charm (Enchantment/Charm)

Level: *2*	Components: *V, S*
Range: *3″*	Casting Time: *5 segments*
Duration: *Special*	Saving Throw: *None*
Area of Effect: *Special*	

Explanation/Description: When this spell is cast, a hypnotic pattern is set up which causes one or more snakes to cease all activity except a semi-erect postured swaying movement. If the snakes are charmed while in a torpor, the duration of the spell is 3 to 6 turns (d4+2); if the snakes are not torpid, but are not aroused and angry, the charm lasts 1 to 3 turns; if the snakes are angry and/or attacking, the *snake charm* spell will last from 5 to 8 melee rounds (d4+4). The cleric casting the spell can charm snakes whose hit points are less than or equal to those of the cleric. On the average, a 1st level cleric could charm snakes with a total of 4 or 5 hit points; a 2nd level cleric 9 hit points, a 3rd level 13 or 14 hit points, etc. The hit points can represent a single snake or several of the reptiles, but the total hit points cannot exceed those of the cleric casting the spell.

Speak With Animals (Alteration)

Level: *2*	Components: *V, S*
Range: *0*	Casting Time: *5 segments*
Duration: *2 rounds/level*	Saving Throw: *None*
Area of Effect: *One animal within 3″ radius of cleric*	

Explanation/Description: By employing this spell, the cleric is empowered to comprehend and communicate with any warm or cold-blooded animal which is not mindless (such as an amoeba). The cleric is able to ask questions, receive answers, and generally be on amicable terms with the animal. This ability lasts for 2 melee rounds for each level of experience of the cleric employing the spell. Even if the bent of the animal is opposite to that of the cleric (evil/good, good/evil), it and any others of the same kind with it will not attack while the spell lasts. If the animal is neutral or of the same general bent as the cleric (evil/evil, good/good), there is a possibility that the animal, and its like associates, will do some favor or service for the cleric. This possibility will be determined by the referee by consulting a special reaction chart, using the charisma of the cleric and his actions as the major determinants. Note that this spell differs from *speak with monsters* (q.v.), for it allows conversation only with basically normal, non-fantastic creatures such as apes, bears, cats, dogs, elephants, and so on.

Spiritual Hammer (Invocation)

Level: *2*	Components: *V, S, M*
Range: *3″*	Casting Time: *5 segments*
Duration: *1 round/level*	Saving Throw: *Special*
Area of Effect: *One opponent*	

Explanation/Description: By calling upon his or her deity, the cleric casting a *spiritual hammer* spell brings into existence a field of force which is shaped vaguely like a hammer. This area of force is hammer-sized, and as long as the cleric who invoked it concentrates upon the *hammer*, it will strike at any opponent within its range as desired by the cleric. The force area strikes as a magical weapon equal to one plus per 3 levels of experience of the spell caster for purposes of being able to strike creatures, although it has no magical plusses whatsoever "to hit", and the damage it causes when it scores a hit is exactly the same as a normal war hammer, i.e. 1-6 versus opponents of man-size or smaller, 1-4 upon larger opponents. Furthermore, the hammer strikes at exactly the same level as the cleric controlling it, just as if the cleric was personally wielding the weapon. As soon as the cleric ceases concentration, the *spiritual hammer* is dispelled. *Note:* If the cleric is behind an opponent, the force can strike

from this position, thus gaining all bonuses for such an attack and negating defensive protections such as shield and dexterity. The material component of this spell is a normal war hammer which the cleric must hurl towards opponents whilst uttering a plea to his or her deity. The hammer disappears when the spell is cast.

Third Level Spells:

Animate Dead (Necromantic)

Level: *3*	Components: *V, S, M*
Range: *1″*	Casting Time: *1 round*
Duration: *Permanent*	Saving Throw: *None*
Area of Effect: *Special*	

Explanation/Description: This spell creates the lowest of the *undead* monsters, skeletons or zombies, from the bones or bodies of dead humans. The effect is to cause these remains to become animated and obey the commands of the cleric casting the spell. The skeletons or zombies will follow, remain in an area and attack any creature (or just a specific type of creature) entering the place, etc. The spell will animate the monsters until they are destroyed or until the magic is dispelled. (See *dispel magic* spell). The cleric is able to animate 1 skeleton or 1 zombie for each level of experience he or she has attained. Thus, a 2nd level cleric can animate 2 of these monsters, a 3rd level 3, etc. The act of animating dead is not basically a good one, and it must be used with careful consideration and good reason by clerics of *good* alignment. It requires a drop of blood, a piece of human flesh, and a pinch of bone powder or a bone shard to complete the spell.

Continual Light (Alteration) Reversible

Level: *3*	Components: *V, S*
Range: *12″*	Casting Time: *6 segments*
Duration: *Permanent*	Saving Throw: *None*
Area of Effect: *6″ radius globe*	

Explanation/Description: This spell is similar to a *light* spell, except that it lasts until negated (by a *continual darkness* or *dispel magic* spell) and its brightness is very great, being nearly as illuminating as full daylight. It can be cast into air, onto an object, or at a creature. In the third case, the *continual light* affects the space about one foot behind the creature if the latter makes its saving throw. Note that this spell will blind a creature if it is successfully cast upon the visual organs, for example. Its reverse causes complete absence of light.

Create Food & Water (Alteration)

Level: *3*	Components: *V, S*
Range: *1″*	Casting Time: *1 turn*
Duration: *Permanent*	Saving Throw: *None*
Area of Effect: *1 cubic foot/level*	

Explanation/Description: When this spell is cast, the cleric causes food and/or water to appear. The food thus created is highly nourishing, and each cubic foot of the material will sustain three human-sized creatures or one horse-sized creature for a full day. For each level of experience the cleric has attained, 1 cubic foot of food and/or water is created by the spell, i.e. 2 cubic feet of food are created by a 2nd level cleric, 3 by a 3rd, 4 by a 4th, and so on; or the 2nd level cleric could create 1 cubic foot of food and 1 cubic foot of water, etc.

Cure Blindness (Abjuration) Reversible

Level: *3*	Components: *V, S*
Range: *Touch*	Casting Time: *1 round*
Duration: *Permanent*	Saving Throw: *None*
Area of Effect: *Creature touched*	

Explanation/Description: By touching the creature afflicted, the cleric employing the spell can permanently cure most forms of blindness. Its reverse, *cause blindness*, requires a successful touch upon the victim, and if the victim then makes the saving throw, the effect is negated.

Cure Disease (Abjuration) Reversible

Level: *3*	Components: *V, S*
Range: *Touch*	Casting Time: *1 turn*

Duration: *Permanent*
Area of Effect: *Creature touched*
Saving Throw: *None*

Explanation/Description: The cleric cures most diseases — including those of a parasitic, bacterial, or viral nature — by placing his or her hand upon the diseased creature. The affliction rapidly disappears thereafter, making the cured creature whole and well in from 1 turn to 1 week, depending on the kind of disease and the state of its advancement when the cure took place. The reverse of the *cure disease* spell is *cause disease*. To be effective, the cleric must touch the intended victim, and the victim must fail the saving throw. The disease caused will begin to affect the victim in 1-6 turns, causing the afflicted creature to lose 1 hit point per turn, and 1 point of strength per hour, until the creature is at 10% of original hit points and strength, at which time the afflicted is weak and virtually helpless.

Dispel Magic (Abjuration)

Level: *3*	Components: *V, S*
Range: *6″*	Casting Time: *6 segments*
Duration: *Permanent*	Saving Throw: *None*
Area of Effect: *3″ cube*	

Explanation/Description: When a cleric casts this spell, it neutralizes or negates the magic it comes in contact with as follows: A *dispel magic* will not affect a specially enchanted item such as a scroll, magic ring, wand, rod, staff, miscellaneous magic item, magic weapon, magic shield, or magic armor. It will destroy magic potions (they are treated as 12th level for purposes of this spell), remove spells cast upon persons or objects, or counter the casting of spells in the area of effect. The base chance for success of a *dispel magic* spell is 50%. For every level of experience of the character casting the *dispel magic* above that of the creature whose magic is to be dispelled (or above the efficiency level of the object from which the magic is issuing), the base chance increases by 5%, so that if there are 10 levels of difference, there is a 100% chance. For every level below the experience/efficiency level of the creature/object, the base chance is reduced by 2%. Note that this spell can be very effective when used upon *charmed* and similarly beguiled creatures. It is automatic in negating the spell caster's own magic.

Feign Death (Necromantic)

Level: *3*	Components: *V, S, M*
Range: *Touch*	Casting Time: *2 segments*
Duration: *1 turn + 1 round/level*	Saving Throw: *None*
Area of Effect: *One person*	

Explanation/Description: Except as noted above, this spell is the same as the third level magic-user spell, *feign death* (q.v.). Note that a character of any level may be affected by the cleric casting this spell, and that the material components are a pinch of graveyard dirt and the cleric's holy/unholy symbol.

Glyph of Warding (Abjuration-Evocation)

Level: *3*	Components: *V, S, M*
Range: *Touch*	Casting Time: *Special*
Duration: *Permanent until discharged*	Saving Throw: *Special*
Area of Effect: *25 square feet per level of the spell caster*	

Explanation/Description: A *glyph of warding* is a powerful inscription magically drawn to prevent unauthorized or hostile creatures from passing, entering, or opening. It can be used to guard a small bridge, ward an entry, or as a trap on a chest or box. When the spell is cast, the cleric weaves a tracery of faintly glowing lines around the warding sigil. For every square foot of area to be protected, 1 segment of time is required to trace the warding lines from the glyph, plus the initial segment during which the sigil itself is traced. A maximum of a 5′ × 5′ area per level can be warded. When the spell is completed, the glyph and tracery become invisible, but any creature touching the protected area without first speaking the name of the glyph the cleric has used to serve as a ward will be subject to the magic it stores. Saving throws apply, and will either reduce effects by one-half or negate them according to the glyph employed. The cleric must use incense to trace this spell, and then sprinkle the area with powdered diamond (at least 2,000 g.p. worth) if it exceeds 50 square feet. Typical glyphs shock for 2 points of electrical damage per level of the spell caster, explode for a like amount of fire damage,

paralyze, blind, or even drain a life energy level (if the cleric is of high enough level to cast this glyph).

Locate Object (Divination) Reversible

Level: *3*	Components: *V, S, M*
Range: *6″ + 1″/level*	Casting Time: *1 turn*
Duration: *1 round/level*	Saving Throw: *None*
Area of Effect: *Special*	

Explanation/Description: This spell aids in location of a known or familiar object. The cleric casts the spell, slowly turns, and knows when he or she is facing in the direction of the object to be located, provided the object is within range, i.e. 7″ for 1st level clerics, 8″ for 2nd, 9″ for 3rd, etc. The casting requires the use of a piece of lodestone. The spell will locate such objects as apparel, jewelry, furniture, tools, weapons, or even a ladder or stairway. By reversal (*obscure object*), the cleric is able to hide an object from location by spell, crystal ball, or similar means. Neither application of the spell will affect a living creature.

Prayer (Conjuration/Summoning)

Level: *3*	Components: *V, S, M*
Range: *0*	Casting Time: *6 segments*
Duration: *1 round/level*	Saving Throw: *None*
Area of Effect: *6″ radius*	

Explanation/Description: This spell exactly duplicates the effects of a *chant* with regard to bonuses of +1 for friendly attacks and saving throws and -1 on like enemy dice. However, once the *prayer* is uttered, the cleric can do other things, unlike a *chant* which he or she must continue to make the spell effective. The cleric needs a silver holy symbol, prayer beads, or a similar device as the material component of this spell.

Remove Curse (Abjuration) Reversible

Level: *3*	Components: *V, S*
Range: *Touch*	Casting Time: *6 segments*
Duration: *Permanent*	Saving Throw: *Special*
Area of Effect: *Special*	

Explanation/Description: Upon casting this spell, the cleric is usually able to remove a curse — whether it be on an object, a person, or in the form of some undesired sending or evil presence. Note that the *remove curse* spell will not remove a cursed shield, weapon or suit of armor, for example, although the spell will typically enable the person afflicted with any such cursed item to be rid of it. The reverse of the spell is *not* permanent; the *bestow curse* lasts for 1 turn for every level of experience of the cleric using the spell. It will lower one ability of the victim to 3 (your DM will determine which by random selection) 50% of the time; reduce the victim's "to hit" and saving throw probabilities by -4 25% of the time; or make the victim 50% likely per turn to drop whatever he, she, or it is holding (or simply do nothing in the case of creatures not using tools) 25% of the time. It is possible for a cleric to devise his or her own curse, and it should be similar in power to those shown. Consult your referee. The target of a *bestow curse* spell must be touched. If the victim is touched, a saving throw is still applicable; and if it is successful, the effect is negated.

Speak With The Dead (Necromantic)

Level: *3*   Components: *V, S, M*
Range: *1*   Casting Time: *1 turn*
Duration: *Special*   Saving Throw: *None*
Area of Effect: *One creature*

Explanation/Description: Upon casting a *speak with the dead* spell, the cleric is able to ask several questions of a dead creature in a set period of time and receive answers according to the knowledge of that creature. Of course, the cleric must be able to converse in the language which the dead creature once used. The length of time the creature has been dead is a factor, since only higher level clerics can converse with the long-dead. Likewise, the number of questions which can be answered and the length of time in which the questions can be asked are dependent upon the level of experience of the cleric. The cleric needs a holy symbol and burning incense in order to cast this spell upon the body, remains, or portion thereof.

Level of Experience	Maximum Length of Time Dead	Time Questioned	Number of Questions
up to 7th	1 week	1 round	2
7th — 8th	1 month	3 rounds	3
9th — 12th	1 year	1 turn	4
13th — 15th	10 years	2 turns	5
16th — 20th	100 years	3 turns	6
21st and up	1,000 years	6 turns	7

Fourth Level Spells:

Cure Serious Wounds (Necromantic) Reversible

Level: *4*   Components: *V,S*
Range: *Touch*   Casting Time: *7 segments*
Duration: *Permanent*   Saving Throw: *None*
Area of Effect: *Creature touched*

Explanation/Description: This spell is a more potent version of the *cure light wounds* spell (q.v.). Upon laying his or her hand upon a creature, the cleric causes from 3 to 17 (2d8+1) hit points of wound or other injury damage to the creature's body to be healed. This healing will affect only those creatures listed in the *cure light wounds* spell explanation. *Cause serious wounds*, the reverse of the spell, operates similarly to the *cause light wounds* spell, the victim having to be touched first, and if the touch is successful, it will inflict 3 to 17 hit points.

Detect Lie (Divination) Reversible

Level: *3*   Components: *V, S, M*
Range: *3"*   Casting Time: *7 segments*
Duration: *1 round/level*   Saving Throw: *None*
Area of Effect: *One person*

Explanation/Description: When the cleric employs this spell, the recipient is immediately able to determine if truth is being spoken. The spell lasts one round for each level of experience of the cleric casting the *detect lie*. Gold dust is necessary for this spell. Its reverse, *undetectable lie*, makes bald-face untruths seem reasonable, or simply counters the *detect lie* spell powers. The reverse spell requires brass dust as its material component.

Divination (Divination)

Level: *4*   Components: *V, S, M*
Range: *0*   Casting Time: *1 turn*
Duration: *Special*   Saving Throw: *None*
Area of Effect: *Special*

Explanation/Description: Similar to an *augury* spell, a *divination* spell is used to determine information regarding an area. The area can be a small woods, large building, or section of a dungeon level. In any case, its location must be known. The spell gives information regarding the relative strength of creatures in the area; whether a rich, moderate or poor treasure is there; and the relative chances for incurring the wrath of evil or good supernatural, super powerful beings if the area is invaded and attacked. The base chance for correct *divination* is 60%, plus 1% for each level of experience of the cleric casting the spell, i.e. 65% at 5th level, 66% at 6th, etc. The Dungeon Master will make adjustments to this base chance considering the facts regarding actual area being divined. If the result is not correct, inaccurate information will be obtained. The material components of the *divination* are a sacrificial creature, incense, and the holy symbol of the cleric. If an unusually potent *divination* is attempted, sacrifice of particularly valuable gems or jewelry and/or magic items may be required.

Exorcise (Abjuration)

Level: *4*   Components: *V, S, M*
Range: *1*   Casting Time: *1-100+ turns*
Duration: *Permanent*   Saving Throw: *None*
Area of Effect: *One creature or object*

Explanation/Description: The spell of *exorcism* will negate possession of a creature or an object by any outside or supernatural force. This includes control of a creature by some force in an object, possession by *magic jar* (q.v.) spell, demonic possession, curse, and even charm, for the *exorcise* spell is similar to a *dispel magic* spell. Furthermore, it will affect a magical item if such is the object of the exorcism. Thus a soul object of any sort which comes under successful exorcism will make the life force of the creature concerned wholly inhabit its nearest material body, wholly and completely. (Cf. **ADVANCED DUNGEONS & DRAGONS, MONSTER MANUAL**, *Demon*.) The *exorcise* spell, once begun, cannot be interrupted, or else it is spoiled and useless. The base chance for success is a random 1% to 100%. Each turn of exorcism the dice are rolled, and if the base chance number, or less, is rolled, the spell is successful. Base chance of success is modified by -1% for each level of difference between the cleric's level of experience and the level of the possessor or possessing magic, where the smaller number is the cleric's level. In the obverse, a +1% cumulative is added. The referee can determine base chance according to the existing circumstances if he or she so desires. Material components for this spell are the holy object of the cleric and holy water (or unholy, in the case of evil clerics, with respect to object and water). A religious artifact or relic can increase the chance of success by from 1% to 50%, according to the power of the artifact or relic.

Lower Water (Alteration) Reversible

Level: *4*   Components: *V, S, M*
Range: *12"*   Casting Time: *1 turn*
Duration: *1 turn/level*   Saving Throw: *None*
Area of Effect: *1" X 1" square/level area*

Explanation/Description: The cleric casting a *lower water* spell causes water or similar fluid in the area of effect to sink away. Lowering is 5% of original effect for every level of experience of the cleric, i.e. 40% at 8th level, 45% at 9th, 50% at 10th, etc. The effect of the spell lasts for 1 turn for each level of experience of the cleric casting it. Likewise, the area of effect increases by level of experience, an 8th level cleric affecting an area of 8" X 8", a 9th level an area of 9" X 9", and so forth. Material components of this spell are the cleric's religious symbol and a pinch of dust. The reverse of the spell causes the water or similar fluid to return to its normal highest level, plus one foot for every level of experience of the cleric casting it.

Neutralize Poison (Alteration) Reversible

Level: *4*   Components: *V, S*
Range: *Touch*   Casting Time: *7 segments*
Duration: *Permanent*   Saving Throw: *None*
Area of Effect: *Creature touched or 1 cubic foot of substance/2 levels*

Explanation/Description: By means of a *neutralize poison* spell, the cleric detoxifies any sort of venom in the creature or substance touched. Note that an opponent, such as a poisonous reptile or snake (or even an envenomed weapon of an opponent) unwilling to be so touched requires the cleric to score a hit in melee combat. Effects of the spell are permanent only with respect to poison existing in the touched creature at the time of the touch, i.e. creatures (or objects) which generate new poison will *not* be permanently detoxified. The reversed spell, *poison*, likewise requires an attack (a "to hit" touch which succeeds), and the victim is allowed a saving throw versus poison. If the latter is unsuccessful, the victim is killed by the poison.

Protection From Evil, 10' Radius (Abjuration) Reversible

Level: *4*	Components: *V, S, M*
Range: *Touch*	Casting Time: *7 segments*
Duration: *1 turn/level*	Saving Throw: *None*
Area of Effect: *20' diameter sphere*	

Explanation/Description: The globe of protection of this spell is identical in all respects to a *protection from evil* (q.v.) spell, except that it encompasses a much larger area and the duration of the *protection from evil, 10' radius* spell is greater. To complete this spell, the cleric must trace a circle 20' in diameter using holy water or blood, incense or smouldering dung as according to the *protection from evil* spell.

Speak With Plants (Alteration)

Level: *4*	Components: *V, S, M*
Range: *0*	Casting Time: *1 turn*
Duration: *1 round/level*	Saving Throw: *None*
Area of Effect: *6" diameter circle*	

Explanation/Description: When cast, a *speak with plants* spell enables the cleric to converse, in very rudimentary terms, with all sorts of living vegetables. Thus, the cleric can question plants as to whether or not creatures have passed through them, cause thickets to part to enable easy passage, require vines to entangle pursuers, and similar things. The spell does not enable the cleric to animate non-ambulatory vegetation. The power of the spell lasts for 1 melee round for each level of experience of the cleric who cast it. All vegetation within the area of effect are under command of the spell. The material components for this spell are a drop of water, a pinch of dung, and a flame.

Sticks To Snakes (Alteration) Reversible

Level: *4*	Components: *V,S,M*
Range: *3"*	Casting Time: *7 segments*
Duration: *2 rounds/level*	Saving Throw: *None*
Area of Effect: *1 cubic "*	

Explanation/Description: By means of this spell the cleric is able to change 1 stick to a snake for each level of experience he or she has attained, i.e. a 9th level cleric can change 9 sticks into 9 snakes. These snakes will attack as commanded by the cleric. There must, of course, be sticks or similar pieces of wood (such as torches, spears, etc.) to turn into snakes. Note that magical items such as staves and spears which are enchanted are *not* affected by the spell. Only sticks within the area of effect will be changed. The probability of a snake thus changed being venomous is 5% per level of experience of the spell caster, so that there is a 55% probability of any given snake created by the spell being poisonous when sticks are turned to snakes by an 11th level cleric, 60% at 12th level, etc. The effect lasts for 2 melee rounds for each level of experience of the spell caster. The material components of the spell are a small piece of bark and several snake scales. The reverse changes *snakes to sticks* for the duration appropriate, or it negates the *sticks to snakes* spell according to the level of the cleric countering the spell, i.e. a 10th level cleric casting the reverse spell can turn only 10 snakes back to sticks.

Tongues (Alteration) Reversible

Level: *4*	Components: *V, S*
Range: *0*	Casting Time: *7 segments*
Duration: *1 turn*	Saving Throw: *None*
Area of Effect: *6" diameter circle*	

Explanation/Description: This spell enables the cleric to speak the language of any creature inside the spell area, whether it is a racial tongue or an alignment language. The reverse of the spell cancels the effect of the *tongues* spell or confuses verbal communication of any sort within the area of effect.

Fifth Level Spells:

Atonement (Abjuration)

Level: *5*	Components: *V, S, M*
Range: *Touch*	Casting Time: *1 turn*
Duration: *Permanent*	Saving Throw: *None*
Area of Effect: *One person*	

Explanation/Description: This spell is used by the cleric to remove the onus of unwilling or unknown deeds from the person who is the subject of the *atonement*. The spell will remove the effects of magical alignment change as well. The person for whom *atonement* is being made must be either truly repentant or not in command of his or her own will so as to be able to be repentant. Your referee will judge this spell in this regard, noting any past instances of its use upon the person. Deliberate misdeeds and acts of knowing and willful nature cannot be atoned for with this spell. The material components of this spell are the cleric's religious symbol, prayer beads or wheel or book, and burning incense.

Commune (Divination)

Level: *5*	Components: *V, S, M*
Range: *0*	Casting Time: *1 turn*
Duration: *Special*	Saving Throw: *None*
Area of Effect: *Special*	

Explanation/Description: By use of a *commune* spell the cleric is able to contact his or her divinity — or agents thereof — and request information in the form of questions which can be answered by a simple "yes" or "no". The cleric is allowed one such question for every level of experience he or she has attained. The answers given will be correct. It is probable that the referee will limit the use of *commune* spells to one per adventure, one per week, or even one per month, for the "gods" dislike frequent interruptions. The material components necessary to a *commune* spell are the cleric's religious symbol, holy/unholy water, and incense.

Cure Critical Wounds (Necromantic) Reversible

Level: *5*	Components: *V, S*
Range: *Touch*	Casting Time: *8 segments*
Duration: *Permanent*	Saving Throw: *None*
Area of Effect: *Creature touched*	

Explanation/Description: The *cure critical wounds* spell is a very potent version of the *cure light wounds* spell (q.v.). The cleric lays his or her hand upon a creature and heals from 6 to 27 (3d 8 + 3) hit points of damage from wounds or other damage. The spell does not affect creatures excluded in the *cure light wounds* spell explanation. Its reverse, *cause serious wounds*, operates in the same fashion as other *cause wounds* spells, requiring a successful touch to inflict the 6-27 hit points of damage. Caused wounds heal as do wounds of other sorts.

Dispel Evil (Abjuration) Reversible

Level: *5*	Component: *V, S, M*
Range: *Touch*	Casting Time: *8 segments*
Duration: *1 round/level*	Saving Throw: *Neg.*
Area of Effect: *Creature touched*	

Explanation/Description: The cleric using this spell causes summoned creatures of evil nature, or monsters enchanted and caused to perform evil deeds, to return to their own plane or place. Examples of such creatures are: aerial servants, demons, devils, djinn, efreet, elementals, and invisible stalkers. Note that this spell lasts for 1 melee round for each level of experience of the caster, and while the spell is in effect all creatures which could be affected by it attack at a -7 penalty on their "to hit" dice when engaging the spell caster. The reverse of the spell, *dispel good*, functions against summoned or enchanted creatures of good alignment or sent to aid the cause of good. The material components for this spell are the cleric's religious object and holy/unholy water.

Flame Strike (Evocation)

Level: *5*	Components: *V, S, M*
Range: *6"*	Casting Time: *8 segments*
Duration: *1 segment*	Saving Throw: *½*
Area of Effect: *1" diameter by 3" high column*	

Explanation/Description: When the cleric calls down a *flame strike* spell, a column of fire roars downward in the exact location called for by the caster. If any creature is within the area of effect of a *flame strike*, it must make a saving throw. Failure to make the save means the creature has sustained 6-48 (6d8) hit points of damage; otherwise, 3-24 (3d8) hit points of damage are taken. The material component of this spell is a pinch of sulphur.

Insect Plague (Conjuration/Summoning)

Level: 5
Range: 36''
Duration: 1 turn/level
Area of Effect: 36'' diameter, 6''
   high cloud

Components: V, S, M
Casting Time: 1 turn
Saving Throw: None

Explanation/Description: When this spell is cast by the cleric, a horde of creeping, hopping, and flying insects swarm in a thick cloud. These insects obscure vision, limiting it to 3''. Creatures within the *insect plague* sustain 1 hit point of damage for each melee round they remain in it due to the bites and stings of the insects, regardless of armor class. The referee will cause all creatures with fewer than five hit dice to check morale. Creatures with two or fewer hit dice will automatically move at their fastest possible speed in a straight line in a random direction until they are not less than 24'' distant from the cloud of insects. Creatures with fewer than five hit dice which fail their morale check will behave likewise. Heavy smoke will drive off insects within its bounds. Fire will also drive insects away; a *wall of fire* in a ring shape will keep the *insect plague* outside its confines, but a *fire ball* will simply clear insects from its blast area for 1 turn. Lightning and cold/ice act likewise. The plague lasts for 1 turn for each level of experience of the cleric casting the spell, and thereafter the insects disperse. The insects swarm in an area which centers around a summoning point determined by the spell caster, which point can be up to 36'' distant from the cleric. The *insect plague* does not move thereafter for as long as it lasts. Note that the spell can be countered by casting a *dispel magic* upon the summoning point. A *cube of force* (a special magic item) would keep insects away from a character seeking the center of the swarm, but invisibility would afford *no* protection. The material components of this spell are a few grains of sugar, some kernels of grain, and a smear of fat.

Plane Shift (Alteration)

Level: 5
Range: Touch
Duration: Permanent
Area of Effect: Creature touched
   (special)

Components: V,S,M
Casting Time: 8 segments
Saving Throw: None

Explanation/Description: When the *plane shift* spell is cast, the cleric moves himself or herself or some other creature to another plane of existence. The recipient of the spell will remain in the new plane until sent forth by some like means. If several persons link hands in a circle, up to seven can be affected by the *plane shift* at the same time. The material component of this spell is a small, forked metal rod — the exact size and metal type dictating to which plane of existence the spell will send the affected creature(s) to. (Your referee will determine specifics regarding how and what planes are reached.) An unwilling victim must be *touched* in order to be sent thusly; and in addition, the creature also is allowed a saving throw, and if the latter is successful the effect of the spell is negated.

Quest (Enchantment/Charm)

Level: 5
Range: 6''
Duration: Until fulfilled
Area of Effect: One creature

Components: V, S, M
Casting Time: 8 segments
Saving Throw: Neg.

Explanation/Description: The *quest* is a spell by means of which the cleric requires the affected creature to perform a service and return to the cleric with proof that the deed was accomplished. The quest can, for example, require the location and return of some important or valuable object, the rescue of a notable person, the release of some creature, the capture of a stronghold, the slaying of a person, the delivery of some item, and so forth. If the *quest* is not properly followed due to disregard, delay, or perversion, the creature affected by the spell loses 1 from its saving throw dice for each day of such action, and this penalty will not be removed until the *quest* is properly discharged or the cleric cancels it. (There are certain circumstances which will temporarily suspend a *quest*, and other which will discharge or cancel it; your Dungeon Master will give you appropriate information as the need to know arises.) The material component of this spell is the cleric's religious symbol.

Raise Dead (Necromantic) Reversible

Level: 5
Range: 3''
Duration: Permanent
Area of Effect: One person

Components: V, S
Casting Time: 1 round
Saving Throw: Special

Explanation/Description: When the cleric casts a *raise dead* spell, he or she can restore life to a dwarf, gnome, half-elf, halfling, or human. The length of time which the person has been dead is of importance, as the cleric can raise dead persons only up to a certain point, the limit being 1 day for each level of experience of the cleric, i.e. a 9th level cleric can raise a person dead for up to 9 days. Note that the body of the person must be whole, or otherwise missing parts will still be missing when the person is brought back to life. Also, the resurrected person must make a special saving throw to survive the ordeal (see **CHARACTER ABILITIES,** Constitution). Furthermore, the raised person is weak and helpless in any event, and he or she will need one full day of rest in bed for each day he or she was dead. The somatic component of the spell is a pointed finger. The reverse of the spell, *slay living*, allows the victim a saving throw, and if it is successful, the victim sustains damage equal only to that caused by a *cause serious wounds* spell, i.e. 3-17 hit points. An evil cleric can freely use the reverse spell; a good cleric must exercise extreme caution in its employment, being absolutely certain that the victim of the *slay living* spell is evil and that his or her death is a matter of great necessity and for good, otherwise the alignment of the cleric will be sharply changed. Note that newly made *undead*, excluding skeletons, which fall within the days of being dead limit are affected by *raise dead* spells cast upon them. The effect of the spell is to cause them to become resurrected dead, providing the constitution permits survival; otherwise, they are simply dead.

True Seeing (Divination) Reversible

Level: 5
Range: Touch
Duration: 1 round/level
Area of Effect: 12'' sight range

Components: V,S,M
Casting Time: 8 segments
Saving Throw: None

Explanation/Description: When the cleric employs this spell, all things within the area of the *true seeing* effect appear as they actually are. Secret doors become plain. The exact location of displaced things is obvious. Invisible things and those which are astral or ethereal become quite visible. Illusions and apparitions are seen through. Polymorphed, changed, or magicked things are apparent. Even the aura projected by creatures becomes visible, so that the cleric is able to know whether they are good or evil or between. The spell requires an ointment for the eyes. The ointment is made from very rare mushroom powder, saffron, and fat. The reverse of the spell, *false seeing*, causes the person to see things as they are not, rich being poor, rough smooth, beautiful ugly. The ointment for the reverse spell is concocted of oil, poppy dust, and pink orchid essence. For both spells, the ointment must be aged for 1-6 months.

Sixth Level Spells:

Aerial Servant (Conjuration/Summoning)

Level: 6
Range: 1''
Duration: 1 day/level
Area of Effect: Special

Components: V, S
Casting Time: 9 segments
Saving Throw: None

Explanation/Description: This spell summons an invisible *aerial servant* (see **ADVANCED DUNGEONS & DRAGONS, MONSTER MANUAL**) to do the bidding of the cleric who conjured it. The creature does not fight, but it obeys the command of the cleric with respect to finding and returning with whatever object or creature that is described to it. Of course, the object or creature must be such as to allow the *aerial servant* to physically bring it to the cleric or his or her assign. The spell caster should keep in mind the consequences of having an *aerial servant* prevented, for any reason, from completion of the assigned duty. The spell lasts for a maximum of 1 day for each level of experience of the cleric who cast it. The *aerial servant* returns to its own plane whenever the spell lapses, its duty is fulfilled, it is dispelled, the cleric releases it, or the cleric is slain. The cleric must have a *protection from evil* spell, or be within a magic circle, thaumaturgic triangle, or pentagram when summoning an *aerial servant* unless the cleric has his or her religious symbol or a religious artifact or relic to use to control the creature. Otherwise, the creature will slay its summoner and return from whence it came. The *aerial servant* will always attack by complete surprise when sent on a mission, and gain the benefit of 4 free melee rounds unless the creature involved is able to detect invisible objects, in which case a six-sided die is rolled, and 1 = 1 free round, 2 = 2 free rounds, 3 = 3 free rounds, 4 = 4 free rounds, and 5 or 6 = 0 free rounds (the opponent is not surprised at all). Each round the *aerial servant* must dice to score a hit, and when a hit is scored, it means the *aerial servant* has grabbed the item or creature it was sent to take and bring back to the cleric. If a creature is involved, the *aerial servant's* strength is compared to the strength of the creature to be brought. If the creature in question does not have a strength rating, roll the appropriate number of the correct type of hit dice for the *aerial servant* and for the creature it has grabbed. The higher total is the stronger.

Animate Object (Alteration)

Level: 6	Components: V, S
Range: 3''	Casting Time: 9 segments
Duration: 1 round/level	Saving Throw: None
Area of Effect: 1 cubic foot/level	

Explanation/Description: This powerful spell enables the cleric casting it to imbue inanimate objects with mobility and a semblance of life. The animated object, or objects, then attack whomever or whatever the cleric first designates. The object can be of any material whatsoever — wood, metal, stone, fabric, leather, ceramic, glass, etc. The speed of movement of the object is dependent upon its means of propulsion and its weight. A large wooden table would be rather heavy, but its legs would give it speed. A rug could only slither along. A jar would roll. Thus a large stone pedestal would rock forward at 1'' per round, a stone statue would move at 4'' per round, a wooden statue 8'' per round, an ivory stool of light weight would move at 12''. Slithering movement is about 1'' to 2'' per round, rolling 3'' to 6'' per round. The damage caused by the attack of an animated object is dependent upon its form and composition. Light, supple objects can only obscure vision, obstruct movement, bind, trip, smother, etc. Light, hard objects can fall upon or otherwise strike for 1-2 hit points of damage or possibly obstruct and trip as do light, supple objects. Hard, medium weight objects can crush or strike for 2-8 hit points of damage, those larger and heavier doing 3-12, 4-16, or even 5-20 hit points of damage. The frequency of attack of animated objects is dependent upon their method of locomotion, appendages, and method of attack. This varies from as seldom as once every five melee rounds to as frequently as once per melee round. The armor class of the object animated is basically a function of material and movement ability with regard to hitting. Damage is dependent upon the type of weapon and the object struck. A sharp cutting weapon is effective against fabric, leather, wood and like substances. Heavy smashing and crushing weapons are useful against wood, stone, and metal objects. Your referee will determine all of these factors, as well as how much damage the animated object can sustain before being destroyed. The cleric can animate 1 cubic foot of material for each level of experience he or she has attained. Thus, a 14th level cleric could animate one or more objects whose solid volume did not exceed 14 cubic feet, i.e. a large statue, two rugs, three chairs, or a dozen average crocks.

Blade Barrier (Evocation)

Level: 6	Components: V, S
Range: 3''	Casting Time: 9 segments
Duration: 3 rounds/level	Saving Throw: None
Area of Effect: Special	

Explanation/Description:The cleric employs this spell to set up a wall of circling, razor-sharp blades. These whirl and flash in endless movement around an immobile point. *Any creature which attempts to pass through the blade barrier* suffers 8-64 (8d8) hit points of damage in doing so. The barrier remains for 3 melee rounds for every level of experience of the cleric casting it. The barrier can cover any area from as small as 5' square to as large as 2'' square, i.e. 20'×20' under ground, 60'×60' outdoors.

Conjure Animals (Conjuration/Summoning)

Level: 6	Components: V, S
Range: 3''	Casting Time: 9 segments
Duration: 2 rounds/level	Saving Throw: None
Area of Effect: Special	

Explanation/Description: The *conjure animals* spell enables the cleric to summon a mammal, or several of them, to his locale in order that the creature(s) can attack the cleric's opponents. The conjured animal(s) remain in the cleric's locale for 2 melee rounds for each level of experience of the cleric conjuring it (them), or until slain. The spell caster can, by means of his incantation, call up one or more mammals with hit dice whose total does not exceed his or her level. Thus, a cleric of 12th level could conjure one mammal with 12 hit dice, two with 6 hit dice each, three with 4 hit dice each, 4 with 3 hit dice each, six with 2 hit dice each, or 12 with 1 hit die each. For every +1 (hit point) of a creature's hit dice, count 1/4 of a hit die, i.e. a creature with 4 +3 hit dice equals a 4 3/4 hit dice creature. The creature(s) summoned by the spell will unfailingly attack the opponent(s) of the cleric by whom the spell was cast.

Find The Path (Divination) Reversible

Level: 6	Components: V, S, M
Range: Touch	Casting Time: 3 rounds
Duration: 1 turn/level	Saving Throw: None
Area of Effect: Creature touched	

Explanation/Description: By use of this spell, the cleric is enabled to find the shortest, most direct route that he or she is seeking, be it the way to or from or out of a locale. The locale can be outdoors or underground, a trap or even a *maze* spell. The spell will enable the cleric to select the correct direction which will eventually lead him or her to egress, the exact path to follow (or actions to take), and this knowledge will persist as long as the spell lasts, i.e. 1 turn for each level of experience of the cleric casting *find the path*. The spell frees the cleric, and those with him or her from a *maze* spell in a single melee round and will continue to do so as long as the spell lasts. The material component of this spell is a set of divination counters of the sort favored by the cleric — bones, ivory counters, sticks, carved runes, or whatever. The reverse, *lose the path*, makes the creature touched totally lost and unable to find its way for the duration of the spell, although it can be led, of course.

Heal (Necromantic) Reversible

Level: 6	Components: V, S
Range: Touch	Casting Time: 1 round
Duration: Permanent	Saving Throw: None
Area of Effect: Creature touched	

Explanation/Description: The very potent *heal* spell enables the cleric to wipe away disease and injury in the creature who receives the benefits of the spell. It will completely cure any and all diseases and/or blindness of the recipient and *heal* all hit points of damage suffered due to wounds or injury, save 1 to 4 (d4). It dispels a *feeblemind* spell. Naturally, the effects can be negated by later wounds, injuries, and diseases. The reverse, *harm*, infects the victim with a disease and causes loss of all hit points, as damage, save 1 to 4 (d4), if a successful touch is inflicted. For creatures not affected by the *heal* (or *harm*) spell, see *cure light wounds*.

Part Water (Alteration)

Level: 6	Components: V, S, M
Range: 2''/level	Casting Time: 1 turn
Duration: 1 turn/level	Saving Throw: None
Area of Effect: Special	

Explanation/Description: By employing a *part water* spell, the cleric is able to cause water or similar liquid to move apart, thus forming a trough. The depth and length of the trough created by the spell is dependent upon the level of the cleric, and a trough 3' deep by 1' by 2'' (20' or 20 yards) is created per level, i.e. at 12th level the cleric would *part water* 36' deep by 12' wide by 24'' (240' or 240 yards) long. The trough will remain as long as the spell lasts or until the cleric who cast it opts to end its effects (cf. *dispel magic*). The material component of this spell is the cleric's religious symbol.

Speak With Monsters (Alteration)

Level: 6	Components: V, S
Range: 3'' radius	Casting Time: 9 segments
Duration: 1 round/level	Saving Throw: None

Explanation/Description: When cast, the *speak with monsters* spell allows the cleric to converse with any type of creature which has any form of communicative ability. That is, the monster will understand the intent of what is said to it by the cleric. The creature or creatures thus spoken to will be checked by your referee in order to determine reaction. All creatures of the same type as that chosen by the cleric to speak to can likewise understand if they are within range. The spell lasts for 1 melee round per level of experience of the cleric casting it, and during its duration conversation can take place as the monster is able and desires.

Stone Tell (Divination)

Level: 6	Components: V, S, M
Range: Touch	Casting Time: 1 turn
Duration: 1 turn	Saving Throw: None
Area of Effect: One cubic yard of stone	

Explanation/Description: When the cleric casts a *stone tell* upon an area, the very stones will speak and relate to the caster who or what has touched them as well as telling what is covered, concealed, or simply behind the place they are. The stones will relate complete descriptions as required. The material components for this spell are a drop of mercury and a bit of clay.

Word Of Recall (Alteration)

Level: 6	Components: V
Range: 0	Casting Time: 1 segment
Duration: Special	Saving Throw: None
Area of Effect: Special	

Explanation/Description: The *word of recall* spell takes the cleric instantly back to his or her sanctuary when the word is uttered. The sanctuary must be specifically designated in advance by the cleric. It must be a well known place, but it can be any distance from the cleric, above or below ground. Transportation by the *word of recall* spell is infallibly safe. The cleric is able to transport, in addition to himself or herself, 250 gold pieces weight cumulative per level of experience. Thus, a 15th level cleric could transport his or her person and 3,750 (375 pounds) gold pieces weight in addition; this extra matter can be equipment, treasure, or living material such as another person.

Seventh Level Spells:

Astral Spell (Alteration)

Level: 7	Components: V, S
Range: Touch	Casting Time: 3 turns
Duration: Special	Saving Throw: None
Area of Effect: Special	

Explanation/Description: By means of the *astral spell* a cleric is able to project his or her astral body into the *Astral Plane*, leaving his or her physical body and material possessions behind on the *Prime Material Plane*, (the plane on which the entire universe and all of its parallels have existence). Only certain magic items which have multi-planed existence can be brought into the *Astral Plane*. As the *Astral Plane* touches upon all of the first levels of the *Outer Planes*, the cleric can travel astrally to any of these *Outer Planes* as he or she wills. The cleric then leaves the *Astral Plane*, forming a body on the plane of existence he or she has chosen to enter. It is also possible to travel astrally anywhere in the *Prime Material Plane* by means of the *astral spell*, but a second body cannot be formed on the *Prime Material Plane*. As a general rule, a person astrally projected can be seen only by creatures on the *Astral Plane*. At all times the astral body is connected to the material by a silvery cord. If the cord is broken, the affected person is killed, astrally and materially, but generally only the psychic wind can normally cause the cord to break. When a second body is formed on a different plane, the silvery cord remains invisibly attached to the new body, and the cord simply returns to the latter where it rests on the *Prime Material Plane*, reviving it from its state of suspended animation. Although astrally projected persons are able to function on the *Astral Plane*, their actions do not affect creatures not existing on the *Astral Plane*. The spell lasts until the cleric desires to end it, or until it is terminated by some outside means (*dispel magic* or destruction of the cleric's body on the *Prime Material Plane*). The cleric can take up to five other creatures with him or her by means of the *astral spell*, providing the creatures are linked in a circle with the cleric. These fellow travelers are dependent upon the cleric and can be stranded. Travel in the *Astral Plane* can be slow or fast according to the cleric's desire. The ultimate destination arrived at is

subject to the conceptualization of the cleric. (See **APPENDIX IV, THE KNOWN PLANES OF EXISTENCE**, for further information on the *Astral Plane* and astral projection.)

Control Weather (Alteration)

Level: 7	Components: V, S, M
Range: 0	Casting Time: 1 turn
Duration: 4-48 hours	Saving Throw: None
Area of Effect: 4-16 square miles	

Explanation/Description: The *control weather* spell allows a cleric to change the weather in the area he or she is in at the time the spell is cast. The spell will affect the weather for from 4 to 48 hours (4d12) in an area of from 4 to 16 square miles (4d4). It requires 1 turn to cast the spell, and an additional 1 to 4 (d4) turns for the effects of the weather to be felt. The *control weather* spell will not radically change the temperature, i.e. from below zero to a 100 degree temperature heat wave. The weather control possible depends upon the prevailing conditions:

CLEAR WEATHER	HOT WEATHER	CALM
Very clear	Warm weather	Dead calm
Light clouds or hazy	Sweltering heat	Light breeze
PARTLY CLOUDY WEATHER	WARM WEATHER	LIGHT WIND
Clear weather	Hot weather	Calm
Cloudy	Cool weather	Strong wind
Mist/Light rain/small hail	COOL WEATHER	STRONG WIND
Sleet/Light snow	Warm weather	Light wind
CLOUDY WEATHER	Cold weather	Gale
Partly cloudy	COLD WEATHER	GALE
Deep clouds	Cool weather	Strong wind
Fog	Arctic cold	Storm
Heavy rain/Large hail		STORM
Driving sleet/Heavy snow		Gale
		Hurricane-
		Typhoon

All three aspects of the weather (clouds/precipitation, temperature, and wind) can be controlled, but only as shown. For example, a day which is *clear, warm,* and with *light wind* can be controlled to become *hazy, hot,* and *calm.* Contradictions are not possible — *fog* and *strong wind,* for example. Multiple *control weather* spells can be used only in succession. The material components for this spell are the cleric's religious symbol, incense, and prayer beads or similar prayer object. Obviously, this spell functions only in areas where there are appropriate climatic conditions.

Earthquake (Alteration)

Level: 7	Components: V, S, M
Range: 12"	Casting Time: 1 turn
Duration: 1 round	Saving Throw: None
Area of Effect: ½" diameter/level	

Explanation/Description: When this spell is cast by a cleric, a local tremor of fairly high strength rips the ground. The shock is over in one melee round. The *earthquake* affects all terrain, vegetation, structures, and creatures in its locale. The area of effect of the *earthquake* spell is circular, the diameter being ½" for every level of experience of the cleric casting it, i.e. a 20th level cleric casts an *earthquake* spell with a 10" diameter area of effect:

Effects are as follows:

TERRAIN		
	Cave or cavern	Collapses roof
	Cliffs	— Crumble causing landslide
	Ground	— Cracks open, causing creatures to fall in and be killed as follows:
		— Size S — 1 in 4 (d4)
		— Size M — 1 in 6 (d6)
		— Size L — 1 in 8 (d8)
	Marsh	— Drains water off to form muddy, rough ground
	Tunnel	— Caves in

VEGETATION

Small growth	— No effect
Trees	— 1 in 3 are uprooted and fall

STRUCTURES

All structures	— Sustain from 5 to 60 points (5d12) of structural damage; those taking full damage are thrown down in rubble

CREATURES

See above

The material components for this spell are a pinch of dirt, a piece of rock, and a lump of clay.

Gate (Conjuration/Summoning)

Level: 7	Components: V, S
Range: 3″	Casting Time: 5 segments
Duration: Special	Saving Throw: None
Area of Effect: Special	

Explanation/Description: The casting of a gate spell has two effects: first, it causes an ultra-dimensional connection between the plane of existence the cleric is on and that plane on which dwells a specific being of great power, the result enabling the being to merely step through the gate, or portal, from its plane to that of the cleric; second, the utterance of the spell attracts the attention of the dweller on the other plane. When casting the spell, the cleric must name the demon, devil, demi-god, god, or similar being he or she desires to make use of the gate and come to the cleric's aid. There is a 100% certainty that something will step through the gate. The actions of the being which comes through will depend on many factors, including the alignment of the cleric, the nature of those in company with him or her, and who or what opposes or threatens the cleric. Your Dungeon Master will have a sure method of dealing with the variables of the situation. The being gated in will either return immediately (very unlikely) or remain to take action.

Holy (Unholy) Word (Conjuration/Summoning)

Level: 7	Components: V
Range: 0	Casting Time: 1 segment
Duration: Special	Saving Throw: None
Area of Effect: 3″ radius	

Explanation/Description: The utterance of a holy (unholy) word has tremendous power. It drives off evil (good) creatures from other planes, forcing them to return to their own plane(s) of existence. It further affects other creatures of differing alignment as follows:

Creature's Hit Dice or Level	General	Effects Move	Attack Dice	Spells
less than 4	kills	-	-	-
4 to 7+	paralyzes 1-4 turns	-	-	-
8 to 11+	stuns 2-8 rounds	-50%	-4	-
12 or more	deafens 1-4 rounds	-25%	-2	50% chance of failure

Affected creatures must be within the 6″ diameter area of effect centering on the cleric casting the spell.

Regenerate (Necromantic) Reversible

Level: 7	Components: V, S, M
Range: Touch	Casting Time: 3 rounds
Duration: Permanent	Saving Throw: None
Area of Effect: Creature touched	

Explanation/Description: When a regenerate spell is cast, body members (fingers, toes, hands, feet, arms, legs, tails, or even the heads of multi-headed creatures), bones, or organs will grow back. The process of regeneration requires but 1 round if the member(s) severed is (are) present and touching the creature, 2-8 turns otherwise. The reverse,

wither, causes the member or organ touched to shrivel and cease functioning in 1 round, dropping off into dust in 2-8 turns. As is usual, creatures must be touched in order to have harmful effect occur. The material components of this spell are a prayer device and holy/unholy water.

Restoration (Necromantic) Reversible

Level: 7	Components: V, S
Range: Touch	Casting Time: 3 rounds
Duration: Permanent	Saving Throw: None
Area of Effect: Creature touched	

Explanation/Description: When this spell is cast, the life energy level of the recipient creature is raised upwards by one. This subsumes previous life energy level drain of the creature by some force or monster. Thus, if a 10th level character had been struck by a wight and drained to 9th level, the restoration spell would bring the character up to exactly the number of experience points necessary to restore him or her to 10th level once again, and restoring additional hit dice (or hit points) and level functions accordingly. Restoration is only effective if the spell is cast within 1 day/level of experience of the cleric casting it of the recipient's loss of life energy. The reverse, energy drain, draws away a life energy level (cf. such "undead" as spectre, wight, vampire). The energy drain requires the victim to be touched. A restoration spell will restore the intelligence of a creature affected by a feeblemind spell (q.v.).

Resurrection (Necromantic) Reversible

Level: 7	Components: V, S, M
Range: Touch	Casting Time: 1 turn
Duration: Permanent	Saving Throw: None
Area of Effect: Person touched	

Explanation/Description: The cleric employing this spell is able to restore life and complete strength to the person he/she bestows the resurrection upon. The person can have been dead up to 10 years cumulative per level of the cleric casting the spell, i.e. a 19th level cleric can resurrect the bones of a person dead up to 190 years. See raise dead for limitations on what persons can be raised. The reverse, destruction, causes the victim of the spell to be instantly dead and turned to dust. Destruction requires a touch, either in combat or otherwise. The material components of the spell are the cleric's religious symbol and holy/unholy water. Employment of this spell makes it impossible for the cleric to cast further spells or engage in combat until he or she has had one day of bed rest for each level of experience of the person brought back to life or destroyed.

Symbol (Conjuration/Summoning)

Level: 7	Components: V, S, M
Range: Touch	Casting Time: 3 segments
Duration: 1 turn/level	Saving Throw: Neg.
Area of Effect: Special	

Explanation/Description: The cleric casting this spell inscribes a symbol in the air or upon any surface, according to his or her wish. The symbol glows for 1 turn for each level of experience of the cleric casting it. The particular symbol used can be selected by the cleric at the time of casting, selection being limited to:

HOPELESSNESS	— Creatures seeing it must turn back in dejection and/or surrender to capture or attack unless they save versus magic. Its effects last for 3 to 12 turns.
PAIN	— Creatures affected suffer -4 on "to hit" dice and -2 on dexterity ability score due to wracking pains. The effects last for 2-20 turns.
PERSUASION	— Creatures seeing the symbol become of the same alignment as and friendly to the cleric who scribed the symbol for from 1 to 20 turns unless a saving throw versus magic is made.

The material components of this spell are mercury and phosphorus. (cf. eighth level magic-user symbol spell.)

Wind Walk (Alteration)

Level: 7
Range: Touch
Duration: 6 turns/level
Area of Effect: Special

Components: V, S, M
Casting Time: 1 round
Saving Throw: None

Explanation/Description: This spell enables the cleric, and possibly one or two other persons, to alter the substance of his or her body to cloud-like vapors. A magical wind then wafts the cleric along at a speed of up to 60″ per turn, or as slow as 6″ per turn, as the spell caster wills. The *wind walk* spell lasts as long as the cleric desires, up to a maximum duration of 6 turns (one hour) per level of experience of the caster. For every 8 levels of experience the cleric has attained, up to 24, he or she is able to touch another and carry that person, or those two persons, along with the *wind walk*. Persons wind walking are not invisible but appear misty and are transparent. If fully clothed in white they are 80% likely to be mistaken for clouds, fog, vapors, etc. The material components of this spell are fire and holy/unholy water.

DRUID SPELLS

Notes Regarding Druid (Cleric) Spells:

The religious symbol of druids is mistletoe. Of lesser importance is holly. Some magical power resides in oak leaves. *All of the druidic spells with a material component assume the use of mistletoe*, as gathered by the druid character in the manner described hereafter. Lesser mistletoe, as well as holly and oak leaves, will reduce spell effectiveness as follows:

ITEM	SPELL RANGE	SPELL DURATION	AREA OF EFFECT
Lesser mistletoe	100%	75%*	100%
Borrowed mistletoe	75%*	50%**	100%
Holly	75%*	50%**	75%*
Oak leaves	50%**	50%**	50%**

  * or +1 on saving throw, if any, if category is not applicable
  ** or +2 on saving throw, if any, if category is not applicable

Greater mistletoe, that is, mistletoe which is properly harvested by the druid, must be gathered by the druid as follows. On Midsummer's Eve, the druid must locate his mistletoe, cut it with a gold or silver sickle and catch it in a bowl before it touches the ground.

Lesser mistletoe is that which is not harvested on the eve of midsummer, or that which the druid takes in a way which is not prescribed (such as picking by hand).

Borrowed mistletoe is any mistletoe which is not personally harvested by the druid.

Holly and oak leaves must be gathered by the druid, but these may be picked or gathered in any manner.

First Level Spells:

Animal Friendship (Enchantment/Charm)

Level: 1
Range: 1″
Duration: Permanent
Area of Effect: One animal

Components: V, S, M
Casting Time: 6 turns
Saving Throw: Neg.

Explanation/Description: By means of this spell the druid is able to show any animal which is of at least *animal* intelligence (but not above semi-intelligent rating) that the druid is disposed to be its friend. If the animal does not make its saving throw versus magic immediately when the spell is begun, it will stand quietly while the druid finishes the spell. Thereafter, it will follow the druid about, and he or she can teach it 3 specific "tricks" or tasks for each point of intelligence it possesses. (Typical tasks are those taught a dog or similar pet, i.e. they cannot be complex.)

Training for each such "trick" must be done over a period of 1 week, and all must be done within 3 months of acquiring the creature. During the training period the animal will not harm the druid, but if the creature is left alone for more than 3 days it will revert to its natural state and act accordingly. The druid may use this spell to attract up to 2 hit dice of animal(s) per level of experience he or she possesses. This also means that the druid can never have more hit dice of animals so attracted and trained than are equal to or less than twice his or her levels of experience. Only *neutral* animals can be attracted, befriended, and trained. The material components of this spell are mistletoe and a piece of food attractive to the animal subject.

Detect Magic (Divination)

Level: 1
Range: 0
Duration: 12 rounds
Area of Effect: 1″ path, 4″ long

Components: V, S, M
Casting Time: 3 segments
Saving Throw: None

Explanation/Description: Except as noted above, this spell is the same as the first level cleric spell of the same name.

Detect Snares & Pits (Divination)

Level: 1
Range: 0
Duration: 4 rounds/level
Area of Effect: 1″ path, 4″ long

Components: V, S, M
Casting Time: 3 segments
Saving Throw: None

Explanation/Description: Upon casting this spell, the druid is able to *detect snares & pits* along the 1″ wide by 4″ long area of effect path and thus avoid such deadfalls. Note that in the underground only simple pits, not all forms of traps, would be detected by means of this spell. Outdoors, the spell detects all forms of traps — deadfalls, missile trips, snares, etc. The spell lasts 4 melee rounds for each level of experience of the druid casting it, i.e. 4 rounds at the 1st level, 8 at the 2nd, 12 (1 turn plus 2 rounds) at the 3rd, etc.

Entangle (Alteration)

Level: 1
Range: 8″
Duration: 1 turn
Area of Effect: 4″ diameter

Components: V, S, M
Casting Time: 3 segments
Saving Throw: ½

Explanation/Description: By means of this spell the druid is able to cause plants in the area of effect to *entangle* creatures within the area. The grasses, weeds, bushes, and even trees wrap, twist, and entwine about creatures, thus holding them fast for the duration of the spell. If any creature in the area of effect makes its saving throw, the effect of the spell is to slow its movement by 50% for the spell duration.

Faerie Fire (Alteration)

Level: 1
Range: 8″
Duration: 4 rounds/level
Area of Effect: 12 linear feet/level
   within a 4″ radius

Components: V
Casting Time: 3 segments
Saving Throw: None

Explanation/Description: When the druid casts this spell, he or she outlines an object or creature with a pale glowing light. The completeness of the lining is dependent upon the number of linear feet the druid is able to affect, about 12′ per level (i.e. one 6′ man or two 3′ kobolds). If there is sufficient power, several objects or creatures can be covered by the *faerie fire*, but one must be fully outlined before the next is begun, and all must be within the area of effect. Outlined objects or creatures (including those otherwise invisible) are visible at 8″ in the dark, 4″ if the viewer is near a bright light source. Outlined creatures are easier to strike, thus opponents gain +2 on "to hit" dice. The *faerie fire* can be blue, green, or violet according to the word of the druid at the time he or she casts the spell. The *faerie fire* does not itself cause any harm to the object or creature lined.

Invisibility To Animals (Alteration)

Level: 1
Range: Touch

Components: S, M
Casting Time: 4 segments

Duration: *1 turn + 1 round/level*
Area of Effect: *Creature touched*

Saving Throw: *None*

Explanation/Description: When an *invisibility to animals* spell is cast by a druid, the recipient of the magic becomes totally undetectable with respect to normal animals with intelligence under 6. Normal animals includes giant-sized varieties, but it excludes any with magical abilities or powers. The magicked individual is able to walk amongst animals or pass through them as if he or she did not exist. For example, this individual could stand before the hungriest of lions or a tyrannosaurus rex and not be molested or even noticed. However, a nightmare, hell hound, or winter wolf would certainly be aware of the individual. The material component of this spell is holly rubbed over the individual.

Locate Animals (Divination)

Level: *1*
Range: *0*
Duration: *1 round/level*
Area of Effect: *2'' path 2'' long/level*

Components: *V, S, M*
Casting Time: *1 round*
Saving Throw: *None*

Explanation/Description: The druid with a *locate animals* spell is able to determine the direction and distance of any of the desired animals within the area of effect. The sought after animal can be of any sort, but the druid must concentrate on the sort desired. The cleric faces in a direction, thinks of the animal desired, and he or she then knows if any such animal is within spell range. During a round of spell effect duration, the druid must face in only one direction, i.e., only a 2'' wide path can be known. The spell lasts 1 round per level of experience of the druid, while the length of the path is 2'' per level of experience.

Pass Without Trace (Enchantment/Charm)

Level: *1*
Range: *Touch*
Duration: *1 turn/level*
Area of Effect: *Creature touched*

Components: *V, S, M*
Casting Time: *1 round*
Saving Throw: *None*

Explanation/Description: When this spell is cast, the recipient can move through any type of terrain — mud, snow, dust, etc. — and leave neither footprint nor scent. Thus, tracking a person or other creature covered by this dweomer is impossible. The material components of this spell are a leaf of mistletoe (which must be burned thereafter and the ashes powdered and scattered) and a sprig of pine or evergreen. *Note:* The area which is passed over will radiate a dweomer for 6-36 turns after the affected creature passes.

Predict Weather (Divination)

Level: *1*
Range: *0*
Duration: *2 hours/level*
Area of Effect: *Nine square miles*

Components: *V, S, M*
Casting Time: *1 round*
Saving Throw: *None*

Explanation/Description: When a *predict weather* spell is cast by a druid, he or she gains 100% accurate knowledge of the weather (sky, temperature, precipitation) in a nine square mile area centering on the druid. For each level of experience of the druid casting the spell, two hours advance weather can be forecast. Thus, at 1st level the druid knows what the weather will be for two hours; at second level he or she knows the weather for 4 hours in advance, etc.

Purify Water (Alteration) Reversible

Level: *1*
Range: *4''*
Duration: *Permanent*
Area of Effect: *1 cubic foot/level, 1'' square area*

Components: *V, S*
Casting Time: *1 round*
Saving Throw: *None*

Explanation/Description: This spell makes dirty, contaminated water clean and pure, suitable for consumption. Up to one cubic foot per level of the druid casting the spell can be thus purified. The reverse of the spell, *contaminate water*, works in exactly the same manner, and even holy/unholy water can be spoiled by its effects.

Shillelagh (Alteration)

Level: *1*
Range: *Touch*
Duration: *1 round/level*
Area of Effect: *One normal oaken club*

Components: *V, S, M*
Casting Time: *1 segment*
Saving Throw: *None*

Explanation/Description: This spell enables the druid to change his own oaken cudgel into a magical weapon which is +1 to hit and inflicts 2-8 hit points of damage on opponents up to man-sized, 2-5 hit points of damage on larger opponents. The druid must wield the *shillelagh*, of course. The material components of this spell are an oaken club, any mistletoe, and a shamrock leaf.

Speak With Animals (Alteration)

Level: *1*
Range: *0*
Duration: *2 rounds/level*
Area of Effect: *One animal type in 4'' radius of druid*

Components: *V, S*
Casting Time: *3 segments*
Saving Throw: *None*

Explanation/Description: Except as noted above, this spell is the same as the second level cleric spell of the same name.

Second Level Spells:

Barkskin (Alteration)

Level: *2*
Range: *Touch*
Duration: *4 rounds + 1 round/level*
Area of Effect: *Creature touched*

Components: *V,S,M*
Casting Time: *3 segments*
Saving Throw: *None*

Explanation/Description: When the druid casts the *barkskin* spell upon a creature, its armor class improves 1 place because the creature's skin becomes as tough as bark. In addition, saving throws versus all attack forms except magic increase by +1. This spell can be placed on the druid casting it or on any other creature he or she touches. In addition to mistletoe, the caster must have a handful of bark from an oak as the material component of the spell.

Charm Person Or Mammal (Enchantment/Charm)

Level: *2*
Range: *8''*
Duration: *Special*
Area of Effect: *One person or mammal*

Components: *V, S*
Casting Time: *4 segments*
Saving Throw: *Neg.*

Explanation/Description: This spell will affect any single person or mammal it is cast upon. The creature then will regard the druid who cast the spell as a trusted friend and ally to be heeded and protected. The spell does not enable the druid to control the charmed creature as if it were an automaton, but any word or action of the druid will be viewed in its most favorable way. Thus, a charmed creature would not obey a suicide command, but might believe the druid if assured that the only chance to save the druid's life is if the creature holds back an onrushing red dragon for "just a round or two". Note also that the spell does not empower the druid with linguistic capabilities beyond those he or she normally possesses. The duration of the spell is a function of the charmed creature's intelligence, and it is tied to the saving throw. The spell may be broken if a saving throw is made, and this saving throw is checked on a periodic basis according to the creature's intelligence:

Intelligence Score	Period Between Checks
3 or less	3 months
4 to 6	2 months
7 to 9	1 month
10 to 12	3 weeks
13 to 14	2 weeks
15 to 16	1 week
17	3 days
18	2 days
19 or more	1 day

If the druid harms, or attempts to harm, the charmed creature by some overt action, or if a *dispel magic* (q.v.) is successfully cast upon the charmed creature, the *charm* will be broken automatically. The spell affects all mammalian animals and persons. The term *person* includes all bipedal human and humanoid creatures of approximately man-size, or less than man-size, including those affected by the *hold person* spell (q.v.). If the recipient of the *charm person/charm mammal* spell makes its saving throw versus the spell, its effect is negated.

Create Water (Alteration)

Level: 2
Range: 1''
Duration: *Permanent*
Area of Effect: *1 cubic foot/level*

Components: V, S
Casting Time: *1 turn*
Saving Throw: *None*

Explanation/Description: The druid can create pure, drinkable water by means of a *create water* spell. He or she creates 1 cubic foot of water for each level of experience attained. The water can be created at a maximum distance of 1'' from the druid.

Cure Light Wounds (Necromantic) Reversible

Level: 2
Range: *Touch*
Duration: *Permanent*
Area of Effect: *Character touched*

Components: V,S,M
Casting Time: *4 segments*
Saving Throw: *None*

Explanation/Description: With the exception of the fact that the druid must have mistletoe (of any sort) to effect this spell, it is the same as the first level cleric *cure light wounds* spell.

Feign Death (Necromantic)

Level: 2
Range: 1''
Duration: *4 rounds +2 rounds/level*
Area of Effect: *One creature*

Components: V, S, M
Casting Time: *3 segments*
Saving Throw: *None*

Explanation/Description: Except as noted above, this spell is the same as the third level magic-user *feign death* spell (q.v.). The material component is a piece of dead oak leaf (in addition to mistletoe, of course).

Fire Trap (Evocation)

Level: 2
Range: *Touch*
Duration: *Permanent until discharged*
Area of Effect: *Object touched*

Components: V, S, M
Casting Time: *1 turn*
Saving Throw: *½*

Explanation/Description: This spell is the same as the fourth level magic-user *fire trap* spell (q.v.) except as shown above and for the fact that the material components are holly berries and a stick of charcoal to trace the outline of the closure.

Heat Metal (Alteration) Reversible

Level: 2
Range: 4''
Duration: *7 rounds*
Area of Effect: *Special*

Components: V, S, M
Casting Time: *4 segments*
Saving Throw: *None*

Explanation/Description: By means of the *heat metal* spell, the druid is able to excite the molecules of ferrous metal (iron, iron alloys, steel) and thus cause the affected metal to become hot. On the first round of the spell, the effect is merely to cause the metal to be very warm and uncomfortable to touch, and this is also the effect on the last melee round of the spell's duration. The second and sixth (next to the last) round effect is to cause blisters and damage; the third, fourth, and fifth rounds the metal becomes searing hot, causing disability and damage to exposed flesh, as shown below:

Metal Temperature	Per Round of Exposure	
	Damage	Disability
very warm	none	none
hot	1-4 hit points	none
searing	2-8 hit points	hands or feet 2-8 days
		head 1-4 turns unconsciousness
		body 1-4 days

Note also that materials such as wood, leather, or flammable cloth will smoulder and burn if exposed to searing hot metal, and such materials will then cause searing damage to exposed flesh on the next round. *Fire resistance* (potion or ring) or a *protection from fire* spell totally negates the effects of a *heat metal* spell, as will immersion in water or snow, or exposure to a *cold* or *ice storm* spell (qq.v.). For each level of experience of the druid casting the spell, he or she is able to affect the metal of one man-sized creature, i.e. arms and armor, or a single mass of metal equal to 500 gold pieces in weight, cumulative. The reverse, *chill metal*, counters a *heat metal* spell or else causes metal to act as follows:

Metal Temperature	Per Round of Exposure	
	Damage	Disability
cold	none	none
icy	1-2 hit points	none
freezing	1-4 hits points	amputation of fingers, toes, nose, or ears

The *chill* metal spell is countered by a *resist cold* spell, or by any great heat, i.e. proximity to a blazing fire (not a mere torch), a magical *flaming sword*, a *wall of fire*, etc.

Locate Plants (Divination)

Level: 2
Range: 0
Duration: *1 turn/level*
Area of Effect: *1'' diameter/level circle*

Components: V, S, M
Casting Time: *1 round*
Saving Throw: *None*

Explanation/Description: When this spell is used by a druid, he or she is able to locate any desired type of plant within the area of effect. Note: the plant type must be singular and concentrated upon. The spell's area of effect centers on, and moves with, the druid.

Obscurement (Alteration)

Level: 2　　　　　　　　　　　　Components: V, S
Range: 0　　　　　　　　　　　　Casting Time: 4 segments
Duration: 4 rounds/level　　　　　Saving Throw: None
Area of Effect: Special

Explanation/Description: This spell causes a misty vapor to arise around the druid. It persists in this locale for 4 rounds per level of experience of the druid casting the spell, and it reduces visibility of any sort (including infravision) to 2' to 8' (2d4). The area of effect is a cubic progression based on the druid's level of experience, a 1" cube at 1st level, a 2" cube at 2nd level, a 3" cube at 3rd level, and so on. Underground, the height of the vapor is restricted to 1", although the length and breadth of the cloud is not so limited. A strong wind will cut the duration of an *obscurement* spell by 75%.

Produce Flame (Alteration)

Level: 2　　　　　　　　　　　　Components: V, S, M
Range: 0　　　　　　　　　　　　Casting Time: 4 segments
Duration: 2 rounds/level　　　　　Saving Throw: None
Area of Effect: Special

Explanation/Description: A bright flame, equal in brightness to a torch, springs forth from the druid's palm when he or she casts a *produce flame* spell. This magical flame lasts for 2 melee rounds for each level of the druid casting the spell. The flame does not harm the druid's person, but it is hot, and it will cause combustion of inflammable materials (paper, cloth, dry wood, oil, etc.). The druid is capable of hurling the magical flame as a missile, with a range of 4". The flame will flash on impact, igniting combustibles within a 3' diameter of its center of impact, and then extinguish itself. The druid can cause it to go out any time he or she desires, but fire caused by the flame cannot be so extinguished.

Trip (Enchantment/Charm)

Level: 2　　　　　　　　　　　　Components: V, S, M
Range: Touch　　　　　　　　　　Casting Time: 4 segments
Duration: 1 turn/level　　　　　　Saving Throw: Neg.
Area of Effect: One 10' long object

Explanation/Description: The spell caster must use a length of vine, a stick, pole, rope, or similar object to cast this magic upon. The *trip* spell causes the object to rise slightly off the ground or floor it is resting on and trip creatures crossing it if they fail to make their saving throw versus magic. Note that only as many creatures can be tripped as are actually stepping across the magicked object, i.e. a 3' long piece of rope could trip only 1 man-sized creature. Creatures moving at a very rapid pace (running) when tripped will take 1-6 (d6) hit points of damage and be stunned for 2-5 (d4+1) rounds if the surface they fall upon is very hard, but if it is turf or non-hard they will merely be stunned for 2-5 segments. Very large creatures such as elephants will not be at all affected by a *trip*. The object magicked will continue to trip all creatures passing over it, including the spell caster, for as long as the spell duration lasts. Creatures aware of the object and its potential add +4 to their saving throw when crossing it. The object is 80% undetectable without magical means of detection.

Warp Wood (Alteration)

Level: 2　　　　　　　　　　　　Components: V, S, M
Range: 1"/level　　　　　　　　　Casting Time: 4 segments
Duration: Permanent　　　　　　　Saving Throw: None
Area of Effect: Special

Explanation/Description: When this spell is cast the druid causes a volume of wood to bend and warp, permanently destroying its straightness, form, and strength. The range of a *warp wood* spell is 1" for each level of experience of the druid casting it. It affects approximately a fifteen inch shaft of wood of up to one inch diameter per level of the druid. Thus, at 1st level, a druid might be able to warp a hand axe handle, or four crossbow bolts, at 5th level he or she could warp the shaft of a typical magic spear. Note that boards or planks can also be affected, causing a door to be sprung or a boat or ship to leak.

Third Level Spells:

Call Lightning (Alteration)

Level: 3　　　　　　　　　　　　Components: V,S,M
Range: 0　　　　　　　　　　　　Casting Time: 1 turn
Duration: 1 turn/level　　　　　　Saving Throw: ½
Area of Effect: 72" diameter

Explanation/Description: When a *call lightning* spell is cast, there must be a storm of some sort in the area — a rain shower, clouds and wind, hot and cloudy conditions, or even a tornado. The druid is then able to call down bolts of lightning from sky to ground. Each bolt will cause damage equal to 2 eight-sided dice (2d8) plus 1 like die (d8) for each level of experience of the druid casting the spell. Thus, a 4th level druid calls down a six-die (6d8) bolt. The bolt of lightning flashes down in a perpendicular stroke at whatever distance the spell caster decides, up to the 36" radial distance maximum. Any creature within a 1" radius of the path or the point where the lightning strikes will take full damage, unless a saving throw is made, in which case only one-half damage is taken. Full/half damage refers to the number of hit dice of the lightning bolt, i.e. if it is of eight dice strength, the victim will take either eight dice (8d8) or four dice (4d8), if the saving throw is made, of damage. The druid is able to call one bolt of lightning every 10 melee rounds (1 turn), to a maximum number of turns equal to the level of experience he or she has attained, i.e. 1 bolt/turn for each level of experience. Note: This spell is normally usable outdoors only.

Cure Disease (Necromantic) Reversible

Level: 3　　　　　　　　　　　　Components: V, S, M
Range: Touch　　　　　　　　　　Casting Time: 1 round
Duration: Permanent　　　　　　　Saving Throw: None
Area of Effect: Creature touched

Explanation/Description: This spell is the same as the 3rd level cleric *cure disease* spell (q.v.), with the exception that the druid must have mistletoe to effect it. It is reversible to *cause disease* also.

Hold Animal (Enchantment/Charm)

Level: 3　　　　　　　　　　　　Components: V, S, M
Range: 8"　　　　　　　　　　　　Casting Time: 5 segments
Duration: 2 rounds/level　　　　　Saving Throw: Neg.
Area of Effect: One to four animals

Explanation/Description: By means of this spell the druid holds one to four animals rigid. Animals affected are normal or giant-sized mammals, birds, or reptiles, but not *monsters* such as centaurs, gorgons, harpies, naga, etc. That is, apes, bears, crocodiles, dogs, eagles, foxes, giant beavers, and similar animals are subject to this spell. The *hold* lasts for 2 melee rounds per level of experience of the druid casting it. It is up to the druid as to how many animals he or she wishes to *hold* with the spell, but the greater the number, the better chance each will have of not being affected by the spell. Note that a maximum body weight of 400 pounds (100 pounds with respect to non-mammals)/animal/level of experience of the druid can be affected, i.e. an 8th level druid can affect up to four 3,200 pound mammals or a like number of 800 pound non-mammals such as birds or reptiles. Each animal gets a saving throw: if only 1 is the subject of the spell, it has a penalty of -4 on its die roll to save; if 2 are subject, they each receive a penalty of -2 on their die rolls; if 3 are subject, they each receive a penalty of -1 on their die rolls; if 4 are subject, each makes a normal saving throw.

Neutralize Poison (Alteration) Reversible

Level: 3　　　　　　　　　　　　Components: V, S
Range: Touch　　　　　　　　　　Casting Time: 5 segments
Duration: Permanent　　　　　　　Saving Throw: None
Area of Effect: Creature touched

Explanation/Description: This spell is the same as the 4th level cleric *neutralize poison* spell (q.v.).

Plant Growth (Alteration)

Level: 3　　　　　　　　　　　　Components: V, S, M
Range: 16"　　　　　　　　　　　Casting Time: 1 round
Duration: Permanent　　　　　　　Saving Throw: None
Area of Effect: 2" × 2" square
　area/level

Explanation/Description: When a *plant growth* spell is cast by the druid, he or she causes normal vegetation to grow, entwine, and entangle to form a thicket or jungle which creatures must hack or force a way through at a movement rate of 1″ per, or 2″ per with respect to larger than man-sized creatures. Note that the area must have brush and trees in it in order to allow this spell to go into effect. Briars, bushes, creepers, lianas, roots, saplings, thistles, thorn, trees, vines, and weeds become so thick and overgrown in the area of effect as to form a barrier. The area of effect is 2″ × 2″ square per level of experience of the druid, in any square or rectangular shape that the druid decides upon at the time of the spell casting. Thus an 8th level druid can affect a maximum area of 16″ × 16″ square, a 32″ × 8″ rectangle, a 64″ × 4″ rectangle, 128″ × 2″ rectangle, etc. The spell's effects persist in the area until it is cleared by labor, fire, or such magical means as a *dispel magic* spell (q.v.).

Protection From Fire (Abjuration)

Level: *3*
Range: *Touch*
Duration: *Special*
Area of Effect: *Creature touched*

Components: *V, S, M*
Casting Time: *5 segments*
Saving Throw: *None*

Explanation/Description: The effect of a *protection from fire* spell differs according to the recipient of the magic — the druid or some other creature. If the spell is cast upon the druid, it confers complete invulnerability to normal fires (torches, bonfires, oil fires, and the like) and to exposure to magical fires such as demon fire, *burning hands*, fiery dragon breath, *fire ball*, *fire seeds*, *fire storm*, *flame strike*, hell hound breath, *meteor swarm*, pyrohydra breath, etc. until an accumulation of 12 hit points of potential damage per level of experience of the druid has been absorbed by the *protection from fire* spell, at which time the spell is negated. Otherwise the spell lasts for 1 turn per level of experience of the druid. If the spell is cast upon another creature, it gives invulnerability to normal fire, gives a bonus of +4 on saving throw die rolls made versus fire attacks, and reduces damage sustained from magical fires by 50%.

Pyrotechnics (Alteration)

Level: *3*
Range: *16″*
Duration: *Special*
Area of Effect: *10 or 100 times the
fire source*

Components: *V, S, M*
Casting Time: *5 segments*
Saving Throw: *None*

Explanation/Description: A *pyrotechnics* spell can have either of two effects. It produces a flashing and fiery burst of glowing, colored aerial *fireworks* which lasts 1 segment per experience level of the druid casting the spell and temporarily blinds those creatures in the area of effect or under it or within 12″ of the area (and in any event in unobstructed line of sight); or it causes a thick writhing stream of *smoke* to arise from the fire source of the spell and form a choking cloud which lasts for 1 round per experience level of the druid casting the spell, covering a roughly globular area from the ground or floor up (or conforming to the shape of a confined area), which totally obscures vision beyond 2′. The spell requires a fire of some sort in range. The area of *pyrotechnics* effect is 10 times the volume of the fire source with respect to *fireworks*, 100 times with respect to *smoke*. In either case, the fire source is immediately extinguished by the employment of the spell.

Snare (Enchantment/Charm)

Level: *3*
Range: *Touch*
Duration: *Permanent until
triggered*
Area of Effect: *2′ diameter circle
plus 1/6′ per level of the spell
caster*

Components: *V,S,M*
Casting Time: *3 rounds*
Saving Throw: *None*

Explanation/Description: This spell enables the druid to make a *snare* which is 90% undetectable without magical aid. The *snare* can be made from any supple vine, a thong, or a rope. When the *snare* spell is cast upon it, the cordlike object blends with the background of its location. One end of the *snare* is tied in a loop which will contract about 1 or more of the limbs of any creature stepping inside the circle (note that the head of a worm or snake could also be thus ensnared). If a strong and supple tree is nearby, the *snare* will be fastened to it, and the dweomer of the spell will cause it to bend and then straighten when the loop is triggered, thus

causing 1-6 hit points of damage to the creature trapped, and lifting it off the ground by the trapped member(s) (or strangling it if the head/neck triggered the *snare*). If no such sapling or tree is available, the cord-like object will tighten upon the member(s) and then enwrap the entire creature, doing no damage, but tightly binding it. The *snare* is magical, so for 1 hour it is breakable only by storm giant or greater strength (23); each hour thereafter, the snare material loses magic so as to become 1 point more breakable per hour — 22 after 2 hours, 21 after 3, 20 after 4 — until 6 full hours have elapsed. At that time, 18 strength will break the bonds. After 12 hours have elapsed, the materials of the *snare* lose all of the magical properties, and the loop opens, freeing anything it had held. The druid must have a snake skin and a piece of sinew from a strong animal to weave into the cord-like object from which he or she will make the *snare*. Only mistletoe is otherwise needed.

Stone Shape (Alteration)

Level: *3*
Range: *Touch*
Duration: *Permanent*
Area of Effect: *Three cubic feet,
plus one cubic foot per level*

Components: *V, S, M*
Casting Time: *1 round*
Saving Throw: *None*

Explanation/Description: This spell is exactly the same as the fifth level magic-user spell, *stone shape* (q.v.), except as noted above and for the requirement of mistletoe as an additional component to enable a druid to cast the spell.

Summon Insects (Conjuration/Summoning)

Level: *3*
Range: *3″*
Duration: *1 round/level*
Area of Effect: *Special*

Components: *V, S, M*
Casting Time: *1 round*
Saving Throw: *None*

Explanation/Description: When a *summon insects* spell is cast by a druid, he or she attracts flying insects 70% of the time. The exact insects called will be bees, biting flies, hornets, or wasps if flying insects are indicated, or biting ants or pinching beetles if non-flying insects are determined. A cloud of the flying type, or a swarm of the crawling sort, will appear after the spell is cast. They will attack any creature the druid points to. The attacked creature will sustain 2 hit points of damage per melee round, and it can do nothing but attempt to fend off these insects during the time it is so attacked. The summoned insects can be caused to attack another opponent, but there will be at least a 1 round delay while they leave the former recipient and attack the new victim, and crawling insects can travel only about 12′ per round (maximum speed over smooth ground). It is possible in underground situations that the druid could summon 1-4 giant ants by means of the spell, but the possibility is only 30% unless giant ants are nearby. The materials needed for this spell are mistletoe, a flower petal, and a bit of mud or wet clay.

Tree (Alteration)

Level: *3*
Range: *0*
Duration: *6 turns + 1 turn/level*
Area of Effect: *Personal*

Components: *V, S, M*
Casting Time: *5 segments*
Saving Throw: *None*

Explanation/Description: By means of this spell the druid is able to assume the form of a small living tree or shrub or that of a large dead tree trunk with but a few limbs. Although the closest inspection will not reveal that this plant is actually a druid, and for all normal tests he or she is, in fact, a tree or shrub, the druid is able to observe all that goes on around his or her person just as if he or she were in human form. The spell caster may remove the dweomer at any time he or she desires, instantly changing from plant to human form, and having full capability of undertaking any action normally possible to the druid. Note that all clothing and gear worn/carried change with the druid. The material components of this spell are mistletoe and a twig from a tree.

Water Breathing (Alteration) Reversible

Level: *3*
Range: *Touch*
Duration: *6 turns/level*
Area of Effect: *Creature touched*

Components: *V, S, M*
Casting Time: *5 segments*
Saving Throw: *None*

Explanation/Description: The recipient of a *water breathing* spell is able to freely breathe underwater for the duration of the spell, i.e. 6 turns for each level of experience of the druid casting the spell. The reverse, *air breathing*, allows water breathing creatures to comfortably survive in the atmosphere for an equal duration.

Fourth Level Spells:

Animal Summoning I (Conjuration/Summoning)

Level: 4
Range: *4"/level*
Duration: *Special*
Area of Effect: *Special*

Components: *V,S,M*
Casting Time: *6 segments*
Saving Throw: *None*

Explanation/Description: By means of this spell, the druid calls up to eight animals of whatever sort the druid names when the summoning is made, if such type are within spell range. These animals can have no more than four hit dice each. The animals summoned will aid the druid by whatever means they possess, staying until a fight is over, a specific mission is finished, the druid is safe, he or she sends them away, etc. The druid may try three times to summon three different sorts of animals, i.e. suppose that wild dogs are first summoned to no avail, then hawks are unsuccessfully called, and finally the druid calls for wild horses which may or may not be within summoning range. Your referee will determine probabilities if the presence of a summoned animal type is not known. Other than various sorts of giant animals, fantastic animals or monsters cannot be summoned by this spell, i.e. no chimerae, dragons, gorgons, manticores, etc.

Call Woodland Beings (Conjuration/Summoning)

Level: 4
Range: *12" + 1"/level*
Duration: *Special*
Area of Effect: *Special*

Components: *V, S, M*
Casting Time: *Special*
Saving Throw: *Neg.*

Explanation/Description: By means of this spell the druid is able to summon certain woodland creatures to his or her location. Naturally, this spell will only work outdoors, but not necessarily only in wooded areas. The druid begins the incantation, and the spell must be continued uninterrupted until some called creature appears or 2 turns have elapsed. (The verbalization and somatic gesturing are easy, so this is not particularly exhausting to the spell caster.) Only 1 type of the following sorts of beings can be summoned by the spell, and they will come only if they are within the range of the call:

2-8 brownies	1-4 satyrs
1-4 centaurs	1-6 sprites
1-4 dryads	1 treant
1-8 pixies	1 unicorn

(Your referee will consult his outdoor map or base the probability of any such creature being within spell range upon the nature of the area the druid is in at the time of spell casting.)

The creature(s) called by the spell are entitled to a saving throw versus magic (at -4) to avoid the summons. Any woodland being answering the *call* will be favorably disposed to the spell caster and give whatever aid it is capable of. However, if the caller or members of the caller's party are of evil alignment, the creatures are entitled to another saving throw versus magic (this time at +4) when they come within 1" of the druid or other evil character with him or her, and these beings will seek immediately to escape if the saving throw is successful. In any event, if the druid requests that the summoned creatures engage in combat on behalf of the druid, they are required to make a loyalty reaction score based on the druid's charisma and whatever dealings he or she has had with the called creature(s). The material components of this spell are a pinecone and 8 holly berries.

Control Temperature, 10' Radius (Alteration)

Level: 4
Range: *0*
Duration: *4 turns + 1 turn/level*
Area of Effect: *20' diameter sphere*

Components: *V, S, M*
Casting Time: *6 segments*
Saving Throw: *None*

Explanation/Description: When this spell is cast by the druid, the

temperature surrounding the druid can be altered by 9 degrees Fahrenheit per level of experience of the spell caster, either upwards or downwards. Thus, a 10th level druid could raise the surrounding temperature from 1 to 90 degrees, or lower it by from 1 to 90 degrees. The spell lasts for a number of turns equal to 4 plus the level of experience of the druid, i.e. when cast by a 10th level druid the spell persists for 14 turns.

Cure Serious Wounds (Necromantic) Reversible

Level: 4
Range: *Touch*
Duration: *Permanent*
Area of Effect: *creature touched*

Components: *V, S, M*
Casting Time: *6 segments*
Saving Throw: *None*

Explanation/Description: This spell is the same as the 4th level cleric *cure serious wounds* spell (q.v.), with the exception of the fact that the spell requires the use of any sort of mistletoe.

Dispel Magic (Abjuration)

Level: 4
Range: *8"*
Duration: *Permanent*
Area of Effect: *4" cube*

Components: *V,S,M*
Casting Time: *6 segments*
Saving Throw: *None*

Explanation/Description: Except as noted above, this spell is the same as the 3rd level cleric *dispel magic* spell (q.v.).

Hallucinatory Forest (Illusion/Phantasm) Reversible

Level: 4
Range: *8"*
Duration: *Permanent*
Area of Effect: *4" square/level*

Components: *V, S, M*
Casting Time: *6 segments*
Saving Throw: *None*

Explanation/Description: By casting this spell the druid causes the appearance of an *hallucinatory forest* to come into existence. The illusionary forest appears to be perfectly natural and is indistinguishable from a real forest. Other druids — as well as such creatures as centaurs, dryads, green dragons, nymphs, satyrs, and treants — will recognize the forest for what it is. All other creatures will believe it is there, and movement and order of march will be affected accordingly. The *hallucinatory forest* will remain until it is magically dispelled by a reverse of the spell or a *dispel magic*. The area shape is either rectangular or square, in general, at least 4" deep, and in whatever location the druid casting the spell desires. The forest can be of less than maximum area if the druid wishes. One of its edges will appear up to 8" away from the druid, according to the desire of the spell caster.

Hold Plant (Enchantment/Charm)

Level: 4
Range: *8"*
Duration: *1 round/level*
Area of Effect: *Special*

Components: *V, S, M*
Casting Time: *6 segments*
Saving Throw: *Neg.*

Explanation/Description: The *hold plant* spell affects vegetable matter as follows: 1) it causes ambulatory vegetation to cease moving; 2) it prevents vegetable matter from entwining, grasping, closing, or growing; 3) it prevents vegetable matter from making any sound or movement which is not caused by wind. The spell effects apply to all forms of vegetation, including parasitic and fungoid types, and those magically animated or otherwise magically empowered. It affects such monsters as green slime, molds of any sort, shambling mounds, shriekers, treants, etc. The duration of a *hold plant* spell is 1 melee round per level of experience of the druid casting the spell. It affects from 1 to 4 plants — or from 4 to 16 square yards of small ground growth such as grass or mold. If but one plant (or 4 square yards) is chosen as the target for the spell by the druid, the saving throw of the plant (or area of plant growth) is made at -4 on the die; if two plants (or 8 square yards) are the target, saving throws are at -2; if three plants (or 12 square yards) are the target, saving throws are at -1; and if the maximum of 4 plants (or 16 square yards of area) are the target, saving throws are normal.

Plant Door (Alteration)

Level: 4
Range: *Touch*

Components: *V, S, M*
Casting Time: *6 segments*

Duration: *1 turn/level*	Saving Throw: *None*
Area of Effect: *Special*	

Explanation/Description: The *plant door* spell opens a magical portal or passageway through trees, undergrowth, thickets, or any similar growth — even growth of a magical nature. The *plant door* is open only to the druid who cast the spell, druids of a higher level, or dryads. The *door* even enables the druid to enter into a solid tree trunk and remain hidden there until the spell ends. If the tree is cut down or burned, the druid must leave before the tree falls or is consumed, or else he or she is killed also. The duration of the spell is 1 turn per level of experience of the druid casting it. If the druid opts to stay within an oak, the spell lasts 9 times longer, if an ash tree it lasts 3 times as long. The path created by the spell is up to 4' wide, 8' high and 12'/level of experience of the druid long.

Produce Fire (Alteration) Reversible

Level: *4*	Components: *V, S, M*
Range: *4''*	Casting Time: *6 segments*
Duration: *1 round*	Saving Throw: *None*
Area of Effect: *12' square*	

Explanation/Description: By means of this spell the druid causes a common-type fire of up to 12' per side in area boundary. While it lasts but a single round, the fire produced by the spell will cause 1-4 hit points of damage on creatures within its area; and it will ignite combustible materials such as cloth, oil, paper, parchment, wood and the like so as to cause continued burning. The reverse, *quench fire* will extinguish any normal fire (coals, oil, tallow, wax, wood, etc.) within the area of effect.

Protection From Lightning (Abjuration)

Level: *4*	Components: *V, S, M*
Range: *Touch*	Casting Time: *6 segments*
Duration: *Special*	Saving Throw: *None*
Area of Effect: *Creature touched*	

Explanation/Description: This spell is exactly the same as the 3rd level *protection from fire* spell (q.v.) except that it applies to electrical/lightning attacks.

Repel Insects (Abjuration-Alteration)

Level: *4*	Components: *V, S, M*
Range: *0*	Casting Time: *1 round*
Duration: *1 turn/level*	Saving Throw: *None*
Area of Effect: *10' radius of the spell caster*	

Explanation/Description: When this spell is cast the druid creates an invisible barrier to all sorts of insects, and normal sorts will not approach within 10' of the druid while the spell is in effect, although any giant insects with 2 or more hit dice will do so if they make a saving throw versus magic, and even those which do so will sustain 1-6 hit points of damage from the passing of the magical barrier. Note that the spell does not in any way affect arachnids, myriapods, and similar creatures — it affects only true insects. The material components of the *repel insects* spell are mistletoe and one of the following: several crushed marigold flowers, a whole crushed leek, 7 crushed stinging nettle leaves or a small lump of resin from a camphor tree.

Speak With Plants (Alteration)

Level: *4*	Components: *V, S, M*
Range: *0*	Casting Time: *1 turn*
Duration: *2 rounds/level*	Saving Throw: *None*
Area of Effect: *8'' diameter circle*	

Explanation/Description: Except as noted above, and that the material component is that typically druidic (mistletoe, *et al.*), the spell is the same as the 4th level cleric spell *speak with plants*.

Fifth Level Spells:

Animal Growth (Alteration) Reversible

Level: *5*	Components: *V, S, M*
Range: *8''*	Casting Time: *7 segments*

Duration: *2 rounds/level*	Saving Throw: *None*
Area of Effect: *Up to 8 animals in a 2'' square area*	

Explanation/Description: When this spell is cast, the druid causes all animals, up to a maximum of 8, within a 2'' square area to grow to twice their normal size. The effects of this growth are doubled hit dice (with resultant improvement in attack potential) and doubled damage in combat. The spell lasts for 2 melee rounds for each level of experience of the druid casting the spell. Note that the spell is particularly useful in conjunction with a *charm person* or *animal* or a *speak with animals* spell. The reverse reduces animal size by one half, and likewise reduces hit dice, attack damage, etc.

Animal Summoning II (Conjuration/Summoning)

Level: *5*	Components: *V, S, M*
Range: *6''/level*	Casting Time: *7 segments*
Duration: *Special*	Saving Throw: *None*
Area of Effect: *Special*	

Explanation/Description: This spell is the same in duration and effect as the 4th level *animal summoning I* spell, except that up to six animals of no more than eight hit dice each can be called, or 12 animals of no more than four hit dice each can be called.

Anti-Plant Shell (Abjuration)

Level: *5*	Components: *V, S, M*
Range: *0*	Casting Time: *7 segments*
Duration: *1 turn/level*	Saving Throw: *None*
Area of Effect: *16' diameter hemisphere*	

Explanation/Description: The *anti-plant shell* spell creates an invisible barrier which keeps out all creatures or missiles of living vegetable material. Thus, the druid (and any creatures within the shell) is protected from attacking plants or vegetable creatures such as shambling mounds or treants. The spell lasts for one turn per level of experience of the druid.

Commune With Nature (Divination)

Level: *5*	Components: *V, S, M*
Range: *0*	Casting Time: *1 turn*
Duration: *Special*	Saving Throw: *None*
Area of Effect: *Special*	

Explanation/Description: This spell enables the druid to become one with nature in the area, thus being empowered with knowledge of the surrounding territory. For each level of experience of the druid, he or she may "know" one fact, i.e. the ground ahead, left or right, the plants ahead, left or right, the minerals ahead, left or right, the water courses/bodies of water ahead, left or right, the people dwelling ahead, left or right, etc. The spell is effective only in outdoors settings, and operates in a radius of one half mile for each level of experience of the druid casting the *commune with nature* spell.

Control Winds (Alteration)

Level: *5*	Components: *V,S,M*
Range: *0*	Casting Time: *7 segments*
Duration: *1 turn/level*	Saving Throw: *None*
Area of Effect: *4''/level radius hemisphere*	

Explanation/Description: By means of a *control wind* spell the druid is able to alter wind force in the area of effect. For every level of his or her experience, the druid is able to increase or decrease wind force by 3 miles per hour. Winds in excess of 30 miles per hour drive small flying creatures (those eagle-sized and under) from the skies and severely inhibit missile discharge. Winds in excess of 45 miles per hour drive even man-sized flying creatures from the skies. Winds in excess of 60 miles per hour drive all flying creatures from the skies and uproot trees of small size, knock down wooden structures, tear off roofs, etc. Winds in excess of 75 miles per hour are of hurricane force and cause devastation to all save the strongest stone constructions. A wind above 30 miles per hour makes sailing difficult, above 45 miles per hour causes minor ship damage, above 60 miles per hour endangers ships, and above 75 miles per hour sinks ships. There is an "eye" of 4'' radius around the druid where the wind is calm. A higher level druid can use a *control winds* spell to counter the effects of a like spell cast by a lower level druid (cf. *control weather*). The spell remains in force for 1 turn for each level of experience of the druid casting it. Once the spell is cast, the wind force increases by 3 miles per hour per round until maximum speed is attained. When the spell is exhausted, the force of the wind diminishes at the same rate. Note that while the spell can be used in underground places, the "eye" will shrink in direct proportion to any confinement of the wind effect, i.e. if the area of effect is a 48" radius, and the confined space allows only a 46" radius, the "eye" will be a 2" radius; and any space under 44" radius will completely eliminate the "eye" and subject the spell caster to the effects of the wind.

Insect Plague (Conjuration/Summoning)

Level: 5	Components: V, S, M
Range: 32"	Casting Time: 1 turn
Duration: 1 turn/level	Saving Throw: None
Area of Effect: 32" diameter, 4" high cloud	

Explanation/Description: Except as noted above, and other than the fact that the material component needed for the spell is mistletoe or the holly or oak leaves substitute, the spell is the same as the 5th level cleric *insect plague* spell (q.v.).

Pass Plant (Alteration)

Level: 5	Components: V, S, M
Range: Touch	Casting Time: 7 segments
Duration: Special	Saving Throw: None
Area of Effect: Special	

Explanation/Description: By using this spell, a druid is able to enter a tree and move from inside it to another of the same type which lies in approximately the direction desired by the spell user and is within the range shown below:

Type of Tree	Range of Area of Effect
Oak	60"
Ash	54"
Yew	48"
Elm	42"
Linden	36"
deciduous	30"
coniferous	24"
other	18"

The tree entered and that receiving the druid must be of the same type, living, and of girth at least equal to the druid. Note that if the druid enters a tree, suppose an ash, and wishes to pass north as far as possible (54"), but the only appropriate ash in range is south, the druid will pass to the ash in the south. The *pass plant* spell functions so that the movement takes only one segment (6 seconds) of a round. The druid may, at his or her option, remain within the receiving tree for a maximum of 1 round per level of experience. Otherwise, he or she may step forth immediately. Should no like tree be in range, the druid simply remains within the tree, does not pass elsewhere, and must step forth in the applicable number of rounds. (See *plant door* for effects of chopping or burning such a tree.)

Sticks to Snakes (Alteration) Reversible

Level: 5	Components: V, S, M
Range: 4"	Casting Time: 7 segments
Duration: 2 rounds/level	Saving Throw: None
Area of Effect: 1" cube	

Explanation/Description: Except as noted above, and for the fact that the material component of the spell is typical for druids, this is the same as the 4th level cleric *sticks to snakes* spell (q.v.).

Transmute Rock to Mud (Alteration) Reversible

Level: 5	Components: V, S, M
Range: 16"	Casting Time: 7 segments
Duration: Special	Saving Throw: None
Area of Effect: 2" cube/level	

Explanation/Description: This spell turns natural rock of any sort into an equal volume of mud. The depth of the mud can never exceed one-half its length and/or breadth. If it is cast upon a rock, for example, the rock affected will collapse into mud. Creatures unable to levitate, fly, or otherwise free themselves from the mud will sink and suffocate, save for lightweight creatures which could normally pass across such ground. The mud will remain until a *dispel magic* spell or a reverse of this spell, *mud to rock*, restores its substance — but not necessarily its form. Evaporation will turn the mud to normal dirt, from 1 to 6 days per cubic 1" being required. The exact time depends on exposure to sun, wind and normal drainage. The *mud to rock* reverse will harden normal mud into soft stone (sandstone or similar mineral) permanently unless magically changed.

Wall of Fire (Evocation)

Level: 5	Components: V, S, M
Range: 8"	Casting Time: 7 segments
Duration: Special	Saving Throw: None
Area of Effect: Special	

Explanation/Description: The *wall of fire* spell brings forth a blazing curtain of magical fire of shimmering color — yellow-green or amber in case of druidical magic. The *wall of fire* inflicts 4 to 16 hit points of damage, plus 1 hit point of damage per level of the spell caster, upon any creature passing through it. Creatures within 1" of the wall take 2-8 hit points of damage, those within 2" take 1-4 hit points of damage. Creatures especially subject to fire may take additional damage, and undead always take twice normal damage. Only the side of the wall away from the spell caster will inflict damage. The opaque *wall of fire* lasts for as long as the druid concentrates on maintaining it, or 1 round per level of experience of the druid in the event he or she does not wish to concentrate upon it. The spell creates a sheet of flame up to 2" square per level of the spell caster, or as a ring with a radius of up to ½" per level of experience from the druid to its flames, and a height of 2". The former is stationary, while the latter moves as the druid moves.

Sixth Level Spells:

Animal Summoning III (Conjuration/Summoning)

Level: 6	Components: V, S, M
Range: 8"/level	Casting Time: 8 segments
Duration: Special	Saving Throw: None
Area of Effect: Special	

Explanation/Description: This spell is the same in duration and effect as the 4th level *animal summoning I* spell except that up to 4 animals of no more than 16 hit dice each can be summoned, or eight of no more than 8 hit dice, or 16 creatures of no more than 4 hit dice each can be summoned.

Anti-Animal Shell (Abjuration)

Level: 6	Components: V, S, M
Range: 0	Casting Time: 1 round
Duration: 1 turn/level	Saving Throw: None
Area of Effect: 20' diameter hemisphere	

Explanation/Description: By casting this spell the druid brings into being a hemispherical force field which prevents the entrance of any sort of animal matter of normal (not magical) nature. Thus, a giant would be kept out, but undead could pass through the shell of force, as could such monsters as aerial servants, demons, devils, etc. The *anti-animal shell* lasts for 1 turn for each level of experience the druid has attained.

Conjure Fire Elemental (Conjuration/Summoning) Reversible

Level: 6	Components: V, S, M
Range: 8"	Casting Time: 6 rounds
Duration: 1 turn/level	Saving Throw: None
Area of Effect: Special	

Explanation/Description: Upon casting a *conjure fire elemental* spell, the druid opens a special gate to the Elemental Plane of Fire, and a strong fire elemental (see **ADVANCED DUNGEONS & DRAGONS, MONSTER MANUAL**) is summoned to the vicinity of the spell caster. It is 85% likely that a 16 die elemental will appear, 9% likely that 2 to 4 *salamanders* (q.v.) will come, a 4% chance exists that an *efreeti* (q.v.) will come, and a 2% chance exists that a huge fire elemental of 21 to 24 hit dice (d4 + 20) will appear. Because of the relationship of druids to natural and elemental forces, the conjuring druid need not fear that the elemental force summoned will turn on him or her, so concentration upon the activities of the fire elemental (or other creatures summoned) or the protection of a magic circle is not necessary. The elemental summoned will help the druid however possible, including attacking opponents of the druid. The fire elemental or other creature summoned remains for a maximum of 1 turn per level of the druid casting the spell — or until it is sent back by attack, a *dispel magic* spell or the reverse of the spell *(dismiss fire elemental)*. Only a druid can dismiss summoned salamanders, efreeti, or ultra-powerful elementals.

Cure Critical Wounds (Necromantic) Reversible

Level: 6	Components: *V, S, M*
Range: *Touch*	Casting Time: *8 segments*
Duration: *Permanent*	Saving Throw: *None*
Area of Effect: *Creature touched*	

Explanation/Description: This spell is the same as the 5th level cleric *cure critical wounds* spell (q.v.), with the exception of the fact that the spell requires the use of any sort of mistletoe.

Feeblemind (Enchantment/Charm)

Level: 6	Components: *V, S*
Range: *16''*	Casting Time: *8 segments*
Duration: *Permanent*	Saving Throw: *Neg.*
Area of Effect: *One creature*	

Explanation/Description: A spell which is solely for employment against those persons or creatures who use magic spells, *feeblemind* causes the victim's brain to become that of a moronic child. The victim remains in this state until a *heal, restoration* or *wish* spell is used to do away with the effects. The spell is of such a nature that the probability of it affecting the target creature is generally enhanced, i.e. saving throws are lowered.

Type of Spells Used by Target Creature	Saving Throw Adjustment
Cleric	+1
Druid	-1
Magic-user (human)	-4
Illusionist	-5
Combination or non-human	-2

Note that the spell has no material component.

Fire Seeds (Conjuration)

Level: 6	Components: *V, S, M*
Range: *4''*	Casting Time: *1 round/seed*
Duration: *Special*	Saving Throw: *½*
Area of Effect: *Special*	

Explanation/Description: The spell of *fire seeds* creates special missiles or timed incendiaries which burn with great heat. The druid may hurl these seeds up to 4'' or place them to ignite upon a command word. Acorns become *fire seed* missiles, while holly berries are used as the timed incendiaries. The spell creates up to four acorn *fire seeds* or eight holly berry *fire seeds*. The acorns burst upon striking their target, causing 2 to 16 hit points (2d8) of damage and igniting any combustible materials within a 1'' diameter of the point of impact. Although the holly berries are too light to make effective missiles, they can be placed, or tossed up to 6' away, to burst into flame upon a word of command. The berries ignite causing 1 to 8 hit points (d8) of damage to any creature in a ½'' diameter burst area, and their fire ignites combustibles in the burst area. The command range for holly berry *fire seeds* is 4''. All *fire seeds* lose their power after the expiration of 1 turn per level of experience of the druid casting the spell, i.e. a 13th level druid has *fire seeds* which will remain potent for a maximum of 13 turns after their creation. Targets of acorn *fire seeds* must be struck by the missile. If a saving throw is made, creatures within the burst area take only one-half damage, but creatures struck directly always take full damage. Note that no mistletoe or other material components beyond acorns or holly berries are needed for this spell.

Transport Via Plants (Alteration)

Level: 6	Components: *V, S*
Range: *Touch*	Casting Time: *3 segments*
Duration: *Special*	Saving Throw: *None*
Area of Effect: *Special*	

Explanation/Description: By means of this spell, the druid is able to enter any large plant and pass any distance to a plant of the same species in a single round regardless of the distance separating the two. The entry plant must be alive. The destination plant need not be familiar to the druid, but it also must be alive. If the druid is uncertain of the destination plant, he or she need merely determine direction and distance, and the *transport via plant* spell will move him or her as near as possible to the desired location. There is a basic 20% chance, reduced 1% per level of experience of the druid, that the transport will deliver the druid to an allied species of plant from 1 to 100 miles removed from the desired destination plant. If a particular destination plant is desired, but the plant is not living, the spell fails and the druid must come forth from the entrance plant within 24 hours. Harm to a plant housing a druid can affect the druid (cf. *plant door*).

Turn Wood (Alteration)

Level: 6	Components: *V, S, M*
Range: *0*	Casting Time: *8 segments*
Duration: *4 rounds/level*	Saving Throw: *None*
Area of Effect: *12'' wide path, 2'' long/level*	

Explanation/Description: When this spell is cast, waves of force roll forth from the druid, moving in the direction he or she faces, and causing all wooden objects in the path of the spell to be pushed away from the druid to the limit of the area of effect. Wooden objects above three inches diameter which are fixed firmly will not be affected, but loose objects (movable mantlets, siege towers, etc.) will move back. Objects under 3 inches diameter which are fixed will splinter and break and the pieces will move with the wave of force. Thus, objects such as wooden shields, spears, wooden weapon shafts and hafts, and arrows and bolts will be pushed back, dragging those carrying them with them; and if a spear is planted in order to prevent this forced movement, it will splinter. The *turn wood* spell lasts for 4 rounds per level of experience of the druid casting it, and the waves of force will continue to sweep down the set path for this period. The wooden objects in the area of effect are pushed back at a rate of 4'' per melee round. The length of the path is 2'' per level of the druid, i.e. a 14th level druid casts a *turn wood* spell with an area of effect 12'' wide by 28'' long, and the spell would last for 56 rounds (5.6 turns). As usual, the above assumes the druid is using greater mistletoe when casting the spell. Note that after casting the spell the path is set, and the druid may then do other things or go elsewhere without affecting the spell's power.

Wall of Thorns (Conjuration/Summoning)

Level: 6	Components: *V, S, M*
Range: *8''*	Casting Time: *8 segments*
Duration: *1 turn/level*	Saving Throw: *None*
Area of Effect: *10'' cube/level*	

Explanation/Description: The *wall of thorns* spell creates a barrier of very tough, pliable green tangled brush bearing needle-sharp thorns as long as a person's finger. Any creature breaking through (or merely impacting upon) the *wall of thorns* takes 8 hit points of damage *plus* an additional amount of hit points equal to the creature's armor class, i.e. 10 or fewer additional hit points of damage, with negative armor classes subtracting from the base 8 hit points of damage. Any creature within the area of effect of the spell when it is cast is considered to have impacted on the *wall of thorns* and in addition must break through to gain movement space. The damage is based on each 1'' thickness of the barrier. If the *wall of thorns* is chopped at, it will take at least 4 turns to cut a path through a 1'' thickness. Normal fire will not harm the barrier, but magical fires will burn away the barrier in 2 turns with the effect of creating a wall of fire while doing so. (See *wall of fire* spell.) The nearest edge of the *wall of thorns* appears up to 8'' distant from the druid, as he or she desires. The spell lasts for 1 turn for each level of experience of the druid casting it, and covers an area of ten cubic inches per level of the caster in whatever form the caster desires. Thus a 14th level druid could create a *wall of thorns* 7'' long by 2'' high (or deep) by 1'' deep (or high), a 1'' high by 1'' wide by 14'' long wall to block a dungeon passage, or any other sort of shape that suited his or her needs.

Weather Summoning (Conjuration/Summoning)

Level: 6	Components: V, S, M
Range: 0	Casting Time: 1 turn
Duration: Special	Saving Throw: None
Area of Effect: Special	

Explanation/Description: The druidic *weather summoning* spell is similar to the *control weather* spell (q.v.) of clerical nature. By casting the spell, the druid calls forth weather commensurate with the climate and season of the area he or she is in at the time. Thus, in spring a tornado, thunderstorm, cold, sleet storm, or hot weather could be summoned. In summer a torrential rain, heat wave, hail storm, etc. can be called for. In autumn, hot or cold weather, fog, sleet, etc. could be summoned. Winter allows great cold, blizzard, or thaw conditions to be summoned. Hurricane-force winds can be summoned near coastal regions in the late winter or early spring. The summoned weather is not under the control of the druid. It might last but a single turn in the case of a tornado, or for hours or even days in other cases. The area of effect likewise varies from about 1 square mile to 100 or more square miles. Note that several druids can act in concert to greatly affect weather, controlling winds and/or working jointly to summon very extreme weather conditions. Within 4 turns after the spell is cast, the trend of the weather to come will be apparent, i.e., clearing skies, gusts of warm or hot air, a chill breeze, overcast skies, etc. Summoned weather will arrive 6 to 17 turns (d12 + 5) after the spell is cast. Anything less than *greater mistletoe* as the material component will sharply curtail the weather extremes desired.

Seventh Level Spells:

Animate Rock (Alteration)

Level: 7	Components: V, S, M
Range: 4"	Casting Time: 9 segments
Duration: 1 round/level	Saving Throw: None
Area of Effect: 2 cubic feet/level	

Explanation/Description: By employing an *animate rock* spell, the druid causes a lithic object of a size up to that indicated to move. (See *animate object*, the Sixth Level cleric spell.) The animated stone object must be separate, i.e. not a piece of a huge boulder or the like. It will follow the desire of the druid casting the spell — attacking, breaking objects, blocking — while the magic lasts. It has no intelligence nor volition of its own, but it follows instructions exactly as spoken. Note that only one set of instructions for one single action (the whole being simply worded and very brief — 12 words or so), can be given to the rock animated. The rock remains animated for 1 melee round per level of experience of the spell caster, and the volume of rock which can be animated is also based on the experience level of the druid — 2 cubic feet of stone per level, i.e. 24 cubic feet at the 12th level.

Chariot Of Sustarre (Evocation)

Level: 7	Components: V, S, M
Range: 1"	Casting Time: 1 turn
Duration: 6 turns + 1 turn/level	Saving Throw: None
Area of Effect: Special	

Explanation/Description: When this spell is cast by a druid, it brings forth a large flaming chariot pulled by two fiery horses which appear in a clap of thunder amidst cloud-like smoke. This vehicle moves at 24" on the ground, 48" flying, and it can carry the druid and up to 8 other man-sized creatures whom he or she first touches so as to enable these creatures to be able to ride aboard this burning transport. Creatures other than the druid and his or her designated passengers will sustain damage equal to that of a *wall of fire* spell if they are within 5' of the horses or chariot, voluntarily or involuntarily. The druid controls the chariot by verbal command, causing the flaming steeds to stop or go, walk, trot, run or fly, turning left or right as he or she desires. Note that the *Chariot of Sustarre* is a physical manifestation, and can sustain damage. The vehicle and steeds are struck only by magical weapons or by water (one quart of which will cause 1 hit point of damage), they are armor class 2, and each requires 30 hit points of damage to dispel. Naturally, fire has absolutely no effect upon either the vehicle or its steeds, but magical fires will affect the riders if they are exposed to them (other than those of the chariot itself). In addition to mistletoe, the druid casting this spell must have a small piece of wood, 2 holly berries, and a fire source at least equal to a torch.

Confusion (Enchantment/Charm)

Level: 7	Components: V, S, M
Range: 8"	Casting Time: 9 segments
Duration: 1 round/level	Saving Throw: Special
Area of Effect: Up to 4" by 4"	

Explanation/Description: This spell causes *confusion* in one or more creatures within spell range. Confused creatures will react as follows:

Die Roll	Action
01-10	Wander away for 1 turn
11-60	Stand confused for 1 round
61-80	Attack nearest creature for 1 round
81-00	Attack druid or his party for 1 round

The spell lasts for 1 melee round for each level of experience of the spell caster. It will affect 2 to 8 creatures, plus a possible additional number of creatures determined by subtracting the level or number of hit dice of the strongest opponent creature within the spell range and area of effect from the level of the druid who cast the spell of *confusion*. If a positive number results, it is added to the random die roll result for number of creatures affected; a negative number is ignored. All creatures affected will be those closest to the druid within the area of effect. Each affected creature must make a saving throw each round, unless they are caused to "wander away for 1 turn" in which case they will go as far away from the druid as is possible in one turn of normal movement, as conditions permit. All saving throws are at -2. Confused creatures act according to the table of actions shown above, but saving throws and actions are checked at the beginning of each round.

Conjure Earth Elemental (Conjuration/Summoning) Reversible

Level: 7	Components: V, S, M
Range: 4"	Casting Time: 1 turn
Duration: 1 turn/level	Saving Throw: None
Area of Effect: Special	

Explanation/Description: When a druid casts a *conjure earth elemental* spell, he or she summons an earth elemental of 16 hit dice to do the druid's bidding. Furthermore, the druid need but command it, and then do as he or she desires, for the elemental does not regard the druid who conjured it with enmity. The elemental remains until destroyed, dispelled, or sent away by dismissal (cf. *conjure fire elemental*).

Control Weather (Alteration)

Level: 7	Components: V, S, M
Range: 0	Casting Time: 1 turn
Duration: 8-96 hours	Saving Throw: None
Area of Effect: 4-32 square miles	

Explanation/Description: The druidic *control weather* spell is more powerful than the clerical spell of the same name (q.v.). The spell caster is able to change weather by two places from the prevailing conditions if *greater mistletoe* is used. It otherwise is the same as the 7th level cleric *control weather* spell.

Creeping Doom (Conjuration/Summoning)

Level: 7	Components: V, S, M
Range: 0	Casting Time: 9 segments
Duration: 4 rounds/level	Saving Throw: None
Area of Effect: Special	

Explanation/Description: When the druid utters the spell of *creeping doom*, he or she calls forth a mass of from 500 to 1000 (d6 + 4) venomous, biting and stinging arachnids, insects and myriapods. This carpet-like mass will swarm in an area of 2" square, and upon command from the druid will creep forth at 1" per round towards any prey within 8", moving in the direction in which the druid commanded. The *creeping doom* will slay any creature subject to normal attacks, each of the small horrors inflicting 1 hit point of damage (each then dies after their attack), so that up to 1,000 hit points of damage can be inflicted on creatures within the path of the *creeping doom*. If the *creeping doom* goes beyond 8" of the summoner, it loses 50 of its number for each 1" beyond 8", i.e. at 10" its number has shrunk by 100. There are a number of ways to thwart or destroy the creatures forming the swarm, all of which methods should be obvious.

Finger Of Death (Enchantment/Charm)

Level: 7	Components: V, S, M
Range: 6''	Casting Time: 5 segments
Duration: *Permanent*	Saving Throw: Neg.
Area of Effect: *One creature*	

Explanation/Description: The *finger of death* spell causes the victim's heart to stop. The druid utters the incantation, points his or her index finger at the creature to be slain, and unless the victim succeeds in making the appropriate saving throw, death occurs. A successful saving throw negates the spell.

Fire Storm (Evocation) Reversible

Level: 7	Components: V, S, M
Range: 16''	Casting Time: 9 segments
Duration: *1 round*	Saving Throw: ½
Area of Effect: *2'' cube/level, minimum 16 cubic ''*	

Explanation/Description: When a *fire storm* spell is cast by a druid, a whole area is shot through with sheets of roaring flame which are equal to a *wall of fire* (q.v.) in effect. Creatures within the area of fire and 1'' or less from the edge of the affected area receive 2 to 16 hit points of damage plus additional hit points equal to the number of levels of experience of the druid unless they make a saving throw, in which case they take only one-half damage. The area of effect is equal to 2 cubic '' per level of the druid, i.e. a 13th level druid can cast a *fire storm* which measures 13'' by 2'' by 1''. The height of the storm is 1'' or 2''; the balance of its area must be in length and width. The reverse spell, *fire quench*, smothers double the area of effect of a *fire storm* with respect to normal fires, and with respect to magical fires it has a 5% chance per level of the caster of extinguishing a magical fire (such as a *fire storm)* of proportions up to the normal area of effect of the non-reversed spell.

Reincarnate (Necromantic)

Level: 7	Components: V, S, M
Range: *Touch*	Casting Time: 1 turn
Duration: *Permanent*	Saving Throw: None
Area of Effect: *Person touched*	

Explanation/Description: Druids have the capability of bringing back the dead in another body if death occurred no more than a week before the casting of the spell. The person reincarnated will recall the majority of his or her former life and form, but the class they have, if any, in their new incarnation might be different indeed. Abilities and speech are likewise often changed. The table below gives the reincarnation possibilities of this spell:

Die Roll	Incarnation
01-03	badger
04-08	bear, black
09-12	bear, brown
13-16	boar, wild
17-19	centaur
20-23	dryad
24-28	eagle
29-31	elf
32-34	faun
35-36	fox
37-40	gnome
41-44	hawk
45-58	human
59-61	lynx
62-64	owl
65-68	pixie
69-70	raccoon
71-75	stag
76-80	wolf
81-85	wolverine
86-00	use magic-user *reincarnation* table

Any sort of player character can be reincarnated. If an elf, gnome or human is indicated, the character must be created. When the corpse is touched, the new incarnation will appear in the area within 1 to 6 turns. (Cf. sixth level magic-user spell *reincarnation.)*

Transmute Metal To Wood (Alteration)

Level: 7	Components: V, S, M
Range: 8''	Casting Time: 9 segments
Duration: *Permanent*	Saving Throw: *Special*
Area of Effect: *One metal object*	

Explanation/Description: The *transmute metal to wood* spell allows the druid casting it to change an object from metal to wood. The volume of metal is equal to a maximum weight of 80 gold pieces per level of experience. Magical objects of metal are only 10% likely to be affected by the spell. Note that even a *dispel magic* spell will not reverse the spell effects. Thus, a metal door changed to wood would be forevermore a wooden door.

MAGIC-USER SPELLS

Notes Regarding Magic-User Spells:

Magic-users employ a greater variety of material components than do other character classes employing spells, i.e. clerics and druids. Some of the required components will be difficult to find and/or expensive, but alternative spells can always be chosen.

The relatively short casting time for those spells with a material component assumes that the magic-user has decided upon which spell he or she will employ, and the material or materials needed are at hand in the numerous pockets and folds of the magic-user's garb. If this is not the case, there will be a delay commensurate to the situation. It has been recommended to the referee that actual time relate to the game time in such situations if at all possible. If it takes 6 seconds to decide on which spell to cast, 1 segment of the round is gone. Having to search through a pack to locate some component is as good as wasting 5 segments — 30 seconds.

Substitute materials might be allowed. This is up to your Dungeon Master. It should be noted that such substitution could affect spell range, duration, area of effect, effect, etc.

In general, reversible or multiple application spells require the magic-user to determine which form he or she is memorizing prior to the adventure. Consult your referee in this regard.

First Level Spells:

Affect Normal Fires (Alteration)

Level: 1	Components: V, S
Range: ½''/level	Casting Time: 1 segment
Duration: *1 round/level*	Saving Throw: None
Area of Effect: *3' diameter fire*	

Explanation/Description: This spell enables the magic-user to cause small fires — from as small as a torch or lantern to as large as a normal bonfire of 3' maximum diameter — to reduce in size and light to become match-like or increase in light so as to become as bright as a *light* spell. Reducing the fire will cut fuel consumption to half normal, and increasing the fire will double consumption. Note that *heat* output is *not* altered in either case!

Burning Hands (Alteration)

Level: 1	Components: V, S
Range: 0	Casting Time: 1 segment
Duration: *1 round*	Saving Throw: None
Area of Effect: *Special*	

Explanation/Description: When the magic-user casts this spell, jets of searing flame shoot from his or her fingertips. Hands can only be held so as to send forth a fan-like sheet of flames, as the magic-user's thumbs must touch each other and fingers must be spread. The *burning hands* send out flame jets of 3' length in a horizontal arc of about 120° in front of the magic-user. Any creature in the area of flames takes 1 hit point of damage for each level of experience of the spellcaster, and no saving throw is possible. Inflammable materials touched by the fire will burn, i.e. cloth, paper, parchment, thin wood, etc.

Charm Person (Enchantment/Charm)

Level: *1*	Components: *V,S*
Range: *12''*	Casting Time: *1 segment*
Duration: *Special*	Saving Throw: *Neg.*
Area of Effect: *One person*	

Explanation/Description: Except as shown above, this spell is the same as the second level druid spell, *charm person or mammal* (q.v.), but the magic-user can charm only persons, i.e. brownies, dwarves, elves, gnolls, gnomes, goblins, half-elves, halflings, half-orcs, hobgoblins, humans, kobolds, lizard men, nixies, orcs, pixies, sprites, and troglodytes. All other comments regarding spell effects apply with respect to persons.

Comprehend Languages (Alteration) Reversible

Level: *1*	Components: *V, S, M*
Range: *Touch*	Casting Time: *1 round*
Duration: *5 rounds/level*	Saving Throw: *None*
Area of Effect: *One written object or speaking creature*	

Explanation/Description: When this spell is cast, the magic-user is able to read an otherwise incomprehensible written message such as a treasure map (but not a magical writing, other than to know it is "magic") or understand the language of a speaking creature. In either case, the magic-user must touch the object to be read or the creature to be understood, and the spell does not enable the spell caster to write or speak the language. The material components of this spell are a pinch of soot and a few grains of salt. The reverse, *confuse languages*, prevents comprehension or cancels a *comprehend languages* spell.

Dancing Lights (Alteration)

Level: *1*	Components: *V, S, M*
Range: *4'' + 1''/level*	Casting Time: *1 segment*
Duration: *2 rounds/level*	Saving Throw: *None*
Area of Effect: *Special*	

Explanation/Description: When a *dancing lights* spell is cast, the magic-user creates, at his or her option, from 1 to 4 lights which resemble either A) torches and/or lanterns (and cast that amount of light), B) glowing spheres of light (such as evidenced by will-o-wisps), or C) one faintly glowing, vaguely man-like shape, somewhat similar to that of a creature from the Elemental Plane of Fire. The *dancing lights* move as the spell caster desires, forward or back, straight or turning corners, without concentration upon such movement by the magic-user. The spell will wink out if the range or duration is exceeded. Range is a base of 4'' plus 1'' for each level of the magic-user who cast the spell. Duration is 2 melee rounds per level of the spell caster. The material component of this spell is either a bit of phosphorus or wytchwood or a glowworm.

Detect Magic (Divination)

Level: *1*	Components: *V, S*
Range: *0*	Casting Time: *1 segment*
Duration: *2 rounds/level*	Saving Throw: *None*
Area of Effect: *1'' path, 6'' long*	

Explanation/Description: The only differences between this spell and the first level cleric *detect magic* spell are noted above (duration, area of effect, and no material component).

Enlarge (Alteration) Reversible

Level: *1*	Components: *V, S, M*
Range: *½''/level*	Casting Time: *1 segment*
Duration: *1 turn/level*	Saving Throw: *Neg.*
Area of Effect: *Special*	

Explanation/Description: This spell causes instant growth of a creature or object. *Enlargement* causes increase in both size and weight. It can be cast upon only a single creature or object. Spell range is ½'' for each level of experience of the magic-user, and its duration is 1 turn per level of experience of the spell caster. The effect of the *enlargement* spell is to increase the size of a living creature (or a symbiotic or community entity) by 20% per level of experience of the magic-user, with a maximum additional growth of 200%. The effect on objects is one-half that of creatures, i.e. 10% per level to a 100% maximum additional *enlargement*. The creature or object must be seen in order to effect the spell. The maximum volume of living material which can be initially affected is 10 cubic feet — for non-living matter, 5 cubic feet — per level of the magic-user. While magical properties are not increased by this spell — a huge +1 sword is still only +1, a staff-sized wand is still only capable of its normal functions, a giant-sized potion merely requires a greater fluid intake to make its magical effects operate, etc. — weight, mass and strength are. Thus, a table blocking a door would be heavier and more effective; a hurled stone would have more mass (and be more hurtful providing *enlargement* took place just prior to impact); chains would be more massive; doors thicker; a thin line turned to a sizable, longer rope; and so on. Likewise, a person 12' tall would be as an ogre, while an 18' tall person would actually be a giant for the duration of the spell. The reverse spell, *reduce*, will negate the effects or actually make creatures or objects smaller in the same ratios as the regular spell application functions. Unwilling victims of the spell, or its reverse, are entitled to a saving throw, which, if successful, indicates the magic does not function, and the spell is wasted. The material component of this spell is a pinch of powdered iron.

Erase (Alteration)

Level: *1*	Components: *V, S*
Range: *3''*	Casting Time: *1 segment*
Duration: *Permanent*	Saving Throw: *Neg.*
Area of Effect: *One scroll or two facing pages*	

Explanation/Description: The *erase* spell removes writings of either magical or mundane nature from a scroll or one or two pages or sheets of paper, parchment or similar surfaces. It will not remove *explosive runes* or a *symbol* (see these spells hereafter), however. There is a basic chance of

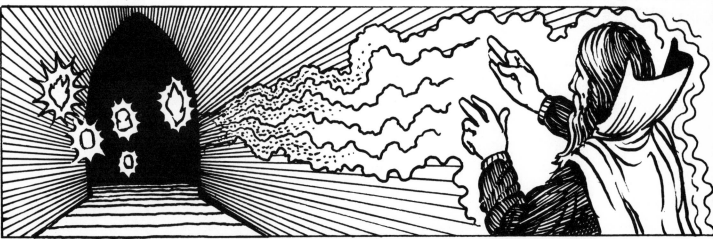

50%, plus 2% per level of experience of the spell caster with respect to magical writings, plus 4% per level for mundane writing, that the spell will take effect. This represents the saving throw, and any percentile dice score in excess of the adjusted percentage chance means the spell fails.

Feather Fall (Alteration)

Level: *1*	Components: *V, M*
Range: *1"/level*	Casting Time: *1/10 segment*
Duration: *1 segment/level*	Saving Throw: *None*
Area of Effect: *Special*	

Explanation/Description: When this spell is cast, the creature(s) or object(s) affected immediately assumes the mass of a feathery piece of down. Rate of falling is thus instantly changed to a mere constant 2' per second or 12' per segment, and no damage is incurred when landing when the spell is in effect. However, when the spell duration ceases, normal rate of fall occurs. The spell can be cast upon the magic-user or some other creature or object up to the maximum range of 1" per level of experience of the spell caster. It lasts for 1 segment for each level of the magic-user. The *feather fall* affects an area of 1 cubic inch, and the maximum weight of creatures and/or objects cannot exceed a combined total equal to a base 2,000 gold pieces weight plus 2,000 gold pieces weight per level of the spell caster. Example: a 2nd level magic-user has a range of 2", a duration of 2 segments, a weight maximum of 6,000 gold pieces (600 pounds) when employing the spell. The spell works only upon free-falling or propelled objects. It will not affect a sword blow or a charging creature, but it will affect a missile. The material component is a small feather or a piece of down somewhere on the person of the spell caster.

Find Familiar (Conjuration/Summoning)

Level: *1*	Components: *V, S, M*
Range: *1 mile/level*	Casting Time: *1-24 hours*
Duration: *Special*	Saving Throw: *Neg.*
Area of Effect: *As spell range*	

Explanation/Description: A familiar is of certain benefit to a magic-user, as the creature adds to the spell caster's hit points, it conveys its sensory powers to its master, and it can converse with and will serve as a guard/scout/spy as well. However, the magic-user has no control over what sort of creature will answer the summoning, or if any at all will come, and the power of the conjuration is such that it can be attempted but once per year. At such time as the magic-user determines to find a familiar, he or she must stoke up a brass brazier with charcoal, and when this is burning well, add 100 g.p. worth of incense, herbs (basil, savory, and catnip for sure), and fat. When these items are burning, the spell caster begins his or her incantation, and it must be continued until the familiar comes or the casting time is finished. Your referee will secretly determine all results. The magic-user has absolutely no control over what sort of a creature appears to become his or her familiar. This will be determined on the table below:

Die Roll (d20)	Familiar	Sensory Powers
1-4	cat, black	excellent night vision & superior hearing
5-6	crow	excellent vision
7-8	hawk	very superior distance vision
9-10	owl, screech	night vision equals human daylight visual ability, superior hearing
11-12	toad	wide angle vision
13-14	weasel	superior hearing & very superior olfactory power
15	special — see sub-table below for details
16-20*	no familiar available within spell range

*Subtract 1 from the die score for each 3 levels of experience of the spell caster, and if the score is 15 or less roll again using d16, and if a 16 is rolled then the result is final.

If a score of 15 is rolled, use the table below for a special familiar:

Alignment of Magic-User	Result of Special Familiar
chaotic evil or neutral chaotic	quasit (see **AD&D, MONSTER MANUAL**)
chaotic good, neutral, or neutral good	pseudo-dragon (see **AD&D, MONSTER MANUAL**)
lawful neutral or lawful good	brownie (see **AD&D, MONSTER MANUAL**)
lawful evil or neutral evil	imp (see **AD&D, MONSTER MANUAL**)

Normal familiars have 2-4 hit points and armor class of 7 (due to size, speed, etc.). Each is abnormally intelligent and totally faithful to the magic-user whose familiar it becomes. The number of the familiar's hit points is added to the hit point total of the magic-user when it is within 12" of its master, but if the familiar should ever be killed, the magic-user will permanently lose double that number of hit points.

If a special familiar is indicated, details of the powers it conveys are given in **ADVANCED DUNGEONS & DRAGONS, MONSTER MANUAL** for all except the brownie. This creature becomes a friend and companion to the magic-user, and he or she will gain dexterity equal to the brownie's (18) and the advantage of never being surprised, as well as +2 on all saving throws. Note that special familiars are entitled to a saving throw versus magic when summoned by the spell, and if they succeed, they will ignore the spell, and **NO** familiar will be available that year to the caster.

A familiar will fight for the life of the magic-user it serves only in a life-and-death situation, and imps and quasits will be 90% likely not to do so at the risk of their own life.

Friends (Enchantment/Charm)

Level: *1*	Components: *V, S, M*
Range: *0*	Casting Time: *1 segment*
Duration: *1 round/level*	Saving Throw: *Special*
Area of Effect: *1" + 1"/level of spell caster radius sphere*	

Explanation/Description: A *friends* spell causes the magic-user to gain a temporary increase of 2-8 points in charisma — or a temporary lowering of charisma by 1-4 points — depending on whether creatures within the area of effect of the spell make — or fail — their saving throw versus magic. Those that fail their saving throw will be very impressed with the spell caster and desire greatly to be his or her friend and help. Those that do not fail will be uneasy in the spell caster's presence and tend to find him or her irritating. Note that this spell has absolutely no effect on creatures of *animal* intelligence or lower. The components for this spell are chalk (or white flour), lampblack (or soot), and vermillion applied to the face before casting the spell.

Hold Portal (Alteration)

Level: *1*	Components: *V*
Range: *2"/level*	Casting Time: *1 segment*
Duration: *1 round/level*	Saving Throw: *None*
Area of Effect: *80 square feet/level*	

Explanation/Description: This spell magically bars a door, gate or valve of wood, metal or stone. The magical closure holds the portal fast just as if it were securely stopped and locked. The range of the spell is 2' per level of experience of the caster, and it lasts for 1 round per level. Note that any extra-dimensional creature (demon, devil, elemental, etc.) will shatter such a held portal. A magic-user of four or more experience levels higher than the spell caster can open the held portal at will. A *knock* spell (q.v.) or *dispel magic* spell (q.v.) will negate the *hold portal*. Held portals can be broken or battered down.

Identify (Divination)

Level: *1*	Components: *V, S, M*
Range: *0*	Casting Time: *1 turn*
Duration: *1 segment/level*	Saving Throw: *Special*
Area of Effect: *One item*	

Explanation/Description: When an *identify* spell is cast, one item may be touched and handled by the magic-user in order that he or she may possibly find what dweomer it possesses. The item in question must be held or worn as would be normal for any such object, i.e. a bracelet must be placed on the spell caster's wrist, a helm on his or her head, boots on the feet, a cloak worn, a dagger held, and so on. Note that any consequences of this use of the item fall fully upon the magic-user, although any saving throw normally allowed is still the privilege of the magic-user. For each segment the spell is in force, it is 15% + 5% per level of the magic-user probable that 1 property of the object touched can become known — possibly that the item has *no* properties and is merely a ruse (the presence of *Nystul's Magic Aura* or a *magic mouth* being detected). Each time a property can be known, the referee will secretly roll to see if the magic-user made his or her saving throw versus magic. If the save was successful, the property is known; if it is 1 point short, a false power will be revealed; and if it is lower than 1 under the required score no information will be gained. The item will never reveal its exact plusses to hit or its damage bonuses, although the fact that it has few or many such plusses can be discovered. If it has charges, the object will never reveal the exact number, but it will give information which is +/-25% of actual, i.e. a wand with 40 charges could feel as if it had 30, or 50, or any number in between. The item to be *identified* must be examined by the magic-user within 1 hour per level of experience of the examiner after it has been discovered, or all readable impressions will have been blended into those of the characters who have possessed it since. After casting the spell and determining what can be learned from it, the magic-user loses 8 points of constitution. He or she must rest for 6 turns per 1 point in order to regain them. If the 8 point loss drops the spell caster below a constitution of 3, he or she will fall unconscious, and consciousness will not be regained until full constitution is restored 24 hours later. The material components of this spell are a pearl (of at least 100 g.p. value) and an owl feather steeped in wine, with the infusion drunk and a live miniature carp swallowed whole prior to spell casting. If a *luckstone* is powdered and added to the infusion, probability increases 25% and all saving throws are made at +4.

Jump (Alteration)

Level: *1*	Components: *V, S, M*
Range: *Touch*	Casting Time: *1 segment*
Duration: *Special*	Saving Throw: *None*
Area of Effect: *Creature touched*	

Explanation/Description: When this spell is cast, the individual is empowered to leap up to 30' forward or 10' backward or straight upward. Horizontal leaps forward or backward are in only a slight arc — about 2'/10' of distance traveled. The *jump* spell does not insure any safety in landing or grasping at the end of the leap. For every 3 additional levels of experience of the magic-user beyond the 1st, he or she is able to empower 1 additional leap, so a 4th level magic-user can cast a *jump* spell which enables the recipient to make 2 leaps, 3 leaps at 7th level, etc. All leaps must be completed within 1 turn after the spell is cast, for after that period has elapsed the spell wears off. The material component of this spell is a grasshopper's hind leg, one for each leap, to be broken when the leap is made.

Light (Alteration)

Level: *1*	Components: *V, S*
Range: *6"*	Casting Time: *1 segment*
Duration: *1 turn/level*	Saving Throw: *None*
Area of Effect: *2" radius globe*	

Explanation/Description: With the exceptions noted above, this spell is the same as the first level cleric *light* spell (q.v.).

Magic Missile (Evocation)

Level: *1*	Components: *V, S*
Range: *6" + 1"/level*	Casting Time: *1 segment*
Duration: *Special*	Saving Throw: *None*
Area of Effect: *One or more creatures in a 10 square foot area*	

Explanation/Description: Use of the *magic missile* spell creates one or more magical missiles which dart forth from the magic-user's fingertip and unerringly strike their target. Each missile does 2 to 5 hit points (d4+1) of damage. If the magic-user has multiple missile capability, he or she can have them strike a single target creature or several creatures, as desired. For each level of experience of the magic-user, the range of his or her

magic missile extends 1" beyond the 6" base range. For every 2 levels of experience, the magic-user gains an additional missile, i.e. 2 at 3rd level, 3 at 5th level, 4 at 7th level, etc.

Mending (Alteration)

Level: *1*	Components: *V, S, M*
Range: *3"*	Casting Time: *1 segment*
Duration: *Permanent*	Saving Throw: *None*
Area of Effect: *One object*	

Explanation/Description: This spell repairs small breaks in objects. It will weld a broken ring, chain link, medallion or slender dagger, providing but one break exists. Ceramic or wooden objects with multiple breaks can be invisibly rejoined to be as strong as new. A hole in a leather sack or wineskin is completely healed over by a *mending* spell. This spell will not repair magic items of any kind. The material components of this spell are two small magnets of any type (lodestone in all likelihood) or two burrs.

Message (Alteration)

Level: *1*	Components: *V,S,M*
Range: *6" + 1"/level*	Casting Time: *1 segment*
Duration: *5 segments + 1 segment/level*	Saving Throw: *None*
Area of Effect: *1/4" path*	

Explanation/Description: When this spell is cast, the magic-user can whisper a message and secretly, or openly, point his or her finger while so doing, and the whispered *message* will travel in a straight line and be audible to the creature pointed at. The *message* must fit spell duration, and if there is time remaining, the creature who received the *message* can whisper a reply and be heard by the spell caster. Note that there must be an open and unobstructed path between the spell caster and the recipient of the spell. The material component of the spell is a short piece of copper drawn fine.

Nystul's Magic Aura (Illusion/Phantasm)

Level: *1*	Components: *V, S, M*
Range: *Touch*	Casting Time: *1 round*
Duration: *1 day/level*	Saving Throw: *Special*
Area of Effect: *Special*	

Explanation/Description: By means of this spell any one item of a weight of 50 g.p. per level of experience of the spell caster can be given an aura which will be noticed if detection of magic is exercised upon the object. If the object bearing the *Nystul's Magic Aura* is actually held by the creature detecting for a dweomer, he, she or it is entitled to a saving throw versus magic, and if this throw is successful, the creature knows that the aura has been placed to mislead the unwary. Otherwise, the aura is simply magical, but no amount of testing will reveal what the magic is. The component for this spell is a small square of silk which must be passed over the object to bear the aura.

Protection From Evil (Abjuration) Reversible

Level: *1*	Components: *V, S, M*
Range: *Touch*	Casting Time: *1 segment*
Duration: *2 rounds/level*	Saving Throw: *None*
Area of Effect: *Creature touched*	

Explanation/Description: With the differences shown above, and the requirement of powdered iron and silver as the material components for tracing the magic circle for *protection from evil*, the spell is the same as the first level cleric *protection from evil* spell (q.v.).

Push (Conjuration/Summoning)

Level: *1*	Components: *V, S, M*
Range: *1" + 1/4"/level*	Casting Time: *1 segment*
Duration: *Instantaneous*	Saving Throw: *Neg.*
Area of Effect: *Special*	

Explanation/Description: Upon pronouncing the syllables of this spell, the magic-user causes an invisible force to strike against whatever object he or she is pointing at. The force of the *push* is not great, being 1 foot pound per level of the magic-user casting the spell, but it can move small objects up to 1' in a direction directly away from the caster, topple an object under the proper conditions, or cause a creature to lose its balance. An example of the latter use is causing a creature attacking to lose its balance when it is attacking, for if the creature fails its saving throw, it will not be able to attack that round. Of course, the mass of the creature attacking cannot exceed the force of the *push* by more than a factor of 50, i.e. a 1st level magic-user cannot effectively *push* a creature weighing more than 50 pounds. A *push* spell employed against an object held by a creature will cause it to subtract the force of the spell in foot pounds (1, 2, 3, etc.) from its chance to hit or add to opponent saving throws as applicable if the creature fails to make its saving throw against magic when the spell is cast. The material component of this spell is a small pinch of powdered brass which must be blown from the palm prior to pointing at the object of the spell.

Read Magic (Divination) Reversible

Level: 1
Range: 0
Duration: 2 rounds/level
Area of Effect: Special

Components: V, S, M
Casting Time: 1 round
Saving Throw: None

Explanation/Description: By means of a *read magic* spell, the magic-user is able to read magical inscriptions on objects — books, scrolls, weapons and the like — which would otherwise be totally unintelligible to him or her. (The personal books of the magic-user, and works already magically read, are intelligible.) This deciphering does not normally invoke the magic contained in the writing, although it may do so in the case of a *curse scroll*. Furthermore, once the spell is cast and the magic-user has read the magical inscription, he or she is thereafter able to read that particular writing without recourse to the use of the *read magic* spell. The duration of the spell is 2 rounds per level of experience of the spell caster. The material component for the spell is a clear crystal or mineral prism. Note that the material is not expended by use. The reverse of the spell, *unreadable magic*, makes such writing completely unreadable to any creature, even with the aid of a *read magic*, until the spell wears off or the magic is dispelled. The material components for the reverse spell are a pinch of dirt and a drop of water.

Shield (Evocation)

Level: 1
Range: 0
Duration: 5 rounds/level
Area of Effect: Special

Components: V, S
Casting Time: 1 segment
Saving Throw: None

Explanation/Description: When this spell is cast, an invisible barrier before the front of the magic-user comes into being. This *shield* will totally negate *magic missile* attacks. It provides the equivalent protection of armor class 2 against hand hurled missiles (axes, darts, javelins, spears, etc.), armor class 3 against small device-propelled missiles (arrows, bolts, bullets, manticore spikes, sling stones, etc.), and armor class 4 against all other forms of attack. The *shield* also adds +1 to the magic-user's saving throw dice vs. attacks which are basically frontal. Note that all benefits of the spell accrue only to attacks originating from the front facing the magic-user, where the *shield* can move to interpose itself properly.

Shocking Grasp (Alteration)

Level: 1
Range: Touch
Duration: One touch
Area of Effect: Creature touched

Components: V, S
Casting Time: 1 segment
Saving Throw: None

Explanation/Description: When the magic-user casts this spell, he or she develops a powerful electrical charge which gives a jolt to the creature touched. The *shocking grasp* delivers from 1 to 8 hit points damage (d8), plus 1 hit point per level of the magic-user, i.e. a 2nd level magic-user would discharge a shock causing 3 to 10 hit points of damage. While the magic-user must only come close enough to his or her opponent to lay a hand on the opponent's body or upon an electrical conductor which touches the opponent's body, a like touch from the opponent does not discharge the spell.

Sleep (Enchantment/Charm)

Level: 1
Range: 3″ + 1″/level
Duration: 5 rounds/level
Area of Effect: Special

Components: V, S, M
Casting Time: 1 segment
Saving Throw: None

Explanation/Description: When a magic-user casts a *sleep* spell, he or she will usually cause a comatose slumber to come upon one or more creatures [other than *undead* and certain other creatures specifically excluded (see **ADVANCED DUNGEONS & DRAGONS, MONSTER MANUAL**) from the spell's effects]. All creatures to be affected by the *sleep* spell must be within a 3″ diameter circle. The number of creatures which can be affected is a function of their life energy levels, expressed as hit dice and hit points:

Creatures Hit Dice	Number Affected By Sleep Spell	
up to 1	4-16	(4d4)
1+1 to 2	2-8	(2d4)
2+1 to 3	1-4	(1d4)
3+1 to 4	1-2	(½d4, round off)
4+1 to 4+4	0-1	(d4, 3 or 4)

The area of effect is determined by the range and area center decided upon by the spell caster. Slapping or wounding will awaken affected creatures, but noise will not do so. Awakening requires 1 complete melee round. Note that sleeping creatures can be slain automatically at a rate of 1 per slayer per melee round. The material component for this spell is a pinch of fine sand, rose petals, or a live cricket.

Spider Climb (Alteration)

Level: 1
Range: Touch
Duration: 1 round + 1 round/level
Area of Effect: Creature touched

Components: V, S, M
Casting Time: 1 segment
Saving Throw: None

Explanation/Description: A *spider climb* spell enables the recipient to climb and travel upon vertical surfaces just as a giant spider is able to do, i.e. at 3″ movement rate, or even hang upside down from ceilings. Note that the affected creature must have bare hands and feet in order to climb in this manner. During the course of the spell the recipient cannot handle objects which weigh less than 50 g.p., for such objects will stick to the creature's hands/feet, so a magic-user will find it virtually impossible to cast spells if under a *spider climb* dweomer. The material components of this spell are a drop of bitumen and a live spider, both of which must be eaten by the spell recipient.

Tenser's Floating Disc (Evocation)

Level: 1
Range: 2″
Duration: 3 turns + 1 turn/level
Area of Effect: Special

Components: V, S, M
Casting Time: 1 segment
Saving Throw: None

Explanation/Description: With this spell, the caster creates the circular plane of null-gravity known as *Tenser's Floating Disc* after the famed wizard of that appellation (whose ability to locate treasure and his greed to recover every copper found are well known). The *disc* is concave, 3' in diameter, and holds 1,000 g.p. weight per level of the magic-user casting the spell. The *disc* floats at approximately 3' above the ground at all times and remains level likewise. It maintains a constant interval of 6' between itself and the magic-user if unbidden. It will otherwise move within its range, as well as along with him at a rate of 6", at the command of the magic-user. If the spell caster moves beyond range, or if the spell duration expires, the *floating disc* winks out of existence and whatever it was supporting is precipitated to the surface beneath it. The material component of the spell is a drop of mercury.

Unseen Servant (Conjuration/Summoning)

Level: *1*	Components: *V, S, M*
Range: *0*	Casting Time: *1 segment*
Duration: *6 turns + 1 turn/level*	Saving Throw: *None*
Area of Effect: *3" radius of spell caster*	

Explanation/Description: The *unseen servant* is a non-visible valet, a butler to step and fetch, open doors and hold chairs, as well as to clean and mend. The spell creates a force which is not strong, but which obeys the command of the magic-user. It can carry only light-weight items — a maximum of 200 gold pieces weight suspended, twice that amount moving across a relatively friction-free surface such as a smooth stone or wood floor. It can only open normal doors, drawers, lids, etc. The *unseen servant* cannot fight, nor can it be killed, as it is a force rather than a creature. It can be magically dispelled, or eliminated after taking 6 hit points of magical damage. The material components of the spell are a piece of string and a bit of wood.

Ventriloquism (Illusion/Phantasm)

Level: *1*	Components: *V,M*
Range: *1"/level, maximum 6"*	Casting Time: *1 segment*
Duration: *2 rounds + 1 round/level*	Saving Throw: *None*
Area of Effect: *One object*	

Explanation/Description: This spell enables the magic-user to make it sound as if his or her voice — or someone's voice or similar sound — is issuing from someplace else, such as from another creature, a statue, from behind a door, down a passage, etc. The spell caster is able to make his or her voice sound as if a different creature were speaking or making the noise; of course, in a language known by him or her, or a sound which the caster can normally make. With respect to such voices and sounds, there is a 10% chance per point of intelligence above 12 of the hearer that the ruse will be recognized. The material component of the spell is a small cone of parchment.

Write (Evocation)

Level: *1*	Components: *V, S, M*
Range: *0*	Casting Time: *1 round*
Duration: *1 hour/level*	Saving Throw: *Special*
Area of Effect: *One magical spell inscription*	

Explanation/Description: By means of this spell a magic-user might be able to inscribe a spell he or she cannot understand at the time (due to level or lack of sufficient intelligence) into the tome or other compilation he or she employs to maintain a library of spells. The magic-user must make a saving throw versus magic to attempt the writing of any spell, +2 if it is only up to 1 level greater than he or she currently uses, 0 at 2 levels higher, and -1 per level from 3 levels higher onwards. If this throw fails, the magic user is subject to 1d4 of damage for every level of the spell he or she was attempting to transcribe into his or her magic book, and furthermore be knocked unconscious for a like number of turns. This damage, if not fatal, can only be healed at the rate of 1-4 points per day, as it is damage to psyche and body. Furthermore, a spell will take 1 hour per level to transcribe in this fashion, and during this period, the magic-user is in a trance state and can always be surprised by any foe. In addition to the writing surface upon which the spell is to be transcribed, the spell caster needs a fine ink composed of rare substances (minimum cost 200 g.p. per bottle, if available at all without manufacture by the magic-user).

Second Level Spells:

Audible Glamer (Illusion/Phantasm)

Level: *2*	Components: *V, M*
Range: *6" + 1"/level*	Casting Time: *2 segments*
Duration: *2 rounds/level*	Saving Throw: *Special*
Area of Effect: *Hearing range*	

Explanation/Description: When the *audible glamer* spell is cast, the magic-user causes a volume of sound to arise, at whatever distance he or she desires (within range), and seeming to recede, close, or remain in a fixed place as desired. The volume of sound caused, however, is directly related to the level of the spell caster. The relative noise is based upon the lowest level at which the spell can be cast, 3rd level. The noise of the *audible glamer* at this level is that of 4 men, maximum. Each additional experience level adds a like volume, so at 4th level the magic-user can have the spell cause sound equal to that of 8 men, maximum. Thus, talking, singing, or shouting, and/or walking, marching or running sounds can be caused. The auditory illusion created by an *audible glamer* spell can be virtually any type of sound, but the relative volume must be commensurate with the level of the magic-user casting the spell. A horde of rats running and squeaking is about the same volume as 8 men running and shouting. A roaring lion is equal to the noise volume of 16 men, while a roaring dragon is equal to the noise volume of no fewer than 24 men. If a character states that he or she does not believe the sound, a saving throw is made, and if it succeeds, the character then hears nothing, or possibly just a faint sound. Note that this spell is particularly effective when cast in conjunction with *phantasmal force* (see below). The material component of the spell is a bit of wool or a small lump of wax.

Continual Light (Alteration)

Level: *2*	Components: *V, S*
Range: *6"*	Casting Time: *2 segments*
Duration: *Permanent*	Saving Throw: *None*
Area of Effect: *6" radius globe*	

Explanation/Description: This spell is the same as the third level cleric spell *continual light*, except that the range is only 6", not 12", and it cannot be reversed by the caster.

Darkness, 15' Radius (Alteration)

Level: *2*	Components: *V, M*
Range: *1"/level*	Casting Time: *2 segments*
Duration: *1 turn + 1 round/level*	Saving Throw: *None*
Area of Effect: *1½" radius globe*	

Explanation/Description: This spell causes total, impenetrable darkness in the area of its effect. Infravision or ultravision are useless. Neither normal nor magical light will work unless a *light* or *continual light* spell is used. In the former event, the *darkness* spell is negated by the *light* spell and vice versa. The material components of this spell are a bit of bat fur and either a drop of pitch or a piece of coal.

Detect Evil (Divination) Reversible

Level: *2*	Components: *V, S*
Range: *6"*	Casting Time: *2 segments*
Duration: *5 rounds/level*	Saving Throw: *None*
Area of Effect: *1" path*	

Explanation/Description: Except as noted above, this spell is the same as the first level cleric *detect evil* (q.v.).

Detect Invisibility (Divination)

Level: *2*	Components: *V,S,M*
Range: *1"/level*	Casting Time: *2 segments*
Duration: *5 rounds/level*	Saving Throw: *None*
Area of Effect: *1" path*	

Explanation/Description: When the magic-user casts a *detect invisibility* spell, he or she is able to clearly see any objects which are invisible, as well as astral, ethereal, hidden, invisible or out of phase creatures. Detection is in the magic-user's line of sight along a 1" wide path to the range limit. The material components of this spell are a pinch of talc and a small sprinkling of powdered silver.

ESP (Divination)

Level: 2	Components: V, S, M
Range: ½''/level, 9'' maximum	Casting Time: 2 segments
Duration: 1 round/level	Saving Throw: None
Area of Effect: One creature per probe	

Explanation/Description: When an ESP spell is used, the caster is able to detect the surface thoughts of any creatures in range — except creatures with no mind (as we know it), such as all of the undead. The ESP is stopped by 2 or more feet of rock, 2 or more inches of any metal other than lead, or a thin sheet of lead foil. The magic-user employing the spell is able to probe the surface thoughts of 1 creature per turn, getting simple instinctual thoughts from lower order creatures. Probes can continue on the same creature from round to round. The caster can use the spell to help determine if some creature lurks behind a door, for example, but the ESP will not always reveal what sort of creature it is. The material component of this spell is a copper piece.

Fools Gold (Alteration)

Level: 2	Components: V, S, M
Range: 1''	Casting Time: 1 round
Duration: 6 turns/level	Saving Throw: None
Area of Effect: 1 cubic foot per level of the magic-user	

Explanation/Description: Copper coins can temporarily be changed to gold pieces, or brass items turned to solid gold for the spell duration by means of this dweomer. Note that a huge amount of copper or brass can be turned to gold by the spell — assume 4,000 g.p. are equal to a cubic foot for purposes of this spell. Any creature viewing fools gold is entitled to a saving throw which must be equal to or less than its intelligence score, but for every level of the magic-user the creature must add 1 to his dice score, so it becomes unlikely that fools gold will be detected if it was created by a high level caster. If the "gold" is struck hard by an object of cold-wrought iron, there is a slight chance it will revert to its natural state, depending on the material component used to create the "gold": if a 50 g.p. citrine is powdered and sprinkled over the metal to be changed, the chance that cold iron will return it to its true nature is 30%; if a 100 g.p. amber stone is powdered, there is a 25% chance that iron will dispel the dweomer; if a 500 g.p. topaz is powdered, the chance drops to 10%; and if a 1,000 g.p. oriental (corundum) topaz is powdered, there is only a 1% chance that the cold iron will reveal that it is fools gold.

Forget (Enchantment/Charm)

Level: 2	Components: V, S
Range: 3''	Casting Time: 2 segments
Duration: Permanent	Saving Throw: Neg.
Area of Effect: 2'' × 2''	

Explanation/Description: By means of this dweomer the spell caster causes creatures within the area of effect to forget the events of the previous round (1 minute of time previous to the utterance of the spell). For every 3 levels of experience of the spell caster another minute of past time is forgotten. Naturally, forget in no way negates any charm, suggestions, geases, quests, or similar spells, but it is possible that the creature who caused such magic to be placed upon the victim of a forget spell could be forgotten by this means. From 1-4 individual creatures can be affected by the spell, at the discretion of the caster. If only 1 is to be affected, the recipient saves versus magic at -2 on the dice; if 2 are spell objects, they save at -1; and if 3 or 4 are to be made to forget by this dweomer, they save normally. A clerical heal or restoration spell, specially cast for this purpose, will restore the lost memories, as will a wish, but other means will not serve to do so.

Invisibility (Illusion/Phantasm)

Level: 2	Components: V, S, M
Range: Touch	Casting Time: 2 segments
Duration: Special	Saving Throw: None
Area of Effect: Creature touched	

Explanation/Description: This spell causes the recipient to vanish from sight and not be detectable by normal vision or even infravision. Of course, the invisible creature is not magically silenced with respect to noises normal to it. The spell remains in effect until it is magically broken or dispelled, or the magic-user or the other recipient cancels it or until he, she or it attacks any creature. Thus, the spell caster or recipient could open doors, talk, eat, climb stairs, etc., but if any form of attack is made, the invisible creature immediately becomes visible, although this will allow the first attack by the creature because of the former invisibility. Even the allies of the spell recipient cannot see the invisible creature, or his, her or its gear, unless these allies can normally see invisible things or employ magic to do so. Note that all highly intelligent creatures with 10 or more hit dice, or levels of experience, or the equivalent in intelligence/dice/levels have a chance to automatically detect invisible objects. The material components of the invisibility spell are an eyelash and a bit of gum arabic, the former encased in the latter.

Knock (Alteration)

Level: 2	Components: V
Range: 6''	Casting Time: 1 segment
Duration: Special	Saving Throw: None
Area of Effect: 10 square feet/level	

Explanation/Description: The knock spell will open stuck or held or wizard-locked doors. It will also open barred or otherwise locked doors. It causes secret doors to open. The knock spell will also open locked or trick-opening boxes or chests. It will loose shackles or chains as well. If it is used to open a wizard-locked door, the knock does not remove the former spell, but it simply suspends its functioning for 1 turn. In all other cases, the knock will permanently open locks or welds — although the former could be closed and locked again thereafter. It will not raise bars or similar impediments (such as a portcullis). The spell will perform two functions, but if a door is locked, barred, and held, opening it will require two knock spells.

Leomund's Trap (Illusion/Phantasm)

Level: 2	Components: V, S, M
Range: Touch	Casting Time: 3 rounds
Duration: Permanent	Saving Throw: None
Area of Effect: Object touched	

Explanation/Description: This false trap is designed to fool the dwarf and/or thief attempting to pilfer or otherwise steal the spell caster's goods. It enables the magic-user to place a dweomer upon any small mechanism or device such as a lock, hinge, hasp, screw-on cap, ratchet, etc. Any examination by a character able to detect traps will be 80% likely to note the Leomund's Trap and believe it to be real. This probability reduces by 4% for each level of experience of the examiner beyond the first. If the supposed "trap" is then to be removed, it is only 20% likely that the creature attempting it will believe he or she has succeeded, +4% probability per level of experience of the remover. Of course, the spell is illusory, nothing will happen if the trap is ignored, and its primary purpose is to frighten away thieves or make them waste precious time. The material component of the spell is a piece of iron pyrite touched to the object to be "trapped". Only one Leomund's Trap may be placed within a 50' by 50' area.

Levitate (Alteration)

Level: 2	Components: V, S, M
Range: 2''/level	Casting Time: 2 segments
Duration: 1 turn/level	Saving Throw: Neg.
Area of Effect: Special	

Explanation/Description: When a levitate spell is cast, the magic-user can place it upon his or her person, or upon some other creature, subject to a maximum weight limit of 1,000 gold pieces equivalence per level of experience, i.e., a third level magic user can levitate up to 300 pounds (3,000 g.p.) maximum. If the spell is cast upon the person of the magic-user, he or she can move vertically at a rate of 20' per round. If cast upon another creature, the magic-user can levitate it at a maximum vertical movement of 10' per round. Horizontal movement is not empowered by this spell, but the recipient could push along the face of a cliff, for example, to move laterally. The spell caster can cancel the spell as desired. If the recipient of the spell is unwilling, that creature is entitled to a saving throw to determine if the levitate spell affects it. The material component of this spell is either a small leather loop or a piece of golden wire bent into a cup shape with a long shank on one end.

Locate Object (Divination) Reversible

Level: 2
Range: 2''/level
Duration: 1 round/level
Area of Effect: Special

Components: V, S, M
Casting Time: 2 segments
Saving Throw: None

Explanation/Description: This spell is the same as the third level cleric *locate object* (q.v.) except that its range differs.

Magic Mouth (Alteration)

Level: 2
Range: Special
Duration: Special
Area of Effect: One object

Components: V, S, M
Casting Time: 2 segments
Saving Throw: None

Explanation/Description: When this spell is cast, the magic-user empowers the chosen object with an enchanted mouth which suddenly appears and speaks the message which the spell caster imparted upon the occurrence of a specified event. The *magic mouth* can speak any message of 25 words or less in a language known by the spell caster, over a 1 turn period from start to finish. It cannot speak magic spells. The *mouth* moves to the words articulated, so if it is placed upon a statue, for example, the mouth of the statue would actually move and appear to speak. Of course, the *magic mouth* can be placed upon a tree, rock, door or any other object excluding intelligent members of the animal or vegetable kingdoms. The spell will function upon specific occurrence according to the command of the spell caster, i.e. speak to the first creature that touches you — or to the first creature that passes within 30'. Command can be as general or specific and detailed as desired, such as the following: ''Speak only when an octogenerian female human carrying a sack of groat clusters sits cross-legged within 1'.'' Command range is ½'' per level of the magic-user, so a 6th level magic-user can command the *magic mouth* to speak at a maximum encounter range of 3'', i.e. ''Speak when a winged creature comes within 3'.'' Until the speak command can be fulfilled, the *magic mouth* will remain in effect, thus spell duration is variable. A *magic mouth* cannot distinguish invisible creatures, alignments, level or hit dice, nor class, except by external garb. The material component of this spell is a small bit of honeycomb.

Mirror Image (Illusion/Phantasm)

Level: 2
Range: 0
Duration: 2 rounds/level
Area of Effect: 6' radius of spell
caster

Components: V, S
Casting Time: 2 segments
Saving Throw: None

Explanation/Description: When a *mirror image* spell is invoked, the spell caster causes from 1 to 4 exact duplicates of himself or herself to come into being around his or her person. These images do exactly what the magic-user does, and as the spell causes a blurring and slight distortion when it is effected, it is impossible for opponents to be certain which are the phantasms and which is the actual magic-user. When an image is struck by a weapon, magical or otherwise, it disappears, but any other existing images remain intact until struck. The images seem to shift from round to round, so that if the actual magic-user is struck during one round, he or she cannot be picked out from amongst his or her images the next. To determine the number of images which appear, roll percentile dice, and add 1 to the resulting score for each level of experience of the magic-user: 25 or less = 1 mirror image, 26-50 = 2, 51-75 = 3, 75 or more = 4. At the expiration of the spell duration all images wink out.

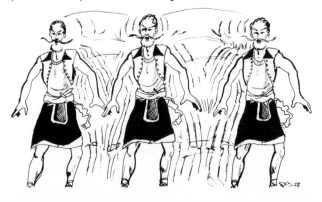

Pyrotechnics (Alteration)

Level: 2
Range: 12''
Duration: Special
Area of Effect: 10 or 100 times the
fire source used

Components: V, S
Casting Time: 2 segments
Saving Throw: None

Explanation/Description: With the exception of the differences noted above, this spell is the same as the third level druid spell *pyrotechnics* (q.v.).

Ray Of Enfeeblement (Enchantment/Charm)

Level: 2
Range: 1'' + 1/4''/level
Duration: 1 round/level
Area of Effect: One creature

Components: V, S
Casting Time: 2 segments
Saving Throw: Neg.

Explanation/Description: By means of a *ray of enfeeblement*, a magic-user weakens an opponent, reducing strength — and attacks which rely upon it — by 25% or more. For every level of experience beyond the third of the magic-user casting the spell, there is an additional 2% strength reduction, so that at 4th level, strength loss is 27%. Range and duration of the spell are also dependent upon the level of experience of the spell caster. For example, if a creature is struck by a *ray of enfeeblement*, it will lose the appropriate percentage of hit points of damage it scores on physical attacks (missiles, thrusting/cutting/crushing weapons, biting, clawing, goring, kicking, constriction, etc.). Your referee will determine any other reductions appropriate to the affected creature. If the target creature makes its saving throw, the spell has no effect.

Rope Trick (Alteration)

Level: 2
Range: Touch
Duration: 2 turns/level
Area of Effect: Special

Components: V, S, M
Casting Time: 2 segments
Saving Throw: None

Explanation/Description: When this spell is cast upon a piece of rope from 5' to 30' in length, one end of the rope rises into the air until the whole is hanging perpendicular, as if affixed at the upper end. The upper end is, in fact, fastened in an extra-dimensional space, and the spell caster and up to five others can climb up the rope and disappear into this place of safety where no creature can find them. The rope cannot be taken into the extra-dimensional space if six persons have climbed it, but otherwise it can be pulled up. Otherwise, the rope simply hangs in air, and will stay there unless removed by some creature. The persons in the extra-dimensional space must climb down the rope *prior* to the expiration of the spell duration, or else they are dropped from the height to which they originally climbed when the effect of the spell wears out. The rope can be climbed by only one person at a time. Note that the *rope trick* spell allows climbers to reach a normal place if they do not climb all the way to the rope's upper end, which is in an extra-dimensional space. The material components of this spell are powdered corn extract and a twisted loop of parchment.

Scare (Enchantment/Charm)

Level: 2
Range: 1''
Duration: 3-12 rounds
Area of Effect: One creature

Components: V, S, M
Casting Time: 2 segments
Saving Throw: Neg.

Explanation/Description: When this spell is directed at any creature with fewer than 6 levels of experience/hit dice, it must save versus magic or fall into a fit of trembling and shaking. The frightened creature will not drop any items held unless it is encumbered. If cornered, the spell recipient will fight, but at -1 on ''to hit'' and damage dice rolls and all saving throws as well. Note that this spell does not have any effect on elves, half-elves, the *undead* (skeletons, zombies, ghouls, shadows, ghasts, wights, wraiths), larvae, lemures, manes, or clerics of any sort. The material component used for this spell is a bit of bone from an *undead* skeleton, zombie, ghoul, ghast or mummy.

Shatter (Alteration)

Level: 2
Range: 6''

Components: V, S, M
Casting Time: 2 segments

Duration: *Permanent*   Saving Throw: *Neg.*
Area of Effect: *One object*

Explanation/Description: The *shatter* spell affects non-magical objects of crystal, glass, ceramic, or porcelain such as vials, bottles, flasks, jugs, windows, mirrors, etc. Such objects are shivered into dozens of pieces by the spell. Objects above 100 gold pieces weight equivalence per level of the spell caster are not affected, but all other objects of the appropriate composition must save versus a "crushing blow" or be shattered. The material component of this spell is a chip of mica.

Stinking Cloud (Evocation)

Level: 2	Components: V, S, M
Range: 3″	Casting Time: 2 segments
Duration: 1 round/level	Saving Throw: Special
Area of Effect: 2″ × 2″ × 2″ cloud	

Explanation/Description: When a *stinking cloud* is cast, the magic-user causes a billowing mass of nauseous vapors to come into being up to 3″ distant from his or her position. Any creature caught within the cloud must save versus poison or be helpless due to nausea from 2 to 5 rounds (d4 + 1). Those which make successful saving throws are helpless only for as long as they remain within the *cloud*, and for the round after they emerge, because of its irritating effects on visual and olfactory organs. The material components of the spell is a rotten egg or several skunk cabbage leaves.

Strength (Alteration)

Level: 2	Components: V, S, M
Range: Touch	Casting Time: 1 turn
Duration: 6 turns/level	Saving Throw: None
Area of Effect: Person touched	

Explanation/Description: Application of this spell increases the strength of the character by a number of points — or tenths of points after 18 strength is attained and the character is in the fighter class. Benefits of the *strength* spell last for the duration of the magic. The amount of additional strength accruing to a character upon whom this spell is cast depends upon his or her class and is subject to all restrictions on strength due to race, sex or class.

Class	Minimum-Maximum Strength Gain
CLERIC	1-6 (d6)
FIGHTER	1-8 (d8)
MAGIC-USER	1-4 (d4)
THIEF	1-6 (d6)
MONK	1-4 (d4)

If a fighter (paladin or ranger as well) has an 18 strength already, from 10% to 80% is added to his extraordinary strength roll. All Strength addition scores above 18 are likewise treated as 1 equalling an extra 10% on the extraordinary strength rating. The material component of this spell is a few hairs or a pinch of dung from a particularly strong animal — ape, bear, ox, etc.

Web (Evocation)

Level: 2	Components: V, S, M
Range: ½″/level	Casting Time: 2 segments
Duration: 2 turns/level	Saving Throw: Neg. or ½
Area of Effect: Special	

Explanation/Description: A *web* spell creates a many-layered mass of strong, sticky strands similar to spider webs, but far larger and tougher. These masses must be anchored to two or more points — floor and ceiling, opposite walls, etc. — diametrically opposed.

The *web* spell covers a maximum area of 8 cubic inches, and the webs must be at least 1″ thick, so a mass 4″ high, 2″ wide, and 1″ deep may be cast. Creatures caught within webs, or simply touching them, become stuck amongst the gluey fibers. Creatures with less than 13 strength must remain fast until freed by another or until the spell wears off. For every full turn entrapped by a *web*, a creature has a 5% cumulative chance of suffocating to death. Creatures with strength between 13 and 17 can break through 1′

of webs per turn. Creatures with 18 or greater strength break through 1′ of webs per round. (N.B. Sufficient mass equates to great strength in this case, and great mass will hardly notice webs.) Strong and huge creatures will break through 1′ of webs per segment. It is important to note that the strands of a *web* spell are flammable. A magic *flaming sword* will slash them away as easily as a hand brushes away cobwebs. Any fire — torch, flaming oil, flaming sword, etc. — will set them alight and burn them away in a single round. All creatures *within* the webs will take 2-8 hits points of damage from the flames, but those freed of the strands will not be harmed. Saving throw is made at -2. If the saving throw versus *web* is made, two results may have occurred. If the creature has room to escape then he is assumed to have jumped free. If there is no room to escape then the webs are only ½ strength.   The material component of this spell is a bit of spider web.

Wizard Lock (Alteration)

Level: 2	Components: V, S
Range: Touch	Casting Time: 2 segments
Duration: Permanent	Saving Throw: None
Area of Effect: 30 square feet/level	

Explanation/Description: When a *wizard lock* spell is cast upon a door, chest or portal, it magically locks it. The wizard-locked door or object can be opened only by breaking, a *dispel magic*, a *knock* spell (qq.v.), or by a magic-user 4 or more levels higher than the one casting the spell. Note that the last two methods do *not remove* the *wizard lock*, they only negate it for a brief duration. Creatures of extra-dimensional nature do not affect a *wizard lock* as they do a held portal (see *hold portal*).

Third Level Spells:

Blink (Alteration)

Level: 3	Components: V, S
Range: 0	Casting Time: 1 segment
Duration: 1 round/level	Saving Throw: None
Area of Effect: Personal	

Explanation/Description: By means of this spell, the magic-user causes his or her material form to "blink" out and back to this plane once again in random period and direction during the duration of each minute the spell is in effect. (Cf. **ADVANCED DUNGEONS & DRAGONS, MONSTER MANU-AL,** *Blink Dog.*) The segment of the round that the spell caster "blinks out" is determined by random roll with 2d4, and during this same segment he or she will appear again 2′ distant from his or her previous position. (Direction is determined by roll of d8: 1 = right ahead, 2 = right, 3 = right behind, 4 = behind, 5 = left behind, 6 = left, 7 = left ahead, 8 = ahead.) If some object is already occupying the space where the spell caster is indicated as "blinking" into, his or her form is displaced in a direction away from original (round starting) position for any distance necessary to appear in empty space, but never in excess of an additional 10′. If that extra distance still dictates the magic-user and another solid object are to occupy the same space, the spell caster is then trapped on the ethereal plane. During and after the *blink* segment of a round, the spell caster can be attacked only by opponents able to strike both locations at once, e.g. a *breath weapon, fireball,* and similar wide area attack forms. Those not so able can only strike the magic-user if they managed to attack prior to the "blink" segment. The spell caster is only 75% likely to be able to perform any acts other than physical attack with a hand-held stabbing or striking weapon during the course of this spell. That is, use of any spell, device, or item might not be accomplished or accomplished in an incorrect manner or in the wrong direction. Your referee will determine success/failure and the results thereof according to the particular action being performed.

Clairaudience (Divination)

Level: 3	Components: V, S, M
Range: Special	Casting Time: 3 segments
Duration: 1 round/level	Saving Throw: None
Area of Effect: Special	

Explanation/Description: The *clairaudience* spell enables the magic-user to concentrate upon some locale and hear in his or her mind whatever noise is within a 6″ radius of his or her determined *clairaudience* locale center. Distance is not a factor, but the locale must be known, i.e. a place familiar to the spell caster or an obvious one (such as behind a door, around a corner, in a copse of woods, etc.). Only sounds which are normally detectable by the magic-user can be heard by use of this spell. Only metal sheeting or magical protections will prevent the operation of the spell. Note that it will function only on the plane of existence on which the magic-user is at the time of casting. The material component of the spell is a small silver horn of at least 100 g.p. value, and casting the spell causes it to disappear.

Clairvoyance (Divination)

Level: *3*
Range: *Special*
Duration: *1 round/level*
Area of Effect: *Special*
Components: *V, S, M*
Casting Time: *3 segments*
Saving Throw: *None*

Explanation/Description: Similar to the *clairaudience* spell, the *clairvoyance* spell empowers the magic-user to see in his or her mind whatever is within sight range from the spell locale chosen. Distance is not a factor, but the locale must be known — familiar or obvious. Furthermore, light is a factor whether or not the spell caster has the ability to see into the infrared or ultraviolet spectrums. If the area is dark, only a 1″ radius from the center of the locale of the spell's area of effect can be clairvoyed; otherwise, the seeing extends to normal vision range. Metal sheeting or magical protections will foil a clairvoyance spell. The spell functions only on the plane on which the magic-user is at the time of casting. The material component of the spell is a pinch of powdered pineal gland from a human or humanoid creature.

Dispel Magic (Abjuration)

Level: *3*
Range: *12″*
Duration: *Permanent*
Area of Effect: *3″ cube*
Components: *V,S*
Casting Time: *3 segments*
Saving Throw: *None*

Explanation/Description: Except as noted above, this spell is the same as the third level cleric spell *dispel magic* (q.v.).

Explosive Runes (Alteration)

Level: *3*
Range: *Touch*
Duration: *Special*
Area of Effect: *1″ radius*
Components: *V, S*
Casting Time: *3 segments*
Saving Throw: *½*

Explanation/Description: By tracing the mystic runes upon a book, map, scroll, or similar instrument bearing written information, the magic-user prevents unauthorized reading of such. The *explosive runes* are difficult to detect, 5% per level of magic use experience of the reader, thieves having only a 5% chance in any event. When read, the *explosive runes* detonate, delivering a full 12 to 30 (6d4 + 6) hit points of damage upon the reader, who gets *no* saving throw, and either a like amount, or half that if saving throws are made, on creatures within the blast radius. The magic-user who cast the spell, as well as any other magic-users he or she instructs, can use the instrument without triggering the runes. Likewise, the magic-user can totally remove them whenever desired. They can otherwise be removed only by a *dispel magic* spell, and the *explosive runes* last until the spell is triggered. The instrument upon which the runes are placed will be destroyed when the explosion takes place unless it is not normally subject to destruction by magical fire.

Feign Death (Necromantic)

Level: *3*
Range: *Touch*
Duration: *6 rounds +1 round/ level*
Area of Effect: *Creature touched*
Components: *V, S*
Casting Time: *1 segment*
Saving Throw: *None*

Explanation/Description: By means of this spell, the caster or any other creature whose levels of experience/hit dice do not exceed the magic-user's own level can be put into a cataleptic state which is impossible to distinguish from actual death. Although the person/creature affected by the *feign death* spell can smell, hear, and know what is going on, no feeling or sight of any sort is possible; thus, any wounding or mistreatment of the body will not be felt and no reaction will occur and damage will be

only one-half normal. In addition, paralysis, poison, or energy level drain will not affect the individual/creature under the influence of this spell, but poison injected or otherwise introduced into the body will become effective when the spell recipient is no longer under the influence of this spell, although a saving throw is permitted. Note that only a willing individual can be affected by *feign death*. The spell caster is able to end the spell effects at any time desired, but it requires 1 full round for bodily functions to begin again.

Fireball (Evocation)

Level: *3*
Range: *10″ + 1″/level*
Duration: *Instantaneous*
Area of Effect: *2″ radius sphere*
Components: *V, S*
Casting Time: *3 segments*
Saving Throw: *½*

Explanation/Description: A *fireball* is an explosive burst of flame, which detonates with a low roar, and delivers damage proportionate to the level of the magic-user who cast it, i.e. 1 six-sided die (d6) for each level of experience of the spell caster. *Exception:* Magic fireball wands deliver 6 die fireballs (6d6), magic staves with this capability deliver 8 die fireballs, and scroll spells of this type deliver a fireball of from 5 to 10 dice (d6 + 4) of damage. The burst of the *fireball* does not expend a considerable amount of pressure, and the burst will generally conform to the shape of the area in which it occurs, thus covering an area equal to its normal spherical volume. [The area which is covered by the *fireball* is a total volume of roughly 33,000 cubic feet (or yards)]. Besides causing damage to creatures, the *fireball* ignites all combustible materials within its burst radius, and the heat of the *fireball* will melt soft metals such as gold, copper, silver, etc. Items exposed to the spell's effects must be rolled for to determine if they are affected. Items which a creature makes its saving throw are considered as unaffected. The magic-user points his or her finger and speaks the range (distance and height) at which the fireball is to burst. A streak flashes from the pointing digit and, unless it impacts upon a material body prior to attaining the prescribed range, flowers into the *fireball*. If creatures fail their saving throws, they all take full hit point damage from the blast. Those who make saving throws manage to dodge, fall flat or roll aside, taking ½ the full hit point damage — each and every one within the blast area. The material component of this spell is a tiny ball composed of bat guano and sulphur.

Flame Arrow (Conjuration/Summoning)

Level: *3*
Range: *Touch*
Duration: *1 segment/level*
Area of Effect: *Each arrow/bolt touched*
Components: *V, S, M*
Casting Time: *3 segments*
Saving Throw: *None*

Explanation/Description: Once the magic-user has cast this spell, he or she is able to touch one arrow or crossbow bolt (quarrel) per segment for the duration of the *flame arrow*. Each such missile so touched becomes magic, although it gains no bonuses "to hit". Each such missile must be discharged within 1 round, for after that period flame consumes it entirely, and the magic is lost. Fiery missiles will certainly have normal probabilities of causing combustion, and any creature subject to additional fire damage will suffer +1 hit point of damage from any *flame arrow* which hits it. The material components for this spell are a drop of oil and a small piece of flint.

Fly (Alteration)

Level: *3*
Range: *Touch*
Duration: *1 turn/level + 1-6 turns*
Area of Effect: *Creature touched*
Components: *V, S, M*
Casting Time: *3 segments*
Saving Throw: *None*

Explanation/Description: This spell enables the magic-user to bestow the power of magical flight. The creature affected is able to move vertically and/or horizontally at a rate of 12″ per move (half that if ascending, twice that if descending in a dive). The exact duration of the spell is always unknown to the spell caster, as the 1-6 turns variable addition is determined by the Dungeon Master secretly. The material component of the *fly* spell is a wing feather of any bird.

Gust Of Wind (Alteration)

Level: *3*
Range: *0*
Components: *V, S, M*
Casting Time: *3 segments*

Duration: *1 segment*　　　　　　Saving Throw: *None*
Area of Effect: *1″ path, 1″ per level in length*

Explanation/Description: When this spell is cast, a strong puff of air originates from the magic-user and moves in the direction he or she is facing. The force of this *gust of wind* is sufficient to extinguish candles, torches, and similar unprotected flames. It will cause protected flames — such as those of lanterns — to wildly dance and has a 5% chance per level of experience of the spell caster to extinguish even such lights. It will also fan large fires outwards 1′ to 6′ in the direction of the wind's movement. It will force back small flying creatures 1″ to 6″ and cause man-sized ones to be held motionless if attempting to move into its force, and similarly slow large flying creatures by 50% for 1 round. It will blow over light objects. Its path is 1″ wide by 1″ of length per level of experience of the magic-user casting the *gust of wind* spell i.e. an 8th level magic-user causes a gust of wind which travels 8″. The material component of the spell is a legume seed.

Haste (Alteration)

Level: *3*　　　　　　　　　Components: *V, S, M*
Range: *6″*　　　　　　　　Casting Time: *3 segments*
Duration: *3 rounds + 1 round/level*　　Saving Throw: *None*
Area of Effect: *4″ × 4″ area, 1 creature/level*

Explanation/Description: When this spell is cast, affected creatures function at double their normal movement and attack rates. Thus, a creature moving at 6″ and attacking 1 time per round would move at 12″ and attack 2 times per round. Spell casting is not more rapid. The number of creatures which can be affected is equal to the level of experience of the magic-user, those creatures closest to the spell caster being affected in preference to those farther away, and all affected by haste must be in the designated area of effect. Note that this spell negates the effects of a *slow* spell (see hereafter). Additionally, this spell ages the recipients due to speeded metabolic processes. Its material component is a shaving of licorice root.

Hold Person (Enchantment/Charm)

Level: *3*　　　　　　　　　Components: *V*
Range: *12″*　　　　　　　　Casting Time: *3 segments*
Duration: *2 rounds/level*　　　Saving Throw: *Neg.*
Area of Effect: *One to four persons*

Explanation/Description: Similar to the second level cleric *hold person* (q.v.), this spell immobilizes creatures, within range, as designated by the magic-user. If three or four persons are attacked, their saving throws are normal; but if two are attacked, their saving throws are made at -1; and if only one creature is attacked, the saving throw versus the *hold person* spell is made at -3 on the die. Partial negation of a *hold person* spell, such as would be possible by a *ring of spell turning*, causes the spell to function as a *slow* spell (q.v.) unless the saving throw is successful. Creatures affected by the spell are: brownies, dryads, dwarves, elves, gnolls, gnomes, goblins, half-elves, halflings, half-orcs, hobgoblins, humans, kobolds, lizard men, nixies, orcs, pixies, sprites, and troglodytes.

Infravision (Alteration)

Level: *3*　　　　　　　　　Components: *V, S, M*
Range: *Touch*　　　　　　　Casting Time: *1 round*
Duration: *12 turns + 6 turns/level*　Saving Throw: *None*
Area of Effect: *Creature touched*

Explanation/Description: By means of this spell the magic-user enables the recipient of *infravision* to see light in the infrared spectrum. Thus, differences in heat wave radiations can be seen up to 6″. Note that strong sources of infrared radiation (fire, lanterns, torches, etc.) tend to blind or cast "shadows" just as such light does with respect to normal vision, so the infravision is affected and does not function efficiently in the presence of such heat sources. (Invisible creatures are not usually detectable by *infravision*, as the infrared light waves are affected by invisibility, just as those of the ultraviolet and normal spectrums are.) The material component of this spell is either a pinch of dried carrot or an agate.

Invisibility, 10' Radius (Illusion/Phantasm)

Level: *3*　　　　　　　　　Components: *V, S, M*
Range: *Touch*　　　　　　　Casting Time: *3 segments*
Duration: *Special*　　　　　Saving Throw: *None*
Area of Effect: *10' radius of creature touched*

Explanation/Description: This spell is essentially the same as *invisibility* (q.v.). Those affected by it cannot see each other. Those affected creatures which attack negate the invisibility only with respect to themselves, not others made invisible, unless the spell recipient causes the spell to be broken.

Leomund's Tiny Hut (Alteration)

Level: *3*　　　　　　　　　Components: *V, S, M*
Range: *0*　　　　　　　　　Casting Time: *3 segments*
Duration: *6 turns/level*　　　Saving Throw: *None*
Area of Effect: *10' diameter sphere*

Explanation/Description: When this spell is cast, the magic-user causes an opaque sphere of force to come into being around his or her person, half of the sphere projecting above the ground or floor surface, the lower hemisphere passing through the surface. This field causes the interior of the sphere to maintain at 70° F. temperature in cold to 0° F., and heat up to 105° F. Cold below 0° lowers inside temperature on a 1° for 1° basis, heat above 105° raises the inside temperature likewise. The *tiny hut* will withstand winds up to 50 m.p.h. without being harmed, but wind force greater than that will destroy it. The interior of the *tiny hut* is a hemisphere, and the spell caster can illuminate it dimly upon command, or extinguish the light as desired. Note that although the force field is opaque from positions outside, it is transparent from within. In no way will *Leomund's Tiny Hut* provide protection from missiles, weapons, spells, and the like. Up to 6 other man-sized creatures can fit into the field with its creator, and these others can freely pass in and out of the *tiny hut* without harming it, but if the spell caster removes himself from it, the spell will dissipate. The material component for this spell is a small crystal bead which will shatter when spell duration expires or the hut is otherwise dispelled.

Lightning Bolt (Evocation)

Level: *3*　　　　　　　　　Components: *V, S, M*
Range: *4″ + 1″/level*　　　　Casting Time: *3 segments*
Duration: *Instantaneous*　　　Saving Throw: *½*
Area of Effect: *Special*

Explanation/Description: Upon casting this spell, the magic user releases a powerful stroke of electrical energy which causes damage equal to 1 six-sided die (d6) for each level of experience of the spell caster to creatures within its area of effect, or 50% of such damage to such creatures which successfully save versus the attack form. The range of the bolt is the location of the commencement of the stroke, i.e. if shot to 6″, the bolt would extend from this point to *n* inches further distance. The *lightning bolt* will set fire to combustibles, sunder wooden doors, splinter up to 1′ thickness of stone, and melt metals with a low melting point (lead, gold, copper, silver, bronze). Saving throws must be made for objects which withstand the full force of a stroke (cf. *fireball*). The area of the *lightning bolt's* effect is determined by the spell caster, just as its distance is. The stroke can be either a forking bolt 1″ wide and 4″ long, or a single bolt ½″ wide and 8″ long. If a 12th level magic-user cast the spell at its maximum range, 16″ in this case, the stroke would begin at 16″ and flash outward from there, as a forked bolt ending at 20″ or a single one ending at 24″. If the full length of the stroke is not possible due to the interposition of a non-conducting barrier (such as a stone wall), the lightning bolt will double and rebound towards its caster, its length being the normal total from beginning to end of stroke, damage caused to interposing barriers notwithstanding. Example: An 8″ stroke is begun at a range of 4″, but the possible space in the desired direction is only 3½″; so the bolt begins at the 3½″ maximum, and it rebounds 8″ in the direction of its creator. The material components of the spell are a bit of fur and an amber, crystal or glass rod.

Monster Summoning I (Conjuration/Summoning)

Level: *3*　　　　　　　　　Components: *V, S, M*
Range: *3″*　　　　　　　　Casting Time: *3 segments*

Duration: *2 rounds + 1 round/level*

Area of Effect: *Special*

Saving Throw: *None*

Explanation/Description: Within 1-4 rounds of casting this spell, the magic-user will cause the appearance of from 2-8 first level monsters (selected at random by the referee, but whose number may be either randomly determined or selected personally by the referee, according to the strength of the monster randomly determined). These monsters will appear in the spot, within spell range, desired by the magic-user, and they will attack the spell user's opponents to the best of their ability until he or she commands that attack cease, or the spell duration expires, or the monsters are slain. Note that if no opponent exists to fight, summoned monsters can, if communication is possible, and if they are physically capable, perform other services for the summoning magic-user. The material components of this spell are a tiny bag and a small (not necessarily lit) candle.

Phantasmal Force (Illusion/Phantasm)

Level: *3*
Range: *8" + 1"/level*
Duration: *Special*
Area of Effect: *8 square inches + 1 square inch/level*

Components: *V, S, M*
Casting Time: *3 segments*
Saving Throw: *Special*

Explanation/Description: When this spell is cast, the magic-user creates a visual illusion which will affect all believing creatures which view the *phantasmal force*, even to the extent of suffering damage from phantasmal missiles or from falling into an illusory pit full of sharp spikes. Note that audial illusion is not a component of the spell. The illusion lasts until struck by an opponent — unless the spell caster causes the illusion to react appropriately — or until the magic-user ceases concentration upon the spell (due to desire, moving, or successful attack which causes damage). Creatures which disbelieve the *phantasmal force* gain a saving throw versus the spell, and if they succeed, they see it for what it is and add +4 to associates' saving throws if this knowledge can be communicated effectively. Creatures not observing the spell effect are immune until they view it. The spell can create the illusion of any object, or creature, or force, as long as it is within the boundaries of the spell's area of effect. This area can move within the limits of the range. The material component of the spell is a bit of fleece.

Protection From Evil, 10' Radius (Abjuration) Reversible

Level: *3*
Range: *Touch*
Duration: *2 rounds/level*
Area of Effect: *10' radius sphere around creature touched*

Components: *V, S, M*
Casting Time: *3 segments*
Saving Throw: *None*

Explanation/Description: This spell is the same as the first level *protection from evil* spell except with respect to its area of effect. See also the first level cleric *protection from evil* spell for general information.

Protection From Normal Missiles (Abjuration)

Level: *3*
Range: *Touch*
Duration: *1 turn/level*
Area of Effect: *Creature touched*

Components: *V, S, M*
Casting Time: *3 segments*
Saving Throw: *None*

Explanation/Description: By means of this spell, the magic-user bestows total invulnerability to hurled and projected missiles such as arrows, axes, bolts, javelins, small stones and spears. Furthermore, it causes a reduction of 1 from each die of damage inflicted by large and/or magical missiles such as ballista missiles, catapult stones, and magical arrows, bolts, javelins, etc. Note, however, that this spell does not convey any protection from such magical attacks as *fireballs*, *lightning bolts*, or *magic missiles*. The material component of this spell is a piece of tortoise or turtle shell.

Slow (Alteration)

Level: *3*
Range: *9" + 1"/level*
Duration: *3 rounds + 1 round/level*
Area of Effect: *4" X 4" area, 1 creature/level*

Components: *V, S, M*
Casting Time: *3 segments*
Saving Throw: *None*

Explanation/Description: A *slow* spell causes affected creatures to move and attack at one-half of the normal or current rate. Thus, it negates a *haste* spell (q.v.), has cumulative effect if cast upon creatures already slowed, and otherwise affects magically speeded or slowed creatures. The magic will affect as many creatures as the spell caster has levels of experience, providing these creatures are within the area of effect determined by the magic-user, i.e. the 4" X 4" area which centers in the direction and at the range called for by the caster. The material component of this spell is a drop of treacle.

Suggestion (Enchantment/Charm)

Level: *3*
Range: *3"*
Duration: *6 turns + 6 turns/level*
Area of Effect: *One creature*

Components: *V, M*
Casting Time: *3 segments*
Saving Throw: *Neg.*

Explanation/Description: When this spell is cast by the magic-user, he or she influences the actions of the chosen recipient by utterance of a few words — phrases, or a sentence or two — suggesting a course of action desirable to the spell caster. The creature to be influenced must, of course, be able to understand the magic-user's *suggestion*, i.e., it must be spoken in a language which the spell recipient understands. The *suggestion* must be worded in such a manner as to make the action sound reasonable; a request asking the creature to stab itself, throw itself onto a spear, immolate itself, or do some other obviously harmful act will automatically negate the effect of the spell. However, a *suggestion* that a pool of acid was actually pure water, and a quick dip would be refreshing, is another matter; or the urging that a cessation of attack upon the magic-user's party would benefit a red dragon, for the group could loot a rich treasure elsewhere through co-operative action, is likewise a reasonable use of the spell's power. The course of action of a *suggestion* can continue in effect for a considerable duration, such as in the case of the red dragon mentioned above. If the recipient creature makes its saving throw, the spell has no effect. Note that a very reasonable *suggestion* will cause the saving throw to be made at a penalty (such as -1, -2, etc.) at the discretion of your Dungeon Master. Undead are not subject to *suggestion*. The material components of this spell are a snake's tongue and either a bit of honeycomb or a drop of sweet oil.

Tongues (Alteration) Reversible

Level: *3*
Range: *0*
Duration: *1 round/level*
Area of Effect: *6" diameter circle*

Components: *V, M*
Casting Time: *3 segments*
Saving Throw: *None*

Explanation/Description: Except as noted above, this spell is the same as the fourth level cleric spell, *tongues* (q.v.). Also, the material component is a small clay model of a ziggurat, which shatters when the spell is pronounced.

Water Breathing (Alteration) Reversible

Level: *3*
Range: *Touch*
Duration: *3 turns/level*
Area of Effect: *Creature touched*

Components: *V, S, M*
Casting Time: *3 segments*
Saving Throw: *None*

Explanation/Description: Except as noted above, and that the material component of the spell is a short reed or piece of straw, this is the same as the third level druid spell, *water breathing* (q.v.).

Fourth Level Spells:

Charm Monster (Enchantment/Charm)

Level: *4*
Range: *6"*
Duration: *Special*
Area of Effect: *Special*

Components: *V, S*
Casting Time: *4 segments*
Saving Throw: *Neg.*

Explanation/Description: This spell is similar to a *charm person* spell (q.v.), but it will affect any living creature — or several creatures of lesser level as explained hereafter. The magic-user casts the *charm monster* spell, and any affected creature regards the spell caster as friendly, an ally or companion to be treated well or guarded from harm. If communication is possible, the charmed creature will follow reasonable requests, instructions, or orders most faithfully (cf. *suggestion* spell). Affected creatures will eventually come out from under the influence of the spell, and the probability of such breaking of a *charm monster* spell is a function of the creature's level, i.e. its number of hit dice:

Monster Level or Hit Dice	Percent Chance/ Week of Breaking Spell
1st or up to 2	5%
2nd or up to 3 + 2	10%
3rd or up to 4 + 4	15%
4th or up to 6	25%
5th or up to 7 + 2	35%
6th or up to 8 + 4	45%
7th or up to 10	60%
8th or up to 12	75%
9th or over 12	90%

Naturally, overtly hostile acts by the person charming the monster will automatically break the spell, or at the very least allow the monster a new saving throw versus the charm. The spell will affect from 2-8 1st level creatures, 1-4 2nd level creatures, 1 or 2 3rd level, or 1 creature of 4th or higher level.

Confusion (Enchantment/Charm)

Level: *4*
Range: *12''*
Duration: *2 rounds + 1 round/level*
Area of Effect: *Up to 6''×6''*

Components: *V, S, M*
Casting Time: *4 segments*
Saving Throw: *Special*

Explanation/Description: Except as noted above, this spell is identical to the seventh level druid spell, *confusion* (q.v.). However, it affects a basic 2-16 creatures. Its material component is a set of three nut shells.

Dig (Evocation)

Level: *4*
Range: *3''*
Duration: *1 round/level*
Area of Effect: *5' cube per level of the magic-user*

Components: *V, S, M*
Casting Time: *4 segments*
Saving Throw: *Special*

Explanation/Description: A *dig* spell enables the caster to excavate 125 cubic feet of earth, sand, or mud per round. The hole thus dug is a cube 5' per side. The material thrown from the excavation scatters evenly around the pit. If the magic-user continues downward beyond 5', there is a chance that the pit will collapse: 15%/additional 5' in depth in earth, 35%/additional 5' depth in sand, and 55%/additional 5' depth in mud. Any creature at the edge (1') of such a pit uses its dexterity score as a saving throw to avoid falling into the hole, with a score equal to or less than the dexterity meaning that a fall was avoided. Any creature moving rapidly towards a pit area will fall in unless it saves versus magic. Any creature caught in the center of a pit just dug will always fall in. The spell caster uses a miniature shovel and tiny bucket to activate a *dig* spell and must continue to hold these material components while each pit is excavated.

Dimension Door (Alteration)

Level: *4*
Range: *0*
Duration: *Special*
Area of Effect: *Spell caster*

Components: *V*
Casting Time: *1 segment*
Saving Throw: *None*

Explanation/Description: By means of a *dimension door* spell, the magic-user instantly transfers himself or herself up to 3'' distance per level of experience of the spell caster. This special form of teleportation allows for no error, and the magic-user always arrives at exactly the spot desired — whether by simply visualizing the area (within spell transfer distance, of course) or by stating direction such as ''30 inches straight downwards,'' or ''upwards to the northwest, 45 degree angle, 42 inches.'' If the magic-user arrives in a place which is already occupied by a solid body, he or she remains in the *Astral Plane* until located by some helpful creature willing to cast a *dispel magic* upon the person, for he or she is stunned and cannot successfully perform any spell casting. If distances are stated and the spell caster arrives with no support below his or her feet (i.e., in mid-air), falling and damage will result unless further magical means are employed. All

that the magic-user wears or carries, subject to a maximum weight equal to 5,000 gold pieces of non-living matter, or half that amount of living matter, is transferred with the spell caster. Recovery from use of a *dimension door* spell requires 7 segments.

Enchanted Weapon (Alteration) Reversible

Level: *4*
Range: *Touch*
Duration: *5 rounds/level*
Area of Effect: *Weapon(s) touched*

Components: *V, S, M*
Casting Time: *1 turn*
Saving Throw: *None*

Explanation/Description: This spell turns an ordinary weapon into a magical one. The weapon is the equivalent of a +1 weapon but has *no* bonuses whatsoever. Thus, arrows, axes, bolts, bows, daggers, hammers, maces, spears, swords, etc. can be made into *enchanted* weapons. Two small (arrows, bolts, daggers, etc.) or one large (axe, bow, hammer, mace, etc.) weapon can be affected by the spell. Note that successful hits by enchanted missile weapons cause the spell to be broken, but that otherwise the spell duration lasts until the time limit based on the level of experience of the magic-user casting it expires, i.e. 40 rounds (4 turns) in the case of an 8th level magic-user. The material components of this spell are powdered lime and carbon.

Extension I (Alteration)

Level: *4*
Range: *0*
Duration: *Special*
Area of Effect: *Special*

Components: *V*
Casting Time: *2 segments*
Saving Throw: *None*

Explanation/Description: By use of an *extension I* spell the magic-user prolongs the *duration* of a previously cast first, second, or third level spell by 50%. Thus, a *levitation* spell can be made to function 1½ turns/level, a *hold person* spell made to work for 3 rounds/level, etc. Naturally, the spell has effect only on such spells where *duration* is meaningful.

Fear (Illusion/Phantasm)

Level: *4*
Range: *0*
Duration: *Special*
Area of Effect: *6'' long cone, 3'' diameter at end, ½' at base*

Components: *V, S, M*
Casting Time: *4 segments*
Saving Throw: *Neg.*

Explanation/Description: When a *fear* spell is cast, the magic-user sends forth an invisible ray which causes creatures within its area of effect to turn away from the spell caster and flee in panic. Affected creatures are likely to drop whatever they are holding when struck by the spell; the base chance of this is 60% at 1st level (or at 1 hit die) above this reduces the probability by 5%, i.e. at 10th level there is only a 15% chance, and at 13th level 0% chance. Creatures affected by *fear* flee at their fastest rate for the number of melee rounds equal to the level of experience of the spell caster. The panic takes effect on the melee round following the spell casting, but dropping of items in hand will take place immediately. Of course, creatures which make their saving throws versus the spell are not affected. The material component of this spell is either the heart of a hen or a white feather.

Fire Charm (Enchantment/Charm)

Level: *4*
Range: *1''*
Duration: *2 rounds/level*
Area of Effect: *30' diameter of fire*

Components: *V, S, M*
Casting Time: *4 segments*
Saving Throw: *Neg.*

Explanation/Description: By means of this spell the magic-user causes a normal fire source such as a brazier, flambeau, or bonfire to serve as a magical agent, for from this source he or she causes a gossamer veil of multi-hued flame to circle the fire at 5' distance. Any creatures observing the fire or the dancing circle of flame around it must save versus magic or be *charmed* into remaining motionless and gazing, transfixed at the flames. While so *charmed*, creatures are subject to *suggestion* spells of 12 or fewer words, saving against their influence at -3. The *fire charm* is broken by any physical attack upon the *charmed* creature, if a solid object is interposed between the creature and the veil of flames so as to obstruct vision, or when the duration of the spell is at an end. Note that the veil of flame is not a magical fire, and passing through it incurs the same type and amount of damage as would be sustained from passing through its original fire source. The material component for this spell is a small piece of multicolored silk of exceptional thinness which the dweomercraefter must throw into the fire source.

Fire Shield: (Evocation-Alteration)

Level: *4*	Components: *V, S, M*
Range: *0*	Casting Time: *4 segments*
Duration: *2 rounds + 1 round/level*	Saving Throw: *None*
Area of Effect: *Personal*	

Explanation/Description: By casting this spell the magic-user appears to immolate himself or herself, but the flames are thin and wispy, shedding light equal only to half that of a normal torch (15' radius of dim light), and colored blue or green if variation A is cast, violet or blue if variation B is employed. Any creature striking the spell caster with body or hand-held weapons will inflict normal damage upon the magic-user, but the attacker will take double the amount of damage so inflicted! The other spell powers depend on the variation of the spell used:

A) The flames are hot, and any cold-based attacks will be saved against at +2 on the dice, and either half normal damage or no damage will be sustained; fire-based attacks are normal, but if the magic-user fails to make the required saving throw (if any) against them, he or she will sustain double normal damage. The material component for this variation is a bit of phosphorous.

B) The flames are cold, and any fire-based attack will be saved against at +2 on the dice, and either half normal damage or no damage will be sustained; cold-based attacks are normal, but if the magic-user fails to make the required saving throw (if any) against them, he or she will sustain double normal damage. The material component for this variation is a live firefly or glow worm or the tail portions of 4 dead ones.

Fire Trap (Evocation)

Level: *4*	Components: *V, S, M*
Range: *Touch*	Casting Time: *3 rounds*
Duration: *Permanent until discharged*	Saving Throw: *½ discharged*
Area of Effect: *Object touched*	

Explanation/Description: Any closable item (book, box, bottle, chest, coffer, coffin, door, drawer, and so forth) is affected by a *fire trap* spell, but the item so trapped cannot have a second spell such as *hold portal* or *wizard lock* placed upon it except as follows: if a *fire trap/hold portal* is attempted, only the spell first cast will work, and the other will be negated (both negated if cast simultaneously). If a *fire trap* is cast after a *wizard lock*, the former is negated, if both are cast simultaneously both are negated, and if a *wizard lock* is cast after placement of a *fire trap* there is a 50% chance that both spells will be negated. A *knock* spell will not affect a *fire trap* in any way — as soon as the offending party enters/touches, the trap will discharge. The caster can use the trapped object without discharging it. When the trap is discharged there will be an explosion of 5' radius, and all creatures within this area must make saving throws versus magic. Damage is 1-4 hit points plus 1 hit point per level of the magic-user who cast the spell, or one-half the total amount for creatures successfully saving versus magic. The item trapped is NOT harmed by this explosion. There is only 50% of the normal chance to detect a *fire trap*, and failure to remove it when such action is attempted detonates it immediately. To place this spell, the caster must trace the outline of the closure with a bit of sulphur or saltpeter.

Fumble (Enchantment/Charm)

Level: *4*	Components: *V, S, M*
Range: *1"/level*	Casting Time: *4 segments*
Duration: *1 round/level*	Saving Throw: *½*
Area of Effect: *1 creature*	

Explanation/Description: When a *fumble* spell is cast, the magic-user causes the recipient of the magic to suddenly become clumsy and

awkward. Running creatures will trip and fall, those reaching for an item will *fumble* and drop it, those employing weapons will likewise awkwardly drop them. Recovery from a fall or of a fumbled object will typically require the whole of the next melee round. Note that breakable items might suffer damage when dropped. If the victim makes his or her saving throw, the *fumble* will simply make him or her effectively operate at one-half normal efficiency (cf. *slow* spell). The material component of this spell is a dab of solidified milk fat.

Hallucinatory Terrain (Illusion/Phantasm)

Level: *4*	Components: *V, S, M*
Range: *2"/level*	Casting Time: *1 turn*
Duration: *Special*	Saving Throw: *None*
Area of Effect: *1" × 1" square area/level*	

Explanation/Description: By means of this spell the magic-user causes an illusion which hides the actual terrain within the area of the spell's effect. Thus, open fields or a road can be made to look as if a swamp or hill or crevasse or some other difficult or impassable terrain existed there. Also, a pond can be made to appear as a grassy meadow, a precipice look as if it were a gentle slope, or a rock-strewn gully made to look as if it were a wide and smooth road. The *hallucinatory terrain* persists until a *dispel magic* spell is cast upon the area or until it is contacted by an intelligent creature. Each level of experience of the magic-user enables him or her to affect a larger area. At 10th level, a magic-user can affect an area up to 10" × 10" square, while at 12th level the spell caster affects a 12" × 12" square area. The material components of this spell are a stone, a twig, and a bit of green plant — leaf or grass blade.

Ice Storm (Evocation)

Level: *4*	Components: *V, S, M*
Range: *1"/level*	Casting Time: *4 segments*
Duration: *1 round*	Saving Throw: *None*
Area of Effect: *Special*	

Explanation/Description: When this spell is cast, the magic-user causes either great hail stones to pound down in an area of 4" diameter and inflict from 3 to 30 (3d10) hit points of damage on any creatures within the area of effect; or the *ice storm* can be made to cause driving sleet to fall in an area of 8" diameter and both blind creatures within its area of effect for the duration of the spell and cause the ground in the area to be icy, thus slowing movement within by 50% and making it 50% probable that a moving creature will slip and fall when trying to move. The material components for this spell are a pinch of dust and a few drops of water. (Note that this spell will negate a *heat metal* spell (q.v.), but its first application will also cause damage in the process.)

Massmorph (Illusion/Phantasm)

Level: *4*	Components: *V, S, M*
Range: *1"/level*	Casting Time: *1 turn*
Duration: *Special*	Saving Throw: *None*
Area of Effect: *11' × 1" square/level*	

Explanation/Description: When this spell is cast upon willing creatures of man-size or smaller, up to 10 such creatures per level of experience of the magic-user can be made to appear as normal trees of any sort. Thus, a company of creatures can be made to appear as a copse, grove, or orchard. Furthermore, these *massmorphed* creatures can be passed through — and even touched — by other creatures without revealing the illusion. Note, however, that blows to the creature-trees will reveal their nature, as damage will be sustained by the creatures struck and blood will be seen. Creatures *massmorphed* must be within the spell's area of effect. Unwilling creatures are not affected. The spell persists until the caster commands it to cease or until a *dispel magic* is cast upon the creatures. The material component of this spell is a handful of bark chips.

Minor Globe Of Invulnerability (Abjuration)

Level: *4*	Components: *V, S, M*
Range: *0*	Casting Time: *4 segments*
Duration: *1 round/level*	Saving Throw: *None*
Area of Effect: *1" diameter sphere*	

Explanation/Description: This spell creates a magical sphere around the caster which prevents any first, second or third level spells from penetrating, i.e. the area of effect of any such spells does not include the area of the *minor globe of invulnerability*. However, any sort of spells can be cast *out* of the magical sphere, and they pass from the caster of the *globe*, through its area of effect, and to their target without effect upon the *minor globe of invulnerability*. Fourth and higher level spells are not affected by the *globe*. It can be brought down by a *dispel magic* spell. The material component of the spell is a glass or crystal bead.

Monster Summoning II (Conjuration/Summoning)

Level: *4*
Range: *4''*
Duration: *3 rounds + 1 round/level*
Area of Effect: *Special*

Components: *V, S, M*
Casting Time: *4 segments*
Saving Throw: *None*

Explanation/Description: This spell is similar to the third level *monster summoning I* spell (q.v.). Its major difference is that 1-6 second level monsters are conjured up. The material components are the same as those of the lesser spell. There is also a 1-4 round delay.

Plant Growth (Alteration)

Level: *4*
Range: *1''/level*
Duration: *Permanent*
Area of Effect: *1'' × 1'' square area/level*

Components: *V, S*
Casting Time: *4 segments*
Saving Throw: *None*

Explanation/Description: Except as noted above, this spell is the same as a third level druid spell, *plant growth* (q.v.).

Polymorph Other (Alteration)

Level: *4*
Range: *½''/level*
Duration: *Permanent*
Area of Effect: *One creature*

Components: *V, S, M*
Casting Time: *4 segments*
Saving Throw: *Neg.*

Explanation/Description: The *polymorph other* spell is a powerful magic which completely alters the form and ability, and possibly the personality and mentality, of the recipient. Of course, creatures with a lower intelligence cannot be polymorphed into something with a higher intelligence, but the reverse is possible. The creature polymorphed must make a "system shock" (cf. **CONSTITUTION**) roll to see if it survives the change. If it is successful, it then acquires all of the form and abilities of the creature it has been polymorphed into. There is a base 100% chance that this change will also change its personality and mentality into that of the creature whose form it now possesses. For each 1 point of intelligence of the creature polymorphed, subtract 5% from the base chance. Additionally, for every hit die of difference between the original form and the form it is changed into by the spell, the polymorphed creature must adjust the base chance percentage by +/-5% per hit die below or above its own number (or *level* in the case of characters). The chance for assumption of the personality and mentality of the new form must be checked daily until the change takes place. (Note that all creatures generally prefer their own form and will not *willingly* stand the risk of being subjected to this spell!) If a one hit die orc of 8 intelligence is *polymorphed* into a white dragon with 6 hit dice, for example, it is 85% (100% - [5% × 8 intelligence] + [(6 - 1) × 5%] = 85%) likely to actually become one in all respects, but in any case it will have the dragon's physical and mental capabilities; and if it does not assume the personality and mentality of a white dragon, it will know what it formerly knew as well. Another example: an 8th level fighter successfully *polymorphed* into a blue dragon would know combat with weapons and be able to employ them with prehensile dragon forepaws if the fighter did not take on dragon personality and mentality. However, the new form of the *polymorphed* creature may be *stronger* than it looks, i.e. a mummy changed to a puppy dog would be very tough, or a brontosaurus changed to an ant would be impossible to squash merely from being stepped on by a small creature or even a man-sized one. The magic-user must use a *dispel magic* spell to change the *polymorphed* creature back to its original form, and this too requires a "system shock" saving throw. The material component of this spell is a caterpillar cocoon.

Polymorph Self (Alteration)

Level: *4*
Range: *0*
Duration: *2 turns/level*
Area of Effect: *The magic-user*

Components: *V*
Casting Time: *3 segments*
Saving Throw: *None*

Explanation/Description: When this spell is cast, the magic-user is able to assume the form of any creature — from as small as a wren to as large as a hippopotamus — and its form of locomotion as well. The spell does *not* give the other abilities (attack, magic, etc.), nor does it run the risk of changing personality and mentality. No "system shock" check is required. Thus, a magic-user changed to an owl could fly, but his or her vision would be human; a change to a black pudding would enable movement under doors or along halls and ceilings, but not the pudding's offensive or defensive capabilities. Naturally, the strength of the new form must be sufficient to allow normal movement. The spell caster can change his or her form as often as desired, the change requiring only 5 segments. Damage to the *polymorphed* form is computed as if it were inflicted upon the magic-user, but when the magic-user returns to his or her own form, from 1 to 12 (d12) points of damage are restored.

Rary's Mnemonic Enhancer (Alteration)

Level: *4*
Range: *0*
Duration: *1 day*
Area of Effect: *The magic-user*

Components: *V, S, M*
Casting Time: *1 turn*
Saving Throw: *None*

Explanation/Description: By means of this spell the magic-user is able to memorize, or retain the memory of, three additional spell levels, i.e. three spells of the first level, or one first and one second, or one third level spell. The magic-user can elect to immediately memorize additional spells or he or she may opt to retain memory of a spell cast by means of the *Enhancer*. The material components of the spell are a piece of string, an ivory plaque of at least 100 g.p. value, and an ink composed of squid secretion and either black dragon's blood or giant slug digestive juice. All components disappear when the spell is cast.

Remove Curse (Abjuration) Reversible

Level: *4*
Range: *Touch*
Duration: *Permanent*
Area of Effect: *Special*

Components: *V, S*
Casting Time: *4 segments*
Saving Throw: *Special*

Explanation/Description: Except as noted above, this spell is the same as the third level cleric spell, *remove curse* (q.v.).

Wall Of Fire (Evocation)

Level: *4*
Range: *6''*
Duration: *Special*
Area of Effect: *Special*

Components: *V, S, M*
Casting Time: *4 segments*
Saving Throw: *None*

Explanation/Description: This spell differs from the fifth level druid spell, *wall of fire* (q.v.) only as indicated above and as stated below: the flame color is either violet or reddish blue, base damage is 2-12 hit points (plus 1 hit point per level), the radius of the ring-shaped *wall of fire* is 1'' + 1/4'' per level of experience of the magic user casting it, and the material component of the spell is phosphorus.

Wall Of Ice (Evocation)

Level: *4*
Range: *1''/level*
Duration: *1 turn/level*
Area of Effect: *Special*

Components: *V, S, M*
Casting Time: *4 segments*
Saving Throw: *None*

Explanation/Description: When this spell is cast, a sheet of strong, flexible ice is created. The wall is primarily defensive, stopping pursuers and the like. The wall is one inch thick per level of experience of the magic-user. It covers a 1'' square area per level, i.e. a 10th level magic-user would cause a *wall of ice* up to 10'' long and 1'' high, or 5'' long and 2'' high, and so forth. Any creature breaking through the ice will suffer 2 hit points of damage per inch of thickness of the wall, fire-using creatures will suffer 3 hit points, cold-using creatures only 1 hit point when breaking through. If this spell is cast to form a horizontal sheet to fall upon opponents, it has the same effect as an *ice storm's* (q.v.) hail stones in the area over which it falls. Magical fires such as fireballs and fiery dragon breath will melt a wall of ice in 1 round, though they will cause a great cloud of steamy fog which will last 1 turn, but normal fires or lesser magical ones will not hasten its melting. The material component of this spell is a small piece of quartz or similar rock crystal.

Wizard Eye (Alteration)

Level: 4	Components: V, S, M
Range: 0	Casting Time: 1 turn
Duration: 1 round/level	Saving Throw: None
Area of Effect: Special	

Explanation/Description: When this spell is employed, the magic-user creates an invisible sensory organ which sends visual information to him or her. The *wizard eye* travels at 3" per round, viewing an area ahead as a human would or 1" per round examining the ceiling and walls as well as the floor ahead and casually viewing the walls ahead. The *wizard eye* can "see" with infravision at 10', or it "sees" up to 60' distant in brightly lit areas. The *wizard eye* can travel in any direction as long as the spell lasts. The material component of the spell is a bit of bat fur.

Fifth Level Spells:

Airy Water (Alteration)

Level: 5	Components: V, S, M
Range: 0	Casting Time: 5 segments
Duration: 1 turn/level	Saving Throw: None
Area of Effect: 2" diameter sphere or 4" diameter hemisphere	

Explanation/Description: The *airy water* spell turns normal liquid such as water or water based infusions or solutions to a less dense, breathable substance. Thus, if the magic-user were desirous of entering an underwater place, he or she would step into the water, cast the spell and sink downwards in a globe of bubbling water which he or she and any companions in the spell's area of effect could move freely in and breathe just as if it were air rather than water. The globe will move with the spell caster. Note that water breathing creatures will avoid a sphere (or hemisphere) of *airy water*, although intelligent ones can enter it if they are able to move by means other than swimming, but no water-breathers will be able to breathe in an area affected by this spell. There is only one word which needs to be spoken to actuate the magic, and the material component of the spell is a small handful of alkaline or bromine salts.

Animal Growth (Alteration) Reversible

Level: 5	Components: V, S
Range: 6"	Casting Time: 5 segments
Duration: 1 round/level	Saving Throw: None
Area of Effect: up to 8 animals in a 2" square area	

Explanation/Description: Except as noted above, and for the fact that the material component of the spell is a pinch of powdered bone, this is the same as the fifth level druid spell *animal growth* (q.v.).

Animate Dead (Necromantic)

Level: 5	Components: V, S, M
Range: 1"	Casting Time: 5 rounds
Duration: Permanent	Saving Throw: None
Area of Effect: Special	

Explanation/Description: Except as noted above, this spell is the same as the third level cleric spell *animate dead* (q.v.).

Bigby's Interposing Hand (Evocation)

Level: 5	Components: V, S, M
Range: 1"/level	Casting Time: 5 segments
Duration: 1 round/level	Saving Throw: None
Area of Effect: Special	

Explanation/Description: *Bigby's Interposing Hand* is a large to huge-sized magic member which appears and places itself between the spell caster and his or her chosen opponent. This disembodied hand then remains between the two, regardless of what the spell caster does subsequently or how the opponent tries to get around it. The size of the *Hand* is determined by the magic-user, and it can be human-sized all the way up to titan-sized. It takes as many hit points of damage to destroy as the magic-user who cast it. Any creature weighing less than 2,000 pounds trying to push past it will be slowed to one-half normal movement. The material component of the spell is a glove.

Cloudkill (Evocation)

Level: 5	Components: V, S
Range: 1"	Casting Time: 5 segments
Duration: 1 round/level	Saving Throw: None
Area of Effect: 4" wide, 2" high, 2" deep cloud	

Explanation/Description: This spell generates a billowing cloud of ghastly yellowish green vapors which is so toxic as to slay any creature with fewer than 4 + 1 hit dice, cause creatures with 4 + 1 to 5 + 1 hit dice to save versus poison at -4 on the dice roll, and creatures up to 6 hit dice (inclusive) to save versus poison normally or be slain by the *cloud*. The cloudkill moves away from the spell caster at 1" per round, rolling along the surface of the ground. A wind will cause it to alter course, but it will not move back towards its caster. A *strong* wind will break it up in 4 rounds, and a greater wind force prevents the use of the spell. Very thick vegetation will disperse the *cloud* in two rounds, i.e. moving through such vegetation for 2". As the vapors are heavier than air, they will sink to the lowest level of the land, even pour down den or sinkhole openings; thus, it is ideal for slaying nests of giant ants, for example.

Conjure Elemental (Conjuration/Summoning)

Level: 5	Components: V, S, M
Range: 6"	Casting Time: 1 turn
Duration: 1 turn/level	Saving Throw: None
Area of Effect: Special	

Explanation/Description: There are actually four spells in one as respects *conjure elemental*. The magic-user is able to conjure an air, earth, fire or water elemental with this spell — assuming he or she has the material component for the particular elemental. A considerable fire source must be in range to conjure that type of elemental; a large amount of water must be likewise available for conjuration of a water elemental. Conjured elementals are very strong — see **ADVANCED DUNGEONS & DRAGONS, MONSTER MANUAL** — typically having 16 hit dice (16d8). It is possible to conjure up successive elementals of different type if the spell caster has memorized two or more of these spells. The type of elemental to be conjured must be decided upon before memorizing the spell. The elemental conjured up must be controlled by the magic-user, i.e. the spell caster must concentrate on the elemental doing his or her commands, or it will turn on the magic-user and attack. The elemental, however, will not cease a combat to do so, but it will *avoid* creatures when seeking its conjurer. If the magic-user is wounded or grappled, his or her concentration is broken. There is always a 5% chance that the elemental will turn on its conjurer regardless of concentration, and this check is made at the end of the second and each succeeding round. The elemental can be controlled up to 3" distant per level of the spell caster. The elemental remains until its form on this plane is destroyed due to damage or the spell's duration expires. Note that water elementals are destroyed if they move beyond 6" of a body of water. The material component of this spell (besides the quantity of the element at hand) is a small amount of:

Air Elemental — burning incense
Earth Elemental — soft clay
Fire Elemental — sulphur and phosphorus
Water Elemental — water and sand

N.B. Special protection from uncontrolled elementals is available by means of a pentacle, pentagram, thaumaturgic triangle, magic circle, or *protection from evil* spell.

Cone Of Cold (Evocation)

Level: 5	Components: V, S, M
Range: 0	Casting Time: 5 segments

Duration: *Instantaneous*   Saving Throw: *½*
Area of Effect: *Special*

Explanation/Description: When this spell is cast, it causes a cone-shaped area originating at the magic-user's hand and extending outwards in a cone ½" long per level of the caster. It drains heat and causes 1 four-sided die, plus 1 hit point of damage (1d4 + 1), per level of experience of the magic-user. For example, a 10th level magic-user would cast a *cone of cold* causing 10d4 + 10 hit points of damage. Its material component is a crystal or glass cone of very small size.

Contact Other Plane (Divination)

Level: 5   Components: *V*
Range: *0*   Casting Time: *1 turn*
Duration: *Special*   Saving Throw: *None*
Area of Effect: *Special*

Explanation/Description: When this spell is cast, the magic-user sends his or her mind to another plane of existence in order to receive advice and information from powers there. As these powers are located at random, and resent such contact in any case, only brief answers will be given. (Your DM will answer all questions with a "yes", "no", "maybe", "never", "irrelevant", etc.) The character can contact an elemental plane or some plane further removed. For every 2 levels of experience of the magic-user one question may be asked. Contact with minds far removed from the plane of the magic-user increases the probability of the spell caster going insane or dying, but the chance of the power knowing the answer, as well as the probability of the being telling the correct answer, are likewise increased by moving to distant planes:

Plane	Likelihood of Insanity*	Likelihood of Knowledge	Probability of Veracity**
Elemental	20%	90%***	75%
1 removed	5%	60%	65%
2 removed	10%	65%	67%
3 removed	15%	70%	70%
4 removed	20%	75%	73%
5 removed	25%	80%	75%
6 removed	30%	85%	78%
7 removed	35%	90%	81%
8 removed	40%	95%	85%
9 or more removed	50%	98%	90%

* For every 1 point of intelligence over 15, the magic user reduces probability of insanity by 5%.

** If the answer is unknown, and the answer is not true, the being will answer definitely. If truth is indicated, it will answer "unknown."

*** Assumes knowledge of questions pertaining to the appropriate elemental plane.

Insanity will strike as soon as 1 question is asked. It will last for 1 week for each removal of the plane contacted, 10 weeks maximum. There is a 1% chance per plane that the magic-user will die before recovering unless a *remove curse* spell is cast upon him or her.

Distance Distortion (Alteration)

Level: 5   Components: *V, S, M*
Range: *1"/level*   Casting Time: *6 segments*
Duration: *1 turn/level*   Saving Throw: *None*
Area of Effect: *100 square " per level*

Explanation/Description: This spell can only be cast when the magic-user has an earth elemental conjured up, but the elemental will not react hostilely to co-operation with the spell caster when he or she announces that his or her intent is to cast a *distance distortion* spell. The magic places the earth elemental in the area of effect, and the elemental then causes the area's dimensions to be distorted in either of two ways: 1) the area will effectively be one-half the distance to those travelling over it, or 2) the

area will be twice the distance to those travelling across it. Thus a 10' × 100' corridor could seem as if it was but 5' wide and 50' long, or it could appear to be 20' wide and 200' long. When the spell duration has elapsed, the elemental returns to its own plane. The true nature of an area affected by *distance distortion* is absolutely undetectable to any creatures travelling along it, although the area will radiate a dim dweomer, and a *true seeing* spell will reveal that an earth elemental is spread within the area. Material needed for this spell is a small lump of soft clay.

Extension II (Alteration)

Level: 5   Components: *V*
Range: *0*   Casting Time: *4 segments*
Duration: *Special*   Saving Throw: *None*
Area of Effect: *Special*

Explanation/Description: This spell is the same as the fourth level *Extension I* spell, except it extends the duration of first through fourth level spells by 50%.

Feeblemind (Enchantment/Charm)

Level: 5   Components: *V, S, M*
Range: *1"/level*   Casting Time: *5 segments*
Duration: *Permanent*   Saving Throw: *Neg.*
Area of Effect: *One creature*

Explanation/Description: Except as noted above, this spell is the same as the sixth level druid spell, *feeblemind* (q.v.). The material component of this spell is a handful of small clay, crystal, glass or mineral spheres.

Hold Monster (Enchantment/Charm)

Level: 5   Components: *V, S, M*
Range: *½"/level*   Casting Time: *5 segments*
Duration: *1 round/level*   Saving Throw: *Neg.*
Area of Effect: *One to four monsters (creatures)*

Explanation/Description: This spell immobilizes from one to four creatures of any type within spell range and in sight of the spell caster. He or she can opt to *hold* one, two, three or four monsters. If three or four are attacked, each saving throw is at normal; if two are attacked, each saving throw is at -1 on the die; and if but one is attacked, the saving throw is at -3 on the die. (Partially-negated *hold monster* spell effects equal those of a *slow* spell.) The material component for this spell is one hard metal bar or rod for each monster to be held. The bar or rod can be small, i.e. the size of a three-penny nail.

Leomund's Secret Chest (Alteration, Conjuration/Summoning)

Level: 5   Components: *V,S,M*
Range: *Special*   Casting Time: *1 turn*
Duration: *60 days*   Saving Throw: *None*
Area of Effect: *One chest of about 2'×2'×3' size*

Explanation/Description: In order to cast this spell the magic-user must have an exceptionally well-crafted and expensive chest constructed for him by master craftsmen. If made principally of wood, it must be of ebony, rosewood, sandalwood, teak or the like, and all of its corner fittings, nails, and hardware must be of platinum. If constructed of ivory, the metal fittings of the chest may be of gold; and if the chest is fashioned from bronze, copper, or silver, its fittings may be of electrum or silver. The cost of such a chest will never be less than 5,000 g.p. Once constructed, the magic-user must have a tiny replica (of the same materials and perfect in every detail) made, so that the miniature of the *chest* appears to be a perfect copy. One magic-user can have but one pair of these *chests* at any given time, and even *wish* spells will not allow exception!

While touching the *chest* and holding the tiny replica, the caster chants the spell. This will cause the large chest to vanish into the ethereal plane. The *chest* can contain one cubic foot of material per level of the magic-user no matter what its apparent size. Living matter makes it 75% likely that the spell will fail, so the *chest* is typically used for securing valuable spell books, magic items, gems, etc. As long as the spell caster has the small duplicate of the magic chest, he or she can recall the large one from the ethereal plane to the locale he or she is in when the chest is desired. If the miniature of the *chest* is lost or destroyed, there is no way, including a *wish*, that the large chest will return.

While on the ethereal plane, there is a 1% cumulative chance per week that some creature/being will find the *chest*. If this occurs there is 10% likelihood that the chest will be ignored, 10% possibility that something will be added to the contents, 30% possibility that the contents will be exchanged for something else, 30% chance that something will be stolen from it, and 20% probability that it will be emptied. In addition, when the *secret chest* is brought back to the Prime Material Plane, an ethereal window is opened and remains open for 5 hours, slowly diminishing in size. As this hole opens between the planes there is a 5% chance that some ethereal monster will be drawn through, with a 1% cumulative reduction in probability each hour thereafter until the window is gone. However, no creature on the Prime Material Plane can locate the *chest*, even with a *gem of seeing*, *true seeing*, etc.

If *Leomund's Secret Chest* is not retrieved before spell duration lapses, there is a cumulative chance of 5% per day that the *chest* will be lost forever, i.e. 5% chance for loss at 61 days, 10% at 62 days, and so forth.

Magic Jar (Possession)

Level: 5
Range: 1''/level
Duration: *Special*
Area of Effect: *One creature*

Components: V, S, M
Casting Time: 1 round
Saving Throw: *Special*

Explanation/Description: *Magic jar* is a very unusual spell. It enables the magic user to take over the mind of the victim and thus control the creature's body. In fact, if the body is human or humanoid, the magic-user can even use the spells he or she knows. The possessor can call upon rudimentary knowledge of the possessed, but not upon the real knowledge, i.e. a possessor will not know the language or spells of the possessed. The spell caster transfers his or her life force to a special container (a large gem or crystal), and from this *magic jar* the life force can sense and attack any creature within the spell range radius, but what the creature is, is not determinable from the *magic jar*. The special life force receptacle must be within spell range of the magic-user's body at the time of spell casting. Possession takes place only if the victim fails to make the required saving throw. Failure to possess a victim leaves the life force of the magic-user in the *magic jar*. Possession attempts require 1 round each. If the body of the spell caster is destroyed, the life force in the *magic jar* is not harmed. If the *magic jar* is destroyed, the life force is snuffed out. Returning to the real body requires 1 round, and can only be done from a *magic jar* in spell range of the body. The saving throw versus a *magic jar* spell is modified by comparing combined intelligence and wisdom scores (intelligence only in non-human or non-humanoid creatures) of the magic-user and victim.

Difference	Die Adjustment
Negative 9 or +	+4
Negative 8 to 6	+3
Negative 5 to 3	+2
Negative 2 to 0	+1
Positive 1 to 4	0
Positive 5 to 8	-1
Positive 9 to 12	-2
Positive 13 or +	-3

A *negative* score indicates the magic-user has a lower score than does his or her intended victim; thus, the victim has a saving throw bonus. The

magic jar is the spell's material component. Note that a possessed creature with any negative difference or a positive difference less than 5 is entitled to a saving throw each round to determine if it is able to displace the possessor's mind, a positive difference of 5 to 8 gains a saving throw each turn, a positive difference of 9 to 12 gains a saving throw each day, and a positive difference of 13 or better gains a saving throw each week. If the *magic jarred* creature regains control of its mind, the magic-user is trapped until he or she can take over the mind for control or escape.

Monster Summoning III (Conjuration/Summoning)

Level: 5
Range: 5''
Duration: *4 rounds + 1 round/level*
Area of Effect: *Special*

Components: V, S, M
Casting Time: 5 segments
Saving Throw: *None*

Explanation/Description: When this spell is cast, 1-4 third level monsters are summoned, coming within 1-4 rounds. See *monster summoning 1* for other details.

Mordenkainen's Faithful Hound (Conjuration/Summoning)

Level: 5
Range: 1''
Duration: *2 rounds/level*
Area of Effect: *Special*

Components: V, S, M
Casting Time: 5 segments
Saving Throw: *None*

Explanation/Description: By means of this spell the magic-user summons up a phantom watchdog which only he or she can see. He or she may then command it to perform as guardian of a passage, room, door, or similar space or portal. The phantom watchdog will immediately commence a loud barking if any creature larger than a cat approaches the place it guards. As the *Faithful Hound* is able to detect invisible, astral, ethereal, out of phase, duo-dimensional, or similarly non-visible creatures, it is an excellent guardian. In addition, if the intruding creature or creatures allow their backs to be exposed to the phantom watchdog, it will deliver a vicious attack as if it were a 10 hit dice monster, striking for 3-18 hit points of damage, and being able to hit opponents of all sorts, even those normally subject only to magical weapons of +3 or greater. The *Faithful Hound* cannot be attacked, but it can be dispelled. Note, however, that the spell caster can never be more than 3'' distant from the area that the phantom watchdog is guarding, or the magic is automatically dispelled. The material components of this spell are a tiny silver whistle, a piece of bone, and a thread.

Passwall (Alteration)

Level: 5
Range: 3''
Duration: *6 turns + 1 turn/level*
Area of Effect: *Special*

Components: V, S, M
Casting Time: 5 segments
Saving Throw: *None*

Explanation/Description: A *passwall* enables the spell caster to open a passage through wooden, plaster, or stone walls; thus he or she and any associates can simply walk through. The spell causes a 5' wide by 8' high by 10' deep opening. Note several of these spells will form a continuing passage so that very thick walls can be pierced. The material component of this spell is a pinch of sesame seeds.

Stone Shape (Alteration)

Level: 5
Range: *Touch*
Duration: *Permanent*
Area of Effect: *One cubic foot per level*

Components: V, S, M
Casting Time: 1 round
Saving Throw: *None*

Explanation/Description: By means of this spell the magic-user can form an existing piece of stone into a shape which will suit his or her purposes. For example, a stone weapon can be made, a special trapdoor fashioned, or an idol sculpted. By the same token, it would allow the spell caster to reshape a stone door, perhaps, so as to escape imprisonment, providing the volume of stone involved was within the limits of the area of effect. While stone coffers can be thus formed, secret doors made, etc., the fineness of detail is not great. The material component of this spell is soft clay which must be worked into roughly the desired shape of the stone object and then touched to the stone when the spell is uttered.

Telekinesis (Alteration)

Level: 5
Range: 1''/level
Duration: 2 rounds + 1
    round/level
Area of Effect: 250 g.p.
    weight/level

Components: V, S
Casting Time: 5 segments
Saving Throw: None

Explanation/Description: By means of this spell the magic-user is able to move objects by will force, by concentrating on moving them mentally. The *telekinesis* spell causes the desired object to move vertically or horizontally. Movement is 2'' the first round, 4'' the second, 8'' the third, 16'' the fourth, and so on, doubling each round until a maximum telekinetic movement of 1,024'' per round is reached. (Heavy objects travelling at high speed can be deadly weapons!) Note that *telekinesis* can be used to move opponents who fall within the weight capacity of the spell, but if they are able to employ as simple a counter-measure as an *enlarge* spell, for example (thus making the body weight go over the maximum spell limit), it is easily countered. Likewise, ambulation or some other form of motive power if the recipient of the spell is not able to ambulate, counters the effect of *telekinesis*, provided the velocity has not reached 16'' per round. The various *Bigby's . . . Hand* spells will also counter this spell, as will many other magics.

Teleport (Alteration)

Level: 5
Range: Touch
Duration: Instantaneous
Area of Effect: Special

Components: V
Casting Time: 2 segments
Saving Throw: None

Explanation/Description: When this spell is used, the magic-user instantly transports himself or herself, along with a certain amount of additional weight which is upon, or being touched by, the spell caster, to a well-known destination. Distance is not a factor, but inter-plane travel is not possible by means of a *teleport* spell. The spell caster is able to *teleport* a maximum weight of 2,500 g.p. equivalence, plus an additional 1,500 g.p. weight for each level of experience above the 10th, i.e. a 13th level magic-user *teleports* a maximum weight of 7,000 g.p. (700 pounds). If the destination area is very familiar to the magic-user (he or she has a clear mental picture through actual proximity to and studying of the area) it is unlikely that there will be any error in arriving exactly in the place desired. Lesser known areas (those seen only magically or from a distance) increase the probability of error. Unfamiliar areas present considerable peril. This is demonstrated below:

Destination Area Is	Probability of Teleporting		
	High	On Target	Low
Very familiar	01-02	03-99	00
Studied carefully	01-04	05-98	99-00
Seen casually	01-08	09-96	97-00
Viewed once	01-16	17-92	93-00
Never seen	01-32	33-84	85-00

Teleporting high means the magic-user will arrive 1'' above ground for every 1% he or she is below the lowest "On Target" probability — only 2'' when the destination is *very familiar,* and as high as 32'' if the destination area was *never seen.* Any low result means the instant death of the magic-user if the area into which he or she teleports to is solid. Note that there is no possibility of teleporting to an area of empty space, i.e. a substantial area of surface must be there, whether a wooden floor, a stone floor, natural ground, etc.

Transmute Rock To Mud (Alteration) Reversible

Level: 5
Range: 1''/level
Duration: Special
Area of Effect: 2 cubic ''/level

Components: V, S, M
Casting Time: 5 segments
Saving Throw: None

Explanation/Description: Except as noted above, and that the material components for the spell are clay and water (or sand, lime and water for the reverse), this spell is the same as the fifth level druid spell, *transmute rock to mud.*

Wall Of Force (Evocation)

Level: 5
Range: 3''
Duration: 1 turn + 1 round/level
Area of Effect: 20' square/level

Components: V, S, M
Casting Time: 5 segments
Saving Throw: None

Explanation/Description: A *wall of force* spell creates an invisible barrier in the locale desired by the caster, up to the spell's range. The *wall of force* will not move and is totally unaffected by any other spells, including *dispel magic,* save a *disintegrate* spell, which will immediately destroy it. Likewise, the *wall of force* is not affected by blows, missiles, cold, heat, electricity, or any similar things. Spells or breath weapons will not pass through it in either direction. The magic-user can, if desired, shape the wall to a hemispherical or spherical shape with an area equal to his or her ability, maximum of 20 square feet per level of experience. The material component for this spell is a pinch of powdered diamond.

Wall Of Iron (Evocation)

Level: 5
Range: ½''/level
Duration: Permanent
Area of Effect: Special

Components: V, S, M
Casting Time: 5 segments
Saving Throw: None

Explanation/Description: When this spell is cast, the magic-user causes a vertical iron wall to spring into being. Typically, this wall is used to seal off a passage or close a breach, for the wall inserts itself into any surrounding material if its area is sufficient to do so. The *wall of iron* is one quarter of an inch thick per level of experience of the spell caster. The magic-user is able to evoke an area of iron wall 15 square feet for each of his or her experience levels, so at 12th level a wall of iron 180 square feet in area can be created. If the wall is created in a location where it is not supported, it will fall and crush any creature beneath it. The wall is permanent, unless attacked by a *dispel magic* spell, but subject to all forces a normal iron wall is subject to, i.e. rust, perforation, etc. The material component of this spell is a small piece of sheet iron.

Wall Of Stone (Evocation)

Level: 5
Range: ½''/level
Duration: Permanent
Area of Effect: Special

Components: V, S, M
Casting Time: 5 segments
Saving Throw: None

Explanation/Description: This spell creates a wall of granite rock which merges into adjoining rock surfaces if the area is sufficient to allow it. It is typically employed to close passages, portals, and breaches against opponents. The *wall of stone* is 1/4' thick and 20' square in area per level of experience of the magic-user casting the spell. Thus, a 12th level magic-user creates a *wall of stone* 3' thick and 240 square feet in surface area (a 12' wide and 20' high wall, for example, to completely close a 10' X 16' passage). The wall created need not be vertical nor rest upon any firm foundation (cf. *wall of iron*); however, it must merge with an existing stone formation. It can be used to bridge a chasm, for instance, or as a ramp. The wall is permanent unless destroyed by a *dispel magic* spell or by normal means such as breaking, chipping or a *disintegrate* spell. The material component is a small block of granite.

Sixth Level Spells:

Anti-Magic Shell (Abjuration)

Level: 6
Range: 0
Duration: 1 turn/level
Area of Effect: 1'/level diameter
    sphere

Components: V, S
Casting Time: 1 segment
Saving Throw: None

Explanation/Description: By means of an *anti-magic shell*, the magic-user causes an invisible barrier to surround his or her person, and this moves with the spell caster. This barrier is totally impervious to all magic and magic spell effects (this includes such attack forms as breath weapons, gaze weapons, and voice weapons). It thus prevents the entrance of spells or their effects, and it likewise prevents the function of any magical items or spells within its confines. It prevents the entrance of charmed, summoned, and conjured creatures. However, normal creatures (assume a normal troll rather than one conjured up, for instance) can pass through the *shell*, as can normal missiles. While a magic sword would not function magically within the *shell*, it would still be a sword.

Bigby's Forceful Hand (Evocation)

Level: 6	Components: V, S, M
Range: 1''/level	Casting Time: 6 segments
Duration: 1 round/level	Saving Throw: None
Area of Effect: Special	

Explanation/Description: *Bigby's Forceful Hand* is a more powerful version of *Bigby's Interposing Hand* (q.v.). It exerts a force in addition to interposing itself, and this force is sufficient to push a creature away from the spell caster if the creature weighs 500 pounds or less, to push so as to slow movement to 1'' per round if the creature weighs between 500 and 2,000 pounds, and to slow movement by 50% of creatures weighing up to 8,000 pounds. It takes as many hit points to destroy as its creator has. Its material component is a glove.

Control Weather (Alteration)

Level: 6	Components: V, S, M
Range: 0	Casting Time: 1 turn
Duration: 4-24 hours	Saving Throw: None
Area of Effect: 4-16 square miles	

Explanation/Description: Except as noted above, and for the differing material components, this spell is the same as the seventh level cleric *control weather* spell (q.v.). The material components of this spell are burning incense, and bits of earth and wood mixed in water.

Death Spell (Conjuration/Summoning)

Level: 6	Components: V, S, M
Range: 1''/level	Casting Time: 6 segments
Duration: Instantaneous	Saving Throw: None
Area of Effect: ½'' square/level	

Explanation/Description: When a *death spell* is cast, it slays creatures in the area of effect instantly and irrevocably. The number of creatures which can be so slain is a function of their hit dice:

Victim's Hit Dice	Maximum Number of Creatures Affected	
less than 2	4-80	(4d20)
2 to 4	3-30	(3d10)
4+1 to 6+3	2-8	(2d4)
6+4 to 8+3	1-4	(1d4)

If a mixed group of creatures is attacked with a *death spell*, use the following conversion:

Creature's Hit Dice:	Equals Creatures with Hit Dice of:			
	less than 2	2 to 4	4+1 to 6+3	6+4 to 8+3
6+4 to 8+3	10	5	2	-
4+1 to 6+3	8	3	-	.5
2 to 4	4	-	.125	.05

First, simply roll the dice to see how many creatures of less than 2 hit dice are affected, kill all these, then use the conversion to kill all 2 to 4 hit dice monsters, etc. If not enough of the number remains to kill the higher levels, they remain. This system can be reversed by applying it to higher hit dice victims first. Example: The 4d20 when rolled indicate a total of 53, 20 of this is used to kill one 6 + 4 to 8 + 3 die creature (20 × .05 = 1), 16 are used to kill two 4 + 1 to 6 + 3 hit dice creatures (16 × .125 = 2), 12 are used to kill three 2 to 4 die creatures (3 × 4 = 12), and 5 remainder can be used to kill off 5 less-than-2 dice creatures (5 × 1 = 5), i.e. 20 + 16 + 12 + 5 = 53. A *death spell* does not affect lycanthropes, undead creatures, or creatures from other than the Prime Material Plane. The material component of this spell is a crushed black pearl with a minimum value of 1000 g.p.

Disintegrate (Alteration)

Level: 6	Components: V, S, M
Range: ½''/level	Casting Time: 6 segments
Duration: Permanent	Saving Throw: Neg.
Area of Effect: Special	

Explanation/Description: This spell causes matter to vanish. It will affect even matter (or energy) of a magical nature, such as *Bigby's Forceful Hand*, but not a *globe of invulnerability* or an *anti-magic shell*. Disintegration is instantaneous, and its effects are permanent. Any living thing can be affected, even undead, and non-living matter up to 1'' cubic volume can be obliterated by the spell. Creatures, and magical material with a saving throw, which successfully save versus the spell are not affected. Only 1 creature or object can be the target of the spell. Its material components are a lodestone and a pinch of dust.

Enchant An Item (Conjuration/Summoning)

Level: 6	Components: V, S, M
Range: Touch	Casting Time: Special
Duration: Special	Saving Throw: Neg.
Area of Effect: One item	

Explanation/Description: This is a spell which must be used by a magic-user planning to create a magic item. The *enchant an item* spell prepares the object to accept the magic to be placed upon or within it. The item to be magicked must meet the following tests: 1) it must be in sound and undamaged condition; 2) the item must be the finest possible, considering its nature, i.e. crafted of the highest quality material and with the finest workmanship; and 3) its cost or value must reflect the second test, and in most cases the item must have a raw materials cost in excess of 100 g.p. With respect to requirement 3), it is not possible to apply this test to items such as ropes, leather goods, cloth, and pottery not normally embroidered, bejeweled, tooled, carved, and/or engraved; however, if such work or materials can be added to an item without weakening or harming its normal functions, these are required for the item to be magicked.

The item to be prepared must be touched manually by the spell caster. This touching must be constant and continual during the casting time which is a base 16 hours plus an additional 8-64 hours (as the magic-user may never work over 8 hours per day, and *haste* or any other spells will not alter time required in any way, this effectively means that casting time for this spell is 2 days + 1-8 days). All work must be uninterrupted, and during rest periods the item being enchanted must never be more than 1' distant from the spell caster, for if it is, the whole spell is spoiled and must be begun again. (Note that during rest periods absolutely no other form of magic may be performed, and the magic-user must remain quiet and in isolation.) At the end of the spell, the caster will "know" that the item is ready for the final test. He or she will then pronounce the final magical syllable, and if the item makes a saving throw (which is exactly the same as that of the magic-user who magicked it) versus magic, the spell is completed. (Note that the spell caster's saving throw bonuses also apply to the item, up to but not exceeding +3.) A result of 1 on the die (d20) always results in failure, regardless of modifications. Once the spell is finished, the magic-user may begin to place the desired dweomer upon the item, and the spell he or she plans to place on or within the item must be cast within 24 hours or the preparatory spell fades, and the item must again be enchanted.

Each spell subsequently cast upon an object bearing an *enchant an item* spell requires 4 hours + 4-8 additional hours *per spell level* of the magic being cast. Again, during casting the item must be touched by the magic-user, and during rest periods it must always be within 1' of his or her person. This procedure holds true for any additional spells placed upon the item, and each successive dweomer must be begun within 24 hours of the last, even if any prior spell failed.

No magic placed on or into an item is permanent unless a *permanency* spell is used as a finishing touch, and this always runs a risk of draining a point of constitution from the magic-user casting the spell. It is also necessary to point out that while it is possible to tell when the basic *(enchant an item)* spell succeeds, it is not possible to tell if successive castings actually take, for each must make the same sort of saving throw as the item itself made. Naturally, items that are charged — rods, staves, wands, *javelins of lightning, ring of wishes,* etc. — can never be made permanent. Scrolls or magic devices can never be used to *enchant an item* or cast magic upon an object so prepared.

The material component(s) for this spell vary according to both the nature of the item being magicked and successive magicks to be cast upon it. For example, a *cloak of displacement* might require the hides of 1 or more displacer beasts, a sword meant to slay dragons could require the blood and some other part of the type(s) of dragon(s) it will be effective against, and a *ring of shooting stars* might require pieces of meteorites and the horn of a ki-rin. These specifics, as well as other information pertaining to this spell, are known by your Dungeon Master.

Extension III (Alteration)

Level: 6
Range: 0
Duration: *Special*
Area of Effect: *Special*

Components: V
Casting Time: 5 segments
Saving Throw: None

Explanation/Description: This spell is the same as the fourth level *Extension I* except that it will extend first through third level spells to double duration and will extend the duration of fourth or fifth level spells by 50% of the indicated duration.

Geas (Enchantment/Charm)

Level: 6
Range: *Touch*
Duration: *Special*
Area of Effect: *Creature touched*

Components: V
Casting Time: 4 segments
Saving Throw: None

Explanation/Description: A geas spell places a magical command upon the creature (usually human or humanoid) to carry out some service, or refrain from some action or course of activity, as desired by the spell caster. The creature must be intelligent, conscious, and under its own volition. While a geas cannot compel a creature to kill itself, or to perform acts which are likely to result in certain death, it can cause almost any other course of action. The spell causes the *geased* creature to follow the instructions until the geas is completed. Failure to do so will cause the creature to grow sick and die within 1 to 4 weeks. Deviation from or twisting of the instructions causes corresponding loss of strength points until the deviation ceases. A *geas* can be done away with by a *wish* spell, but a *dispel magic* or *remove curse* will not negate it. Your referee will instruct you as to any additional details of a geas, for its casting and fulfillment are tricky, and an improperly cast geas is null and void immediately (cf. *wish).*

Glassee (Alteration)

Level: 6
Range: *Touch*
Duration: *1 round/level*
Area of Effect: *Special*

Components: V, S, M
Casting Time: 1 round
Saving Throw: None

Explanation/Description: By means of this spell the magic-user is able to make a section of metal, stone or wood as transparent as glass to his gaze, or even make it into transparent material as explained hereafter. Normally, up to four inches of metal can be seen through, stone up to 6′ thick can be made transparent, and 20′ of wood can be affected by the *glassee* spell. The spell will not work on lead, gold or platinum. The magic-user can opt to make the *glassee* apply to himself or herself only, and apply it up to once per round while spell duration lasts; or the caster can actually make a transparent area, a one-way window, in the material affected. Either case gives a viewing area 3′ wide by 2′ high. The material component of the spell is a small piece of crystal or glass.

Globe Of Invulnerability (Abjuration)

Level: 6
Range: 0

Components: V, S, M
Casting Time: 1 round

Duration: *1 round/level*
Area of Effect: *1″ diameter sphere*

Saving Throw: None

Explanation/Description: This spell is the same as the fourth level *minor globe of invulnerability* (q.v.), except as regards casting time and for the fact that it prevents the functioning of first through fourth level spells affecting the magic-user within the *globe,* while he or she can cast spells through it, of course.

Guards And Wards (Evocation, Alteration, Enchantment/Charm)

Level: 6
Range: 0
Duration: *6 turns/level*
Area of Effect: *1″ radius/level, extending from 2″ diameter sphere*

Components: V, S, M
Casting Time: 3 turns
Saving Throw: None

Explanation/Description: This special and powerful spell is primarily used to defend the magic-user's stronghold. The following take place in the area of effect upon casting of the spell:

1. All corridors become misty, and visibility is reduced to 10′.

2. All doors are *wizard locked.*

3. One door per level of experience of the magic-user is covered by an illusion as if it were a plain wall.

4. Stairs are filled with *webs* from top to bottom.

5. Where there are choices in direction — such as a cross or side passage — a minor confusion-type spell functions so as to make it 50% probable that intruders will believe they are going in the exact opposite direction.

6. The whole area radiates magic.

7. The magic-user can place *one* of the following additional magics:

    A. *Dancing lights* in four corridors, or

    B. *Magic mouths* in two places, or

    C. *Stinking Clouds* in two places, or

    D. *Gust of wind* in one corridor or room, or

    E. *Suggestion* in one place.

Note that items 3 and 7 function only when the magic-user is totally familiar with the area of the spell's effect. *Dispel magic* can remove one effect, at random, per casting of a dispel. A *remove curse* will not work. The material components of the spell are burning incense, a small measure of sulphur and oil, a knotted string, a small amount of umber hulk blood, and a small silver rod.

Invisible Stalker (Conjuration/Summoning)

Level: 6
Range: 1″
Duration: *Special*
Area of Effect: *Special*

Components: V, S, M
Casting Time: 1 round
Saving Throw: None

Expalantion/Description: This spell summons an *invisible stalker* from the Elemental Plane of Air. This 8 hit die monster will obey and serve the spell caster in performance of whatever tasks are set before it. However, the creature is *bound* to serve; it does not do so from loyalty or desire. Therefore, it will resent prolonged missions or complex tasks, and it will attempt to pervert instructions accordingly (for complete details of the *invisible stalker,* consult **ADVANCED DUNGEONS & DRAGONS, MONSTER MANUAL**). The invisible stalker will follow instructions even at hundreds or thousands of miles distance. The material components of this spell are burning incense and a piece of horn carved into a crescent shape.

Legend Lore (Divination)

Level: 6
Range: 0
Duration: *Special*
Area of Effect: *Special*

Components: V, S, M
Casting Time: *Special*
Saving Throw: None

Explanation/Description: The *legend lore* spell is used to determine information available regarding a known person, place or thing. If the person or thing is at hand, or if the magic-user is in the place in question, the likelihood of the spell producing results is far greater and the casting time is only 1 to 4 turns. If detailed information on the person, place or thing is known, casting time is 1 to 10 days. If only rumors are known, casting time is 2 to 12 weeks. During the casting, the magic-user cannot engage in other activities other than routine: eating, sleeping, etc. When completed, the divination will reveal if legendary material is available. It will often reveal where this material is — by place name, rhyme, or riddle. It will sometimes give certain information regarding the person, place or thing (when the object of the *legend lore* is at hand), but this data will always be in some cryptic form (rhyme, riddle, anagram, cipher, sign, etc.). The spell is cast with incense and strips of ivory formed into a rectangle, but some item must be sacrificed in addition — a potion, magic scroll, magic item, creature, etc. Naturally, *legend lore* will reveal information only if the person, place or thing is noteworthy or legendary.

Lower Water (Alteration) Reversible

Level: *6*	Components: *V, S, M*
Range: *8''*	Casting Time: *1 turn*
Duration: *5 rounds/level*	Saving Throw: *None*
Area of Effect: *½'' X ½'' square area/level*	

Explanation/Description: Except as noted above, and for the facts that the reverse spell raises water only ½/level of experience of the spell caster, and the material components for the spell are a small vial of water and a small vial of dust, it is the same as the fourth level cleric spell, *lower water* (q.v.).

Monster Summoning IV (Conjuration/Summoning)

Level: *6*	Components: *V, S, M*
Range: *6''*	Casting Time: *6 segments*
Duration: *5 rounds + 1 round/level*	Saving Throw: *None*
Area of Effect: *Special*	

Explanation/Description: This spell summons 1 to 3 fourth level monsters, and they appear within 1 to 3 rounds. See *monster summoning I* for other details.

Move Earth (Alteration)

Level: *6*	Components: *V, S, M*
Range: *1''/level*	Casting Time: *Special*
Duration: *Permanent*	Saving Throw: *None*
Area of Effect: *Special*	

Explanation/Description: When cast, the *move earth* spell moves dirt (clay, loam, sand) and its other components. Thus, embankments can be collapsed, hillocks moved, dunes shifted, etc. The area to be affected will dictate the casting time; for every 4'' square area, 1 turn of casting time is required. If terrain features are to be moved — as compared to simply caving in banks or walls of earth — it is necessary that an earth elemental be subsequently summoned to assist. All spell casting and/or summoning must be completed before any effects occur. In no event can rock prominences be collapsed or moved. The material components for this spell are a mixture of soils (clay, loam, sand) in a small bag, and an iron blade.

Otiluke's Freezing Sphere (Alteration-Evocation)

Level: *6*	Components: *V, S, M*
Range: *Special*	Casting Time: *6 segments*
Duration: *Special*	Saving Throw: *Special*
Area of Effect: *Special*	

Explanation/Description: *Otiluke's Freezing Sphere* is a multi-purpose dweomer of considerable power. If the caster opts, he or she may create a globe of matter at *absolute zero* temperature which spreads upon contact with water or liquid which is principally composed of water, so as to freeze it to a depth of 6 inches over an area equal to 100 square feet per level of the magic-user casting the spell. The ice so formed lasts for 1 round per level of the caster. The spell can also be used as a thin ray of cold which springs from the caster's hand to a distance of 1'' per level of the magic-user; this ray will inflict 4 hit points of damage per level of the caster upon the creature struck, with a saving throw versus magic applicable, and all damage negated if it is successful (as the ray is so narrow a save indicates it missed), but the path of the ray being plotted to its full distance, as anything else in its path must save (if applicable) or take appropriate damage. Finally, *Otiluke's Freezing Sphere* can be cast so as to create a small globe about the size of a sling stone, cool to the touch, but not harmful. This globe can be cast, and it will shatter upon impact, inflicting 4-24 hit points of cold damage upon all creatures within a 10' radius (one-half damage if saving throw versus magic is made). Note that if the globe is not thrown or slung within a time period equal to 1 round times the level of the spell caster, it automatically shatters and causes cold damage as stated above. This timed effect can be employed against pursuers, although it can also prove hazardous to the spell caster and/or his or her associates as well. The material components of the spell depend upon in which form it is to be cast. A thin sheet of crystal about an inch square is needed for the first application of the spell, a white sapphire of not less than 1,000 g.p. value for the second application of the spell, and a 1,000 g.p. diamond is minimum for the third application of the spell. All components are lost when the spell is cast.

Part Water (Alteration)

Level: *6*	Components: *V, S, M*
Range: *1''/level*	Casting Time: *1 turn*
Duration: *5 rounds/level*	Saving Throw: *None*
Area of Effect: *Special*	

Explanation/Description: Except as shown above, and also that the material components for this spell are two small sheets of crystal or glass, this spell is the same as the sixth level cleric spell, *part water* (q.v.).

Project Image (Alteration, Illusion/Phantasm)

Level: *6*	Components: *V, S, M*
Range: *1''/level*	Casting Time: *6 segments*
Duration: *1 round/level*	Saving Throw: *None*
Area of Effect: *Special*	

Explanation/Description: By means of this spell, the magic-user creates a non-material duplicate of himself or herself, projecting it to any spot within spell range which is desired. This image performs actions identical to the magic-user — walking, speaking, spell-casting — as the magic-user determines. A special channel exists between the image of the magic-user and the actual magic-user, so spells cast actually originate from the image. The image can be dispelled only by means of a *dispel magic* spell (or upon command from the spell caster), and attacks do not affect it. The image *must* be within view of the magic-user projecting it at all times, and if his or her sight is obstructed, the spell is broken. The material component of this spell is a small replica (doll) of the magic-user.

Reincarnation (Necromantic)

Level: *6*	Components: *V, S, M*
Range: *Touch*	Casting Time: *1 turn*
Duration: *Permanent*	Saving Throw: *None*
Area of Effect: *Person touched*	

Explanation/Description: This spell is similar to the seventh level druid spell of the same name (q.v.). It does not require any saving throw for system shock or resurrection survival. The corpse is touched, and a new incarnation of the person will appear in the area in 1 to 6 turns, providing the person has not been dead for longer than 1 day per level of experience of the magic-user. The new incarnation will be:

Die Roll	Incarnation
01-05	bugbear
06-11	dwarf
12-18	elf
19-23	gnoll
24-28	gnome
29-33	goblin
34-40	half-elf
41-47	halfling
48-54	half-orc
55-59	hobgoblin
60-73	human

74-79	kobold
80-85	orc
86-90	ogre
91-95	ogre mage
96-00	troll

Note: Very good or very evil persons will not be *reincarnated* as creatures whose general alignment is the opposite. The material components of the spell are a small drum and a drop of blood.

Repulsion (Abjuration)

Level: 6	Components: V, S, M
Range: 1"/level	Casting Time: 6 segments
Duration: 1 round/2 levels	Saving Throw: None
Area of Effect: 1" path	

Explanation/Description: When this spell is cast, the magic-user is able tc cause all creatures in the path of the area of effect to move away from his or her person. Repulsion is at 3" per round, or at the motive speed of the creature attempting to move towards the spell caster. The repelled creature will continue to move away for the balance of a complete move even though this takes it beyond spell range. The material component of this spell is a pair of small magnetized iron bars attached to two small canine statuettes, one ivory and one ebony.

Spiritwrack (Evocation/Abjuration)

Level: 6	Components: V, M
Range: 1" + 1"/level	Casting Time: Special
Duration: Special	Saving Throw: Special
Area of Effect: Special	

Explanation/Description: A *spiritwrack* spell is a very strong protection/punishment spell against the powerful creatures of the nether planes (Abyssal, Hades, Hell, etc.), but to employ the magic, the spell caster must know the name of the being at whom he or she will direct the energy. Prior to actual utterance of a *spiritwrack* spell the magic-user must prepare an illuminated sheet of vellum, carefully inscribed in special inks made from powdered rubies and the ichor of a slain demon of type I, II, or III and covered with gold leaf in a continuous border. The spell caster must personally prepare this document, including the being's name thereon. (This will require from 8-32 hours of time and cost 1,000 g.p. for vellum, special pens, gold leaf, and other miscellaneous materials alone; the cost of the powdered rubies is a minimum of 5,000 g.p. for each document.) If the demon, devil, or other powerful being from a nether outer plane is present in some form (and not possessing another creature's body instead), the magic-user can then begin actual spell incantation.

Immediately upon beginning the reading of the document, the being named will be rooted to the spot unless it makes its *magic resistance* percentage (adjusted for the level of the magic-user) as a saving throw; and even if such a saving throw is made, the monster feels greatly uncomfortable, and if it has not been magically forced to the locale and so held there, it is 90% likely to retreat to its own (or another) plane, as the named being is powerless to attack the magic-user while he or she is reading the spell document. This first part of the document continues for 1 full round, with the discomfort to the named being becoming greater at the end. During the second minute of the incantation, the being named undergoes acute pain and loses 1 hit point per hit die it possesses. At the end of this round of reading, the being is in wracking pain. The third and final round of utterance of the condemnation will cause a loss to the being of 50% of its existing hit points, horrible pain, and at the end consign it to some confined space on its own plane — there to remain in torture for a number of years equal to the level of the magic-user who prepared the document.

Obviously, the being so dealt with will be the sworn foe of the magic-user forever afterwards, so the magic-user will be loath to finish the spell but rather use it as a threat to force submission of the being. Each round of reading will cause the being forced to listen to be a cumulative 25% likely to concede even without any other offerings or payment.

Stone To Flesh (Alteration) Reversible

Level: 6	Components: V, S, M
Range: 1"/level	Casting Time: 6 segments

Duration: Permanent	Saving Throw: Special
Area of Effect: One creature	

Explanation/Description: The *stone to flesh* spell turns any sort of stone into flesh — if the recipient stone object was formerly living, it will restore life (and goods), although the survival of the creature is subject to the usual system shock survival dice roll. Any formerly living creature, regardless of size, can be thus returned to flesh. Ordinary stone can be likewise turned to flesh at a volume of 9 cubic feet per level of experience of the spell caster. The reverse will turn flesh of any sort to stone, just as the stone to flesh spell functions. All possessions on the person of the creature likewise turn to stone. This reverse of the spell will require a saving throw be allowed the intended victim. The material components of the spell are a pinch of earth and a drop of blood; lime and water and earth are used for the reverse.

Tenser's Transformation (Alteration-Evocation)

Level: 6	Components: V,S,M
Range: 0	Casting Time: 6 segments
Duration: 1 round/level	Saving Throw: None
Area of Effect: Personal	

Explanation/Description: *Tenser's Transformation* is a sight guaranteed to astound any creature not aware of its power, for when the magic-user casts the dweomer, he or she undergoes a startling transformation. The size and strength of the magic-user increase to heroic proportions, so he or she becomes a formidable fighting machine, for the spell causes the caster to become a berserk fighter! The magic-user's hit points double, and all damage he or she sustains comes first from the magical points gained; so if damage does not exceed original hit points, none is actually taken, but if damage beyond the additional amount is sustained, each point counts as 2 (double damage). The armor class of the magic-user is a full 4 factors better than that he or she possessed prior to casting the spell (AC 10 goes to 6, AC 9 to 5, AC 8 to 4, etc.), all attacks are at a level equal to those of a fighter of the same level as the magic-user (i.e., the spell caster uses the combat table normally restricted to fighters), and although he or she can employ a dagger only in attacking, damage inflicted by the weapon is at +2 *additional* hit points, and 2 such attacks per round are made by the magic-user. However, it is worth noting that this spell must run its full course, and the magic-user will continue attacking until all opponents are slain, he or she is killed, the magic is dispelled, or the *Transformation* duration expires. The material component for casting this dweomer is a potion of *heroism* (or *superheroism*) which the magic-user must consume during the course of uttering the spell.

Seventh Level Spells:

Bigby's Grasping Hand (Evocation)

Level: 7	Components: V, S, M
Range: 1"/level	Casting Time: 7 segments
Duration: 1 round/level	Saving Throw: None
Area of Effect: Special	

Explanation/Description: *Bigby's Grasping Hand* is a superior version of the sixth level *Bigby's Forceful Hand* spell (q.v.), being like it in many ways. The *Grasping Hand* can actually hold motionless a creature or object of up to 1,000 pounds weight, or move creatures as a double strength *Forceful Hand*. The material component is a leather glove.

Cacodemon (Conjuration/Summoning)

Level: 7	Components: V, S, M
Range: 1"	Casting Time: Special
Duration: Special	Saving Throw: Special
Area of Effect: Creature summoned	

Explanation/Description: This perilous exercise in dweomercraeft summons up a powerful demon of type IV, V, or VI, depending upon the demon's name being known to the magic-user. Note that this spell is *not* of sufficient power to bring a demon of greater power, and lesser sorts are not called as they have no known names. In any event, the spell caster *must* know the name of the type IV, V, or VI demon he or she is summoning. As the spell name implies, the demon so summoned is most angry and evilly disposed. The spell caster must be within a circle of *protection* (or a thaumaturgic triangle with *protection from evil*) and the demon confined within a pentagram (circled pentacle) if he or she is to avoid being slain or carried off by the summoned *cacodemon*. The summoned demon can be treated with as follows:

1) The magic-user can require the monster to perform a desired course of action by force of threat and pain of a *spiritwrack* spell (q.v.), allowing freedom whenever the demon performs the full extent of the service, and forcing the demon to pledge word upon it. This is exceedingly dangerous, as a minor error in such a bargain will be seized upon by the monster to reverse the desired outcome or simply to kill and devour the summoner. Furthermore, the demon will bear great enmity for the magic-user forever after such forced obedience, so the spell caster had better be most powerful and capable.

2) By tribute of fresh human blood and the promise of 1 or more human sacrifices, the summoner can bargain with the demon for willing service. Again, the spell caster is well advised to have ample protection and power to defend himself or herself, as the demon might decide the offer is insufficient — or it is easier to enjoy the summoner's slow death — and decide not to accept the bargain as offered. Although the demon will have to abide by a pledge, as his name is known, he will have to hold only to the exact word of the arrangement, not to the spirit of the agreement. On the other hand, only highly evil magic-users are likely to attempt to strike such a bargain, and the summoned *cacodemon* might be favorably disposed towards such a character, especially if he or she is also chaotic.

3) The summoned demon can be the object of a *trap the soul* spell (q.v.). In this case, the magic-user will not speak with or bargain for the demon's services, although the *cacodemon* might be eager to reach an accord with the dweomercraefter before he is forced into imprisonment. The trapping of the demon is risky only if proper precautions have not been taken, for failure to confine the monster usually means only that it is able to escape to its own plane. Once trapped, the demon must remain imprisoned until the possessor of his object of confinement breaks it and frees him, and this requires one service from the now loosed monster. If the individual(s) freeing the demon fails to demand a service when the monster asks what is required of him, the demon is under no constraint not to slay the liberator(s) on the spot, but if a service is required, the creature must first do his best to perform it and then return to the Abyss.

The duration of service of any demon must be limited unless the demon is willing to serve for an extended period. Any required course of action or service which effectively requires an inordinate period of time to perform, or is impossible to perform, is 50% likely to free the demon from his obligations and enable him to be unconstrained in his vengeance upon the spell caster if he or she is not thereafter continually protected, for a demon so freed can remain on the plane it was summoned to for as long as 666 days.

The demon summoned will be exceptionally strong, i.e. 8 hit points per hit die.

Casting time is 1 hour per type (numeric) of the demon to be summoned. If there is any interruption during this period, the spell fails. If there is an interruption while the *cacodemon* is summoned, it is 10% probable that it will be able to escape its boundaries and attack the magic-user, this percentage rising cumulatively each round of continued interruption.

Each demon is entitled to a saving throw versus this summoning spell. If a score higher than the level of the magic-user summoning is rolled with 3d6 (2d10 with respect to type VI demons), that particular spell failed to bring the desired demon. When this occurs, it is certain that the named demon is imprisoned or destroyed or the name used was not perfectly correct, so the spell caster will have to call upon another name to bring forth a *cacodemon*.

The components of this spell are 5 flaming black candles; a brazier of hot coals upon which must be burned sulphur, bat hairs, lard, soot, mercuric-nitric acid crystals, mandrake root, alcohol, and a piece of parchment with the demon's name inscribed in runes inside a pentacle; and a dish of blood from some mammal (preferably a human, of course) placed inside the area where the *cacodemon* is to be held.

Charm Plants (Enchantment/Charm)

Level: 7	Components: V, S, M
Range: 3″	Casting Time: 1 turn
Duration: *Permanent*	Saving Throw: *Neg.*
Area of Effect: *Special*	

Explanation/Description: The *charm plants* spell allows the spell caster to bring under command vegetable life forms, communicate with them, and these plants will obey instructions to the best of their ability. The spell will *charm plants* in a 3″ × 1″ area. While the spell does not endow the vegetation with new abilities, it does allow the magic-user to command the plants to use whatever they have in order to fulfill his or her instructions, and if the plants in the area of effect do have special or unusual abilities, these will be used as commanded by the magic-user. The saving throw applies only to intelligent plants, and it is made at -4 on the die roll. The material components of the spell are a pinch of humus, a drop of water and a twig or leaf.

Delayed Blast Fire Ball (Evocation)

Level: 7	Components: V, S, M
Range: 10″ + 1″/level	Casting Time: 7 segments
Duration: *Special*	Saving Throw: ½
Area of Effect: 2″ radius globe	

Explanation/Description: This spell creates a *fire ball* with +1 on each of its dice of damage, and it will not release its blast for from 1 to 50 segments (1/10 to 5 rounds), according to the command upon casting by the magic-user. In other respects, the spell is the same as the third level *fire ball* spell (q.v.).

Drawmij's Instant Summons (Conjuration/Summoning)

Level: 7	Components: V, S, M
Range: *Infinite + special*	Casting Time: 1 segment
Duration: *Instantaneous*	Saving Throw: *None*
Area of Effect: *One small object*	

Explanation/Description: When this spell is cast, the magic-user teleports some desired item from virtually any location directly to his or her hand. The object must be singular, can be no larger than a sword is long, have no more mass and weight than a shield (about 75 g.p. weight), and it must be non-living. To prepare this spell, the magic-user must hold a gem of not less than 5,000 g.p. value in his or her hand and utter all but the final word of the conjuration. He or she then must have this same gem available to cast the spell. All that is then required is that the magic-user utter the final word while crushing the gem, and the desired item is transported instantly into the spell caster's right or left hand as he or she desires. The item must, of course, have been previously touched during the initial incantation and specifically named, and only that particular item will be summoned by the spell. If the item is in the possession of another creature, the spell will not work, but the caster will know who the possessor is and roughly where he, she, or it is located when the *summons* is cast. Items can be summoned from other planes of existence, but only if such items are not in the possession (not necessarily physical grasp) of another creature. For each level of experience above the 14th, the magic-user is able to summon a desired item from 1 plane further removed from the plane he or she is upon at the time the spell is cast, i.e. 1 plane at 14th level, but 2 at 15th, 3 at 16th, etc. Thus, a magic-user of 16th level could effect the spell even if the item desired was on the second layer of one of the outer planes, but at 14th level the magic-user would be able to summon the item only if it were on one of the Elemental Planes or the Astral or the Ethereal Plane.

Duo-Dimension (Alteration)

Level: 7	Components: V, S, M
Range: 0	Casting Time: 7 segments
Duration: *3 rounds + 1 round/level*	Saving Throw: *None*
Area of Effect: *Personal*	

Explanation/Description: A *duo-dimension* spell causes the caster to have only two dimensions, height and width but no depth. He or she is thus invisible when a sideways turn is made, and this invisibility can only be detected by means of a *true seeing* spell or similar means. In addition, the *duo-dimensional* magic-user can pass through the thinnest of spaces as long as they have the proper height according to his or her actual length —

going through the space between a door and its frame is a simple matter. The magic-user can perform all actions on a normal basis. He or she can *turn* and become invisible, move in this state, and appear again next round and cast a spell, disappearing on the following round. Note that when *turned* the magic-user cannot be affected by any form of attack, but when visible he or she is subject to triple the amount of damage normal for an attack form, i.e. a dagger thrust would inflict 3-12 hit points of damage if it struck a *duo-dimensional* magic-user. Furthermore, the magic-user has a portion of his or her existence on the Astral Plane when the spell is in effect, and he or she is subject to possible notice from creatures thereupon. If noticed, it is 25% probable that the magic-user will be entirely brought to the Astral Plane by attack from the astral creature.

The material components of this spell are a thin, flat ivory likeness of the spell caster (which must be of finest workmanship, gold filigreed, and enameled and gem-studded at an average cost of 5,000 to 10,000 g.p.) and a strip of parchment. As the spell is uttered, the parchment is given a half twist and joined at the ends. The figurine is then passed through the parchment loop, and both disappear forever.

Limited Wish (Conjuration/Summoning)

Level: *7*	Components: *V*
Range: *Unlimited*	Casting Time: *Special*
Duration: *Special*	Saving Throw: *Special*
Area of Effect: *Special*	

Explanation/Description: A *limited wish* is a very potent but difficult spell. It will fulfill literally, but only partially or for a limited duration, the utterance of the spell caster. Thus, the actuality of the past, present or future might be altered (but possibly only for the magic-user unless the wording of the *limited wish* is most carefully stated) in some limited manner. The use of a *limited wish* will not substantially change major realities, nor will it bring wealth or experience merely by asking. The spell can, for example, restore some hit points (or all hit points for a limited duration) lost by the magic-user. It can reduce opponent hit probabilities or damage, it can increase duration of some magical effect, it can cause a creature to be favorably disposed to the spell caster, and so on (cf. *wish*). The *limited wish* can possibly give a minor clue to some treasure or magic item. Greedy desires will usually end in disaster for the wisher. Casting time is the actual number of seconds — at six per segment — to phrase the *limited wish.*

Mass Invisibility (Illusion/Phantasm)

Level: *7*	Components: *V, S, M*
Range: *1"/level*	Casting Time: *7 segments*
Duration: *Special*	Saving Throw: *None*
Area of Effect: *Special*	

Explanation/Description: This is the same as an *invisibility* spell (q.v.) except that it can hide creatures in a 3" X 3" area, up to 300 to 400 man-sized creatures, 30 to 40 giants, or 6 to 8 large dragons.

Monster Summoning V (Conjuration/Summoning)

Level: *7*	Components: *V, S, M*
Range: *7"*	Casting Time: *6 segments*
Duration: *6 rounds + 1 round/level*	Saving Throw: *None*
Area of Effect: *Special*	

Explanation/Description: This spell summons 1-2 fifth level monsters, and they will appear in 1-3 rounds. See *monster summoning I* for other details.

Mordenkainen's Sword (Evocation)

Level: *7*	Components: *V, S, M*
Range: *3"*	Casting Time: *7 segments*
Duration: *1 round/level*	Saving Throw: *None*
Area of Effect: *Special*	

Explanation/Description: Upon casting this spell, the magic-user brings into being a shimmering sword-like plane of force. The spell caster is able to mentally wield this weapon (to the exclusion of activities other than movement), causing it to move and strike as if it were being used by a fighter. The basic chance for *Mordenkainen's Sword* to hit is the same as the chance for a sword wielded by a fighter of one-half the level of the

spell caster, i.e. if cast by a 14th level magic-user, the weapon has the same hit probability as a sword wielded by a 7th level fighter. The sword has no magical "to hit" bonuses, but it can hit any sort of opponent, even those normally struck only by +3 weapons or astral, ethereal or out of phase; and it will hit *any* armor class on a roll of 19 or 20. It inflicts 5-20 hit points on opponents of man-size or smaller, and 5-30 on opponents larger than man-sized. It can be used to subdue. It lasts until the spell duration expires, a *dispel magic* is used successfully upon it, or its caster no longer desires it. The material component is a miniature platinum sword with a grip and pommel of copper and zinc which costs 500 g.p. to construct, and which disappears after the spell's completion.

Phase Door (Alteration)

Level: *7*	Components: *V*
Range: *Touch*	Casting Time: *7 segments*
Duration: *1 usage/2 levels*	Saving Throw: *None*
Area of Effect: *Special*	

Explanation/Description: When this spell is cast, the magic-user attunes his or her body, and a section of wall is affected as if by a *passwall* spell (q.v.). The *phase door* is invisible to all creatures save the spell caster, and only he or she can use the space or passage the spell creates, disappearing when the phase door is entered, and appearing when it is exited. The *phase door* lasts for 1 usage for every 2 levels of experience of the spell caster. It can be dispelled only by a casting of *dispel magic* from a higher level magic-user, or by several lower level magic-users, casting in concert, whose combined levels of experience are more than double that of the magic-user who cast the spell.

Power Word, Stun (Conjuration/Summoning)

Level: *7*	Components: *V*
Range: *½"/level*	Casting Time: *1 segment*
Duration: *Special*	Saving Throw: *None*
Area of Effect: *One creature*	

Explanation/Description: When a *power word, stun* is uttered, any creature of the magic-user's choice will be stunned — reeling and unable to think coherently or act — for 2 to 8 (2d4) melee rounds. Of course, the magic-user must be facing the creature, and it must be within the spell caster's range of ½" per level of experience. Creatures with 1 to 30 hit points will be stunned for 4-16 (4d4) rounds, those with 31 to 60 hit points will be stunned for 2 to 8 (2d4) rounds, those with 61 to 90 hit points will be stunned for 1 to 4 (d4) rounds, and creatures with over 90 hit points will not be affected. Note that if a creature is weakened due to any cause so that its hit points are below the usual maximum, the *current* number of hit points possessed will be used.

Reverse Gravity (Alteration)

Level: *7*	Components: *V, S, M*
Range: *½"/level*	Casting Time: *7 segments*
Duration: *1 segment*	Saving Throw: *None*
Area of Effect: *3" X 3" square area*	

Explanation/Description: This spell reverses gravity in the area of effect, causing all unfixed objects and creatures within it to "fall" upwards. The *reverse gravity* lasts for 1 second (1/6 segment) during which time the objects and creatures will "fall" 16' up. If some solid object is encountered in this "fall", the object strikes it in the same manner as a normal downward fall. At the end of the spell duration, the affected objects and creatures fall downwards. As the spell affects an area, objects tens, hundreds or even thousands of feet in the air can be affected. The material components of this spell are a lodestone and iron filings.

Simulacrum (Illusion/Phantasm)

Level: *7*	Components: *V, S, M*
Range: *Touch*	Casting Time: *Special*
Duration: *Permanent*	Saving Throw: *None*
Area of Effect: *One creature*	

Explanation/Description: By means of this spell the magic-user is able to create a duplicate of any creature. The duplicate appears exactly the same as the real. There are differences: the *simulacrum* will have only 51% to 60% (50% + 1% to 10%) of the hit points of the real creature, there will be personality differences, there will be areas of knowledge which the duplicate does not have, and a *detect magic* spell will instantly reveal it as a *simulacrum*, as will a *true seeing* spell. At all times the *simulacrum* remains under the absolute command of the magic-user who created it, although no special telepathic link exists, so command must be exercised in the normal manner. The spell creates the form of the creature, but it is only a zombie-like creature. A *reincarnation* spell must be used to give the duplicate a vital force, and a *limited wish* spell must be used to empower the duplicate with 40% to 65% (35% + 5% to 30%) of the knowledge and personality of the original. The level, if any, of the *simulacrum*, will be from 20% to 50% of the original creature. The duplicate creature is formed from ice or snow. The spell is cast over the rough form, and some piece of the creature to be duplicated must be placed inside the snow or ice. Additionally, the spell requires powdered ruby. The *simulacrum* has no ability to become more powerful, i.e. it cannot increase its levels or abilities.

Statue (Alteration)

Level: 7   Components: V, S, M
Range: *Touch*   Casting Time: 7 segments
Duration: 6 turns/level Saving Throw: *Special*
Area of Effect: *Creature touched*

Explanation/Description: When a *statue* dweomer is cast, the magic-user or other creature is apparently turned to solid stone, along with any garments and equipment worn or carried. The initial transformation from flesh to stone requires 1 full round after the spell is cast. Thereafter the creature can withstand any inspection and appear to be a stone statue, although a faint magic will be detected from the stone if it is checked for. Despite being in this condition, the petrified individual can see, hear, and smell normally. Feeling is only as acute as that which will actually affect the granite-hard substance of the individual's body, i.e. chipping is equal to a slight wound, but breaking off one of the statue's arms is another matter. The individual under the magic of a *statue* spell can return to normal state in 1/6 of a segment, and then return to *statue* state in the same period if he or she so desires, as long as the spell duration is in effect. During the initial transformation from flesh to stone, the creature must make a saving throw of 82% or less, with -1 deducted from the dice roll score for each point of his or her constitution score, so an 18 constitution indicates certain success. Failure indicates system shock and resultant death. The material components of this spell are lime, sand, and a drop of water stirred by an iron bar such as a nail or spike.

Vanish (Alteration)

Level: 7   Components: V
Range: *Touch*   Casting Time: 2 segments
Duration: *Special*   Saving Throw: *None*
Area of Effect: *Special*

Explanation/Description: When the magic-user employs this spell, he or she causes an object to *vanish*. The magic-user can cause the object to be teleported (see *teleport* spell) if it weighs up to a maximum of 500 g.p. per level of experience of the spell caster, i.e. a 14th level magic-user can *vanish* and cause to reappear at his or her desired location 7000 g.p. weight. Greater objects can be made to *vanish*, but they are simply placed into the ethereal plane and replaced with stone. Thus, a door can be made to disappear, and it will be replaced by a stone wall of 1' thickness, or equal in thickness to the door, whichever is greater. The maximum volume of material which can be affected is 3 cubic feet per level of experience. Thus, both weight and volume limit the spell. A *dispel magic* which is successful will bring back vanished items from the ethereal plane.

Eighth Level Spells:

Antipathy/Sympathy (Enchantment/Charm)

Level: 8   Components: V, S, M
Range: 3"   Casting Time: 6 turns
Duration: 12 turns/level Saving Throw: *Special*
Area of Effect: *Special*

Explanation/Description: This spell allows the magic-user to set up certain vibrations which will tend to either repel or attract a specific type of living, intelligent creature or characters of a particular alignment. The magic-user must decide which effect is desired with regard to what creature or alignment type before beginning the dweomercraefting, for the components of each application differ. The spell cannot be cast upon living creatures.

Antipathy: This dweomer causes the affected creature or alignment type to feel an overpowering urge to leave the area or not touch the affected item. If a saving throw versus magic is successful, the creature may stay/touch the item, but the creature will feel very uncomfortable, and a persistent itching will cause it to suffer the loss of 1 point of dexterity per round the area or item is remained in or touched, subject to a maximum of 4 points. Failure to save versus magic forces the creature/alignment type to abandon the magicked area or item, shunning it permanently and never willingly enter/touch it until the spell is removed or expires. The material component for this application of the spell is a lump of alum soaked in vinegar.

Sympathy: By casting the *sympathy* application of the spell, the magic-user can cause a particular type of creature or alignment of character to feel elated and pleased to be in an area or with the prospect of touching or possessing an object or item. The desire to stay in the area or touch/possess the magicked object/item will be overpowering, and unless a saving throw versus magic is made, the creature or character will stay or refuse to release the object. If the saving throw is successful, the creature or character is released from the enchantment, but a subsequent saving throw must be made from 1-6 turns later, and if this one fails, the affected creature will return to the area or object. The material components of this spell are 1,000 g.p. worth of crushed pearls and a drop of honey.

Note that the particular kind of creature to be affected must be named specifically, i.e. red dragons, hill giants, wererats, lammasu, catoblepas, vampires, etc. Likewise, the specific alignment type for characters must be named, i.e. chaotic evil, chaotic good, lawful neutral, neutral, etc.

If this spell is cast upon an area, a 10' per side cube can be magicked per level of experience of the magic-user. If an object or item is magicked, only that single thing can be enchanted, but affected creatures/characters save versus the magic thereon at -2.

Bigby's Clenched Fist (Evocation)

Level: 8   Components: V, S, M
Range: ½"/level   Casting Time: 8 segments
Duration: 1 round/level Saving Throw: *None*
Area of Effect: *Special*

Explanation/Description: *Bigby's Clenched Fist* spell brings forth a huge, disembodied hand which is balled into a fist. This magical member is under the mental control of the spell caster, and he or she can cause it to strike an opponent each round. No other spell casting or magical activity may be undertaken for the duration of the spell. The *Clenched Fist* never misses, but the effectiveness of its blow varies from round to round.

Die Roll	Result
1-12	glancing blow — 1 to 6 hit points
13-16	solid punch — 2 to 12 hit points
17-19	hard punch — 3 to 18 hit points and opponent is stunned next round
20	crushing blow — 4 to 24 hit points and opponent is stunned for next 3 rounds

Note: Any *stunned* opponent allows the magic-user to add +4 to his or her die roll to determine how well the *fist* strikes, as the opponent is not capable of dodging or defending against the attack effectively. (This spell can be used with any of the other *Hand* spells of the Archmage Bigby.) The material component of this spell is a leather glove and a small device consisting of four rings joined so as to form a slightly curved line, with an "I" upon which the bottoms of the rings rest, the whole fashioned of an alloyed metal of copper and zinc. The *Fist* is destroyed by damage equal to the hit points of its caster being inflicted upon it.

Clone (Necromantic)

Level: 8   Components: V, S, M
Range: *Touch*   Casting Time: 1 turn
Duration: *Permanent*   Saving Throw: *None*
Area of Effect: *Special*

Explanation/Description: This spell creates a duplicate of a person. This clone is in all respects the duplicate of the individual, complete to the level of experience, memories, etc. However, the duplicate *is* the person, so that if the original and a duplicate exist at the same time, each knows of the other's existence; and the original person and the *clone* will each desire to do away with the other, for such an alter-ego is unbearable to both. If one cannot destroy the other, one (95%) will go insane (75% likely to be the *clone)* and destroy itself, or possibly (5%) both will become mad and commit suicide. These probabilities will occur within 1 week of the dual existence. The material component of the spell is a small piece of the flesh of the person to be duplicated. Note that the *clone* will become the person as he or she existed at the time at which the flesh was taken, and all subsequent knowledge, experience, etc. will be totally unknown to the *clone.* Also, the *clone* will be a physical duplicate, and possessions of the original are another matter entirely. Note that a clone takes from 2-8 months to grow, and only after that time is dual existence established.

Glassteel (Alteration)

Level: *8*
Range: *Touch*
Duration: *Permanent*
Area of Effect: *Object touched*

Components: *V, S, M*
Casting Time: *8 segments*
Saving Throw: *None*

Explanation/Description: The *glassteel* spell turns crystal or glass into a transparent substance which has the tensile strength and unbreakability of actual steel. Only a relatively small volume of material can be affected, a maximum weight of 10 pounds per level of experience of the spell caster, and it must form one whole object. The material components of this spell are a small piece of glass and a small piece of steel.

Incendiary Cloud (Alteration-Evocation)

Level: *8*
Range: *3"*
Duration: *4 rounds + 1-6 rounds*
Area of Effect: *Special*

Components: *V, S, M*
Casting Time: *2 segments*
Saving Throw: *½*

Explanation/Description: An *incendiary cloud* spell exactly resembles the smoke effects of a *pyrotechnics* spell (q.v.), except that its minimum dimensions are a cloud of 10' height by 20' length and breadth. This dense vapor cloud billows forth, and on the 3rd round of its existence it begins to flame, causing ½ hit point per level of the magic-user who cast it. On the 4th round it does 1 hit point of damage per level of the caster, and on the 5th round it again drops to ½ h.p. of damage per level of the magic-user as its flames burn out. Any successive rounds of existence are simply harmless smoke which obscures vision within its confines. Creatures within the cloud need make only 1 saving throw if it is successful, but if they fail the first, they roll again on the 4th and 5th rounds (if necessary) to attempt to reduce damage sustained by one-half. In order to cast this spell the magic-user must have an available fire source (just as with a *pyrotechnics* spell), scrapings from beneath a dung pile, and a pinch of dust.

Mass Charm (Enchantment/Charm)

Level: *8*
Range: *½"/level*
Duration: *Special*
Area of Effect: *Special*

Components: *V*
Casting Time: *8 segments*
Saving Throw: *Neg.*

Explanation/Description: A *mass charm* spell affects either persons or monsters just as a *charm person* spell or a *charm monster* spell (qq.v.) does. The *mass charm,* however, will affect a number of creatures whose combined levels of experience and/or hit dice does not exceed twice the level of experience of the spell caster. All affected creatures must be within the spell range and within a maximum area of 3" by 3". Note that the creatures' saving throws are unaffected by the number of recipients (cf. *charm person* and *charm monster),* but all target creatures are subject to a penalty of -2 on the saving throw because of the efficiency and power of a *mass charm* spell.

Maze (Conjuration/Summoning)

Level: *8*
Range: *½"/level*
Duration: *Special*
Area of Effect: *One creature*

Components: *V,S*
Casting Time: *3 segments*
Saving Throw: *None*

Explanation/Description: An extra-dimensional space is brought into being upon utterance of a *maze* spell. The recipient will wander in the shifting labyrinth of force planes for a period of time which is totally dependent

upon its intelligence. (Note: Minotaurs are not affected by this spell.)

Intelligence of Mazed Creature	Time Trapped in Maze
under 3	2 to 8 turns
3 to 5	1 to 4 turns
6 to 8	5 to 20 rounds
9 to 11	4 to 16 rounds
12 to 14	3 to 12 rounds
15 to 17	2 to 8 rounds
18 and up	1 to 4 rounds

Mind Blank (Abjuration)

Level: *8*
Range: *3"*
Duration: *1 day*
Area of Effect: *One creature*

Components: *V,S*
Casting Time: *1 segment*
Saving Throw: *None*

Explanation/Description: When the very powerful *mind blank* spell is cast, the recipient is totally protected from all devices and/or spells which detect, influence, or read emotions and/or thoughts. Protection includes *augury, charm, command, confusion, divination, empathy* (all forms), *ESP, fear, feeblemind, mass suggestion, phantasmal killer,* possession, rulership, *soul trapping, suggestion,* and *telepathy.* Cloaking protection also extends to prevention of discovery or information gathering by *crystal balls* or other scrying devices, *clairaudience, clairvoyance, communing,* contacting other planes, or wish-related methods (*wishing, limited wish, alter reailty*). Of course, exceedingly powerful deities would be able to penetrate the spell's powers. Note that this spell also protects from psionic-related detection and/or influence such as *domination* (or *mass domination),* hypnosis, *invisibility* (the psionic sort is mind related), and *precognition,* plus those powers which are already covered as spells.

Monster Summoning VI (Conjuration/Summoning)

Level: *8*
Range: *8"*
Duration: *7 rounds + 1 round/level*
Area of Effect: *Special*

Components: *V, S, M.*
Casting Time: *8 segments*
Saving Throw: *None*

Explanation/Description: This spell summons 1 or 2 sixth level monsters, the creature(s) appearing in 1 to 3 rounds. See *monster summoning I* for other details.

Otto's Irresistible Dance (Enchantment/Charm)

Level: *8*
Range: *Touch*
Duration: *2-5 rounds*
Area of Effect: *Creature touched*

Components: *V*
Casting Time: *5 segments*
Saving Throw: *None*

Explanation/Description: When *Otto's Irresistible Dance* is placed upon a creature, the spell causes the recipient to begin dancing, feet shuffling and tapping. This dance makes it impossible for the victim to do anything other than caper and prance, this cavorting lowering the armor class of the creature by -4, making saving throws impossible, and negating any consideration of a shield. Note that the creature must be touched — possibly as if melee combat were taking place and the spell caster were striking to do damage.

Permanency (Alteration)

Level: 8
Range: *Special*
Duration: *Permanent*
Area of Effect: *Special*

Components: V,S,M
Casting Time: *2 rounds*
Saving Throw: *None*

Explanation/Description: This spell affects the duration of certain other spells, making the duration *permanent*. The spells upon which a personal permanency will be effective are:

comprehend languages	protection from evil
detect evil	protection from normal missiles
detect invisibility	read magic
detect magic	tongues
infravision	unseen servant

The magic-user casts the desired spell and then follows with the *permanency* spell. Each *permanency* spell lowers the magic-user's constitution by 1 point. The magic-user cannot cast these spells upon other creatures. In addition to personal use, the *permanency* spell can be used to make the following object/creature or area effect spells lasting:

enlarge	prismatic sphere
fear	stinking cloud
gust of wind	wall of fire
invisibility	wall of force
magic mouth	web

The former application of *permanency* can be dispelled only by a magic-user of greater level than the spell caster was when he or she initially cast it. The *permanency* application to other spells allows it to be cast simultaneously with any of the latter when no living creature is the target, but the *permanency* can be dispelled normally, and thus the entire spell negated.

Polymorph Any Object (Alteration)

Level: 8
Range: *½"/level*
Duration: *Variable*
Area of Effect: *Special*

Components: V,S,M
Casting Time: *1 round*
Saving Throw: *Special*

Explanation/Description: This spell changes one object (living or otherwise) into another. When used as a *polymorph other* or *stone to flesh*, simply treat the spell as a more powerful version, with saving throws made at -4 on the die. When it is cast in order to change other objects, the duration of the spell will depend on how radically removed the original was from its magicked state, as well as how different in size. This will be determined by your Dungeon Master by comparing:

kingdom — animal, vegetable, mineral
class — mammals, bipeds, fungi, metals, spheres, etc.
relationship — twig is to tree, sand is to beach, etc.
size — smaller, equal, larger
shape — comparative resemblance of the original to the polymorphed state
intelligence — particularly with regard to a change in which the end product is more intelligent

Change in *kingdom* makes the spell work for hours or turns, i.e. hours if one removed, turns if two removed. Other changes likewise affect spell duration. Thus, changing a lion to an androsphinx would be permanent, but turning a turnip to a purple worm would be a change of only hours duration; turning a tusk into an elephant would be permanent, but turning a twig into a sword would be only a change of several turns duration. All *polymorphed* objects radiate a strong magic, and if a *dispel magic* spell is used upon them, they will return to their natural form. Note that a *stone to flesh*, or its reverse, will affect objects under this spell. The material components of this spell are mercury, gum arabic, and smoke. N.B.: *System shock* applies to living creatures, as do the restrictions noted regarding *polymorph others* and *stone to flesh* (qq.v.).

Power Word, Blind (Conjuration/Summoning)

Level: 8
Range: *½"/level*
Duration: *Special*
Area of Effect: *3" diameter*

Components: V
Casting Time: *1 segment*
Saving Throw: *None*

Explanation/Description: When a *power word, blind* is cast, one or more creatures within spell range and area of effect will become temporarily sightless. The spell affects up to 100 hit points of creatures, but the duration is dependent upon how many hit points of creatures are affected. If 50 or less points are affected, blindness lasts for 2 to 5 (d4+1) turns, if 51 or more hit points of creatures are affected, the spell duration is but 2 to 5 rounds. Note that the spell caster must indicate which creatures he or she desires to affect with the spell, noting one as target center, prior to determining results. Creatures with over 100 hit points are not affected. Blindness can be removed by *cure blindness* or *dispel magic*.

Serten's Spell Immunity (Abjuration)

Level: 8
Range: *Touch*
Duration: *1 turn/level*
Area of Effect: *Creature(s) touched*

Components: V,S,M
Casting Time: *1 round/recipient*
Saving Throw: *None*

Explanation/Description: By use of this spell the magic-user is able to confer virtual immunity to certain spells and magical attack forms upon those he or she touches and magicks. For every 4 levels of experience of the magic-user, 1 creature can be protected by the *Serten's Spell Immunity* spell, but the duration of the protection is similarly disbursed upon these additional figures. (Example: A 16th level magic-user can cast the dweomer upon 1 creature and it will last 16 turns, or he or she can place it upon 2 creatures for an 8 turn duration, or upon 4 creatures for but 4 turns duration.) The protection gives a bonus to saving throws as follows:

Beguiling, Charm, Suggestion	+9
Command, Domination, Fear, Hold, Scare	+7
Geas, Quest	+5

The material component of this spell is a diamond which must be crushed and sprinkled over the spell recipients, and each such creature must also have in its possession a diamond of any size, intact and carried on its person.

Symbol (Conjuration/Summoning)

Level: 8
Range: *Touch*
Duration: *Special*
Area of Effect: *Special*

Components: V,S,M
Casting Time: *8 segments*
Saving Throw: *Special*

Explanation/Description: A *symbol* spell causes the creation of magical runes which affect creatures which pass over, touch, read, or pass through a portal upon which the *symbol* is inscribed. Upon casting the spell, the magic-user inscribes the *symbol* upon whatever surface he or she desires. Likewise, the spell caster is able to place the *symbol* of his or her choice, using any one of the following:

Death —	One or more creatures whose total hit points do not exceed 80 are slain.
Discord —	All creatures are affected and immediately fall to loudly bickering and arguing; furthermore, there is a 50% probability that creatures of different alignment will attack each other. The bickering lasts for 5-20 rounds; the fighting for 2-8 rounds.
Fear —	This *symbol* operates as an extra-strong *fear* spell, causing all creatures to save vs. the spell at -4 on the die or panic and flee as if affected by a *fear* spell (q.v.).
Hopelessness —	All creatures are affected and must turn back in dejection unless they save versus magic. Affected creatures will submit to the demands of any opponent, i.e. surrender, get out, etc.; the *hopelessness* lasts for 3 to 12 (3d4) turns, and during this period it is 25% probable that affected creatures will take no action during any round, and 25% likely that those taking action will turn back or retire from battle, as applicable.

Insanity —	One or more creatures whose total hit points do not exceed 120 will become insane and remain so, acting as if a *confusion* spell (q.v.) had been placed upon them until a *heal, restoration,* or *wish* spell is used to remove the madness.
Pain —	All creatures are affected, having wracking pains shooting through their bodies, which causes them to have -2 on dexterity and -4 on attack dice for from 2-20 turns.
Sleep —	All creatures under 8+1 hit dice will immediately fall into a catatonic slumber and cannot be awakened for 5 to 16 (d12 + 4) turns.
Stunning —	One or more creatures whose total hit points do not exceed 160 will be *stunned* and reeling for 3-12 (3d4) rounds, dropping anything it or they hold in manipulative members.

The type of symbol cannot be recognized without it being read and thus activating its effects. The material components of this spell are powdered black opal and diamond dust worth not less than 5000 g.p. each.

Trap The Soul (Conjuration/Summoning)

Level: 8	Components: V,S,M
Range: 1″	Casting Time: *Special + 1 segment*
Duration: *Permanent until broken*	Saving Throw: *Neg.*
Area of Effect: *One creature*	

Explanation/Description: This spell is similar to the *magic jar*, except that the *trap the soul* spell forces the subject creature's life force (and its material body, if any) into a special prison magicked by the spell caster. The subject of the spell must be seen by the caster, and the magic-user must know the subject's true name as well when the final word is uttered. Preparatory to the actual casting of the *trap the soul*, the magic-user must prepare the soul prison, a gem of 1,000 g.p. value for every hit die or level of experience the creature whose soul is to be trapped possesses, i.e. it requires a gem of 10,000 g.p. value to trap a 10 hit dice (or 10th level) creature by placing an *enchant an item* spell upon it and then placing a *maze* spell into the gem, thereby forming the prison for the soul to be trapped. There are 2 manners in which the soul of the victim can be imprisoned. The final word of the spell can be spoken when the creature is within spell range, but this entitles it to exercise its magic resistance (if any) and a saving throw versus magic as well, and if the latter is successful, the gem shatters. The second method of soul trapping is far more insidious, for it tricks the victim into accepting a trigger object inscribed with the final spell word which will automatically place the creature's soul into the trap. If this method is used, it will be necessary to name the triggering item when the prison gem is magicked. A *sympathy* spell may be placed on the trigger item. As soon as the subject creature picks up or accepts the trigger item, its soul is automatically transferred to the gem. The gem prison will hold the soul trapped until time indefinite, or until it is broken and the soul is released, allowing the material body to reform. If the creature trapped is a powerful creature from another plane (and this could actually mean a character trapped by some inhabitant of another plane of existence when the character is not on the Prime Material Plane), it can be required to perform a service immediately upon being freed. Otherwise, the creature can go totally free once the gem imprisoning it is broken.

Ninth Level Spells:

Astral Spell (Evocation)

Level: 9	Components: V,S
Range: *Touch*	Casting Time: 9 segments
Duration: *Special*	Saving Throw: *None*
Area of Effect: *Special*	

Explanation/Description: Except as noted above, this spell is the same as the seventh level cleric spell, *astral spell* (q.v.).

Bigby's Crushing Hand (Evocation)

Level: 9	Components: V,S,M
Range: ½″/level	Casting Time: 9 segments

Duration: *1 round/level*	Saving Throw: *None*
Area of Effect: *Special*	

Explanation/Description: *Bigby's Crushing Hand* causes the appearance of a huge disembodied hand which is similar to *Bigby's Forceful Hand* and *Bigby's Clenched Fist* (qq.v.). The *Crushing Hand* is under the mental control of the spell caster, and he or she can cause it to grasp and squeeze an opponent. Damage from this constriction depends on the number of rounds it acts upon the victim:

1st round	1-10 hit points
2nd & 3rd rounds	2-20 hit points
4th & beyond	4-40 hit points

The *Hand* can sustain hit points equal to those of the magic-user who created it before being dispelled. The material components of the spell are a glove of snake skin and the shell of an egg.

Gate (Conjuration/Summoning)

Level: 9	Components: V,S
Range: 3″	Casting Time: 9 segments
Duration: *Special*	Saving Throw: *None*
Area of Effect: *Special*	

Explanation/Description: Except as noted above, this spell is the same as the seventh level cleric spell, *gate* (q.v.).

Imprisonment (Abjuration) Reversible

Level: 9	Components: V,S
Range: *Touch*	Casting Time: 9 segments
Duration: *Permanent*	Saving Throw: *None*
Area of Effect: *1 creature*	

Explanation/Description: When an *imprisonment* spell is cast and the victim is touched, the recipient is entombed in a state of suspended animation (cf. *temporal stasis*) in a small sphere far below the surface of the earth. The victim remains there unless a reverse of the spell, with the creature's name and background, is cast. Magical search by *crystal ball*, a *locate objects* spell or similar means will not reveal the fact that a creature is *imprisoned*. The reverse *(freedom)* spell will cause the appearance of the victim at the spot he, she or it was entombed and sunk into the earth. There is a 10% chance that 1 to 100 other creatures will be freed from imprisonment at the same time if the magic-user does not perfectly get the name and background of the creature to be freed. The spell only works if the name and background of the victim are known.

Meteor Swarm (Evocation)

Level: 9	Components: V,S
Range: 4″ + 1″/level	Casting Time: 9 segments
Duration: *Instantaneous*	Saving Throw: ½
Area of Effect: *Special*	

Explanation/Description: A *meteor swarm* is a very powerful and spectacular spell which is similar to a *fireball* in many aspects. When it is cast, either four spheres of 2′ diameter or eight spheres of 1′ diameter spring from the outstretched hand of the magic-user and streak in a straight line up to the distance demanded by the spell caster, up to the maximum range. Any creature in the straight line path of these missiles will receive the full effect of the missile, or missiles, without benefit of a saving throw. The "meteor" missiles leave a fiery trail of sparks, and each bursts as a *fireball* (q.v.). The large spheres each do 10 to 40 hit points of damage, the four bursting in a diamond or box pattern. Each has a 3″ diameter area of effect, and each sphere will be 2″ apart, along the sides of the pattern, so that there are overlapping areas of effect, and the center will be exposed to all four blasts. The eight small spheres have one-half the diameter (1½'') and one-half the damage potential (5-20). They burst in a pattern of a box within a diamond or vice versa, each of the outer sides 2'' long, and the inner sides being 1'' long. Note that the center will have 4 areas of overlapping effect, and there are numerous peripheral areas which have two overlapping areas of effect. A saving throw for each area of effect will indicate whether full hit points of damage, or half the indicated amount of damage, will be sustained by creatures within each area, except as already stated with regard to the missiles impacting.

Monster Summoning VII (Conjuration/Summoning)

Level: 9	Components: V,S,M
Range: 9''	Casting Time: 9 segments
Duration: 8 rounds + 1 round/level	Saving Throw: None
Area of Effect: Special	

Explanation/Description: This spell summons 1 or 2 seventh level monsters which appear 1 round after the spell is cast, or 1 8th level monster which will appear 2 rounds after the spell is cast. See *monster summoning I* for other details.

Power Word, Kill (Conjuration/Summoning)

Level: 9	Components: V
Range: ¼''/level	Casting Time: 1 segment
Duration: Permanent	Saving Throw: None
Area of Effect: 2'' diameter	

Explanation/Description: When a *power word, kill* is uttered, one or more creatures within the spell range and area of effect will be slain. The *power word* will destroy a creature with up to 60 hit points, or it will kill 2 or more creatures with 10 or fewer hit points, up to a maximum of 120 hit points. The option to attack a single creature, or multiple creatures, must be stated along with the spell range and area of effect center.

Prismatic Sphere (Abjuration, Conjuration/Summoning)

Level: 9	Components: V
Range: 0	Casting Time: 7 segments
Duration: 1 turn/level	Saving Throw: Special
Area of Effect: 2'' diameter sphere	

Explanation/Description: This spell enables the magic-user to conjure up an opaque globe of shimmering, multi-colored spheres of light to surround him or her which give protection from all forms of attack. This scintillating sphere flashes all the seven colors of the visible spectrum, and each of these spheres of color has a different power and purpose. Any creature with fewer than eight hit dice will be blinded for from 2 to 8 turns by the colors of the sphere. This phenomenon is immobile and only the spell caster can pass in and out the *prismatic sphere* without harm. Note that typically the upper hemisphere of the globe will be visible, as the spell caster is at the center of the sphere, so the lower half is usually hidden by the floor surface he or she is standing upon. The colors and effects of the *prismatic sphere*, as well as what will negate each globe, are:

Color of Globe	Order of Globe	Effects of Globe	Spell Negated By
red	1st	prevents all non-magical missiles — inflicts 10 hit points of damage	cone of cold
orange	2nd	prevents all magical missiles — inflicts 20 hit points of damage	gust of wind
yellow	3rd	prevents poisons, gasses, and petrification — inflicts 40 hit points of damage	disintegrate
green	4th	prevents all breath weapons — save vs. poison or dead	passwall
blue	5th	prevents location/detection and psionics — save vs. petrification or turned to stone	magic missile
indigo	6th	prevents all magical spells — save vs. wand or insane	continual light
violet	7th	force field protection — save vs. magic or sent to another plane	dispel magic

Note that a *rod of cancellation* will destroy a *prismatic sphere*. Otherwise, anything entering the sphere will be destroyed, any creature subject to the effects of each and every globe as indicated, i.e. 70 hit points of damage plus death, petrification, insanity and/or instantaneous transportation to another plane, and only the four latter effects are subject to saving throws. The individual globes may be destroyed by appropriate magical attacks in consecutive order, the 1st globe destroyed before any others, then the 2nd, etc.

Shape Change (Alteration)

Level: 9	Components: V,S,M
Range: 0	Casting Time: 9 segments
Duration: 1 turn/level	Saving Throw: None
Area of Effect: The spell caster	

Explanation/Description: With this spell, the magic-user is able to assume the form of any creature short of a demi-god, greater devil, demon prince, singular dragon type, greater demon or the like. The spell caster becomes the creature he or she wishes, and has all of the abilities save those dependent upon intelligence, for the mind of the creature is that of the spell caster. Thus, he or she can change into a griffon, thence to an efreet, and then to a titan, etc. These creatures have whatever hit points the magic-user has at the time of the *shape change*. Each alteration in form requires 1 segment. No system shock is incurred. Example: A wizard is in combat and assumes the form of a will o' wisp, and when this form is no longer useful, the wizard changes into a stone golem and walks away. When pursued, the golem-shape is changed to that of a flea, which hides upon a horse until it can hop off and become a bush. If detected as the latter, the magic-user can become a dragon, pool of water, or just about anything else. The material component of the spell is a jade circlet worth no less than 5000 g.p. which will shatter at the expiration of the magic's duration. In the meantime, it is left in the wake of the *shape change*, and premature shattering will cause the magic to be dispelled.

Temporal Stasis (Alteration) Reversible

Level: 9	Components: V,S,M
Range: 1''	Casting Time: 9 segments
Duration: Permanent	Saving Throw: None
Area of Effect: One creature	

Explanation/Description: Upon casting this spell, the magic-user places the recipient creature into a state of suspended animation. This cessation of time means that the creature does not grow older. Its body functions virtually cease. This state persists until the magic is removed by a *dispel magic* spell or the reverse of the spell (*temporal reinstatement*) is uttered. Note that the reverse requires only a single word and no somatic or material components. The material component of a *temporal stasis* spell is a powder composed of diamond, emerald, ruby, and sapphire dust, one stone of each type being required.

Time Stop (Alteration)

Level: 9	Components: V
Range: 0	Casting Time: 9 segments
Duration: ½ segment/level + 1-8 segments	Saving Throw: None
Area of Effect: 3'' diameter sphere	

Explanation/Description: Upon casting a *time stop* spell, the magic-user causes the flow of time to stop in the area of effect, and outside this area the sphere simply seems to shimmer for an instant. During the period of spell duration, the magic-user can move and act freely within the area where time is stopped, but all other creatures there are frozen in their actions, for they are literally between ticks of the time clock, and the spell duration is subjective to the caster. No creature can enter the area of effect without being stopped in time also, and if the magic-user leaves it, he or she immediately negates the spell. When spell duration ceases, the magic-user will again be operating in normal time.

Wish (Conjuration/Summoning)

Level: 9
Range: *Unlimited*
Duration: *Special*
Area of Effect: *Special*

Components: V
Casting Time: *Special*
Saving Throw: *Special*

Explanation/Description: The *wish* spell is a more potent version of a *limited wish* (q.v.). If it is used to alter reality with respect to hit points sustained by a party, to bring a dead character to life, or to escape from a difficult situation by lifting the spell caster (and his or her party) from one place to another, it will not cause the magic-user any disability. Other forms of *wishes*, however, will cause the spell caster to be weak (-3 on strength) and require 2 to 8 days of bed rest due to the stresses the *wish* places upon time, space, and his or her body. Regardless of what is wished for, the exact terminology of the *wish* spell is likely to be carried through. (This discretionary power of the referee is necessary in order to maintain game balance. As wishing another character dead would be grossly unfair, for example, your DM might well advance the spell caster to a future period where the object is no longer alive, i.e. putting the wishing character out of the campaign.)

ILLUSIONIST SPELLS

Notes Regarding Illusionist (Magic-User) Spells:

There are fewer illusionist spells than there are magic-user spells, and there is some duplication; at seventh level the list includes all first level magic-user spells, several of which are taken as if they were but one spell of seventh level. The illusions of this class grow progressively more powerful as levels increase; the phantasms take on some actual substance, and even other sorts of spells used by illusionists are potent (cf. *phantasmal killer, shades, prismatic spray*).

There are some illusionist spells which have no verbal (V) component. Also, these spells typically need fewer material components than do those of other classes. A notable exception is the *vision* spell which needs great material outlay.

First Level Spells:

Audible Glamer (Illusion/Phantasm)

Level: 1
Range: 6" + 1"/level
Duration: 3 rounds/level
Area of Effect: *Hearing range*

Components: V,S
Casting Time: 5 segments
Saving Throw: *Special*

Explanation/Description: Except as noted above, this spell is the same as the second level magic-user spell, *audible glamer* (q.v.).

Change Self (Illusion/Phantasm)

Level: 1
Range: 0
Duration: 2-12 rounds + 2
  rounds/level
Area of Effect: *The illusionist*

Components: V,S
Casting Time: 1 segment
Saving Throw: None

Explanation/Description: This spell enables the illusionist to alter the appearance of his or her form — including clothing and equipment — to appear 1' shorter or taller; thin, fat, or in between; human, humanoid, or any other generally man-shaped bipedal creature. The duration of the spell is 2 to 12 (2d6) rounds base plus 2 additional rounds per level of experience of the spell caster.

Color Spray (Alteration)

Level: 1
Range: 1"/level
Duration: 1 segment
Area of Effect: ½" × 2" × 2"
  wedge

Components: V,S,M
Casting Time: 1 segment
Saving Throw: *Special*

Explanation/Description: Upon casting this spell, the illusionist causes a vivid fan-shaped spray of clashing colors to spring forth from his or her hand. From 1 to 6 creatures within the area of effect can be affected. The spell caster is able to affect 1 level or hit die of creatures for each of his or her levels of experience. Affected creatures are struck unconscious for 2 to 8 rounds if their level is less than or equal to that of the spell caster; they are blinded for 1 to 4 rounds if their level or number of hit dice is 1 or 2 greater than the illusionist; and they are stunned (cf. *power word, stun,* seventh level magic-user spell) for 2 to 8 segments if their level or number of hit dice is 3 or more greater than the spell caster. All creatures above the level of the spell caster and all creatures of 6th level or 6 hit dice are entitled to a saving throw versus the *color spray* spell. The material components of this spell are a pinch each of powder or sand colored red, yellow and blue.

Dancing Lights (Alteration)

Level: 1
Range: 4" + 1"/level
Duration: 2 rounds/level
Area of Effect: *Special*

Components: V,S,M
Casting Time: 1 segment
Saving Throw: None

Explanation/Description: This spell is the same as the first level magic-user spell, *dancing lights* (q.v.).

Darkness (Alteration)

Level: 1
Range: 1"/level
Duration: 2-8 rounds + 1
  round/level
Area of Effect: *15' radius globe*

Components: V,S
Casting Time: 1 segment
Saving Throw: None

Explanation/Description: Except as noted above, this spell is the same as the second level magic-user spell of *darkness* (q.v.).

Detect Illusion (Divination)

Level: 1
Range: *Touch*
Duration: 3 rounds + 2 rounds/
  level
Area of Effect: *Line of sight 1" wide,
  1"/level long*

Components: V,S,M
Casting Time: 1 segment
Saving Throw: None

Explanation/Description: By means of this spell the illusionist is able to see an illusion and know it for exactly that. Note that it can be used to enable others to see illusions as unreal if the spell caster touches the creature with both hands and the creature looks at the illusion while so touched. The material component is a piece of yellow tinted crystal, glass, or mica.

Detect Invisibility (Divination)

Level: 1
Range: 1"/level
Duration: 5 rounds/level
Area of Effect: *1" path*

Components: V,S,M
Casting Time: 1 segment
Saving Throw: None

Explanation/Description: Except as noted above, this spell is the same as the second level magic-user spell, *detect invisibility* (q.v.).

Gaze Reflection (Alteration)

Level: 1
Range: 0
Duration: 1 round
Area of Effect: *Special*

Components: V,S
Casting Time: 1 segment
Saving Throw: None

Explanation/Description: The *gaze reflection* spell creates a mirror-like area of air before the illusionist. Any gaze attack, such as that of a basilisk or a medusa, will be reflected back upon the gazer if it looks upon the spell caster.

Hypnotism (Enchantment/Charm)

Level: *1*	Components: *V,S*
Range: *3''*	Casting Time: *1 segment*
Duration: *1 round + 1 round/level*	Saving Throw: *Neg.*
Area of Effect: *One to six creatures*	

Explanation/Description: The gestures of the illusionist, along with his or her droning incantation, cause from 1 to 6 creatures to become susceptible to *suggestion* (see the third level magic-user *suggestion* spell). The *suggestion* must be given after the *hypnotism* spell is cast, and until that time the success of the spell is unknown. Note that the subsequent *suggestion* is not a spell, but simply a vocalized urging. Creatures which make their saving throw are not under hypnotic influence.

Light (Alteration)

Level: *1*	Components: *V,S,*
Range: *6''*	Casting Time: *1 segment*
Duration: *1 turn/level*	Saving Throw: *None*
Area of Effect: *2'' radius globe*	

Explanation/Description: This spell is the same as the first level magic-user *light* spell (q.v.) (cf. first level cleric *light* spell.)

Phantasmal Force (Illusion/Phantasm)

Level: *1*	Components: *V,S,M*
Range: *6'' + 1''/level*	Casting Time: *1 segment*
Duration: *Special*	Saving Throw: *Special*
Area of Effect: *4 square'' + 1'' square/level*	

Explanation/Description: Except as noted above, this spell is the same as the third level magic-user spell, *phantasmal force* (q.v.).

Wall Of Fog (Alteration)

Level: *1*	Components: *V,S,M*
Range: *3''*	Casting Time: *1 segment*
Duration: *2-8 rounds + 1 round/level*	Saving Throw: *None*
Area of Effect: *Special*	

Explanation/Description: By casting this spell, the illusionist creates a wall of misty vapors in whatever area within the spell range he or she desires. The *wall of fog* obscures all sight, normal and/or infravisual, beyond 2'. The area of effect is a cube of 2'' per side per level of experience of the spell caster. The misty vapors persist for 3 or more rounds unless blown away by a strong breeze (cf. *gust of wind*). The material component is a pinch of split dried peas.

Second Level Spells:

Blindness (Illusion/Phantasm)

Level: *2*	Components: *V*
Range: *3''*	Casting Time: *2 segments*
Duration: *Special*	Saving Throw: *Neg.*
Area of Effect: *One creature*	

Explanation/Description: The *blindness* spell causes the recipient creature to become blind and able to see only a grayness before its eyes. Various *cure* spells will not remove this effect, and only a *dispel magic* or the spell caster can do away with the blindness if the creature fails its initial saving throw versus the spell.

Blur (Illusion/Phantasm)

Level: *2*	Components: *V,S*
Range: *0*	Casting Time: *2 segments*
Duration: *3 rounds + 1 round/level*	Saving Throw: *None*
Area of Effect: *The illusionist*	

Explanation/Description: When a *blur* spell is cast, the illusionist causes

the outline of his or her form to become blurred, shifting and wavery. This distortion causes all missile and melee combat attacks to be made at -4 on the first attempt and -2 on all successive attacks. It also allows a +1 on the saving throw die roll for any direct magical attack.

Deafness (Illusion/Phantasm)

Level: *2*	Components: *V,S,M*
Range: *6''*	Casting Time: *2 segments*
Duration: *Special*	Saving Throw: *Neg.*
Area of Effect: *One creature*	

Explanation/Description: The *deafness* spell causes the recipient creature to become totally deaf and unable to hear any sounds (cf. *blindness*). This *deafness* can be done away with only by means of a *dispel magic* or by the spell caster. The victim is allowed a saving throw. The material component of the spell is beeswax.

Detect Magic (Divination)

Level: *2*	Components: *V,S*
Range: *0*	Casting Time: *2 segments*
Duration: *2 rounds/level*	Saving Throw: *None*
Area of Effect: *1'' path, 6'' long*	

Explanation/Description: This spell is similar to the first level cleric and the first level magic-user spell, *detect magic* (qq.v.).

Fog Cloud (Alteration)

Level: *2*	Components: *V,S*
Range: *1''*	Casting Time: *2 segments*
Duration: *4 rounds + 1 round/level*	Saving Throw: *None*
Area of Effect: *4'' wide, 2'' high, 2'' deep cloud*	

Explanation/Description: The *fog cloud* is a billowing mass of misty vapors which is of similar appearance to a *cloudkill* (q.v.), the fog being greenish. The spell caster creates the *fog cloud* and it moves away from him or her at a 1'' per round rate. Although it behaves in most respects just as if it were a *cloudkill*, the only effect of the fog is to obscure vision, just as a *wall of fog* does.

Hypnotic Pattern (Illusion/Phantasm)

Level: *2*	Components: *S,M*
Range: *0*	Casting Time: *2 segments*
Duration: *Special*	Saving Throw: *Neg.*
Area of Effect: *3'' × 3'' square area*	

Explanation/Description: When this spell is cast the illusionist creates a weaving, turning pattern of subtle colors in the air. This *hypnotic pattern* will cause any creature looking at it to become fascinated and stand gazing at it as long as the spell caster continues to maintain the shifting interplay of glowing lines. Note that the spell can captivate a maximum of 24 levels, or hit dice, of creatures, i.e. 24 creatures with 1 hit die each, 12 with 2 hit dice, etc. All creatures affected must be within the area of effect, and each is entitled to a saving throw. The illusionist need not utter a sound, but he or she must gesture appropriately while holding a glowing stick of incense or a crystal rod filled with phosphorescent material.

Improved Phantasmal Force (Illusion/Phantasm)

Level: *2*	Components: *V,S,M*
Range: *6'' + 1''/level*	Casting Time: *2 segments*
Duration: *Special*	Saving Throw: *Special*
Area of Effect: *4 square'' + 1'' square/level*	

Explanation/Description: Except as noted above, and as detailed hereafter, this spell is the same as the third level magic-user *phantasmal force* spell (q.v.). The spell caster can maintain the illusion with minimal concentration, i.e. he or she can move at half normal speed (but not cast other spells). Some minor sounds are included in the effects of the spell, but not understandable speech. Also, by concentration on the form of the phantasm, the *improved phantasmal force* will continue for 2 rounds after the illusionist ceases to concentrate upon the spell.

Invisibility (Illusion/Phantasm)

Level: 2
Range: *Touch*
Duration: *Special*
Area of Effect: *Creature touched*

Components: *V,S*
Casting Time: *2 segments*
Saving Throw: *None*

Explanation/Description: Except as noted above, this spell is the same as the second level magic-user spell, *invisibility* (q.v.).

Magic Mouth (Alteration)

Level: 2
Range: *Special*
Duration: *Special*
Area of Effect: *One object*

Components: *V,S,M*
Casting Time: *2 segments*
Saving Throw: *None*

Explanation/Description: This spell is the same as the second level magic-user *magic mouth* spell (q.v.).

Mirror Image (Illusion/Phantasm)

Level: 2
Range: *0*
Duration: *3 rounds/level*
Area of Effect: *6' radius of spell caster*

Components: *V,S*
Casting Time: *2 segments*
Saving Throw: *None*

Explanation/Description: Except as noted above, and except for the fact that there are 2-5 (d4 +1) *mirror images* created, this spell is the same as the second level magic-user spell, *mirror image* (q.v.).

Misdirection (Illusion/Phantasm)

Level: 2
Range: *3''*
Duration: *1 round/level*
Area of Effect: *Special*

Components: *V,S*
Casting Time: *2 segments*
Saving Throw: *Neg.*

Explanation/Description: By means of this spell the illusionist *misdirects* the information from a detection-type spell, i.e. *detect charm, detect evil, detect invisibility, detect lie, detect magic,* and *detect snares & pits.* While the detection spell functions, the information it reveals will indicate the wrong area, creature, or the opposite of the truth with respect to *detect evil* or *detect lie.* The illusionist directs the spell effect upon the creature or item which is the object of the detection spell. If the caster of the detection-type spell fails his or her saving throw, the *misdirection* takes place.

Ventriloquism (Illusion/Phantasm)

Level: 2
Range: *1''/level, Maximum 9''*
Duration: *4 rounds + 1 round/level*
Area of Effect: *One object*

Components: *V,M*
Casting Time: *2 segments*
Saving Throw: *None*

Explanation/Description: Except as noted above, this spell is the same as the first level magic-user spell, *ventriloquism* (q.v.).

Third Level Spells:

Continual Darkness (Alteration)

Level: 3
Range: *6''*
Duration: *Permanent*
Area of Effect: *3'' radius globe*

Components: *V,M*
Casting Time: *3 segments*
Saving Throw: *None*

Explanation/Description: When this spell is cast, a globe of impenetrable darkness is created. The effects of this darkness, as well as the material component of the spell, are the same as the second level magic-user spell, *darkness, 15' radius* (cf. *continual light*).

Continual Light (Alteration)

Level: 3
Range: *6''*
Duration: *Permanent*
Area of Effect: *6'' radius globe*

Components: *V,S*
Casting Time: *3 segments*
Saving Throw: *None*

Explanation/Description: This spell is the same as the second level cleric *continual light* spell (q.v.), except as noted above.

Dispel Illusion (Abjuration)

Level: 3
Range: *1''/level*
Duration: *Permanent*
Area of Effect: *Special*

Components: *V,S*
Casting Time: *3 segments*
Saving Throw: *None*

Explanation/Description: By means of this spell, the spell caster can dispel any *phantasmal force* — with or without *audible glamer* — cast by a non-illusionist; and the spell has the same chance of dispelling any illusion/phantasm spells of another illusionist as a *dispel magic* spell (q.v.) does, i.e. 50% base chance adjusted by 2% downward, or 5% upward, for each level of experience lesser/greater of the illusionist casting the *dispel illusion* compared to the illusionist casting the spell to be dispelled.

Fear (Illusion/Phantasm)

Level: 3
Range: *0*
Duration: *Special*
Area of Effect: *6'' long cone, 3''*
   diameter at end, ½'' at base

Components: *V,S*
Casting Time: *3 segments*
Saving Throw: *Neg.*

Explanation/Description: Except as noted above, this spell is the same as the fourth level magic-user spell, *fear* (q.v.).

Hallucinatory Terrain (Illusion/Phantasm)

Level: 3
Range: *2'' + 2''/level*
Duration: *Special*
Area of Effect: *4'' × 4'' square area*
   + 1'' × 1'' square area/level

Components: *V,S,M*
Casting Time: *5 rounds*
Saving Throw: *None*

Explanation/Description: Except as noted above, this spell is the same as the fourth level magic-user *hallucinatory terrain* spell (q.v.).

Illusionary Script (Illusion/Phantasm)

Level: 3
Range: *Special*
Duration: *Permanent*
Area of Effect: *Creature reading the script*

Components: *V,S,M*
Casting Time: *Special*
Saving Throw: *None*

Explanation/Description: This spell enables the illusionist to write instructions or other information on parchment, paper, skin, etc. The *illusionary script* appears to be some form of foreign or magical writing. Only the person (or class of persons or whatever) whom the illusionist desires to read the writing will be able to do so, although another illusionist will recognize it for *illusionary script.* Others attempting to read it will become confused as from a *confusion* spell (q.v.) for 5 to 20 turns, minus 1 turn for each level of experience he or she has attained. The material component of the spell is a lead-based ink which requires special manufacture by an alchemist.

Invisibility, 10' Radius (Illusion/Phantasm)

Level: 3
Range: *Touch*
Duration: *Special*
Area of Effect: *10' radius of creature touched*

Components: *V,S*
Casting Time: *3 segments*
Saving Throw: *None*

Explanation/Description: Except as noted above, this spell is the same as the third level magic-user spell, *invisibility, 10' radius* (q.v.). See also the second level magic-user spell, *invisibility.*

Non-detection (Abjuration)

Level: 3
Range: *0*
Duration: *1 turn/level*
Area of Effect: *5' radius of spell caster*

Components: *V,S,M*
Casting Time: *3 segments*
Saving Throw: *None*

Explanation/Description: By casting this spell, the illusionist makes himself or herself invisible to divination spells such as *clairaudience, clairvoyance, "detects",* and *ESP*. It also prevents location by such magic items as *crystal balls* and *ESP medallions*. The material component of the spell is a pinch of diamond dust.

Paralyzation (Illusion/Phantasm)

Level: *3*
Range: *1''/level*
Duration: *Special*
Area of Effect: *2'' × 2'' area*

Components: *V,S*
Casting Time: *3 segments*
Saving Throw: *Neg.*

Explanation/Description: The *paralyzation* spell enables the spell caster to create illusionary muscle slowdown in creatures whose combined hit dice do not exceed twice the total level of experience of the illusionist. If the recipient creatures fail their saving throws, they become paralyzed, and a *dispel illusion* or *dispel magic* spell must be used to remove the effect, or the illusionist may dispel it at any time he or she desires.

Rope Trick (Alteration)

Level: *3*
Range: *Touch*
Duration: *2 turns/level*
Area of Effect: *Special*

Components: *V,S,M*
Casting Time: *3 segments*
Saving Throw: *None*

Explanation/Description: This spell is the same as the second level magic-user spell, *rope trick* (q.v.).

Spectral Force (Illusion/Phantasm)

Level: *3*
Range: *6'' + 1''/level*
Duration: *Special*
Area of Effect: *4 square'' + 1 square/level*

Components: *V,S,M*
Casting Time: *3 segments*
Saving Throw: *Special*

Explanation/Description: The *spectral force* spell creates an illusion in which sound, smell and thermal illusions are included. It is otherwise similar to the second level *improved phantasmal force* spell (q.v.). The spell will last for 3 rounds after concentration.

Suggestion (Enchantment/Charm)

Level: *3*
Range: *3''*
Duration: *4 turns + 4 turns/level*
Area of Effect: *One creature*

Components: *V,M*
Casting Time: *3 segments*
Saving Throw: *Neg.*

Explanation/Description: Except as noted above, this spell is the same as the third level magic-user spell, *suggestion* (q.v.).

Fourth Level Spells:

Confusion (Enchantment/Charm)

Level: *4*
Range: *8''*
Duration: *1 round/level*
Area of Effect: *Up to 4'' × 4''*

Components: *V,S,M*
Casting Time: *4 segments*
Saving Throw: *Special*

Explanation/Description: Except as noted above, this spell is the same as the fourth level magic-user *confusion* spell (q.v.). See also the seventh level druid *confusion* spell.

Dispel Exhaustion (Illusion/Phantasm)

Level: *4*
Range: *Touch*
Duration: *3 turns/level*
Area of Effect: *1 to 4 persons*

Components: *V,S*
Casting Time: *4 segments*
Saving Throw: *None*

Explanation/Description: By means of this spell, the illusionist is able to restore 50% of lost hit points to all persons (humans, demi-humans and humanoids) he or she touches during the round it is cast, subject to a maximum of four persons. The spell gives the illusion to the person touched that he or she is fresh and well. Stamina is renewed, but when the

spell duration expires, the recipient drops back to their actual hit point strength. The spell will allow recipients to move at double speed for 1 round every turn (cf. *haste* spell).

Emotion (Enchantment/Charm)

Level: *4*
Range: *1''/level*
Duration: *Special*
Area of Effect: *4'' × 4'' area*

Components: *V,S*
Casting Time: *4 segments*
Saving Throw: *Neg.*

Explanation/Description: When this spell is cast, the illusionist can project his or her choice of 1 of the following 4 emotions:

1. *Fear:* This is the same as the spell of the same name, but as it is not illusionary, the saving throw is made at -2. It counters/is countered by *rage*.

2. *Hate:* The effect of *hate* is to raise morale, saving throw dice, "to hit" dice, and damage done by +2. It counters/is countered by *hopelessness*.

3. *Hopelessness:* This has the same effect as the *hopelessness* symbol. It counters/is countered by *hate*.

4. *Rage:* The *rage* emotion causes the recipient to become berserk, attack at a +1 on the "to hit" dice, do +3 hit points of damage, and gives a temporary +5 hit points to the enraged creature. The recipient will fight without shield, and regardless of life as well. It counters/is countered by *fear*.

The spell lasts as long as the illusionist continues to concentrate on projecting the chosen *emotion*.

Improved Invisibility (Illusion/Phantasm)

Level: *4*
Range: *Touch*
Duration: *4 rounds + 1 round/level*
Area of Effect: *Creature touched*

Components: *V,S*
Casting Time: *4 segments*
Saving Throw: *None*

Explanation/Description: This spell is similar to *invisibility*, but the recipient is able to attack, either by missile discharge, melee combat, or spell casting and remain unseen. Note, however, that there are sometimes telltale traces, a shimmering, so that an observant opponent can attack the invisible spell recipient. Such attacks are at -4 on the "to hit" dice, and all saving throws are made at +4.

Massmorph (Illusion/Phantasm)

Level: *4*
Range: *1''/level*
Duration: *Special*
Area of Effect: *1'' × 1'' square/level*

Components: *V,S*
Casting Time: *4 segments*
Saving Throw: *None*

Explanation/Description: Except as noted above, this spell is the same as the fourth level magic-user spell, *massmorph* (q.v.).

Minor Creation (Alteration)

Level: 4
Range: Touch
Duration: 6 turns/level
Area of Effect: Special

Components: V,S,M
Casting Time: 1 turn
Saving Throw: None

Explanation/Description: This spell enables the illusionist to create an item of non-living, vegetable nature, i.e. soft goods, rope, wood, etc. The item created cannot exceed 1 cubic foot per level of the spell caster in volume. (Cf. **ADVANCED DUNGEONS & DRAGONS, MONSTER MANUAL,** *Djinni.*) Note the limits of the spell's duration. The spell caster must have at least a tiny piece of matter of the same type of item he or she plans to create by means of the *minor creation* spell, i.e. a bit of twisted hemp to create rope, a splinter of wood to create a door, and so forth.

Phantasmal Killer (Illusion/Phantasm)

Level: 4
Range: ½''/level
Duration: 1 round/level
Area of Effect: One creature

Components: V,S
Casting Time: 4 segments
Saving Throw: Special

Explanation/Description: When this spell is cast, the illusionist creates the illusion of the most fearsome thing imagined, simply by forming the fears of the subject creature's subconscious mind into something which its conscious mind can visualize — the most horrible beast. Only the spell caster and the spell recipient can see the *phantasmal killer*, but if it succeeds in scoring a hit, the victim dies (from fright). The beast attacks as a 4 hit dice monster with respect to its victim. It is invulnerable to all attacks, and it can pass through any barriers, for it exists only in the beholder's mind. The only defense against a *phantasmal killer* is an attempt to disbelieve, which can be tried but once, or slaying or rendering unconscious the illusionist who cast the spell. Note that the saving throw against this spell is not standard. The subject must roll three six-sided dice (3d6) and score a sum equal to or less than its intelligence ability score in order to disbelieve the apparition. The dice score is modified as follows:

Condition	Modifier*
Complete surprise	+2
Surprise	+1
Subject previously attacked by this spell	-1 per previous attack
Subject is an illusionist	-2
Subject is wearing a *helm of telepathy*	-3 plus the ability to turn the *phantasmal killer* upon its creator if disbelieved

*Note that magic resistance and wisdom factors also apply, magic resistance being checked first to determine spell operation (or -1 to -5 on dice if spell resistance is as that of a dwarf, gnome, etc.), and then wisdom bonus applies as a minus to the dice roll to match or score less than intelligence.

If the subject of the attack by a *phantasmal killer* succeeds in disbelieving and is wearing a *helm of telepathy*, the beast can be turned upon the illusionist, and then he or she must disbelieve it or be subject to its attack and possible effects.

Shadow Monsters (Illusion/Phantasm)

Level: 4
Range: 3''
Duration: 1 round/level
Area of Effect: 2'' × 2''

Components: V,S
Casting time: 4 segments
Saving Throw: Special

Explanation/Description: The *shadow monsters* spell enables the illusionist to create semi-real phantasms of one or more monsters. The total hit dice of the shadow monster or monsters thus created cannot exceed the level of experience of the illusionist; thus a 10th level illusionist can create one creature which has 10 hit dice (in normal circumstances), two which have 5 hit dice (normally), etc. All *shadow monsters* created by one spell must be of the same sort, i.e. hobgoblins, orcs, spectres, etc. They have 20% of the hit points they would normally have. To determine this, roll the appropriate hit dice and multiply by .20, any score less than .4 is dropped

— in the case of monsters with one (or fewer) hit dice, this indicates the monster was not successfully created — and scores of .4 or greater are rounded up to one hit point. If the creature or creatures viewing the *shadow monsters* fail their saving throw and believe the illusion, the *shadow monsters* perform as normal with respect to armor class and attack forms. If the viewer or viewers make their saving throws, the *shadow monsters* are armor class 10 and do only 20% of normal melee damage (biting, clawing, weapon, etc.), dropping fractional damage less than .4 as done with hit points. Example: A *shadow monster* dragonne attacks a person knowing it is only quasi-real. The monster strikes with 2 claw attacks and 1 bite, hitting as a 9 die monster. All 3 attacks hit, and the normal damage dice are rolled: d8 scored 5, d8 scores 8, 3d6 scores 11 and each total is multiplied by .2 (.2 × 5 = 1, .2 × 8 = 1.6 = 2, .2 × 11 = 2.2 = 2) and 5 hit points of real damage are scored upon the victim.

Fifth Level Spells:

Chaos (Enchantment/Charm)

Level: 5
Range: ½''/level
Duration: 1 round/level
Area of Effect: up to 4'' × 4''

Components: V,S,M
Casting Time: 5 segments
Saving Throw: Special

Explanation/Description: This spell is similar to the seventh level druid *confusion* spell (q.v.), but all creatures in the area of effect are confused for the duration of the spell. Only fighters other than paladins or rangers and illusionists are able to combat the spell effects and are thus allowed a saving throw. Similarly, monsters which do not employ magic and have intelligences of 4 (semi-intelligent) or less are entitled to saving throws.

The material component for this spell is a small disc of bronze and a small rod of iron.

Demi-Shadow Monsters (Illusion/Phantasm)

Level: 5
Range: 3''
Duration: 1 round/level
Area of Effect: 2'' × 2''

Components: V,S
Casting Time: 5 segments
Saving Throw: Special

Explanation/Description: This spell is similar to the fourth level spell, *shadow monsters*, except that the monsters created are of 40% hit points. Damage potential is 40% of normal, and they are armor class 8.

Major Creation (Alteration)

Level: 5
Range: 1''
Duration: 6 turns/level
Area of Effect: Special

Components: V,S,M
Casting Time: 1 turn
Saving Throw: None

Explanation/Description: This spell is comparable to a *minor creation* spell (q.v.) except that it allows the illusionist to create mineral objects. If vegetable objects are created, they have a duration of 12 turns per level of experience of the spell caster.

Maze (Conjuration/Summoning)

Level: 5
Range: ½''/level
Duration: Special
Area of Effect: One Creature

Components: V,S
Casting Time: 5 segments
Saving Throw: None

Explanation/Description: This spell, except as noted above, is the same as the eighth level magic-user *maze* spell (q.v.).

Projected Image (Alteration, Illusion/Phantasm)

Level: 5	Components: V,S,M
Range: ½"/level	Casting Time: 5 segments
Area of Effect: *Special*	Saving Throw: *None*

Explanation/Description: Except as shown above, this spell is the same as the sixth level magic-user spell *project image* (q.v.).

Shadow Door (Illusion/Phantasm)

Level: 5	Components: S
Range: 1"	Casting Time: 2 segments
Duration: 1 round/level	Saving Throw: *None*
Area of Effect: *Special*	

Explanation/Description: By means of this spell, the illusionist creates the illusion of a door. The illusion also permits the illusionist to appear to step through this "door" and disappear, when in reality he or she has darted aside, and can then flee totally invisible for the spell duration. Creatures viewing this are deluded into seeing/entering an empty 10' × 10' room if they open the "door". Only a *true seeing* spell, a *gem of seeing*, or similar magical means will discover the illusionist.

Shadow Magic (Illusion/Phantasm)

Level: 5	Components: V,S
Range: 5" + 1"/level	Casting Time: 5 segments
Duration: *Special*	Saving Throw: *Special*
Area of Effect: *Special*	

Explanation/Description: The *shadow magic* spell allows the illusionist to cast a quasi-real magic-user spell. This spell can be *magic missile, fireball, lightning bolt*, or *cone of cold* and will have normal effects upon creatures in the area of effect if they fail to make their saving throws. If saving throws are made, the *shadow magic* spell will inflict but 1 hit point of damage per level of experience of the illusionist casting it, regardless of which quasi-real spell was cast.

Summon Shadow (Conjuration/Summoning)

Level: 5	Components: V,S,M
Range: 1"	Casting Time: 5 segments
Duration: 1 round + 1 round/level	Saving Throw: *None*
Area of Effect: 1" × 1"	

Explanation/Description: When this spell is cast, the illusionist conjures up 1 *shadow* (see ADVANCED DUNGEONS & DRAGONS, MONSTER MANUAL) for every three levels of experience he or she has attained. These monsters are under the control of the spell caster and will attack his or her enemies on command. The *shadows* will remain until slain or turned or the spell duration expires. The material component for this spell is a bit of smoky quartz.

Sixth Level Spells:

Conjure Animals (Conjuration/Summoning)

Level: 6	Components: V,S
Range: 3"	Casting Time: 6 segments
Duration: 1 round/level	Saving Throw: *None*
Area of Effect: *Special*	

Explanation/Description: Except as shown above, this spell is the same as the sixth level cleric spell, *conjure animals* (q.v.).

Demi-Shadow Magic (Illusion/Phantasm)

Level: 6	Components: V,S
Range: 6" + 1"/level	Casting Time: 6 segments
Duration: *Special*	Saving Throw: *Special*
Area of Effect: *Special*	

Explanation/Description: This spell is similar to the fifth level *shadow magic* spell (q.v.), but in addition to the quasi-real spells listed thereunder it enables the illusionist to cast a quasi-real *wall of fire, wall of ice*, or *cloudkill*. If recognized as *demi-shadow magic* (the victim makes its saving throw), the *magic missile, fireball, et al.* do 2 hit points of damage per

level of experience of the spell caster, the *wall* spells cause 1-4 hit points of damage per level, and the *cloudkill* will slay only creatures with fewer than 2 hit dice.

Mass Suggestion (Enchantment/Charm)

Level: 6	Components: V,M
Range: 3"	Casting Time: 6 segments
Duration: 4 turns + 4 turns/level	Saving Throw: Neg.
Area of Effect: One creature/level	

Explanation/Description: This spell is the same as the third level *suggestion* spell, except that the illusionist is able to cast the spell upon more than one subject, provided the prospective recipients of the *suggestion* are within the 3" range. One creature per level of experience the spell caster has attained can be affected. If only one creature is the subject, its saving throw is at -2. The suggestion must be the same for all hearing it.

Permanent Illusion (Illusion/Phantasm)

Level: 6	Components: V,S,M
Range: 1"/level	Casting Time: 6 segments
Duration: *Permanent*	Saving Throw: *Special*
Area of Effect: 4 square" + 1 square"/level	

Explanation/Description: This spell creates a lasting *spectral force* (q.v.) which requires no concentration. It is subject to *dispel magic*, of course.

Programmed Illusion (Illusion/Phantasm)

Level: 6	Components: V,S,M
Range: 1"/level	Casting Time: 6 segments
Duration: *Special*	Saving Throw: *Special*
Area of Effect: 4 square" + 1 square"/level	

Explanation/Description: By means of this spell, the illusionist sets up a *spectral forces* spell (q.v.) which will activate upon command or when a specified condition occurs (cf. *magic mouth*). The illusion will last for a maximum of 1 round per level of the spell caster.

Shades (Illusion/Phantasm)

Level: 6	Components: V,S
Range: 3"	Casting Time: 6 segments
Duration: 1 round/level	Saving Throw: *Special*
Area of Effect: 2" × 2"	

Explanation/Description: This spell is related to *shadow monsters* and *demi-shadow monsters* (qq.v.), but the monsters created are of 60% hit points and damage potential and are of armor class 6.

True Sight (Divination)

Level: 6	Components: V,S
Range: Touch	Casting Time: 1 round
Duration: 1 round/level	Saving Throw: *None*
Area of Effect: 6" light range	

Explanation/Description: This spell is very like the fifth level cleric spell, *true seeing* (q.v.). However, while the *true sight* spell allows the illusionist to see its actual or former form, it does not allow determination of alignment.

Veil (Illusion/Phantasm)

Level: 6	Components: V,S
Range: 1"/level	Casting Time: 3 segments
Duration: 1 turn/level	Saving Throw: *None*
Area of Effect: 2" × 2"/level	

Explanation/Description: The *veil* spell enables the illusionist to instantly change the appearance of his or her surroundings and/or party or create *hallucinatory terrain* (q.v.) so as to fool even the most clever creatures unless they have *true seeing/sight*, a *gem of seeing*, or similar magical aid. The *veil* can make a sumptuous room seem a filthy den and even touch will conform to the visual illusion. If *hallucinatory terrain* is created, touch will not cause it to vanish.

Seventh Level Spells:

Alter Reality (Illusion/Phantasm, Conjuration/Summoning)

Level: 7	Components: *Special*
Range: *Unlimited*	Casting Time: *Special*
Duration: *Special*	Saving Throw: *Special*
Area of Effect: *Special*	

Explanation/Description: The *alter reality* spell is similar to the seventh level magic-user *limited wish* spell (q.v.). In order to effect the magic fully, the illusionist must depict the enactment of the alteration of reality through the casting of a *phantasmal force*, as well as verbalization in a limited form, before the spell goes into action.

Astral Spell (Alteration)

Level: 7	Components: *V,S*
Range: *Touch*	Casting Time: *3 turns*
Duration: *Special*	Saving Throw: *None*
Area of Effect: *Special*	

Explanation/Description: This spell is the same as the seventh level cleric spell, *astral spell* (q.v.).

Prismatic Spray (Abjuration, Conjuration/Summoning)

Level: 7	Components: *V,S*
Range: 0	Casting Time: *7 segments*
Duration: *Instantaneous*	Saving Throw: *Special*
Area of Effect: *7'' long plane, 1½'' wide at end, ½'' wide at base*	

Explanation/Description: When this spell is cast, the illusionist causes 7 rays of the *prismatic sphere* spell (q.v.) to spring from his or her hand. Any creature in the area of effect will be touched by 1 or more of the rays. To determine which ray strikes the concerned creature, roll an eight-sided die:

1 = red	5 = blue
2 = orange	6 = indigo
3 = yellow	7 = violet
4 = green	8 = struck by 2 rays, roll again twice ignoring any 8's

Saving throws apply only with respect to those prismatic color rays which call for such.

Prismatic Wall (Abjuration, Conjuration/Summoning)

Level: 7	Components: *V,S*
Range: 1''	Casting Time: *7 Segments*
Duration: *1 turn/level*	Saving Throw: *Special*
Area of Effect: *Special*	

Explanation/Description: The *prismatic wall* spell is similar to the *prismatic sphere* spell (q.v.). It differs only in that the spell creates a wall, or curtain, of scintillating colors. The wall is of maximum proportions of 4' wide per level of experience of the spell caster and 2' high per level of experience.

Vision (Divination)

Level: 7	Components: *V,S,M*
Range: 0	Casting Time: *7 segments*
Duration: *Special*	Saving Throw: *None*
Area of Effect: *The Illusionist*	

Explanation/Description: At such time as the illusionist wishes to gain supernatural guidance, he or she casts a *vision* spell, calling upon whatever power he or she desires aid from, and asking the question for which a vision is to be given to answer. Two six-sided dice are rolled. If they total 2 to 6, the power is annoyed and will cause the illusionist, by ultra-powerful *geas* or *quest*, to do some service, and no question will be answered. If the dice total 7 to 9, the power is indifferent, and some minor *vision*, possibly unrelated to the question, will be given. A score of 10 or

better indicates the *vision* is granted. Note that the material component of the spell is the sacrifice of something valued by the spell caster and/or by the power supplicated. The more precious the sacrifice, the better the chance of spell success, for a very precious item will give a bonus of +1 on the dice, one that is extremely precious will add +2, and a priceless/nonesuch will add +3.

First Level Magic-user Spells

Level: 7	Components: *
Range: *	Casting Time: *
Duration: *	Saving Throw: *
Area of Effect: *	

*As appropriate to the spell in question

Explanation/Description: The illusionist gains four of the following first level magic-user spells at the 14th level of experience and an additional one as each additional level of experience is gained. The spells are:

Affect Normal Fires	Mending
Burning Hands	Message
Charm Person	Nystul's Magic Aura
Comprehend Languages	Protection from Evil
Enlarge	Read Magic
Erase	Shield
Feather Fall	Shocking Grasp
Friends	Sleep
Hold Portal	Tenser's Floating Disc
Magic Missile	Unseen Servent

The illusionist may learn any spell or spells from the preceding list. He or she must seek the spells in the same manner as a magic-user. If the illusionist chooses to take this "spell", he or she actually takes four or more first level magic-user spells as a seventh level spell.

SPELL CASTING

The casting of spells during the course of an adventure will be discussed at length hereafter in the section of this book which deals with all aspects of an expedition into underground or outdoors settings.

Each character able to cast spells can remember only a certain number at any given level. (This number can be modified by magical means.) Once a spell is cast, *that particular spell* is wiped from the mind, forgotten, but another spell of the same type can still be remembered, i.e. the spell caster can have several of the same spell memorized and prepared for, within the number limits for his or her particular class and level.

Most spells can be cast during the course of a single melee round, although some — particularly high level ones — require more time. Casting a spell requires certain actions, and if these are interrupted, the spell cannot be cast and it is lost from memory. A good example of this is a magic-user about to cast a *fireball* spell being struck by an arrow when in the midst of the spell. Magical silence or physical gagging will prevent *verbal* (V) spell completion. Magical immobility prevents any spell casting. Physical restraint, including grappling, grasping, binding, etc. prevents proper *somatic* (S) spell completion, for gestures must be exact and movements free and as prescribed. Despite these restrictions, there is no doubt that spells in general are potent offensive and defensive weapons, providing the caster does not hesitate, i.e. he or she must know which spell is being cast when the melee round begins.

As each spell is cast, it is crossed off the character's list of spells memorized for that particular expedition. The same is true for any material components which are required for the spell cast; the component(s) must be ready and then crossed off as expended.

Scroll Spells: Use of scroll spells is similar to the casting of normal (memorized) spells. They too disappear when read off the scroll, for their magical properties and energies are bound up in the characters, runes, signs, sigils, and words written for the particular spell. Being written, the scroll spell requires no *somatic* or *material* components. The time required to cast (read) a scroll spell is exactly that shown for the memorized spell. Of course, this assumes the scroll is in hand and ready to read. In general, scroll spells will be 12th level as regards range and duration and area of effect. Notable variations occur in projectile attack spells (*magic missile*, *fireball, lightning bolt*) which have variable strength. Other information regarding scroll spells will be given by your Dungeon Master as the need arises.

THE ADVENTURE

When you go on an *adventure*, you, and in all probability one or more other characters, will go to explore some *underground* labyrinth or area of land *outdoors*. Your Dungeon Master will have carefully prepared a map of the place you and your party are to enter, a map showing all outstanding features of the place, with numbers and/or letters to *key encounter/special interest* areas. Your DM will give you certain information prior to the *adventure* — you might have to ask questions of the local populace, or you might have heard rumors or know of legends — so your party can properly equip itself for the expedition, hire men-at-arms, and obtain mounts or whatever in order to have the best possible chance for success in *dungeon* or *wilderness* setting. Of course, going about a *city* or *town* might in itself be interesting, informative, and dangerous, so a third sort of adventure can occur at any time, the *city* or *town adventure*. These three major types of adventures have elements in

and the standard map-making equipment. Travel will be at a slow rate in unknown areas, for your party will be exploring, looking for foes to overcome, and searching for new finds of lost temples, dungeons, and the like. If the expedition continues for several days, there will be a need to hunt for game to provide food, unless some inhabited area is found — a thorp, hamlet, village, or town — in which case your party will then be able to have another short adventure.

Town Adventures: Cities, towns, and sometimes even large villages provide the setting for highly interesting, informative, and often hazardous affairs and incidents. Even becoming an active character in a campaign typically requires interaction with the populace of the habitation, locating quarters, buying supplies and equipment, seeking information. These same activities in a completely strange town require forethought and skill. Care must be taken in all one says and does. Questions about rank, profession, god and alignment are perilous, and use of an alignment tongue is socially repulsive in most places. There are usually beggars, bandits, and drunks to be dealt with; greedy and grasping merchants and informants to do business with; inquiring officials or suspicious guards to be answered. The taverns house many potential helpful or useful

common and differences; so each will be described separately. The various elements of all sorts of adventures are given thereafter. Your campaign referee has detailed information, including charts, tables, and matrices, so he or she will be completely equipped for conducting any sort of adventure.

Dungeon Expeditions: Adventures into the underworld mazes are the most popular. The party equips itself and then sets off to enter and explore the dungeons of some castle, temple or whatever. Light sources, poles for probing, rope, spikes, and like equipment are the main tools for such activity. And, since none of the party will know the dungeon's twists and turns, one or more of the adventurers will have to keep a record, a map, of where the party has been. Thus you will be able to find your way out and return for yet more adventuring. As your party is exploring and mapping, movement will be slow, and it is wise to have both front and rear guards. In the dungeon will be chambers and rooms — some inhabited, some empty; there will be traps to catch those unaware, tricks to fool the unwise, monsters lurking to devour the unwary. The rewards, however, are great — gold, gems, and magic items. Obtaining these will make you better able to prepare for further expeditions, more adept in your chosen profession, more powerful in all respects. All that is necessary is to find your way in and out, to meet and defeat the guardians of the treasures, to carry out the wealth...

Outdoor Exploration: Adventuring into unknown lands or howling wilderness is extremely perilous at best, for large bands of men, and worse, might roam the area; there are dens of monsters, and trackless wastes to contend with. Protracted expeditions are, therefore, normally undertaken by higher level characters. Forays of limited duration are possible even for characters new to adventuring, and your DM might suggest that your party do some local exploration — perhaps to find some ruins which are the site of a dungeon or to find a friendly clan of dwarves, etc. Mounts are necessary, of course, as well as supplies, missile weapons,

characters, but they also contain clever and dangerous adversaries. Then there are the unlit streets and alleys of the city after dark . . . And what lies in wait in the deserted ruins of some lost ancient city? Meat and drink for the doughty **ADVANCED D&D**er!

Preparation for one of these adventures is highly important, and one can lead directly into another sort altogether. Here are the basic considerations you will need to know to prepare your character for success.

ENCUMBRANCE

Whatever you select to carry will have both weight and volume (or bulk). Equipment for adventuring is necessary, but too much is deadly. In order to be able to move with reasonable rapidity and freedom, the number of items carried and apparel worn must suit encumbrance restrictions. (Remember that the volume of something can be as critical as its weight, i.e. 20 pounds of feathers in a sack are cumbersome.) To be useful, items generally must be readily accessible, so this consideration must also be borne in mind. Lastly, as the main purpose of adventuring is to bring back treasure, provision for carrying out a considerable amount of material must also be made. The table below gives you a guideline respecting weight and bulk carried and how movement is affected:

Encumbrance	Movement	Reaction and Initiative
normal gear — about 35# and no great bulk	12″ — subject can run quickly	normal or better
heavy gear — armor and/or equipment of about 70# or fairly bulky	9″ — subject can make a lumbering run	normal, no bonuses

| very heavy gear — armor and/or equipment of 105# and bulky (such as plate armor) | 6″ — subject can trot for short distances | slowed |
| encumbered — armor and/or equipment over 105# weight and/or (very) bulky | 3″ to 4″ — no trotting possible | slowed greatly |

Strength penalties or bonuses will modify these guidelines. Weight is usually stated in gold pieces, 10 gold pieces equalling 1# (pound). Volume can only be calculated from known comparisons, as the size and shape of objects varies from individual to individual, i.e. how big is a tapestry?

MOVEMENT — TIME AND DISTANCE FACTORS

Movement rate is always shown by a numeral followed by the sign for inches thus, 9″. The number of inches moved is scaled to circumstances and time by modifying either the distance represented or the time period or both.

Movement in the Dungeon: The movement distance in the dungeon is 1″ to 10′ over a turn of 10 minutes duration while exploration and mapping are in progress. If the party is following a known route or map, the movement rate is 5 times greater, so each move takes 1/5 of a turn (2 rounds). If the party is fleeing, all movement — excluding encumbered movement, is 10 times faster, so each move takes only 1/10 of a turn, or 1 round. This same movement rate applies to combat situations, so by converting each 1″ movement rate to 10′, and then taking 1/10 of the round (using segments), the distance a character or monster can travel during the course of combat is easily found:

	Distance Traveled in One	
Movement Rate	**Round (1 minute)**	**Segment (6 seconds)**
6″	60′	6′
9″	90′	9′
12″	120′	12′
15″	150′	15′
18″	180′	18′

If moving but 12′ in 6 seconds seems slow, consider the conditions — whether prolonged physical exertion or the threat of hostile counter to the movement.

Movement Outdoors: The major difference in outdoor movement is distance and time. Each 1″ equals the number of miles a character or creature can travel in one-half day's trekking. Terrain will vary the movement rate. When an encounter occurs, the movement rate is handled in the same manner as combat movement in the dungeon.

Movement in Cities: When your party is in an inhabited area, movement turns are at the same rate as when combat in the dungeon takes place, i.e. 6″ = 60′ and each move is 1 minute long. This assumes that no map is being made. Mapping takes 10 times as long, so movement when mapping is the same as in a dungeon.

Note: No mapping is possible when a party is moving at fast speed such as when pursued or pursuing. Light must be available to make or read a map; infravision is not suitable in such circumstances. Marks, dropped objects, or a trailing string or line are typically useless devices in dungeons, as they will be obliterated, moved, or destroyed by passing creatures.

LIGHT

Infravision, the ability to see radiation in the infra-red spectrum, is an ability possessed by most of the creatures dwelling below ground and nocturnal animals. Some characters have this ability due to race or by magical means. However, as many characters can only see in light which is normal to the human visual spectrum, and mapping requires light also, some form of light generating device is necessary for activities in dungeons or at night. The table below gives the properties of the usual light sources:

Light Source	Radius of Illumination	Burning Time
Torch	40′	6 turns (1 hour)
Lantern	30′	24 turns*
Bullseye Lanthorn	80′**	24 turns*
Magic Dagger	10′	infinite
Magic Short Sword	15′	infinite
Magic Long Sword	20′	infinite

*Illumination is from burning 1 pot (pint) of fine oil
**Illumination is 1″ wide only and can be masked by shutter.

INFRAVISION

As previously mentioned, infravision is the ability to see into the infrared spectrum. Thus heat radiation becomes visible and differences in temperature allow infrared sight. Warm things are bright, cool things grey, very cold things are black. Most infravision extends to 60′ distance. Dungeon-dwelling monsters have infravision to 120′. All infravision is spoiled if a light source is shedding illumination upon the creature possessing the infrared sight capability. Similarly, great heat will spoil the capability.

Thieves hiding in shadows are successful with respect to infravision only if there is a heat/light source nearby to mask their body heat, or a very cold object or radiation to provide similar cover.

ULTRAVISION

Ultravision is the ability to see radiation in the ultraviolet spectrum — gamma rays, x-rays, etc. Creatures with this ability can see in normal nighttime darkness; that is, they see at night as well as a human can see at dusk because of the continual bombardment of ultraviolet radiation upon the earth.

SILENT MOVEMENT

Characters typically make a certain amount of noise, and thus alert opponents of their presence. But thieves, as well as characters able to move quietly because of a magical device such as boots of elvenkind have a chance to be absolutely silent when moving. This chance to be absolutely silent is given as a percentage, +/- modifiers, and the character must roll percentile dice to score less than or equal to the percentage chance he or she has to move without sound. Success indicates silent movement and an improved chance to surprise an opponent or slip past it.

INVISIBLE MOVEMENT

By various magical means it is possible to become invisible and move about. Invisibility bestowed by a cloak of elvenkind extends to what it covers. A ring or spell of invisibility offers superior invisibility. Note that none mask light, so the invisible character cannot move about with a light source and be unseen, for the light will be noticed even though its bearer and possibly its source are not.

SURPRISE

Surprise is simply the unexpected, unprepared for. Characters can be surprised just as creatures they encounter can. Noise and light can negate chances for surprise with respect to characters or creatures they encounter. Surprise is usually expressed as a 2 in 6 chance for all parties concerned, i.e. a six-sided die is rolled with a 1 or 2 indicating surprise. Some monsters are more capable of surprising foes than the normal 2 in 6 probability, and some cannot be surprised as easily, so they have a reduced probability — 1 in 6, 1 in 8, etc. Each 1 of surprise equals 1 segment (six seconds) of time lost to the surprised party, and during the lost time the surprising party can freely act to escape or attack or whatever. If both parties are surprised, then the effect is negated or reduced:

Surprise Dice Difference	Lost Segments
0	0
1 (2-1, 3-2, etc.)	1
2 (3-1, 4-2, etc.)	2
3 (4-1, 5-2, etc.)	3

Assume the party of characters, moving silently and invisibly, comes upon a monster. They have 4 of 6 chances to surprise, and the monster has 2 in 6. A six-sided die is rolled for the party, another for the monster. Both sides could be surprised, neither could be surprised, or either could be surprised. This is shown on the table below:

Party's Die	Monster's Die	Surprise Effect
3 to 6	5 or 6	none
1	1	both surprised
2	2	both surprised
1 or 2	5 or 6	party surprised
3 to 6	1 to 4	monster surprised
1	2 to 4	monster surprised
2	1	party surprised

Noise or light can negate the chance of surprising a monster. Similarly, if the party is aware of a monster, the party cannot be surprised by it unless it is also aware of them — in the latter case, it might be able to hide and ambush the party.

If surprise exists, the surprising party can use the time segments to flee/escape, close, or attack. Distance of 10' or less can usually be closed and an attack made in 1 segment. Physical attacks during surprise situations are also possible on a 1 per segment basis, whether the form is by weapon, projectile, or method intrinsic to the creature (claws, fangs, etc.), even a breath weapon use; magic spells require the proper number of segments of casting time, regardless of surprise.

See also **INITIATIVE** hereafter.

TRAPS, TRICKS, AND ENCOUNTERS

During the course of an adventure, you will undoubtedly come across various forms of traps and tricks, as well as encounter monsters of one sort or another. While your DM will spend considerable time and effort to make all such occurrences effective, you and your fellow players must do everything within your collective power to make them harmless, unsuccessful or profitable. On the other hand, you must never allow preparedness and caution to slow your party and make it ineffective in adventuring. By dealing with each category here, the best approach to negating the threat of a trap, trick, or encounter can be developed.

Traps: Traps are aimed at *confining, channeling, injuring,* or *killing* characters. *Confining traps* are typified by areas which are closed by bars or stone blocks, although some might be pits with valves which close and can then only be opened by weight above. Most confinement areas will have another entrance by which a capturing or killing creature(s) will enter later. It is usually impossible to avoid such areas, as continual minute scrutiny makes exploration impossible and assures encounters with wandering/patrolling monsters. When confined, prepare for attack, search for ways out, and beware of being channeled. *Channeling traps* are often related to confining ones. Walls which shift and doors which allow entry but not egress are typical. While they cannot be avoided, such traps can be reacted to much as a confining trap is. However, they also pose the problem of finding a way back. Careful mapping is a good remedy. *Injuring traps,* traps which wear the strength of the party away prior to the attaining of their goal, are serious. Typical injuring traps are blades which scythe across a corridor when a stone in the floor is stepped on, arrows which fire when a trip rope is yanked, or spears released when a door is opened. Use of a pole or spear as a prod ahead might help with these, and likewise such a prod could discover pits in the floor. The safest remedy is to have some healing at hand — potions or spells — so as to arrive relatively undamaged. *Killing traps* are typical of important areas or deep dungeon levels. Deep pits with spikes, poisoned missiles, poisoned spikes, chutes to fire pits, floors which tilt to deposit the party into a pool of acid or before an angry red dragon, ten ton blocks which fall from the ceiling, or locked

rooms which flood are examples of killing areas. Again, observation and safety measures (poles, spikes thrown ahead, rope, etc.) will be of some help, and luck will have to serve as well.

In summation, any trap can be bad and many can mean a character's or the entire party's demise. Having proper equipment with the party, a cleric for healing, a dwarf for trap detection, and a magic-user to *knock* open doors and locks go a long way towards reducing the hazard. Observation and clever deduction, as well as proper caution, should negate a significant portion of traps.

Tricks: So many tricks can be used that it is quite impossible to thoroughly detail any reasonable cross-section here. As imagination is the only boundary for what sort of tricks can be placed in a dungeon, it is incumbent upon the players to use their own guile. Many tricks are *irksome* only; others are irksome and *misleading.* Assume that there are several rooms with a buzzing sound discernible to those who listen at the doors and/or enter them. Does this cause the party to prepare for battle only to find nothing? Or is there some trick of acoustics which allows sound from a nearby hive of giant wasps to permeate the rooms? If the latter, the party might grow careless and enter yet another "buzzing" room unprepared so as to be surprised by angry wasps. *Illusions* can annoy, delay, mislead or *kill* a party. There can be illusionary creatures, pits, fires, walls and so on. But consider an illusion of a pile of gold cast upon a pit of vipers. Slanting (or sloping) passages, space distortion areas, and teleporters are meant to *confuse* or *strand* the party. They foul maps, take the group to areas they do not wish to enter, and so on. The same is true of sinking/rising (elevator) rooms, sliding rooms, and chutes. As an example of the latter, consider a chute at the bottom of a pit, or one at the end of a corridor which slopes *upwards* — so that the effect is to deposit the party on the original level but seemingly on one deeper. Rooms can turn so as to make directions wrong, secret doors can open into two areas if they are properly manipulated, and seemingly harmless things can spell death.

Tricks are best countered by forethought and discernment. They can be dealt with by the prepared and careful party, but rashness can lead to real trouble. Your DM will be using his imagination and wit to trick you, and you must use your faculties to see through or at least partially counter such tricks.

Encounters: A "monster" can be a kindly wizard or a crazed dwarf, a friendly brass dragon or a malicious manticore. Such are the possibilities of encounters in dungeon, wilderness, or town. Chance meetings are known as encounters with *wandering monsters.* Finding a creature where it has been placed by the referee is usually referred to as a *set encounter.*

Wandering monsters can be totally random or pre-planned. A party wandering in the woods outdoors or on a deserted maze in the dungeon might run into nearly any sort of monster. If the woods were the home of a tribe of centaurs, or the dungeon level one constructed by a band of orcs, certain prescribed encounters would randomly occur, however. At prescribed intervals, your DM will generate a random number to find if any meeting with a wandering monster occurs. Avoiding or fleeing such encounters is often wise, for combat wears down party strength, and wandering monsters seldom have any worthwhile treasure. If monsters pursue, you can consider hurling down food or treasure behind. Thus, the pursuing monsters may be lured into stopping to eat or gather coins or gems. When confrontation is unavoidable, be wary of tricks, finish off hostile creatures quickly, and get on with the business of the expedition. As determination of chance encounters is usually a factor of time, do not waste it — and your party — endlessly checking walls for secret doors, listening at every door, etc. As noise is a factor your DM will consider in the attraction of additional monsters, never argue or discuss what course of action your party is to follow in an open place or for long periods. A fight will take time and cause plenty of noise, so move on quickly after combat with wandering monsters. Pre-planning and organization are essential to all successful play, no less here than elsewhere.

Set encounters are meetings with monsters placed by your DM. All such encounters will be in, or near, the monster's (or monsters') lair; so, unlike encounters with wandering monsters, these incidents promise a fair chance for gain if the monster or monsters are successfully dealt with. A successful expedition usually is aimed at a particular monster or group of lairs discovered during previous excursions. Note: a lair is wherever the monster dwells — even such places as a castle, guard house, temple or other construction.

All encounters have the elements of *movement* and *surprise* (previously discussed), as well as *initiative, communication, negotiation,* and/or *combat.* These aspects of adventuring, as well as *damage, healing, saving throws, obedience,* and *morale* must now be considered.

INITIATIVE

The initiative factor affects who can do what and when during the course of an encounter of any sort. Surprise, already covered heretofore, obviates the need for initiative checks, as the surprising party has complete freedom of action for a time. However, surprise eventually wanes, and then, just as in other circumstances, the relative weight of action must be determined. Initiative allows one group, the party or the monster(s), to begin some course of action prior to the other group.

Actions affected by initiative are many and include slamming a door, fleeing, moving to grapple or melee, a call for a truce or surrender, firing wands, discharging missiles, beginning a spell, and so on.

The initiative check is typically made with 2 six-sided dice, 1d6 for the party, and another of a different size or color for the creatures encountered. This check is made each round of play where first action is a factor. Because a round is a full minute long, dexterity seldom is a factor in the determination of which side acts first. However, if one group is *slowed* or *hasted,* or one or more members of the group are, the initiative will always go to the *non-slowed* or *hasted* side. In most other cases, the group with the higher die score will always act first. For effects of initiative in fighting, see **COMBAT** hereafter.

COMMUNICATION

In order to determine the intent of a possibly friendly or neutral monster or to pass along your intentions or desires, some form of communication is necessary. Speech might do for human-types, as the common tongue is known by most. But what of an encounter with a giant, blink dogs, or dozens of similar creatures? An open and raised right hand is possible, and simply refraining from hostile moves will possibly allow for further exchange. Remember though, that you cannot bribe a band of ogres to allow you to pass through unless you can communicate clearly.

NEGOTIATION

Most DMs love communication and negotiations, for this allows them to assume an active role in actual play. Your referee will assume the persona proper to the creature your party is dealing with — be it shy and hostile, stupid, greedy, helpful, misinformed, or whatever. Intelligent monsters will always balance the offer versus the expectation. A lone ogre is likely, even with his rather dim wit, to recognize that a strong party will kill him if he attacks or demands too much, so a small bribe is better than a risky combat to get flesh to eat and pretty baubles to have. On the other hand, weakness will be exploited by any basically hostile monster unless it seems certain that more can be gained by other action. Be resigned to pay amounts in excess of the actual value received. As a player, you must *earn* what you gain. Negotiation usually gives you a chance to get on with the earning process, or live to come back and fight another day. Always be wary and use your wits, look at all facets of the situation, and then use your best judgment accordingly. In many cases a payment, bribe, toll, share or ransom fee will enable success or survival, and negotiation is a useful tool to the expert adventurer.

COMBAT

This broad heading covers all forms of attack and fighting. It includes clerical *turning undead, magical control, spell attacks, breath and gaze weapon attacks, magical device attacks, missile discharge,* and *melee* (hand-to-hand combat). Combat occurs when communication and negotiation are undesired or unsuccessful. The clever character does not attack first and ask questions (of self or monster) later, but every adventure will be likely to have combat for him or her at some point.

Turning Undead:

Clerics are empowered with the ability to turn away *undead* creatures, as well as certain lesser demons, devils, godlings and paladins through the power of their profession and holy/unholy symbols. The cleric's level of experience dictates the level of success he or she can expect to achieve in this action. As level of experience increases, the cleric is actually able to destroy undead by the power of his or her religion; or in the case of evil clerics, destroy or *command to service* such undead if they are of the same

alignment as the cleric, or neutral such as skeletons or zombies. Success also depends on opportunity, of course. The cleric must be in a position to step before the undead, and he or she must have time to speak and hold forth the religious symbol in order to turn (or command) undead, and this of course precludes other spell activity.

Magical Control:

Magical control is given over certain creatures by means of potions, scrolls, rings and similar magical means. A potion ingested will allow a character a chance to control the actions of a dragon, a scroll read will prevent elementals from attacking, a ring will allow its wearer to command mammals. All such actions affect monsters encountered and are part of combat. Opportunity to employ the magical means of control must be available, so surprise, initiative, and melee situations must be considered. A potion cannot be found, opened and swallowed while a giant is beating upon the character with a club. A scroll cannot be read in the whirlwind of an air elemental's attack. And it is too late to command a hungry weasel not to attack when it is already feasting on prey!

Spell Combat:

Unless combat is spell versus spell, many such attacks will happen near the *end* of a melee round. This is because the spell requires a relatively lengthy time to cast, generally longer as spell level increases, so high level spells may take over a full melee round to cast. Furthermore, if the spell caster is struck, grabbed, or magically attacked (and fails to make the requisite saving throw — explained later), the spell will be spoiled and fail. Spell combat includes cleric and magic-user, as well as monster-oriented spells. Curative spells are handled likewise.

Breath Weapon Attacks:

Some creatures have *breath weapons* — notably dragons, gorgons, winter wolves, etc. — and some have *gaze weapons* — notably umber hulks, basilisks, medusae, catoblepas, etc. These attack forms will affect those in the area of breath effect or those upon whom the gaze falls. Precautions can be taken to avoid or minimize breath and gaze weapons' effects. Most allow the victim a saving throw which will reduce or negate the weapon effect if successful. These attack forms are speedy, and they will usually be unpreventable if the creature which generates them is alive when its action during a melee round occurs.

Magical Device Attacks:

Magical device attacks include rods, staves, wands, some rings, and a few other miscellaneous items. These devices are similar to breath and gaze attacks in that their area of effect is usually large and affects multiple creatures, saving throws apply, and the attack is quickly accomplished by pointing the device and discharging it.

Missile Discharge:

This aspect of combat includes catapult missiles, giant-hurled rocks, the discharge of spikes from a manticore's tail, throwing such things as flasks of oil, torches, vials of holy water, bottles of poison, magic weapons (*javelins of lightning,* fireball missiles from a necklace, etc.), poison spitting, the hurling of axes, hammers, javelins, spears, etc., and shooting sling missiles, arrows, bolts and so forth from slings and bows.

Melee Combat:

This form of fighting includes the use of hand-held weapons, natural weaponry (claws, horns, teeth, etc.), grappling, and special or magical touch attacks, i.e. poison, petrification, paralysis, energy level loss, etc. As with most other combat forms, the first "blow" will be struck by the side gaining initiative during the round. Surviving opponents will then be allowed their attacks. Note that *haste* and *slow* spells will have the effects heretofore mentioned. Fighters able to strike more than once during a round will attack once before opponents not able to do so, regardless of initiative, but if fighter and fighter melee, initiative tells. Position and weapon length will sometimes affect the order of attack in melee combat.

Participants in a melee can opt to attack, parry, fall back, or flee. *Attack* can be by weapon, bare hands, or grappling. *Parrying* disallows any return attack that round, but the strength "to hit" bonus is then subtracted from the opponent's "to hit" dice roll(s), so the character is less likely to be hit. *Falling back* is a retrograde move facing the opponent(s) and can be used in conjunction with a parry, and opponent creatures are able to follow if not otherwise engaged. *Fleeing* means as rapid a withdrawal from combat as possible; while it exposes the character to rear attack at the time, subsequent attacks can only be made if the opponent is able to follow the fleeing character at equal or greater speed.

Example of Combat:

A party of 5 characters — a magic-user, a cleric, a thief, a human fighter, and a dwarf fighter surprise an illusionist with 20 orcs. The opponents are 30' distant, and the magic-user immediately begins casting a *sleep* spell. The cleric also prepares to cast a spell, *silence, 15' radius*. Meanwhile, the thief darts to the rear of the party to attempt to hide in the shadows and attack from behind when opportunity presents itself; the human fighter nocks an arrow and shoots it at the illusionist; and the dwarf hurls an axe. The surprise segment is over, and initiative is determined. The illusionist/orcs win initiative, and while the former begins a spell of his own, the latter rush to attack, hurling spears as they come. A spear hits the magic-user, so the *sleep* spell is spoiled. The orcs are attacked by the fighters, the cleric casts his spell upon the illusionist, and the magical *silence* both spoils his *prismatic spray* spell and enhances the chances for the thief's attack, for he is successfully slinking and sliding around in the shadows. Thus, after surprise and 1 melee round, the party has inflicted 2 hits upon the illusionist, spoiled his spell attack, and felled one orc and wounded another. They have taken 3 spear hits and had one of their spell attacks ruined.

Initiative is now checked for the second round. The illusionist/orcs again win initiative and attack first, 5 orcs going after each fighter to grapple, 6 rushing the magic-user, and 3 heading for the cleric. The fighters are pulled down, as is the magic-user, but the cleric avoids their grasp. The illusionist begins casting another spell, one which requires no verbal component; he does not hear the thief behind him. It is now the party's turn in the round. The cleric smites 1 of the onrushing orcs and kills it, and the thief stabs the illusionist from behind with his sword, killing him; the fighters and magic-user are held fast by orcs, so they can do nothing. Round 2 is over.

The initiative roll in the third round goes to the party. The cleric kills another orc, while the thief rushes at the orcs holding the nearest fighter. It is now the orcs' turn, and as their leader is dead and they still face 2 powerful opponents, they will check morale. It is probable that they will kill the pinned characters with dagger thrusts if their morale does not break, or that they will release the pinned characters and run away if their morale is bad.

COMBAT PROCEDURES

Most magical combat and breath weapons do not require the attacker to determine if the weapon hits, but the target creatures are allowed saving throws to see if they avoided the attack or at least partially negated it. Other attacks require a "to hit" dice roll by the attackers, and damage is always scored if the hit is made. A further saving throw might be required if the hit scored has other possible effects such as death due to poison, paralyzation, etc. Whether or not a hit is scored depends on the power of the attacker and the armor class of the defender. Each of these topics is discussed below:

Saving Throw:

The chance to avoid or partially negate magical and breath attack forms is known as the *save*. (Note that magic items and even normal items and weapons must be saved for due to such attacks, falls or blows. Consider the fate of a cloak when exposed to dragon fire, a suit of magic armor struck by a lightning bolt, or a magic hammer flying through a *cone of cold* prior to striking its target.) Your Dungeon Master has tables which show the saving throw scores for these attack forms, by class of character, by level of experience in class. These base numbers are modified by the power of the attack, and by magical protections and character class and race.

Armor Class:

The type of armor worn, the inclusion of a shield, magical factors, and dexterity are inclusions in overall armor class. The size ratio is also important at times, i.e. a dwarf adds 4 factors to his armor class if his opponent is a giant. For example, splint mail is armor class 4, and if a shield is added the armor class becomes 3, but suppose it is a magical +1 shield; then armor class becomes 2. Now assume that the character has a

displacer cloak, so the armor class becomes 0, and furthermore, because the character has a 16 dexterity, a final bonus of +2 is given, and the armor class of this character is -2. If the character is a dwarf, a giant attempting to hit him or her would have to hit AC -6, because of the size differential penalty.

Now let us take this character through a few attacks. First the dwarf is engaged in melee against a band of 7 hobgoblins. His shield bonus is good only against a maximum of 3 opponents, so 4 hobgoblins would attack at armor class 0. Furthermore, as the dwarf can only see and react to opponents before him, these same 4 hobgoblins would also attack the dwarf without the latter getting dexterity bonuses, so their attacks would be against armor class 2. Similarly, if giants hurled boulders at the dwarf, rather than struck at him with their weapons, his dexterity and size bonuses would not accrue to him, so instead of AC -6, the boulders would attack a target with AC 0.

First Strike:

The 1 minute melee round assumes much activity — rushes, retreats, feints, parries, checks, and so on. Once during this period each combatant has the opportunity to get a real blow in. Usually this is indicated by initiative, but sometimes other circumstances will prevail. High level fighters get multiple blows per round, so they will usually strike first and last in a round. *Slowed* creatures always strike last. *Hasted/speeded* creatures strike first. A solid formation of creatures with long weapons will strike opponents with shorter weapons first, a rushing opponent will be struck first by a pole arm/spear set in its path. Your DM will adjudicate such matters with common sense. When important single combats occur, then dexterities and weapons factors will be used to determine the order and number of strikes in a round.

Weapon Factors:

You have already seen information regarding the damage each type of weapon does, how heavy each is, how long and how much space each needs, and each weapon's relative speed factor. The same charts also give relative efficiency against armor types. Your referee will use these factors in determination of melee combats by relating them to his *Attack Matrices*.

Monster Attack Damage:

Monsters with weapons will generally attack much as characters do. Those with natural weaponry such as claws, talons, teeth, fangs, tusks, horns, etc. will use the matrix for monster attacks. There are exceptions to both cases.

Attack and Saving Throw Matrices:

Your DM has matrices for each class of character by level groups, showing the scores required to hit the various sorts of armor and armor classifications. Normal men such as men-at-arms are always considered at level 0. Monsters are classed by their hit dice. All creatures use the same saving throw matrices; the modifier is relative class, i.e. fighter, thief, etc. Items save on a special matrix.

DAMAGE

Damage is meted out in hit points. If any creature reaches 0 or negative hit points, it is dead. Certain magical means will prevent actual death, particularly a *ring of regeneration* (cf. **MONSTER MANUAL**, *Troll*).

FALLING DAMAGE

Falling into pits, from ledges, down shafts, and so forth will certainly cause damage unless the fall is broken. While such falls could break limbs and other bones, it is probable that your referee will simply use a hit points damage computation based on 1d6 for each 10' of distance fallen to a maximum of 20d6, plus or minus adjustments for the surface fallen upon. This treatment gives characters a better survival chance, although it is not as "realistic" as systems to determine breaks, sprains, dislocations, internal organ damage, etc.

HEALING

There are numerous ways to restore lost hit points. The most mundane is by resting and allowing time to do the job. For each day of rest, 1 hit point of damage is restored. After 30 game days have passed, hit points accrue at the rate of 5 per day thereafter. The "laying on of hands" by paladins, spells, potions, and various magical devices will quickly restore many lost hit points. A *wish* spell can be used to restore lost hit points to several characters at once. Hit points can never exceed the total rolled for the character, plus bonuses.

OBEDIENCE

This aspect of play has three facets. The leader and caller of a party might order one course of action while various players state that their characters do otherwise. Your DM will treat such situations as confused and muddled, being certain to penalize the group accordingly.

Obedience also applies to hirelings and henchmen. Loyalty and morale are factors here, as is the existing situation where obedience is called for.

Finally, certain magic items, particularly magic swords, tend to be argumentative and may refuse to obey uncertain, demanding, weak, or foolish masters.

If in doubt regarding obedience, the sure test is the one where you ask yourself if *your* character would do it. This test applies only to creatures, not magically endowed items. If you ask a henchman to try on a cloak, it is probable that he and all of your other henchmen and hirelings will expect that the garment will become his. Likewise, if a servitor is asked to sample the contents of a potion bottle, the item is then regarded as the servitor's property by all onlookers. Obedience is based on such considerations, i.e. fairness, justness, rewards, hazards, love, respect, fear, and similar repute and emotion.

MORALE

Morale properly refers to the state of mind of "troops" during combat or stress situations. Stupid creatures tend to fight to the death. So do creatures with a set purpose in mind — elite, guards, and fanatical creatures. Your character will never have to check morale status, nor will any other player character, for each player provides this personally. Some are brave, some foolish, some cautious, some cowardly. Your character's *henchmen* will probably have to check morale, so too will *hirelings*. Powerful monsters will never check morale, and even weak ones will probably not do so as long as they have leadership.

When you require your henchmen and/or hirelings to take risks which your character is not personally taking, or when in hazardous situations with or without your character, or when faced with a defeated and fleeing enemy just overcome, or when given the prospect of rich loot, these are times when the campaign referee will usually require morale checks. Obedience, actions, reactions, etc. will be decided by such morale checks.

In addition to the influence your character's charisma has, the loyalty rating of henchmen and hirelings will be influenced by past treatment, current situation, and the behavior of any of their fellows nearby. Your lieutenants, if any, will provide a steadying influence. Higher level characters are unlikely to have poor morale unless they are faced with an obviously hopeless situation (at least as far as they can see it) and/or when they are low in hit points.

If you treat your henchmen and hirelings fairly, pay them well, and give them arms and equipment which allow them to effectively engage in combat by maximizing their protection and offensive potential, their morale base will be good. Furthermore, if you do not require them to take risks which your character does not take, if their mortality is not high, and their "master" does not abandon them to their fate as long as another course is possible, the "troops" will be likely to be firm in the face of nearly any threat. Lack of action, setbacks, and similar things reduce morale. A good player pays strict attention to these considerations.

MAPPING

One player must keep a map of the expedition's trek, and if two players make maps the chances for the success of the expedition improve. Graph paper with 5 or 6 lines to the inch is suggested for underground map making. A sheet of small size hex grid is usual for outdoors maps. Both sorts of paper should always be on hand.

Never become concerned if your map is not exact, if it is off 10' here or 20' there. As long as it gives your party an idea as to where they are and how to get back, it is serving its purpose. Always make notes on the map to

show danger — traps, tricks, monsters.

ORGANIZATION

Organize your party by showing which characters are where. Show marching order for a 10' passage, a 20' passage, door openings, etc. Always prepare for rear actions as well as frontal combats. Assign one individual as leader. This character will "call", i.e. tell the referee where the party will go and what they will do. Miniature figures are a great aid here. The DM will usually require a marching order to be drawn on a piece of paper if figures are not at hand.

EXPERIENCE

Experience is the measure of a character's ability in his or her chosen profession, the character's class. Each player character begins the campaign at 1st level with no experience points accumulated. Thereafter, as he or she completes adventures and returns to an established base of operations, the Dungeon Master will award experience points to the character for treasure gained and opponents captured or slain and for solving or overcoming problems through professional means. Characters with high scores in their major characteristic ability area might be entitled to an experience points bonus (see **CHARACTER ABILITIES**). When a sufficient number of experience points have been gained, the character will gain an experience level (see **CHARACTER CLASSES**). It is important to keep in mind that most humans and demi-humans are "0 level". They do not have the ability to gain experience levels. Player characters are unusual and superior.

Gaining experience points through the acquisition of gold pieces and by slaying monsters might be questioned by some individuals as non-representative of how an actual character would become more able in his or her class. Admittedly, this is so, if the existence of spell casting clerics, druids, magic-users, and illusionists is (unrealistically) granted; likewise, dwarven superheroes, paladins, elven thieves, half-orc assassins, and the like might gain real experience from altogether different sorts of activities. This is a game, however, a fantasy game, and suspension of disbelief is required. If one can accept the existence of 12' tall giants, why not the rewarding of experience points for treasure gained? While praying and religious-oriented acts are more properly the activities for which a cleric would gain experience points, this is not the stuff of exciting swords & sorcery adventure. So too, fighters need physical training and weapons practice, magic-users long hours of study in tomes of arcane lore, and thieves the repetition of their manual skills and discernitory prowess; but none of this is suitable to gaming. It is, therefore, discarded and subsumed as taking place on a character's "off hours".

As a rule, one point of experience will be awarded for one gold piece gained by a character, with copper pieces, silver pieces, electrum pieces, platinum pieces, gems, jewelry, and like treasure being converted to a gold piece value. Magic items gained and retained have only a low experience point value, for they benefit the character through their use. Magic items gained and sold immediately are treated as gold pieces, the selling price bringing an award in experience on the stated one for one basis. Experience points awarded for treasure gained — monetary or magical — are modified downward if the guardian of the treasure (whether a monster, device, or obstacle, such as a secret door or maze) was generally weaker than the character who overcame it. A 4th level character versus a single orc is an overmatch, and only about 10% of the treasure value gained could count towards experience points; but if nine or ten orcs were involved, the experience points awarded would generally be on the one for one basis.

Monsters captured or slain always bring a full experience point award. Captured monsters ransomed or sold bring a gold piece: experience point ratio award. Monsters slain gain a set point award. Low hit point/dice monsters have a low experience point amount. Monsters with high hit point/dice have large experience point awards. Special abilities such as magic resistance, spell capability, gaze or breath weapons, regeneration, and the like also increase experience points amounts.

Finally, clerics' major aims are to use their spell abilities to aid during any given encounter, fighters aim to engage in combat, magic-users aim to cast spells, thieves aim to make gain by stealth, and monks aim to use their unusual talents to come to successful ends. If characters gain treasure by pursuit of their major aims, then they are generally entitled to a full share of earned experience points awarded by the DM.

Your DM will award your character(s) experience points as explained. He or she has detailed information respecting this subject, and a chart of experience points to be given for monsters slain, with bonus points shown for special abilities of monsters. After being awarded points, you will be expected to add any bonus due for high major characteristic ability, total the whole, and record the number of experience points now possessed by the character. Remember, character *henchmen* will gain only one-half of total experience. Your referee might require you to inform him or her of new experience point totals in order to keep records. This prevents any "fudging" on the part of over-zealous players.

POISON

It is not generally possible to envenom a weapon. This is because the poison will not readily adhere to the blade or head of the weapon (and for purposes of the game widespread use of poison is highly undesirable in any event). However, let us suppose that your Dungeon Master will allow poisons as follows:

1. Poison potions discovered in an adventure can be used as missiles to be hurled into the maws of monsters or can be offered as "gift" potions to intelligent captors.

2. Missiles — arrows, bolts, darts, javelins, and spears — can be envenomed with a toxin sufficient to cause any creature hit by such a missile to make a saving throw versus poisoning or die. (Suppose that this poison is such that saving throws are made at +2 on the victim's die roll.)

3. Blades can likewise be coated with a toxic resin or similarly viscous fluid so as to make sword or axe strokes cause a poison saving throw to be made by the first creature initially struck by such a weapon.

With respect to the first case, the resolution of the matter is simply a checking of the appropriate tables to find if the potion hit the mouth, if the reaction caused the captor to taste the potion, etc.

The second and third cases, however, make it too easy for interesting play. Imagine: Party sees red dragon, party discharges a volley of poisoned missiles, monster dies, and party seizes dragon hoard. Therefore, the DM will typically make every character employing poisoned weapons check to see if they nick themselves handling their weapons, to determine what happens to missiles which fail to strike the opponent, etc. It is also likely that the DM will establish sanctions regarding the use of poisons on a continuing basis, i.e. characters of *good* alignment cannot use such toxic substances as it constitutes foul and unfair practice; or characters found with poisoned weapons will be immediately slain and their corpses burned and ashes scattered. In a similar vein, most communities view poisoning and poisons as highly undesirable due to the difficulty of protecting against ingestion of such fatal substances. Any individual (or group) making indiscriminate use of poison will have social pressure and/or legal action brought against him or her. For example:

The Thieves Guild is an accepted part of communal society, and so long as they contain their activities to cutting purses, picking pockets, burglarizing homes, waylaying late-night revelers, all is well. Then the guild decides to poison a whole establishment, a large gold smithing and jewelry making firm, in order to loot the entire place. Such activity would arouse the ire of the citizens, tradesmen, and city officials. Furthermore, the Assassins Guild will probably view the action as a threat to their existence and an infringement on their prerogatives as well. The socially unsanctioned use of poison would call to mind the use, usually accepted if not liked, of toxins by assassins. Premeditated murder, particularly on a grand scale, is likewise the exclusive precinct of the Assassins Guild. Taken in a lesser context, an individual employing an envenomed sword is calling unfavorable attention to the use of poisons, possibly confusing his or her role with that of a guild member, and so trespassing.

The upshot of this is to consult your DM with respect to the permissible usage of poisons. Keep in mind the principal reason for restriction of the use of poison — the game must offer challenge. If poison is limited or specially treated, you will understand and co-operate.

SUCCESSFUL ADVENTURES

Few players are so skillful at fantasy role playing games as to not benefit from advice. Also, many readers will be new to this form, if not totally uninitiated. So what follows are some basic guidelines as to how good players approach the game, and as continued success tends towards even more achievement, those who play well might actually become great.

The most common form of **ADVANCED DUNGEONS & DRAGONS** play is the underground adventure, whether in dungeons, cave complexes, temple mazes and labyrinths, or whatever. The main thrust of this section will logically aim at improving play in just those sorts of settings. The outdoor and city adventure will be touched on thereafter. Now assume that a game is scheduled tomorrow, and you are going to get ready for it well in advance so as to have as much actual playing time as possible — no sense in spending precious adventuring minutes with the mundane preparations common to the game.

First get in touch with all those who will be included in the adventure, or if all are not available, at least talk to the better players so that you will be able to *set an objective* for the adventure. Whether the purpose is so simple as to discover a flight of stairs to the next lowest unexplored level or so difficult as to find and destroy an altar to an alien god, some firm objective should be established and then adhered to as strongly as possible. Note, however, that inflexibility or foolish stubbornness is often fatal. More about that a bit later.

Once the objective has been established, consider how well the party playing will suit the needs which it has engendered. Will the characters have the means of accomplishing the goal? Is it well-balanced, so that it can cope with typical problems expected in the fullfillment of the objective? Will it be necessary to find mercenary non-player characters or hire men-at-arms in order to give the party the necessary muscle? Is any special equipment needed? When agreement regarding these and any similar questions has been reached, each participant must ready his or her character, but preparations must be made with the welfare of the whole group in mind.

Co-operation amongst party members is a major key to success, particularly when the characters are relatively low-level. Later, when players have characters of 9th, 10th, or even higher level it will be a slightly different matter, for then some adventures will be with but one or two player characters participating, and the balance of the group will be made up of henchmen whose general co-operation is relatively assured. But to gain the upper levels, it is essential that a character survive, and *survival at lower levels is usually dependent upon group action and team spirit.* Co-operation must begin when the party prepares for the adventure and continue through safe return to base and division of spoils — including the special treatment required for any unfortunate characters cursed, diseased, maimed, or killed.

Each character has a selection of equipment which he or she will carry on the adventure. Particulars should be given to the party if any equipment is possibly redundant, newly conceived, or of possible special use considering the established goal for the adventure. In like manner, spells must be selected in co-operation with other spell-users in general, so that attack, defense, and assistance modes will be balanced properly and compliment the strengths and weaknesses of the party as a whole. Characters must know each other's strengths and weaknesses, physical and mental, in order to meet the problem posed with the correct character or combination thereof. Does the group have sufficient equipment of the elementary sort to meet both expected and unexpected challenges (ropes, spikes, poles, torches, oil, etc.)? Are we burdening ourselves with too much because of simple duplication (too many torches, everybody has a 10' pole, and so on)? Do we have as broad a spectrum of spells as possible so as to be able to have a good chance against the unexpected, considering the objective and what it requires in spells? Is there some magic item which one of the party members possesses that will be of special help, or general assurance of survival, in this adventure? All this should be done before play begins, for it is time consuming, and the readying of a party can require several hours if there are more than six characters involved.

At the same time preparations for the upcoming expedition are under way, each player should see that his or her character has made proper preparations as well. These preparations include the safety of henchmen and/or goods which are to remain behind, wealth safely hidden or placed, instructions as to what to do if the character fails to return left with a

trusted person, and a "will" of some sort written out so that the DM will not balk at the arrangements made to assure the smooth transition of goods to the devoted "relative" of the defunct character if those sore straits should ever come to pass.

With everything just about all set to go, a few more touches will be of great help. Assign formations for the group — 10' corridor, 20' corridor, door opening, and any other formation which your party might commonly assume. It is always a wise idea to have the very short characters in the front rank, elves and dwarves to the flanks, and at least one sturdy fighter in the rear if the party is sufficiently large. Draw these formations out on paper (possibly your referee will require copies for reference), identifying each character carefully. The leader who is to make decisions and give directions for the party must be in the front rank, or in the second rank if he or she is tall compared to the characters before. The leader should keep a sketch or trailing map as the adventure gets underway, and another member of the expedition should keep a carefully drawn map as well.

A word about mapping is in order. *A map is very important because it helps assure that the party will be able to return to the surface.* Minor mistakes are not very important. It makes no difference if there is a 20' error somewhere as long as the chart allows the group to find its way out! As it is possible that one copy of the party's map might be destroyed by mishap or monster, the double map is a good plan whenever possible — although some players have sufficiently trained recall so as to be able to find their way back with but small difficulty, and these individuals are a great boon to the group. If pursuit prevents mapping, always go in a set escape pattern if possible — left-straight-right-straight, etc. Such patterns are easy to reverse. In mazes always follow one wall or the other, left or right, and you will never get lost. If transported or otherwise lost, begin mapping on a fresh sheet of paper, and check for familiar or similar places as you go along. Never become despondent; fight until the very end.

When everything is all set, it will take only a very few minutes to organize the group for the adventure once time for actual play begins. Your referee will certainly appreciate this, for his or her enjoyment comes from adventuring, not from waiting for a party to get their act together. With your objective all set, it will also be a relatively quick trek to the "jumping off" area, as the expedition leader will be able to give clear and concise directions on how to get there to the DM, and that means there will be few monster dice, for the party is marching along quickly down known passages, not mapping or otherwise tarrying.

Avoid unnecessary encounters. This advice usually means the difference between success and failure when it is followed intelligently. Your party has an objective, and wandering monsters are something which stand between them and it. The easiest way to overcome such difficulties is to avoid the interposing or trailing creature if at all possible. Wandering monsters typically weaken the party through use of equipment and spells against them, and they also weaken the group by inflicting damage. Very few are going to be helpful; fewer still will have anything of any value to the party. Run first and ask questions later. In the same vein, shun encounters with creatures found to be dwelling permanently in the dungeon (as far as you can tell, that is) unless such creatures are part of the set objective or the monster stands between the group and the goal it has set out to gain. *Do not be sidetracked.* A good referee will have many ways to distract an expedition, many things to draw attention, but ignore them if at all possible. The mappers must note all such things, and another expedition might be in order another day to investigate or destroy something or some monster, but always stay with what was planned if at all possible, and wait for another day to handle the other matters. This not to say that something hanging like a ripe fruit ready to be plucked must be bypassed, but be relatively certain that what appears to be the case actually is. Likewise, there are times when objectives must be abandoned.

If the party becomes lost, the objective must immediately be changed to discovery of a way out. If the group becomes low on vital equipment or spells, it should turn back. The same is true if wounds and dead members have seriously weakened the group's strength. The old statement about running away to fight another day holds true in the game. It is a wise rule to follow.

On the other hand, if the party gains its set goal and is still quite strong, some other objectives can be established, and pursuit of them can then be followed. It is of utmost importance, however, to always carry slain members of the expedition with the party if at all possible, so even if but a lone character is lost, it is usually best to turn back and head for the surface.

Co-operation assumes *mutual trust and confidence,* and this is enhanced when members are certain that the survivors will do their best to see that any slain character is carried forth from the dungeon to be resurrected if at all possible. All members of the expedition should be ready and willing to part with any goods, money, and magic items in order to save lives. Failing that, each should be willing to fight to the death to assure the survival and success of the party. This will happen when mutual trust exists. What about evil alignment? selfish neutrals? unco-operative players?

Intelligent players of evil alignment will certainly be ready to help in order to further their own ends. This is not to say that they will be chummy with those of good alignment, but on a single expedition basis it is possible to arrange situations where they are very likely to desire to be helpful in order to benefit themselves and their cause. Generally evil characters, particularly chaotic evil ones, are prone to be troublesome and hurtful to the party. They should accordingly be shunned when possible. Selfish neutrals are similar to evil characters, but their price is usually easier to meet, and it is therefore easier to integrate them into an expedition which will depend on co-operation for success. The character of good alignment who is basically unco-operative — often acting as an evil or (selfish) neutral would — is another matter, for such players usually join under the pretense of being helpful and willing to act in the best interest of the party. Undoubtedly the best way to take care of such players is to expel them from the group as soon as circumstances permit. Do this as often as is necessary to either change the player's mind about co-operation, or until he or she becomes tired of having their characters consigned to oblivion because of their attitude.

So much for the underworld adventure. Most of what was said regarding successful expeditions there also applies to outdoor and city adventures as well. Preparation and mutual aid are keys to these sorts of adventures also. It is not usually possible to return to home base in the wilderness, but a place of refuge can be found and used in order to rebuild a party's strength. The party should avoid confrontations with monsters which are obviously superior and always seek to engage monsters at an advantage. City adventures are the toughest of all, for they are more difficult to plan and prepare for. Yet with care, and a careful adherence to co-operative principles, they can be successfully handled with the guidelines stated above. Setting out with an objective in mind, having sufficient force to gain it, and not drawing undue attention to the party in the course of accomplishing the goal should serve to bring such adventures to successful conclusion.

Superior play makes the game more enjoyable for all participants, DM and players alike. It allows more actual playing time. It makes play more interesting. The DM will have to respond to superior play by extending himself or herself to pose bigger and better problems for the party to solve. This in turn means more enjoyment for the players. Successful play means long-lived characters, characters who will steadily, if not rapidly, gain levels. You will find that such characters become like old friends; they become almost real. Characters with stories related about their exploits — be they cleverly wrought gains or narrow escapes — bring a sense of pride and accomplishment to their players, and each new success adds to the luster and fame thus engendered. The DM will likewise revel in telling of such exploits...just as surely as he or she will not enjoy stories which constantly relate the poor play of his or her group! Some characters will meet their doom, some will eventually retire in favor of a new character of a different class and/or alignment; but playing well is a reward unto itself, and old characters are often remembered with fondness and pride as well. If you believe that **ADVANCED DUNGEONS & DRAGONS** is a game worth playing, you will certainly find it doubly so if you play well.

APPENDICES

APPENDIX I: PSIONICS

Psionics are various powers derived from the brain, and they enable characters so endowed to perform in ways which resemble magical abilities. If your DM opts to include psionic abilities in your campaign, they will be determined for humans (and possibly dwarves and halflings) as follows:

Characters with one or more unmodified intelligence, wisdom or charisma ability scores of 16 or higher *might* have psionic ability. Whether or not this ability is possessed is then determined by a dice roll using percentile dice. Any score of 00 (100%) indicates the ability exists. For each 1 point of intelligence above 16 add 2½ to the dice roll, for each 1 point of wisdom above 16 add 1½ to the dice roll, and for each 1 point of charisma above 16 add ½ to the dice roll (drop all fractions).

Example: A character has intelligence of 17, wisdom of 12, and charisma of 17. There are 2½ points to be added to the psionic potential roll because intelligence is 1 above 16, and ½ point for charisma 1 above 16, total 2½ + ½ = +3. The dice are rolled, and any score of 97 or greater indicates psionic ability exists in the character.

If psionics are possessed, it is necessary to determine the ability (or strength) and the number of powers the character has. Psionics in no way affect the performance of the character in his or her chosen class, except as possible behavioral modifiers.

PSIONIC ABILITY

The psionically endowed character rolls percentile dice, adding 1 point to the total for each unmodified point of intelligence, wisdom and charisma score above 12. In addition, if 2 of these scores are above 16, the number of points is doubled, and if all 3 scores are above 16, the number of points is quadrupled. The base score (01-00 (100)) plus bonuses (1-72), if any, are added together. The total is the *psionic strength* of the individual; it is the strength for attack and for defense. *Psionic ability is double psionic strength*, i.e. 10 to 344. One-half of *psionic ability* is attack strength, one-half is defense strength.

Strengths can be used up in attack and defense during psionic combat and in employment of psionic powers. These expenditures are detailed later, as is how they can be regained. Once *psionic ability* is determined it can never change except due to brain injury (which will destroy it), or the acquisition of magical devices (which artificially alter it). Use of strength points, or regaining them, does not alter psionic ability.

PSIONIC POWERS

Psionic powers include *attack modes*, *defense modes*, and *disciplines* (the magic-like powers). The number of each power is determined by further dice rolls; attack/defense modes are selected by choice, disciplines by random selection.

Attack Modes:

Roll percentile dice, and consult the following table:

01-25	1 attack mode
26-50	2 attack modes
51-75	3 attack modes
76-95	4 attack modes
96-00	5 attack modes

Attack Mode	Point Cost per Usage	Attack Range		
		Short	Medium	Long
A. Psionic Blast	20	2″	4″	6″
B. Mind Thrust	4	3″	6″	9″
C. Ego Whip	7	4″	8″	12″
D. Id Insinuation	10	6″	12″	18″
E. Psychic Crush	14	5″	-	-

Psionic Blast is a wave of brain force, in effect much like "stunning news" to the mind. It is costly in attack point expenditure, but it is the only psionic attack which can affect non-psionic creatures. The attack is a cone-shaped wave of force ½″ diameter at its source and 2″ diameter at its terminus (6″ distance).

Mind Thrust is a stabbing attack which seeks to short the synapses of the defender. The attack is individual.

Ego Whip attacks the ego, either by feelings of inferiority and worthlessness or by superiority and megalomania. The attack affects but a single creature.

Id Insinuation seeks to loose the uncontrolled subconscious mind of the defender, pitting it against the super-ego. The attack affects all psionically aware creatures in a 2″ × 2″ area within attack range.

Psychic Crush is a massive assault upon all neurons in the brain, attempting to destroy all by a massive overload of signals. This mode of attack affects but one defender. If it is used the user may defend with only mode G, *Thought Shield*, or have no defense at all.

Point Cost per Usage: This shows the number of psionic attack points of strength which the attacker must expend in using the attack mode.

Attack Range: This table shows the various distances at which the various attack modes will function. Effects of attacks are reduced at medium and long ranges.

If all attack points are expended, or too few remain to use any attack mode listed, the creature may defend only.

Defense Modes:

Roll percentile dice and consult the following table:

01-25	2 defense modes
26-75	3 defense modes
76-90	4 defense modes
91-00	5 defense modes

Defense Mode	Point Cost per Usage	Area Protected
F. Mind Blank	1	Individual only
G. Thought Shield	2	Individual only
H. Mental Barrier	3	Individual only
I. Intellect Fortress	8	10′r. of individual
J. Tower of Iron Will	10	3′r. of individual

The individual must always have defense mode F. Others are optionally selected.

Mind Blank attempts to hide the mind from attack, making its parts unidentifiable.

Thought Shield cloaks the mind so as to hide first one part, then another. This defense can be kept up at all times, unlike the others.

Mental Barrier is a carefully built thought repetition wall which exposes only that small area.

Intellect Fortress is a defense which calls forth the powers of the ego and super-ego to stop attacks.

Tower of Iron Will relies only upon the super-ego to build an unassailable haven for the brain.

Point Cost per Usage: This shows the number of psionic defense points of strength which the attacker must expend to use the defense mode when under psionic attack.

Area Protected: If the defense mode has an area of protection beyond the individual, it offers its defense, or the defense used by any individual within its radius, whichever is better. Suppose 3 psionics are defending in a group; the first puts up defense mode F, another I, and the third puts up J. The first selects from defense modes F, I or J; the other two from either I or J, whichever does the most efficient job of damage reduction. Non-psionics in the area are given +2 by an *Intellect Fortress*, +6 by a *Tower of Iron Will*, on saving throws versus *Psionic Blast*.

If all defense points are expended, the individual has NO defense and can be attacked on a special combat table which offers the possibility of stunning, mental wounding or crippling, and death as well as loss of psionic strength points.

PSIONIC DISCIPLINES

The psionically endowed character determines how many disciplines he or she is able to exercise by use of the following table (one roll of percentile dice):

Die Score	Number of Disciplines	
	Minor	Major
01-10	1	0
11-25	2	0
26-40	3	0
41-55	2	1
56-70	3	1
71-80	4	1
81-90	3	2
91-95	5	1
96-00	4	2

Once the number of disciplines possessed is known, the character determines by random die rolling which disciplines he or she knows. If the same one is indicated a second time, simply re-roll until a different one is indicated. Only a few are excluded to certain classes. Only one discipline (minor) can immediately be gained, with one additional discipline (all minor first) gained with the acquisition of each 2 additional levels of experience in the character's profession.

Note that the employment of these powers costs psionic strength points, the equivalent of 1 point each of attack and defense points.

TABLE OF PSIONIC DISCIPLINES

Minor (Devotions) (d12, d6)	Major (Sciences) (d20)
1. Animal Telepathy	Astral Projection
2. Body Equilibrium	Aura Alteration
3. Body Weaponry (excludes magic-users)	Body Control
4. Cell Adjustment	Dimension Door
5. Clairaudience	Dimension Walk
6. Clairvoyance	Energy Control
7. Detection of Good or Evil	Etherealness
8. Detection of Magic	Mass Domination (excludes thieves)
9. Domination (excludes thieves)	Mind Bar
10. Empathy (excludes fighters)	Molecular Manipulation
11. ESP	Molecular Rearrangement
12. Expansion (excludes clerics)	Probability Travel
13. Hypnosis	Telekinesis
14. Invisibility	Telempathic Projection (excludes fighters)
15. Levitation	Telepathy
16. Mind Over Body	Telepathic Projection
17. Molecular Agitation	Teleportation
18. Object Reading (excludes thieves)	Shape Alteration
19. Precognition	Roll again (or select one*)
20. Reduction (excludes clerics)	Roll again (or get two minors ones*)
21. Sensitivity to Psychic Impressions	
22. Suspend Animation	*Consult your referee for his ruling on this.
23. Roll again (or select one*)	
24. Roll again (or select one*)	

The level of mastery of any discipline equals the level of experience of the character who possesses it unless otherwise specified.

MINOR DEVOTIONS

Animal Telepathy

Range: *Special*
Duration: *Time of Concentration*
Strength Point Cost: *1/round*
Saving Throw: None

Area of Effect: *1" wide directional path*

Explanation/Description: This discipline allows the possessor to communicate with various forms of living things, the type of animal life and the range determined by the level of mastery of the possessor. *Animal telepathy* allows clear communication but no command or influence beyond the possessor's own persuasiveness. The discipline operates as follows:

Level of Mastery	Range	Type of Animal Life which can be Communicated with
first	6" + 1"/level	mammals
third	5" + 1"/level	marsupials, et. al.
fifth	3" + 1"/level	avians
sixth	2" + 1"/level	reptiles
seventh	1" + 1"/level	amphibians
eighth	1"/level	fish and similar creatures
tenth	2" + 1"/2levels	arachnids and myriapodae
twelfth	1" + 1"/2 levels	"monsters"
fourteenth+	1"/2 levels	plants

Search for creatures can be made at the rate of one path of area (1" width × range) per round.

Body Equilibrium

Range: *0*
Duration: *Time of concentration*
Area of Effect: *Individual*
Strength Point Cost: *1/round*
Saving Throw: *None*

Explanation/Description: This discipline allows the user to adjust the weight of his or her body to correspond with the surface upon which he or she is. Thus, the possessor can walk upon water, quicksand, mud or whatever. With respect to falling, this discipline has the effect of the magic-user spell, *feather fall* (q.v.).

Body Weaponry

Range: *0*
Duration: *Time of concentration*
Area of Effect: *Individual*
Strength Point Cost: *1/round*
Saving Throw: *None*

Explanation/Description: The *body weaponry* discipline allows the possessor to use his or her body as both weapon and armor by altering the molecules in the body as needed. The table below shows the equivalent armor class and weapon according to the level of mastery. Note the class distinctions:

Level of Mastery	Armor Class for			Weapon Equivalent
	Cleric	Fighter	Thief	
first	9	9	9	club
second	8	8	8	dagger
third	7	7	7	axe, hand
fourth	6	6	7	mace
fifth	5	5	6	axe, battle
sixth	4	4	5	morning-star*
seventh	3	3	5	sword, broad
eighth	3	2	4	sword, long
ninth	2	1	4	sword, long +1**
tenth	2	1	3	sword, long +2
eleventh	1	0	3	sword, long +3
twelfth +	1	0	2	sword, long +4

* maximum weapon equivalent for a thief
** maximum weapon equivalent for a cleric

If the psionic wears armor and uses weapons, the *body weaponry* factors do not apply during that period, but are not otherwise affected.

Cell Adjustment

Range: *0*
Duration: *Permanent*
Area of Effect: *Creature touched*
Strength Point Cost: *Special*
Saving Throw: *None*

Explanation/Description: By means of psionic attunement to the cells of an injured creature, the possessor of this ability is able to heal wounds at a strength point cost of 1 per hit point of wounds healed, or cure diseases at a strength point cost of 20 for a mild, early stage disease (and up to 70 for an advanced stage of plague or leprosy). The maximum healing/curing ability depends upon the class of the psionic and his or her level of mastery:

> Cleric — 5 points/level
> Fighter — 4 points/level
> Magic-User — 3 points/level
> Thief — 2 points/level

Clairaudience

Range: *Special*
Duration: *Time of Concentration*
Area of Effect: *Special*

Strength Point Cost: *5/round*
Saving Throw: *None*

Explanation/Description: This discipline is the same as the magic-user spell, *clairaudience* (q.v.), except that unknown areas up to 30' distant can be scanned.

Clairvoyance

Range: *Special*
Duration: *Time of Concentration*
Area of Effect: *Special*

Strength Point Cost: *5/round*
Saving Throw: *None*

Explanation/Description: This discipline is the same as the magic-user spell, *clairvoyance* (q.v.), except that unknown areas up to 20' distant can be scanned.

Detection of Good/Evil

Range: *3"*
Duration: *Time of Concentration*
Area of Effect: *One creature or object*

Strength Point Cost: *2/round*
Saving Throw: *Special*

Explanation/Description: By means of this discipline the aura of creatures and objects can be viewed. As level of mastery goes up, the aura of objects becomes more visible. An unsuccessful attempt at reading an aura means it cannot be discerned, and further attempts cannot be made until reaching the next level of mastery. Note the chart below:

Level	Chance for Aura Reading		
of Mastery	Creature	Exact Alignment	Object
first	30%	0%	5%
second	40%	5%	10%
third	50%	10%	15%
fourth	60%	15%	20%
sixth	70%	25%	35%
eighth	80%	35%	50%
tenth	90%	45%	65%
twelfth	100%	55%	80%
fourteenth	100%	65%	95%

Creatures above 14th level/hit dice are entitled to a saving throw versus magic with regard to determination of their exact alignment.

Detection of Magic

Range: *3"*
Duration: *Time of Concentration*
Area of Effect: *½" wide path*

Strength Point Cost: *3/round*
Saving Throw: *None*

Explanation/Description: This discipline allows detection of the aural force of magic and also the type of spell (abjuration, conjuration/summoning, etc.) or magic which has been detected. Determination of type of magic is 5% per level of mastery of the psionic, i.e. at 5th mastery level there is a 25% chance.

Domination

Range: *3"*
Duration: *Time of Concentration*
Area of Effect: *One creature*

Strength Point Cost: *Special*
Saving Throw: *Neg.*

Explanation/Description: By exercise of the discipline of *domination*, the

psionic forces the mind of another creature to accept signals from his or her own brain, thus causing the former to do his or her will. Contacting the mind to be dominated costs 5 strength points, and the creature must then save versus magic. If the saving throw is not made, the psionic must then expend additional points equal to the dominated creature's level/hit dice (treat + 1 to + 4 on the creature's hit dice as 1 additional hit die, +5 or more as 2 additional hit dice, with respect only to races of creatures not classed as character races) for each round the creature is controlled. Furthermore, if the creature dominated is forced to do something totally against its nature or self-destructive, the expenditure of strength points is doubled or trebled accordingly.

Empathy

Range: *1"/level of mastery*
Duration: *1 turn/use*
Area of Effect: *1" wide path*

Strength Point Cost: *3/use*
Saving Throw: *None*

Explanation/Description: This discipline allows the basic needs, drives and/or emotions generated by any unshielded sentient mind to be sensed by the possessor of the psionic power. Thus, he or she can sense thirst, hunger, fear, fatigue, pain, rage, hatred, uncertainty, curiosity, hostility, friendliness, love and like emotions. The discipline functions in a directional path determined by the direction in which the possessor is facing.

ESP

Range: *9"*
Duration: *Time of Concentration*
Area of Effect: *1" wide path*

Strength Point Cost: *2/round*
Saving Throw: *None*

Explanation/Description: This discipline allows the user to "tune in" to the unshielded thoughts of the minds of any creatures within range when the power is employed. In most respects it is identical to the magic-user spell, *ESP* (q.v.). Thoughts received in non-understood languages will be meaningless. Non-intelligent creatures will transmit "pictures" or raw drives.

Expansion

Range: *0*
Duration: *1 turn/level of mastery*
Area of Effect: *Individual*

Strength Point Cost: *5/round*
Saving Throw: *None*

Explanation/Description: *Expansion* allows the psionic to cause his or her body to become larger in size, with proportionate increase in mass and strength. This increase is limited to a maximum of 1' growth per level of mastery of the discipline. With each 1' growth the possessor gains +1 on hit points of damage. Compare the table below:

Level of Mastery	Maximum Height Increase	Damage Bonus	Strength Equivalent
first	1'	+ 1	(17)
second	2'	+ 2	(18)
third	3'	+ 3	(18/51)
fourth	4'	+ 4	(18/76)
fifth	5'	+ 5	(18/91)
sixth	6'	+ 6	(18/00) ogre
seventh	7'	+ 7	hill giant
eighth	8'	+ 8	stone giant
ninth	9'	+ 9	frost giant
tenth	10'	+10	fire giant
eleventh	11'	+11	cloud giant
twelfth	12'	+12	storm giant

If the possessor of this discipline already has strength equal to that gained by growth, there is no bonus.

Note that apparel worn can be caused to expand with the body, as can weapons used, but magical items so treated have a 5% chance of being destroyed (d20, 1 in 20).

Hypnosis

Range: *3"*
Duration: *Special*

Strength Point Cost: *Special*
Saving Throw: *Special*

Area of Effect: One level/hit die per
 level of mastery cumulative

Explanation/Description: This discipline is similar to *suggestion* and *charm person/charm monster* spells (qq.v.) It affects only creatures with intelligence greater than 7 and less than 17, i.e. the stupid and unusually bright are not subject to *hypnosis*. By employing this discipline, the psionic is able to instruct the creature as to a course of action which seems reasonable — no orders to kill self, friends, associates, etc. — and plant a post-hypnotic suggestion as well, the latter having a 5% per day cumulative chance of wearing off and not affecting the creature in whose mind it was implanted. *Hypnosis* affects 1 level or hit die of creatures per level of mastery of the possessor. Thus at 1st level of mastery but a single 1st level character or monster with up to 1 hit die can be *hypnotized*; but at 2nd level 2 additional effect levels are added, so up to 3 levels/hit dice can be hypnotized:

Level of Mastery	Levels/Hit Dice Affected
first	1 = 1
second	1 + 2 = 3
third	1 + 2 + 3 = 6
fourth	1 + 2 + 3 + 4 = 10
fifth	1 + 2 + 3 + 4 + 5 = 15
...etc.	

The strength point cost is 1 per level/hit die hypnotized. Creatures with 15 or 16 intelligence or over 10th level/10 hit dice are entitled to a saving throw versus magic; if it is successful, the *hypnosis* has no effect.

Invisibility

Range: *0*
Duration: *1 turn/expenditure*
Area of Effect: One level/hit die per
 level of mastery cumulative

Strength Point Cost: *3/turn*
Saving Throw: *None*

Explanation/Description: This discipline closely resembles the *invisibility* spell (q.v.), but it is weaker in some ways, more powerful in others. It enables the possessor to become invisible to creatures with only as many levels or hit dice as the psionic has cumulative levels of mastery: 1 at 1st level, 1 + 2 at 2nd level, 1 + 2 + 3 at 3rd level, etc. However, psionic *invisibility* cannot be detected by any form of magic, only a *mind bar* being able to prevent the power from operating with respect to that particular creature, for this power affects minds, not light waves or similar physical manifestations.

Levitation

Range: *0*
Duration: *1 turn/level of mastery*
Area of Effect: *Individual*

Strength Point Cost: *3/turn*
Saving Throw: *None*

Explanation/Description: This discipline is similar to the magic-user spell, *levitation* (q.v.). *Levitation* need not be exercised in a continuous period, i.e. a 1st level psionic can use the discipline on multiple occasions so long as the total duration of all uses together is 1 turn or less.

Mind Over Body

Range: *0*
Duration: *2 days/level of mastery*
Area of Effect: *Individual*

Strength Point Cost: *5/day*
Saving Throw: *None*

Explanation/Description: This discipline allows the possessor to suppress or mentally satisfy the need for water, food, rest and/or sleep. For each level of mastery, the psionic can use the discipline for up to 2 consecutive days, so at 2nd level, he or she can go 4 days without water, food, rest or sleep; at third level 6 days, etc. At some point, however, the possessor must spend an equal number of days of complete rest so as to restore this power. While the individual is not harmed, the discipline cannot be used again until complete rest is taken.

Molecular Agitation

Range: *Sight*
Duration: *Special*
Area of Effect: *One item or creature*

Strength Point Cost: *1/round*
Saving Throw: *None*

Explanation/Description: The power of *molecular agitation* enables the possessor to cause the molecules of an item to move more rapidly than is normal. Although only a small number of molecules can be so moved, continued exercise of the ability will have the following effects after 10 rounds:

Type of Material	Molecular Agitation Effect
paper, parchment, straw	aflame, burning brightly
dry wood, heavy cloth	scorching and smouldering
water, wine	boiling (if a small amount)
flesh	blistering*
metal	hot to touch**

*each round thereafter the victim will sustain 1 hit point of damage, cumulative, 1 that round, 2 the next, 3 the next, etc.

**at this point the effect is the same as the druid spell, *heat metal* (q.v.).

While the amount of material that the psionic can affect by molecular agitation does not appreciably increase, the time requirement does shorten by 1 round per level of mastery, so that at 10th level and beyond, the molecular agitation effect shown above requires only 1 round to achieve. Note that the item affected must be in the view (*clairvoyance* included) of the psionic individual.

Object Reading

Range: *Touch*
Duration: *1 round*
Area: *Object touched*

Strength Point Cost: *1/round*
Saving Throw: *None*

Explanation/Description: This ability enables the possessor to detect psychic impressions left on an object by its previous owner. Thus, by handling an artifact found in a dungeon, the psionic would possibly be able to tell its owner's race, alignment and probably fate. If the object had a long and legendary history he would have visions of its past, back through history. Not all objects (and certainly not all magical objects) give off these impressions, however.

Precognition

Range: *0*
Duration: *Special*
Area of Effect: *Special*

Strength Point Cost: *Special*
Saving Throw: *None*

Explanation/Description: The discipline of *precognition* is the ability to estimate the best probable course of action, or to estimate the probable outcome of an undertaking; this power applies only to the relatively immediate future. Estimation becomes more accurate with increased levels of possessing the ability, providing the number of unknown factors remains constant. Precognition accuracy is also a factor of combined intelligence and wisdom scores:

Total Intelligence and Wisdom Scores	Precognition Probability by Difficulty		
	Low	Medium	High
under 30	40%	30%	20%
30-33	50%	35%	25%
34-35	65%	45%	35%
36 & up	70%	50%	40%

For every level the ability is possessed, the probability of being able to correctly precognate goes up by a percentage equal to the level (2 levels equals 2%, 3 levels equals 3%, etc.) but never beyond a maximum precognition probability of 90%. The expenditure of psionic strength is directly related to the number of unknown factors which must be ascertained, i.e. if there are six basically solvable unknown factors then it costs 6 points, and the cost is not known to the individual precognating until after the fact. (In order to precognate the results of a melee, for example, each attack must be made and counted as an unknown, and in a melee with several individuals involved with several monsters, the cost per melee round could easily be 10 or more points.) If the psionically endowed individual has insufficient points to completely precognate, then the precognition ceases at the point when he has no longer any strength to continue. Time is also a factor of precognating — a short duration means a typically low difficulty factor. If 1-4 turns is considered a short time, 5-30 turns is of medial difficulty, and anything beyond 30 turns (5 hours) becomes a high difficulty precognition; however, unknown factors will alter this rule, so that a short time precognition with many (basically unsolvable) unknowns becomes a high difficulty precognition. N.B. Precognition relies entirely upon the referee, and he will exercise utmost care in handling this ability usage.

Reduction

Range: *0*
Strength Point Cost: *2/turn*
Duration: *1 turn/level of mastery*
Saving Throw: *None*
Area of Effect: *Individual*

Explanation/Description: *Reduction* is the discipline which allows the possessor to alter his or her body size so as to make it up to 1' shorter (and accordingly less massive) per level of mastery. After fifth level of mastery, size reduction is 50% of the remainder per level, so if a human 6' tall was at 7th level of mastery, he or she could reduce body size to 3 inches (-1' per level to 5th, 50% of 1' at 6th, and 50% of ½' at 7th), to 1½ inches at 8th level, 3/4 inches at 9th, 3/8 inches at 10th, etc.

Suspend Animation

Range: *0*
Strength Point Cost: *6*
Duration: *Special*
Saving Throw: *None*
Area of Effect: *Individual*

Explanation/Description: This discipline allows the possessor to virtually cease all life functions (as far as any but minute examination can determine, the individual is dead). The psionic is able to program his or her body to awaken again after a set period of time has elapsed, so normal functions will then resume. With each level of mastery of this ability the individual is able to suspend animation for 1 week per level cumulative (1 week during the 1st level of possession, 3 weeks during the 2nd level of possession, etc.) The sleeping individual cannot be awakened before the time he or she has "set" himself or herself to reawaken. For each week spent in suspended animation, the individual must spend one day of normal activity before being able to return to suspended animation. Air is not needed, and temperatures can be as low as 35 degrees Farenheit.

Sensitivity to Psychic Impressions

Range: *2" sphere*
Strength Point Cost: *1/round*
Duration: *1 round*
Saving Throw: *None*
Area: *1" to every side*

Explanation/Description: Deaths and other highly dramatic events leave a "psychic residue" in the very earth and stones where they occur which may last for centuries. The possessor of this ability can sense emotions, perhaps see momentary visions, of those who have died or suffered some powerful emotion in a place just by standing in it for a moment.

MAJOR SCIENCES

Astral Projection

Range: *Special*
Strength Point Cost: *10*
Duration: *Special*
Saving Throw: *None*
Area of Effect: *Individual*

Explanation/Description: This discipline is very similar to the cleric *astral spell* (q.v.). Only the psionic individual can use this power to travel, however, unlike the magic *astral spell*. For information on astral travel see **APPENDIX IV, THE KNOWN PLANES OF EXISTENCE.**

Aura Alteration

Range: *Touch*
Strength Point Cost: *Special*
Duration: *Special*
Saving Throw: *None*
Area of Effect: *Individual*

Explanation/Description: *Aura alteration* is a power which can be used two different ways: it can be used to change the personal aura of the individual (to disguise true alignment and show one which is different from the actual) or it can be used to recognize and alter unfavorable (cursed, geased, or quested) aura in another. The strength point cost for the former application is 10 points per factor change (good/evil, evil/good, neutral/evil, evil/neutral, neutral/good, good/neutral, lawful/chaotic, chaotic/lawful, etc.). A neutral character wishing to

appear as neutral evil would pay 10 strength points, but a change to chaotic evil would cost 20. Such alteration lasts 6 turns. The latter application of *aura alteration* allows curses, geases and quests to be removed. The strength point cost to recognize the aura is:

Aura	Strength Point Cost
curse	¼ point/level of curse
geas	½ point/level of magic-user
quest	1 point/level of cleric

(round all fractions up to the nearest whole number)

Actual removal of the undesired aura costs 8 times the recognition cost.

Body Control

Range: *0*
Strength Point Cost: *2/turn*
Duration: *1 turn/level of mastery*
Saving Throw: *None*
Area of Effect: *Individual*

Explanation/Description: This devotion allows the possessor to exist in hostile environments or elements or withstand substances or radiations destructive to his or her body, viz. cold, heat, poisonous gases, acids, flame, etc. For each level of mastery the possessor can withstand what would normally inflict 1 hit of damage to his or her body in a single exposure. Thus, at 2nd level of mastery burning oil would not affect the individual. The duration of such body control is 1 turn maximum for each level of mastery. For example, the 2nd level of mastery psionic mentioned above could withstand burning oil for 2 turns. This discipline allows breathing under water at 1st level.

Dimension Door

Range: *0*
Strength Point Cost: *10*
Duration: *Instantaneous*
Saving Throw: *None*
Area of Effect: *Individual*

Explanation/Description: This psionic power is basically the same as the magic-user spell, *dimension door* (q.v.).

Dimension Walk

Range: *0*
Strength Point Cost: *1/turn*
Duration: *Time of concentration*
Saving Throw: *None*
Area of Effect: *Individual*

Explanation/Description: *Dimension walk* is the name for the psionic discipline which enables the possessor to move through the dimensions, by inter-dimensional travel, rather than along them. Thus great distances can be covered in short periods of time. The base distance covered by 1 turn of *dimension walking* is 7 leagues, i.e. 10 minutes of travelling time for 21 miles. However, this mode of travel is difficult for the inexperienced, and even misleading to some experienced travelers. There is a 10% chance that the walker will go in the wrong direction, the opposite of that desired. This 10% is reduced by 1% for every level of mastery of the science above the 1st, to a minimum risk of 1% at 10th level, but there is always that 1% chance of going in the wrong direction. Furthermore, *dimension walking* is always a journey fraught with missteps, and this causes differences in the time required to travel the desired distance; usually longer at low mastery levels but sometimes shorter at high levels of mastery. Each level of mastery is based on 700 leagues of travel.

Level of Mastery	Time Alteration %				
	01-20	21-45	46-75	76-90	91-00
first, second	+200	+150	+50	0	0
third through fifth	+150	+100	+25	0	0
sixth, seventh	+100	+50	+10	0	0
eighth	+50	+25	0	0	-10
ninth	+25	+10	0	-10	-25
tenth	+10	0	0	-25	-50

Percentile dice are rolled at journey's end. Whether the traveller went in the wrong direction or not, the dice are rolled to determine the alteration in the time required to travel the desired distance. Example: the psionic individual is at 4th level of mastery and desires to *dimension walk* to an island 600 miles distant (east). The distance of 600 miles is 200 leagues, or about 29 turns travel time. The 2d20 are rolled twice, once to see if the character went the wrong direction (7% chance to go west), once to see how long the trip actually took — a result of 38 in this case indicates that the trip was 100% longer than the base rate, so it took 58 turns (580 minutes, or 9 hours and 40 minutes). No hostile encounters occur during *dimension walks.*

Energy Control

Range: *0*   Strength Point Cost: *Special*
Duration: *Special*   Saving Throw: *None*
Area of Effect: *10' radius of individual*

Explanation/Description: This science allows the possessor to channel energies directed at or in the presence of his or her body so as to make such energies harmless or dissipate them. If a spell or energy weapon (fiery breath, lightning, cold, etc.) is directed towards the psionic individual's area, it will not harm him or her provided the individual expends 1 strength point per spell level (or die of damage normally delivered by the energy).

Etherealness

Range: *0*   Strength Point Cost: *6/turn*
Duration: *Time of Concentration*   Saving Throw: *None*
Area of Effect: *Individual + Special*

Explanation/Description: This discipline enables the psionic to shift his material body to an ethereal state. At each level of mastery the possessor of this ability is also able to cause up to 50 gold pieces weight of material which he or she is touching to likewise become *ethereal*, i.e. 50 g.p. weight at 1st level of mastery, 100 g.p. weight at 2nd, 150 at 3rd, etc. The *ethereal* individual is able to function on the *Ethereal Plane.* (For details of this see **APPENDIX IV: THE KNOWN PLANES OF EXISTENCE.**) He or she can likewise alter bodily vibrations to materialize in the various planes touched by the *Ethereal* (the *Elemental* and *Positive* and *Negative Material Planes*).

Mass Domination

Range: *3''*   Strength Point Cost: *Special*
Duration: *Special*   Saving Throw: *Neg.*
Area of Effect: *Special*

Explanation/Description: *Mass domination* is the power of being able to *dominate* (see **MINOR DEVOTIONS,** *Domination*) up to 5 creatures at one time and to do so for extended periods of time. At each level of mastery, the possessor of this ability is able to use the power of an additional level/hit die creature, i.e. at 1st level of mastery the power affects up to 5 creatures of 2nd level or 2 hit dice, etc. *Mass domination* lasts for 5 turns per level of mastery of the psionic exercising the science. It requires 10 strength points to contact the minds to be dominated, and 1 additional strength point per level/hit die of creatures dominated to establish the command. Thereafter, there is no additional expenditure of strength while the duration of the domination lasts. Creatures under a *mass domination* attempt are entitled to a saving throw versus magic to determine if the power affects them. Such saving throws are made at -4 on the dice. Reduce the period of domination by 1 turn for every point of intelligence, wisdom, and/or charisma over 14 possessed by each affected creature. Creatures under the influence of *mass domination* will never act in any manner which is obviously self-destructive or against their basic nature.

Mind Bar

Range: *0*   Strength Point Cost: *5/day*
Duration: *As set by individual*   Saving Throw: *Special*
Area of Effect: *Individual*

Explanation/Description: The science of constructing a *mind bar* protects the individual from such magical attacks as *charm, confusion, ESP, fear, feeblemind, magic jar, sleep, suggestion.* It prevents the possessor from suffering telepathic influence or possession by such creatures as demons or devils. Psionic (or magical) powers of *domination* (any form), *empathy, hypnosis,* or *telepathy* do not work against an individual with a *mind bar*; and he or she can see a psionic trying to use the discipline of *invisibility.* A *mind bar* can be placed upon the physical body while *astrally projecting.* The chance for success of a *mind bar* is 10% per level of mastery, i.e. 100%

at 10th level. At 11th level of mastery and beyond, there is a 10% per level chance that the possessor of this power will be able to locate the source of any attack upon his or her mind the instant it is made, and this includes psionic attacks, as well as attempts to *magic jar* or possess him or her (in the two latter cases this means identification of the *magic jar* or amulet of the being attempting the attack!).

Molecular Manipulation

Range: *1''*   Strength Point Cost: *50*
Duration: *Permanent*   Saving Throw: *None*
Area of Effect: *Special*

Explanation/Description: By exercise of this science, the possessor is able to alter the molecular arrangement of an item so as to make it weak and fragile and easily broken. The ability increases with each level of mastery as shown below:

Level of Mastery	Able to Manipulate the Equivalent of
first	thin cord
second	thick cord, leather thong
third	thick rope, leather strap, thin wire
fourth	thick wire, 1/12' thick wooden board
fifth	light iron chain, 1/6' thick wooden board
sixth	heavy iron chain, light steel chain
seventh	stock and shackles, 1' thick wooden board
eighth	iron bar of 1/12' diameter, heavy steel chain
ninth	iron bar of 1/6' diameter, steel bar of 1/12' diameter
tenth	2' thick stone wall (man-sized hole)
eleventh	magical chain armor, magical dagger
twelfth	magical splint armor, magical mace
thirteenth	magical shield, magical axe or flail
fourteenth	magical plate armor, magical sword

The science requires 1 round to exercise the *molecular manipulation.* All magical items so attacked are entitled to a saving throw versus magical fire, with each basic +1 giving the item +1 on the saving throw dice.

Molecular Rearrangement

Range: *Touch*   Strength Point Cost: *Special*
Duration: *Permanent*   Saving Throw: *None*
Area of Effect: *Special*

Explanation/Description: This science allows the possessor to rearrange the molecules of metals so as to transmute one to another. Up to 10 gold piece weight of metal can be transmuted per level of mastery. The change, however, is dependent upon the relative softness of the metals involved, and the level of mastery of the psionic as well.

Level of Mastery	Metals Which can be Affected
first through third	gold, lead, and others very soft
fourth through sixth	copper, silver, tin, zinc, et. al. (brass)
seventh through ninth	platinum, nickel, iron, et. al. (bronze)
tenth through twelfth	steel
thirteenth through fifteenth	Mithril, steel alloys
sixteenth and up	adamantite

The cost is 1 strength point per gold piece weight changed. This science is so demanding that it can be exercised only once per month.

Probability Travel

Range: *0*   Strength Point Cost: *Special*
Duration: *Special*   Saving Throw: *None*
Area of Effect: *Special*

Explanation/Description: *Probability travel* is a form of *astral projection*, but it actually brings the body of the *probability traveller*, and possibly 1 or more others, to the planes outside the *Prime Material*. When this science is exercised, the individual is able to cross into parallel worlds or various planes, including those normally reached by the *Ethereal Plane*, as that plane can be reached and then used to get to those it touches upon. The cost is 10 strength points per world or plane entered or crossed. At 5th level of mastery the possessor can bring up to 2 other persons with him or her at an additional strength point expenditure of 5 points per person per world or plane; and at 10th level up to 8 other persons can be brought along at a cost of 2 points apiece. Note that this form of travel does offer the hazard of ending up in a place not desired. There is a basic 20% chance at 1st level of mastery, and the risk declines at 1% per level thereafter.

Telekinesis

Range: *3'' + 1''/level of mastery*   Strength Point Cost: *3/round*
Duration: *Special*   Saving Throw: *None*
Area of Effect: *Special*

Explanation/Description: This ability resembles the magic-user spell *telekinesis* (q.v.). The psionic individual is able to use the science to mentally move (*telekinese*) objects weighing up to a maximum of 30 gold piece weight equivalence, cumulative, per level of mastery, i.e. 30 g.p. weight at 1st level of mastery, 90 g.p. (30 + 60) at 2nd, 180 g.p. (30 + 60 + 90) at 3rd, 300 g.p. (30 + 60 + 90 + 120) at 4th, 450 g.p. (30 + 60 + 90 + 120 + 150) at 5th etc. Duration is a function of the psionic strength of the individual. The object to be *telekinesed* must be in clear sight of the psionically endowed individual.

Telempathic Projection

Range: *1''*   Strength Point Cost: *Special*
Duration: *1 round/level of mastery*   Saving Throw: *Special*
Area of Effect: *1'' wide path*

Explanation/Description: This science is similar to the devotion of *empathy* (q.v.). However, the possessor is able to send an emotion et. al.

Telepathy

Range: *Special*   Strength Point Cost: *1/round*
Duration: *Time of Concentration*   Saving Throw: *None*
Area of Effect: *Special*

Explanation/Description: This discipline allows the possessor to communicate mind-to-mind with any other creature with intelligence of 5 or greater. This obviates the need for knowledge of the language of the creature. The creature to be communicated with must be in sight or be well-known mentally by the possessor of this science. In the latter case distance is not a factor as long as the telepath and the receiver are on the same plane of existence and not separated by distances greater than 186,000 miles (1 light second). *Telepathic* waves can traverse greater distances only if all individuals involved are *telepathic*. Note that multiple-mind communications by *telepathy* are possible. While normal communications are possible, no special form of influence is gained by the exercise of *telepathy*.

Telepathic Projection

Range: *Special*   Strength Point Cost: *Special*
Duration: *Time of Concentration*   Saving Throw: *Neg.*
Area of Effect: *Special*

Explanation/Description: *Telepathic projection* enables both telepathic communication, but only with other creatures endowed with *telepathy* or *ESP* (cf. *Telepathy*), and telepathic suggestion. The former is accomplished at a strength point cost which is identical to *telepathy* (q.v.)

The latter allows the possessor to either implant a *suggestion* (exactly as per the spell of the same name) in one or more creatures' minds or attempt to actually possess the mind of a single creature. The influence function of *telepathic projection* requires that all creatures contacted be within sight range of the psionic individual, or within a distance equal to 6'' + 1''/level/level of the individual if the minds are known. (Thus, 7'' at 1st level, 9'' at 2nd level, 12'' at 3rd level, etc. — 6 + 1, 6 + 1 + 2, 6 + 1 + 2 + 3, 6 + 1 + 2 + 3 + 4, and so on.) Likewise, the number of

creatures influenced is based on the level of mastery, being 1 level/hit die of creatures per level of the psionic, cumulative, i.e. 1 level/hit die at 1st level, 3 levels/hit dice at 2nd, 6 levels at 3rd, etc. The cost for influence is dependent upon which tack is taken. *Suggestion* requires 1 point per level/hit die for contact, 1 point per level/hit die for implantation of the suggestion. *Possession* requires 2 points for every point of intelligence, and 1 for every point of wisdom and charisma, of the creature to be possessed. All influence is subject to the right of the influenced to make a saving throw versus magic, and if this is successful, neither *suggestion* nor *possession* are successful.

Shape Alteration

Range: *0*   Strength Point Cost: *Special*
Duration: *Until again altered*   Saving Throw: *None*
Area of Effect: *Individual*

Explanation/Description: The science of shape alteration closely resembles the magic-user spell, *polymorph self*. The reader is referred to that spell for informational purposes. By means of this discipline, the individual is able to alter his or her body size, form and composition to nearly any other, the garments and equipment he or she wears and carries being altered to conform to parts of the new body shape assumed. Note that *shape alteration* bestows the normal means of respiration and locomotion of the new form assumed, and strength proportionate to the size and characteristics, but no other characteristics peculiar to a certain life form are thus gained, i.e. assuming the shape of a red dragon does *not* allow the individual a fiery breath weapon. Note also that the new shape might preclude the use of weapons, spells, etc. The strength point cost for *shape alteration* is 3 points, plus any of the following additional costs:

Alteration	Strength Point Cost
each +/-1,000 g.p. weight equivalent in a body	1/1,000 g.p. weight equivalent
vegetable material to animal material or vice versa*	1/100 g.p. weight equivalent
mineral material to vegetable material or vice versa*	2/100 g.p. weight equivalent
mineral material to animal material or vice versa*	3/100 g.p. weight equivalent

* includes alteration of garments and equipment if any class exceeds 50 g.p. weight.

Example: The psionic individual wishes to make a shape alteration to become a red dragon. The individual is a fighter wearing/carrying 200 g.p. weight equivalent of vegetable material and 500 g.p. weight equivalent of mineral material. The latter add 19 points of psionic strength costs to the basic cost of 3, or 19 + 3 = 22. The dragon size desired is assumed to be about 5 tons, or 10,000 pounds, or 100,000 g.p. weight equivalent. This means that 100 psionic strength points are required here, and the total cost for the whole alteration is 122 points. Assuming the individual has this strength, the equipment et al. would become parts of the dragon shape — the armor scales, weapons claws, etc.

Teleportation

Range: *0*   Strength Point Cost: *20*
Duration: *Instantaneous*   Saving Throw: *None*
Area of Effect: *Individual + special*

Explanation/Description: This discipline is very similar to the magic-user spell, *teleport* (q.v.). The only major difference is that psionic energy points must be expended to use the power. Also, if points above the required 20 are expended, the psionic individual is able to alter the percentage probabilities of mis-teleporting (coming in too low or too high) by 1% per additional psionic strength point expended either to correct low and/or high mis-teleporting.

PSIONIC COMBAT

During psionic combat the creatures involved can engage in no other activity. The procedure is as follows: Combatants select their defense modes, attack modes, and opponent (if multiple creatures per side are involved). This information is recorded, and the defenses and attacks are matrixed to determine results. Expeditures for defense, attack and combat losses are noted and taken from the appropriate totals of involved creatures. Psionic combat takes place at a rate of 1 exchange per segment, 10 exchanges per melee round.

If the attention of a creature is distracted by physical attack or spell damage or effect (such as *charm*, *hold*, etc.) it cannot engage in attack, although its defenses remain.

Non-psionic creatures can be attacked psionically only by attack mode A., *psionic blast*. This attack mode cannot be used by distracted creatures as shown above.

MULTIPLE PSIONIC OPERATIONS

Psionic creatures can operate together to increase the range of psionic disciplines where range is a factor and such increase is otherwise possible. Where applicable, the multiple individuals link their minds and this then adds a cumulative 50% to the range of the discipline, so that 2 individuals operating together have 200% of the range normally possible. However, range base is always that of the weakest individual in the group. It is possible for 2 or more creatures to operate to increase psionic combat powers. Such operation must be in "series", with the additional creatures adding 20% of their total strength (all fractions rounded *up*) to the next individual in the chain. *Example:* Creature A has 100 points of strength, so 20 points are transferred to creature B to bring its total to 140, and B then transfers 28 points to creature C whose base strength is 130 points but now has 158 points, and C passes 158 × .20, or 32 points to creature D. All series should feed from weakest to strongest. Only the final link in the series can attack or be attacked, but all creatures in the series will be affected by whatever happens to the final link individual. The final creature attacks and defends for all in the series link.

USE OF PSIONIC POWERS

Use of psionic powers, or related magic spells (such as *clairaudience*, *clairvoyance*, *ESP*, *detection*, *levitation*, etc.) does not attract the attention of creatures (or monsters) with psionic powers unless they are within range and attuned to such activity. A perusal of **ADVANCED DUNGEONS & DRAGONS, MONSTER MANUAL**, will reveal which sorts of creatures are to be expected and guarded against if psionic powers are exercised.

RECOVERY OF PSIONIC STRENGTH POINTS

Psionic strength points expended in any way can be restored by refraining from any psionic activity for varying periods. Of course, psionic disciplines which do not require continuing strength point outlay to maintain their effects can be in operation during recovery periods. The rate of restoration of psionic strength points depends upon the physical activity of the individual during the period. Note attack and defense points are considered as ½ strength point, as it is quite possible to have disparate amounts of one or the other of these points after combat.

Physical Activity*	Psionic Strength Recovered
hard exertion	none
walking and like activity	3 points/hour
sitting and talking or reading	6 points/hour
resting and meditating	12 points/hour
sleeping	24 points/hour

*The least favorable class must always be used for each hour of time spent in restoration of psionic strength.

Note that there are 6 turns in an hour, but no points can be recovered in less than one-hour periods.

APPENDIX II: BARDS

As this character class subsumes the functions of two other classes, fighters and thieves, and tops them off with magical abilities, it is often not allowed by Dungeon Masters. Even though this presentation is greatly modified from the original bard character class, it is offered as supplemental to the system, and your DM will be the final arbiter as to the inclusion of bards in your campaign.

BARD ABILITIES

A bard must have scores of 15 or better in the following abilities: *strength*, *wisdom*, *dexterity* and *charisma*. Furthermore, a bard must have at least a 12 score in intelligence and a 10 in constitution.

BARD RACE

A bard must be human or half-elven.

THE CLASS

Bards begin play as *fighters*, and they must remain exclusively fighters until they have achieved at least the 5th level of experience. Anytime thereafter, and in any event prior to attaining the 8th level, they must change their class to that of *thieves*. Again, sometime between 5th and 9th level of ability, bards must leave off thieving and begin clerical studies as *druids*; but at this time they are actually *bards* and under druidical tutelage. Bards must fulfill the requirements in *all* the above classes before progressing to Bards Table I. They must always remain *neutral*, but can be *chaotic*, *evil*, *good* or *lawful* neutral if they wish.

Bards Table I:

Experience Points	Experience Level	6-Sided Dice for Accumulated Hit Points	Level Title	Number of Spells by Druid Spell Level 1	2	3	4	5
0 — 2,000	1	0*	Rhymer	1	-	-	-	-
2,001 — 4,000	2	1	Lyrist	2	-	-	-	-
4,001 — 8,000	3	2	Sonnateer	3	-	-	-	-
8,001 — 16,000	4	3	Skald	3	1	-	-	-
16,001 — 25,000	5	4	Racaraide	3	2	-	-	-
25,001 — 40,000	6	5	Joungleur	3	3	-	-	-
40,001 — 60,000	7	6	Troubador	3	3	1	-	-
60,001 — 85,000	8	7	Minstrel	3	3	2	-	-
85,001 — 110,000	9	8	Muse	3	3	3	-	-
110,001 — 150,000	10	9	Lorist	3	3	3	1	-
150,001 — 200,000	11	10	Bard	3	3	3	2	-
200,001 — 400,000	12	10+1	Master Bard	3	3	3	3	-
400,001 — 600,000	13	10+2	M. Bard 13th	3	3	3	3	1
600,001 — 800,000	14	10+3	M. Bard 14th	3	3	3	3	2
800,001 — 1,000,000	15	10+4	M. Bard 15th	3	3	3	3	3
1,000,001 — 1,200,000	16	10+5	M. Bard 16th	4	3	3	3	3
1,200,001 — 1,400,000	17	10+6	M. Bard 17th	4	4	3	3	3
1,400,001 — 1,600,000	18	10+7	M. Bard 18th	4	4	4	3	3
1,600,001 — 1,800,000	19	10+8	M. Bard 19th	5	4	4	4	3
1,800,001 — 2,000,000	20	10+9	M. Bard 20th	5	4	4	4	4
2,000,001 — 2,200,000	21	10+10	M. Bard 21st	5	5	4	4	4
2,200,001 — 3,000,000	22	10+11	M. Bard 22nd	5	5	5	4	4
3,000,001 — up	23	10+12	M. Bard 23rd	5	5	5	5	5

*See notes hereafter.

Notes Regarding Bards Table I:

Experience Points are strictly those gained as a bard, all previously earned are not considered here.

Experience Level is likewise that of the bard class only. There is no level beyond the 23rd. The bard gains druidic powers as a druid of the same level, with the exception of druidic spells as explained below.

6-sided Dice for Accumulated Hit Points shows an asterisk after the initial ''0'' to indicate that the bard has as many hit dice as he or she has previously earned as a fighter (plus the possible addition of those earned as a thief if that class level exceeds the class level of fighter). All bard hit dice (and additional hit points) are additions to existing hit dice — none are lost for becoming a bard.

Number of Spells by Druid Spell level shows the number and level of druid (cleric) spells which the bard is able to use during one day. The bard selects which spells he or she wishes to have for that day (praying to see if his god will grant them) and casts them exactly as a druid of that level would, but never beyond the 12th level of druid ability until the 23rd level is reached. 23rd level bards cast their spells at 13th level druid ability. Bards can read scrolls which contain druid spells.

Bards Table II:

Level of Experience	College	Additional Languages Known	Charm Percentage	Legend Lore and Item Knowledge Percentage
1	(Probationer)	0*	15%	0%
2	Fochlucan	0	20%	5%
3	Fochlucan	0	22%	7%
4	Fochlucan	1	24%	10%
5	Mac-Fuirmidh	0	30%	13%
6	Mac-Fuirmidh	1	32%	16%
7	Mac-Fuirmidh	1	34%	20%
8	Doss	0	40%	25%
9	Doss	1	42%	30%
10	Doss	1	44%	35%
11	Canaith	0	50%	40%
12	Canaith	1	53%	45%
13	Canaith	1	56%	50%
14	Cli	0	60%	55%
15	Cli	1	63%	60%
16	Cli	1	66%	65%
17	Anstruth	0	70%	70%
18	Anstruth	1	73%	75%
19	Anstruth	1	76%	80%
20	Ollamh	1	80%	85%
21	Ollamh	1	84%	90%
22	Ollamh	1	88%	95%
23	Magna Alumnae	1	95%	99%

Notes Regarding Bards Table II:

College is the important distinction to a bard, and he or she will not associate with a bard of a lesser college. The exception to this rule are the *Magna Alumnae* who will happily aid (by advice and suggestion) any other bard of any level.

Additional Languages Known shows the number of *new* languages the character gains upon achieving each level. Unlike other characters, the bard need not study to learn these new tongues — this is subsumed as previous work. The asterisk at 1st level is there to indicate that the character already knows certain languages from previous classes.

Charm Percentage is the chance the bard has of successfully casting a *charm person* (or *charm monster*) spell with his or her music. This charming ability does *not* negate any immunities or the saving throw versus magic.

Legend Lore and Item Knowledge Percentage shows the chance that the

bard has of knowing something about a legendary person, place or thing or of knowing what a particular magic item is. The latter ability is limited to weapons, armor, potions, scrolls, and those items of magical nature which the bard can employ or which bear magical inscriptions; for all bards know runes, glyphs, characters, symbols, etc. Naturally, any knowledge gained by bards while in their former classes is also retained at all levels.

Bards Table III: Armor and Weapons Permitted

Armor	Shield	Weapons*	Oil	Poison
leather or magical chainmail only	none	club, dagger, dart, javelin, sling, scimiter, spear, staff, sword**	yes	never (except by *neutral evil* bards)

*includes any magical weapons of the named type
**bastard, broad, long, short

BARDS

A bard always engages in combat at the level he or she attained as a fighter. A bard is able to function as a thief of the level previously attained. All saving throws are made on the most favorable table, with the actual bard level considered as that of a druid. He or she must always have a stringed instrument.

The bard's poetic ability raises the morale of associated creatures by 10%. It likewise can inspire ferocity in attack, so hit probability die rolls are given a bonus of +1. Both of these characteristics require 2 rounds of poetics to inspire the desired effect, i.e. 2 rounds of poetics will raise morale and cause ferocity, but 1 round will do neither. The effects last for 1 complete turn. Note that while engaged in this activity, the bard can engage in melee combat but not in any singing or spell casting.

A bard's singing and playing negates the song effects of harpies and prevents similar attacks which rely upon song. It will likewise still the noise of shriekers, for these creatures are soothed by the vibrations of the bard's instrument.

The singing and playing of the bard likewise has a chance of charming most creatures. Creatures within 4'' of the bard must be diced for if they are not already associated with the bard and those possibly affected (See Table II) must save versus magic or be charmed and sit entranced while the bard sings. Note that even those creatures not charmed will listen to the bard's singing and playing for 1 full round. Charmed creatures are subject to *suggestion* (as if it were the spell of that name) from the bard, and if the bard implants a *suggestion* in his singing, the charmed creatures must save versus magic at -2 on their dice rolls or be subject to the full impact of the *suggestion*. Those which save are totally free of the bard's musical charming, however. The charming can be attempted on the same creature but once per day. Loud noise or physical attack will immediately negate charming, but not *suggestion*.

Due to training, a bard has knowledge of many legendary and magical items after 1st level of experience, and this knowledge increases as the bard progresses upwards in level. If some legendary knowledge is appropriate and the dice score indicates that the bard has knowledge in the area, then his or her ability will deliver information similar to the magic-user spell, *legend lore* (q.v.). Without actually touching an item, the bard also has a like chance of determining its magical properties and alignment. This latter ability is limited to:

    armor
    misc. weapons
    misc. magic items — if usable by a druid, fighter or thief*
    potions
    rings
    rods et al. — if usable by a druid, fighter or thief*
    scrolls
    swords

*unless inscribed with magical writing, in which case the bard *can* read what is written at the very least

Artifacts and relics are legendary in nature and not considered as miscellaneous magic items.

Except as previously noted, bards are able to use magic items which are permitted to druids, fighters and thieves. Magical books/librams/tomes which pertain to druids, fighters, or thieves are also beneficial (or baneful) to bards, and these items can raise fighting or thieving ability of a bard beyond the norm. (If a writing is baneful, treat the bard as the least favorable of his three classes.) Miscellaneous magic items of a musical nature are superior when employed by a bard:

Drums of Panic — Saving throw is made at a -1 on the die
Horn of Blasting — 50% greater damage
Lyre of Building — Double effects
Pipes of the Sewer — Double number of rats in one-half
         the usual time

Bards will never serve another as a henchman for longer than 1 to 4 months. They are unable to employ henchmen other than druids, fighters or thieves of human, half-eleven, or elven race. It is possible for a bard to have 1 henchman upon attaining 5th level, 2 henchmen can be maintained upon reaching 8th level, 3 at 11th, 4 at 14th, 5 at 17th, 6 at 20th and any number at 23rd. This is subject to the bard's charisma rating, of course. Only bards of 23rd level will settle down and construct a stronghold of any sort.

Note: If bards are permitted in your campaign, there is a possibility that your DM will also include certain magical items usable only by bards.

APPENDIX III: CHARACTER ALIGNMENT GRAPH

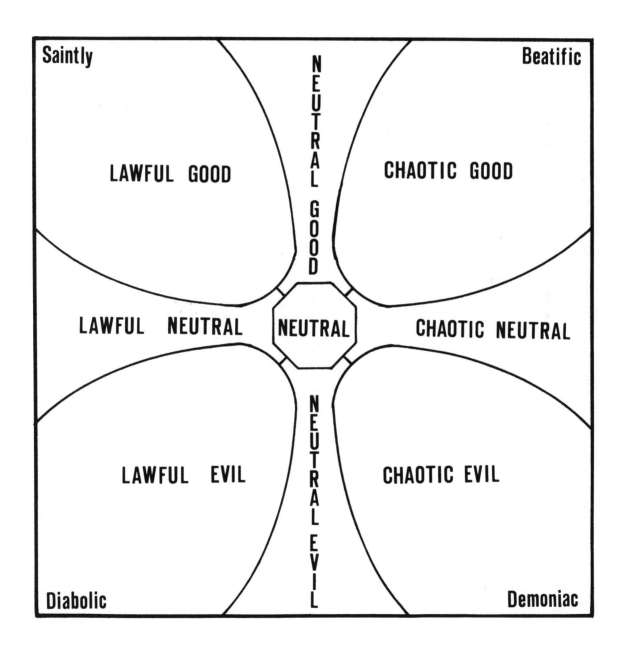

APPENDIX IV: THE KNOWN PLANES OF EXISTENCE

There exist an infinite number of parallel universes and planes of existence in the fantastic "multiverse" of **ADVANCED DUNGEONS & DRAGONS**. All of these "worlds" co-exist, but how "real" each is depends entirely upon the development of each by the campaign referee. The chart and explanations which follow show only the various planes tied to that of normal existence. The parallel universes are not shown, and their existence might or might not be actual.

THE INNER PLANES 1-8

1. The *Prime Material Plane* (or *Physical Plane*) houses the universe and all of its parallels. It is the plane of Terra, and your campaign, in all likelihood.

2. The *Positive Material Plane* is a place of energy and light, the place which is the source of much that is vital and active, the power supply for good.

3. The *Negative Material Plane* is the place of anti-matter and negative force, the source of power for undead, the energy area from which evil grows.

4. The *Elemental Plane of Air*.

5. The *Elemental Plane of Fire*.

6. The *Elemental Plane of Earth*.

7. The *Elemental Plane of Water*.

8. The *Ethereal Plane* is that which surrounds and touches all of the other *Inner Planes*, the endless parallel worlds of the universe, without being a part of any of them. Any creature able to become ethereal and then return to material form can use this plane to move from one to another of the Inner Planes; this is explained fully in the following paragraphs.

THE OUTER PLANES: 9-25

9. The *Astral Plane* radiates from the *Prime Material* to a non-space where endless vortices spiral to the parallel *Prime Material Planes* and to the *Outer Planes* as well. Thus, this plane can be used to travel the universe(s) or to the *Outer Planes* which are the homes of powerful beings, the source of alignment (religious/philosophical/ethical ideals), the deities. Note that the *Astral Plane* touches only the upper layers of the *Outer Planes*. Use of this plane is explained later.

10. The *Seven Heavens* of absolute lawful good.

11. The *Twin Paradises* of neutral good lawfuls.

12. The planes of *Elysium* of neutral good.

13. The *Happy Hunting Grounds* of neutral good chaotics.

14. The planes of *Olympus* of absolute good chaotics.

15. The planes of *Gladsheim* (*Asgard, Valhalla, Vanaheim*, etc.) of chaotic good neutrals.

16. The planes of *Limbo* of neutral (absolute) chaos (entropy).

17. The Planes of *Pandemonium* of chaotic evil neutrals.

18. The **666** layers of the *Abyss* of absolute chaotic evil.

19. The planes of *Tarterus* of evil chaotic neutrals.

20. *Hades'* "Three Glooms" of absolute (neutral) evil.

21. The furnaces of *Gehenna* of lawful evil neutrals.

22. The *Nine Hells* of absolute lawful evil.

23. The nether planes of *Acheron* of lawful evil neutrals.

24. *Nirvana* of absolute (neutral) lawfuls.

25. The planes of *Arcadia* of neutral good lawfuls.

ETHEREAL TRAVEL

A character can achieve the ethereal state by various means which include magical ointment (*oil of etherealness*), magical items, magic spells and psionic discipline. It is possible to move to or about any plane which the *Ethereal Plane* permeates, and it is also possible to move from plane to plane ethereally.

All movement and travel in the *Ethereal Plane* is subject to certain hazards. Some monsters are able to function partially in this plane. Some monsters roam freely in the *Ethereal Plane*. The worst hazard, however, is the *ether cyclone*, a strong moving force which can cause the individual to enter a different world or plane or become lost in the ether for many, many days when it blows across the stretches of this multi-plane.

Ethereal travel is tireless and rapid. Creatures in ethereal state need neither food, drink, rest, or sleep.

Your referee has complete tables for encounters in the *Ethereal Plane* as well as for movement of the *ether cyclone* and its results.

ASTRAL TRAVEL

Astral travel is possible by various means including magic spells and psionic discipline. The *Astral Plane* touches only the endless *Prime Material Plane* and the 16 "first levels" of the *Outer Planes*. The *Astral Plane* does not touch any of the *Inner Planes* other than the *Prime Material Plane*. It is possible to move about in or to any of the universes or to the first level of the *Outer Planes* by means of astral travel.

Travel on the *Astral Plane* can be dangerous due to the functioning or presence of monsters in or upon the plane. The *psychic wind* is the most dangerous, however, for it can either blow the traveller about so as to cause him or her to become lost (thus coming to some undesired world or plane or be out of touch for many days) or snap the silver cord (cf. *astral spell, astral projection*) and kill the individual irrevocably.

As with ethereal travel, movement through the *Astral Plane* is speedy, and while there the individual needs no food, drink, rest or even sleep.

Along with ethereal encounter and travel tables, your DM has similar information pertaining to like activities on the *Astral Plane*. This information will be revealed to you through experience (and possibly by other means) as the need arises.

ETHEREAL AND ASTRAL COMBAT

It is possible to cast spells, melee, etc. on either the *Ethereal* or *Astral Plane*. These activities generally affect only others on the same plane, but can affect other creatures who exist partially or function on either or both planes. Magic spells can be cast from the *Ethereal* to the *Prime Material Plane*, but not from the *Astral* to the *Prime Material*, except as noted above.

Certain magic weapons will remain magical in either of these planes, but some will not, so be prepared for the worst. Only very powerful creatures (demon princes, arch devils, godlings, gods, etc.) can do more than destroy the astral body, causing the *silver cord* to return to the material body and preventing further astral travel for a period of time. Very powerful beings might be able to snap the silver cord, thus killing the astral and material bodies simultaneously. Ethereal combat damage is actual damage. Note also that all is lost if the material body is destroyed while the astral body is in that plane.

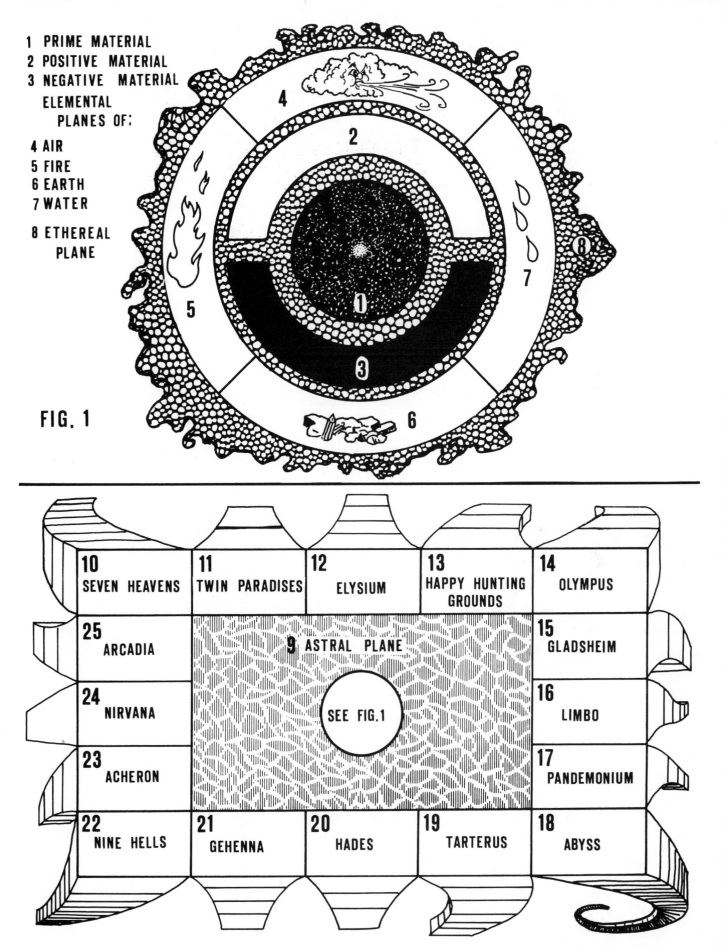

1 PRIME MATERIAL
2 POSITIVE MATERIAL
3 NEGATIVE MATERIAL

ELEMENTAL
PLANES OF:

4 AIR
5 FIRE
6 EARTH
7 WATER

8 ETHEREAL
PLANE

FIG. 1

10 SEVEN HEAVENS	11 TWIN PARADISES	12 ELYSIUM	13 HAPPY HUNTING GROUNDS	14 OLYMPUS
25 ARCADIA	9 ASTRAL PLANE			15 GLADSHEIM
24 NIRVANA		SEE FIG.1		16 LIMBO
23 ACHERON				17 PANDEMONIUM
22 NINE HELLS	21 GEHENNA	20 HADES	19 TARTERUS	18 ABYSS

APPENDIX V:

SUGGESTED AGREEMENTS FOR DIVISION OF TREASURE

Agreements:

1. *Equal shares* (share and share alike) is a simple division by the total number of characters involved.

2. *Shares by level* is a division whereby all* character levels of experience are added and the total treasure divided by this sum. One share of treasure is given for each experience level.

3. *Equal shares plus bonus* is a method to reward excellence and leadership. Treasure is divided by the sum of all characters, plus two or three. The outstanding character or characters, as determined by vote, each gain one extra share.

   *For multi-classed characters add one-half of the lesser class(es) levels to the greater class levels to determine total experience levels for the division of treasure. Characters with two classes receive shares for the class levels they are *permitted* to employ (cf. **THE CHARACTER WITH TWO CLASSES**).

Modifiers:

1. Non-player characters who are henchmen of a player character count as one-half character or for one half of their levels and cannot gain bonus shares.

2. A character incapacitated or killed (but subsequently brought back to life) is eligible to share only in treasure gained prior to such incapacity or death.

3. Characters who are uncooperative, who obstruct the party, attack party members, or are the proximate cause of the incapacitation or death of a party member shall forfeit from one-quarter to all of their share(s) as penalty for their actions.

Magical Treasure:

While it is a simple matter to total coins and precious items which can be sold for an established amount of money, the division of magic items is far more difficult. It is therefore necessary for party members to determine how magic will be divided. As the number of items which will be gained is unknown, selection of a system of division is not possible until after the adventure is concluded.

1. *If but one or two items of magic are gained* these can be grouped singly or paired to equal a share of treasure. If one is of relatively small worth, it can be grouped with money to equal one share.

2. *Three or more magic items:*
   a) best item
   b) next best item
   c) third + fourth items
   d) "x" amount of money as compensation for not getting any magic items

3. *Three or more magic items, alternate method:*
   a) best item
   b) second item + "x" amount of money
   c) fourth item + "3x" amount of money

Magic items thus parcelled are then diced for, the character with the highest roll selecting first, and then the second highest scoring character choosing next, etc. It is suggested that each character be given a number of rolls equal to his or her level of experience, the highest of these rolls being the one retained. Non-player character henchmen are typically allowed but a single roll.

Variations on the above systems are, of course, possible. Systems should always be established prior to the inception of the adventure whenever possible.

ADVANCED DUNGEONS & DRAGONS

PLAYERS HANDBOOK

REFERENCE SHEETS

(THESE PAGES ARE PERFORATED FOR EASY
REMOVAL IF DESIRED)
© 1978 — TSR GAMES

THE MONETARY SYSTEM

The basic unit of exchange is the *gold piece* (g.p. hereafter). There are coins of lesser and greater value, and these are shown on the table below. It is also common to use gems of various sorts and values as coin.

10 copper pieces (c.p.)	= 1 silver piece
20 silver pieces (s.p.)	= 1 g.p.
2 electrum pieces (e.p.)	= 1 g.p.
1 platinum piece (p.p.)	= 5 g.p.

Thus:

200 c.p. = 20 s.p. = 2 e.p. = 1 g.p. = 1/5 p.p.

It is assumed that the size and weight of each coin is relatively equal to each other coin, regardless of type.

STARTING MONEY

Cleric	30-180 g.p. (3d6)
Fighter	50-200 g.p. (5d4)
Magic-user	20-80 g.p. (2d4)
Thief	20-120 g.p. (2d6)
Monk	5-20 g.p. (5d4)

BASIC EQUIPMENT AND SUPPLIES COSTS

Armor

Banded	90 g.p.	Ring	30 g.p.
Chain	75 g.p.	Scale	45 g.p.
Helmet, great	15 g.p.	Shield, large	15 g.p.
Helmet, small	10 g.p.	Shield, small	10 g.p.
Leather	5 g.p.	Shield, small, wooden	1 g.p.
Padded	4 g.p.	Splinted	80 g.p.
Plate	400 g.p.	Studded	15 g.p.

Arms

Arrow, normal, single	2 s.p.	Javelin	10 s.p.
Arrow, normal, dozen	1 g.p.	Lance	6 g.p.
Arrow, silver, single	1 g.p.	Mace, footman's	8 g.p.
Axe, battle	5 g.p.	Mace, horseman's	4 g.p.
Axe, hand or throwing	1 g.p.	Morning Star	5 g.p.
Bardiche	7 g.p.	Partisan	10 g.p.
Bec de corbin	6 g.p.	Pick, Military, footman's	8 g.p.
Bill-Guisarme	6 g.p.	Pick, Military, horseman's	5 g.p.
Bow, composite short	75 g.p.	Pike, awl	3 g.p.
Bow, composite, long	100 g.p.	Quarrel (or Bolt), light, single	1 s.p.
Bow, long	60 g.p.	
Bow, short	15 g.p.	Quarrel (or Bolt), heavy, score	2 g.p.
Crossbow, heavy	20 g.p.	
Crossbow, light	12 g.p.	Ranseur	4 g.p.
Dagger and scabbard	2 g.p.	Scimitar	15 g.p.
Dart	5 s.p.	Sling & Bullets, dozen	15 s.p.
Fauchard	3 g.p.	Sling Bullets, score	10 s.p.
Fauchard — Fork	8 g.p.	Spear	1 g.p.
Flail, footman's	3 g.p.	Spetum	3 g.p.
Flail, horseman's	8 g.p.	Sword, bastard, & scabbard	25 g.p.
Fork, Military	4 g.p.	
Glaive	6 g.p.	Sword, broad, & scabbard	10 g.p.
Glaive-Guisarme	10 g.p.	Sword, long & scabbard	15 g.p.
Guisarme	5 g.p.	Sword, short & scabbard	8 g.p.
Guisarme — Voulge	7 g.p.	Sword, two-handed	30 g.p.
Halberd	9 g.p.	Trident	4 g.p.
Hammer, Lucern	7 g.p.	Voulge	2 g.p.
Hammer	1 g.p.		

Clothing

Belt	3 s.p.	Cloak	5 s.p.
Boots, high, hard	2 g.p.	Girdle, broad	2 g.p.
Boots, high, soft	1 g.p.	Girdle, normal	10 s.p.
Boots, low, hard	1 g.p.	Hat	7 s.p.
Boots, low, soft	8 s.p.	Robe	6 s.p.
Cap	1 s.p.		

Herbs

Belladona, sprig	4 s.p.	Wolvesbane, sprig	10 s.p.
Garlic, bud	5 c.p.		

Livestock

Chicken	3 c.p.	Horse, medium war	225 g.p.
Cow	10 g.p.	Horse, riding (light)	25 g.p.
Dog, guard	25 g.p.	Mule	20 g.p.
Dog, hunting	17 g.p.	Ox	15 g.p.
Donkey	8 g.p.	Pigeon	2 c.p.
Goat	1 g.p.	Piglet	1 g.p.
Hawk, large	40 g.p.	Pig	3 g.p.
Hawk, small	18 g.p.	Pony	15 g.p.
Horse, draft	30 g.p.	Sheep	2 g.p.
Horse, heavy war	300 g.p.	Songbird	4 c.p.
Horse, light war	150 g.p.		

Miscellaneous Equipment & Items

Backpack, leather	2 g.p.	Pouch, belt, large	1 g.p.
Box, iron, large	28 g.p.	Pouch, belt, small	15 s.p.
Box, iron, small	9 g.p.	Quiver, 1 doz. arrows cap.	8 s.p.
Candle, tallow	1 c.p.	Quiver, 1 score arrows cap.	12 s.p.
Candle, wax	1 s.p.	Quiver, 1 score bolts cap.	15 s.p.
Case, bone, map or scroll	5 g.p.	Quiver, 2 score bolts cap.	1 g.p.
Case, leather, map or scroll	15 s.p.	Rope, 50'	4 s.p.
Chest, wooden, large	17 s.p.	Sack, large	16 c.p.
Chest, wooden, small	8 s.p.	Sack, small	10 c.p.
Lantern, bullseye	12 g.p.	Skin for water or wine	15 s.p.
Lantern, hooded	7 g.p.	Spike, iron, large	1 c.p.
Mirror, large metal	10 g.p.	Thieves' picks & tools	30 g.p.
Mirror, small, silver	20 g.p.	Tinder Box, with flint & steel	1 g.p.
Oil, flask of	1 g.p.	Torch	1 c.p.
Pole, 10'	3 c.p.		

Provisions

Ale, pint	1 s.p.	Mead, pint	5 s.p.
Beer, small, pint	5 c.p.	Rations, iron, 1 week	5 g.p.
Food, merchant's meal	1 s.p.	Rations, standard, 1 week	3 g.p.
Food, rich meal	1 g.p.	Wine, pint, good	10 s.p.
Grain, horse meal, 1 day	1 s.p.	Wine, pint, watered	5 s.p.

Religious Items

Beads, Prayer	1 g.p.	Symbol, Holy*, wooden	7 s.p.
Incense, stick	1 g.p.	Water, Holy*, vial	25 g.p.
Symbol, Holy*, iron	2 g.p.	* or Unholy	
Symbol, Holy*, silver	50 g.p.		

Tack and Harness

Barding, chain	250 g.p.	Saddle	10 g.p.
Barding, leather	100 g.p.	Saddle Bags, large	4 g.p.
Barding, plate	500 g.p.	Saddle Bags, small	3 g.p.
Bit and Bridle	15 s.p.	Saddle Blanket	3 s.p.
Harness	12 s.p.		

Transport

Barge (or Raft), small	50 g.p.	Galley, small	10,000 g.p.
Boat, small	75 g.p.	Ship, merchant, large	15,000 g.p.
Boat, long	150 g.p.	Ship, merchant, small	5,000 g.p.
Cart	50 g.p.	Ship, war	20,000 g.p.
Galley, large	25,000 g.p.	Wagon	150 g.p.

COMBINED WEAPONS TABLES (SELECTED INFORMATION)

Weapon Type	Approximate Weight in Gold Pieces	Length	Space Required	Speed Factor	Damage vs. Opponent Size S or M	Size L
Arrow	2		see below		1-6	1-6
Axe, Battle	75	c. 4'	4'	7	1-8	1-8
Axe, Hand or throwing	50	c. 1½'	1'	4	1-6	1-4
Bardiche	125	c. 5'	5'	9	2-8	3-12
Bec de corbin	100	c. 6'	6'	9	1-8	1-6
Bill-Guisarme	150	8'+	2'	10	2-8	1-10
Bo Stick	15	c. 5'	3'	3	1-6	1-3
Club	30	c. 3'	1'-3'	4	1-6	1-3
Dagger	10	c. 15"	1'	2	1-4	1-3
Dart	5		see below		1-3	1-2
Fauchard	60	8'+	2'	8	1-6	1-8
Fauchard-Fork	80	8'	2'	8	1-8	1-10
Flail, footman's	150	c. 4'	6'	7	2-7	2-8
Flail, horseman's	35	c. 2'	4'	6	2-5	2-5
Fork, Military	75	7'+	1'	7	1-8	2-8
Glaive	75	8'+	1'	8	1-6	1-10
Glaive — Guisarme	100	8'+	1'	9	2-8	2-12
Guisarme	80	6'+	2'	8	2-8	1-8
Guisarme-Voulge	150	7'+	3'	10	2-8	2-8
Halberd	175	5'+	5'	9	1-10	2-12
Hammer, Lucern	150	5'+	5'	9	2-8	1-6
Hammer	50	c. 1½'	5'	4	2-5	1-4
Javelin	20		see below		1-6	1-6
Jo Stick	40	c. 3'	2'	2	1-6	1-4
Lance* (light horse)	50	c. 14'	1'	8	1-6	1-8
Lance* (medium horse)	100	10'	1'	7	2-7	2-12
Lance* (heavy horse)	150	12'	1'	6	3-9	3-18
Mace, footman's	100	c. 2½'	4'	7	2-7	1-6
Mace, horseman's	50	c. 1½'	2'	6	1-6	1-4
Morning Star	125	c. 4'	5'	7	2-8	2-7
Partisan	80	7'+	3'	9	1-6	2-7
Pick, Military, footman's	60	c. 4'	4'	7	2-7	2-8
Pick, Military, horseman's	40	c. 2'	2'	5	2-5	1-4
Pike, Awl	80	18'+	1'	13	1-6	1-12
Quarrel (or Bolt), light	1		see below		1-4	1-4
Quarrel (or Bolt) heavy	2		see below		2-5	2-7
Ranseur	50	8'+	1'	8	2-8	2-8
Scimitar	40	c. 3'	2'	4	1-8	1-8
Sling bullet	2		see below		2-5	2-7
Sling stone	1		see below		1-4	1-4
Spear**	40-60	5'-13'+	1'	6-8	1-6	1-8
Spetum	50	8'+	1'	8	2-7	2-12
Staff, Quarter	50	6'-8'	3'	4	1-6	1-6
Sword, Bastard	100	c. 4½'	4'+	6	2-8	2-16
Sword, Broad	75	c. 3½'	4'	5	2-8	2-7
Sword, Long	60	c. 3½'	3'	5	1-8	1-12
Sword, Short	35	c. 2'	1'	3	1-6	1-8
Sword, Two-handed	250	c. 6'	6'	10	1-10	3-18
Trident	50	4'-8'+	1'	6-8	2-7	3-12
Voulge	125	8'+	2'	10	2-8	2-8

HURLED WEAPONS AND MISSILES

	Fire Rate	Range S	M	L
Axe, hand	1	1	2	3
Bow, composite, long	2	6	12	21
Bow, composite, short	2	5	10	18
Bow, long	2	7	14	21
Bow, short	2	5	10	15
Club	1	1	2	3
Crossbow, heavy	½	8	16	24
Crossbow, light	1	6	12	18
Dagger	2	1	2	3
Dart	3	1½	3	4½
Hammer	1	1	2	3
Javelin	1	2	4	6
Sling (bullet)	1	5	10	20
Sling (stone)	1	4	8	16
Spear	1	1	2	3

ARMOR CLASS TABLE

Type of Armor	Armor Class Rating
None	10
Shield only	9
Leather or padded armor	8
Leather or padded armor + shield/ studded leather/ring mail	7
Studded leather or ring mail + shield/ scale mail	6
Scale mail + shield/chain mail	5
Chain mail + shield/splint mail/ banded mail	4
Splint or banded mail + shield/ plate mail	3
Plate mail + shield	2

See Text (pages 36-38) for complete information on these tables.

ADVANCED
DUNGEONS & DRAGONS®
PLAYERS HANDBOOK
REFERENCE SHEETS
(THESE PAGES ARE PERFORATED FOR EASY
REMOVAL IF DESIRED)
© 1978 — TSR GAMES

SPELL TABLES

CLERICS

Number	1st Level	2nd Level	3rd Level
1	Bless	Augury	Animate Dead
2	Command	Chant	Continual Light
3	Create Water	Detect Charm	Create Food & Water
4	Cure Light Wounds	Find Traps	Cure Blindness
5	Detect Evil	Hold Person	Cure Disease
6	Detect Magic	Know Alignment	Dispel Magic
7	Light	Resist Fire	Feign Death
8	Protection From Evil	Silence 15' Radius	Glyph Of Warding
9	Purify Food & Drink	Slow Poison	Locate Object
10	Remove Fear	Snake Charm	Prayer
11	Resist Cold	Speak With Animals	Remove Curse
12	Sanctuary	Spiritual Hammer	Speak With Dead

Number	4th Level	5th Level	6th Level	7th Level
1	Cure Serious Wounds	Atonement	Aerial Servant	Astral Spell
2	Detect Lie	Commune	Animate Object	Control Weather
3	Divination	Cure Critical Wounds	Blade Barrier	Earthquake
4	Exorcise	Dispel Evil	Conjure Animals	Gate
5	Lower Water	Flame Strike	Find The Path	Holy (Unholy) Word
6	Neutralize Poison	Insect Plague	Heal	Regenerate
7	Protection from Evil 10' Radius	Plane Shift	Part Water	Restoration
8	Speak With Plants	Quest	Speak With Monsters	Resurrection
9	Sticks to Snakes	Raise Dead	Stone Tell	Symbol
10	Tongues	True Seeing	Word Of Recall	Wind Walk

DRUIDS (Clerics)

Number	1st Level	2nd Level	3rd Level	4th Level
1	Animal Friendship	Barkskin	Call Lightning	Animal Summoning I
2	Detect Magic	Charm Person Or Mammal	Cure Disease	Call Woodland Beings
3	Detect Snares & Pits	Create Water	Hold Animal	Control Temperature 10' Radius
4	Entangle	Cure Light Wounds	Neutralize Poison	Cure Serious Wounds
5	Faerie Fire	Feign Death	Plant Growth	Dispel Magic
6	Invisibility To Animals	Fire Trap	Protection From Fire	Hallucinatory Forest
7	Locate Animals	Heat Metal	Pyrotechnics	Hold Plant
8	Pass Without Trace	Locate Plants	Snare	Plant Door
9	Predict Weather	Obscurement	Stone Shape	Produce Fire
10	Purify Water	Produce Flame	Summon Insects	Protection From Lightning
11	Shillelagh	Trip	Tree	Repel Insects
12	Speak With Animals	Warp Wood	Water Breathing	Speak With Plants

Number	5th Level	6th Level	7th Level
1	Animal Growth	Animal Summoning III	Animate Rock
2	Animal Summoning II	Anti-Animal Shell	Chariot Of Sustarre
3	Anti-Plant Shell	Conjure Fire Elemental	Confusion
4	Commune With Nature	Cure Critical Wounds	Conjure Earth Elemental
5	Control Winds	Feeblemind	Control Weather
6	Insect Plague	Fire Seeds	Creeping Doom
7	Pass Plant	Transport Via Plants	Finger Of Death
8	Sticks To Snakes	Turn Wood	Fire Storm
9	Transmute Rock To Mud	Wall Of Thorns	Reincarnate
10	Wall Of Fire	Weather Summoning	Transmute Metal To Wood

MAGIC-USERS

Number	1st Level	2nd Level	3rd Level	4th Level	5th Level
1	Affect Normal Fires	Audible Glamer	Blink	Charm Monster	Airy Water
2	Burning Hands	Continual Light	Clairaudience	Confusion	Animal Growth
3	Charm Person	Darkness 15' Radius	Clairvoyance	Dig	Animate Dead
4	Comprehend Languages	Detect Evil	Dispel Magic	Dimension Door	Bigby's Interposing Hand
5	Dancing Lights	Detect Invisibility	Explosive Runes	Enchanted Weapon	Cloudkill
6	Detect Magic	ESP	Feign Death	Extension I	Conjure Elemental
7	Enlarge	Fools Gold	Fireball	Fear	Cone Of Cold
8	Erase	Forget	Flame Arrow	Fire Charm	Contact Other Plane
9	Feather Fall	Invisibility	Fly	Fire Shield	Distance Distortion
10	Find Familiar	Knock	Gust Of Wind	Fire Trap	Extension II
11	Friends	Leomund's Trap	Haste	Fumble	Feeblemind
12	Hold Portal	Levitate	Hold Person	Hallucinatory Terrain	Hold Monster
13	Identify	Locate Object	Infravision	Ice Storm	Leomund's Secret Chest
14	Jump	Magic Mouth	Invisibility 10' Radius	Massmorph	Magic Jar
15	Light	Mirror Image	Leomund's Tiny Hut	Minor Globe of Invulnerability	Monster Summoning III
16	Magic Missile	Pyrotechnics	Lightning Bolt	Monster Summoning II	Mordenkainen's Faithful Hound
17	Mending	Ray Of Enfeeblement	Monster Summoning I	Plant Growth	Passwall
18	Message	Rope Trick	Phantasmal Force	Polymorph Other	Stone Shape
19	Nystul's Magic Aura	Scare	Protection From Evil 10' Radius	Polymorph Self	Telekinesis
20	Protection From Evil	Shatter	Protection From Normal Missiles	Rary's Mnemonic Enhancer	Teleport
21	Push	Stinking Cloud	Slow	Remove Curse	Transmute Rock To Mud
22	Read Magic	Strength	Suggestion	Wall Of Fire	Wall Of Force
23	Shield	Web	Tongues	Wall Of Ice	Wall Of Iron
24	Shocking Grasp	Wizard Lock	Water Breathing	Wizard Eye	Wall Of Stone
25	Sleep				
26	Spider Climb				
27	Tenser's Floating Disc				
28	Unseen Servant				
29	Ventriloquism				
30	Write				

Number	6th Level	7th Level	8th Level	9th Level
1	Anti-Magic Shell	Bigby's Grasping Hand	Antipathy/Sympathy	Astral Spell
2	Bigby's Forceful Hand	Cacodemon	Bigby's Clenched Fist	Bigby's Crushing Hand
3	Control Weather	Charm Plants	Clone	Gate
4	Death Spell	Delayed Blast Fireball	Glassteel	Imprisonment
5	Disintegrate	Drawmij's Instant Summons	Incendiary Cloud	Meteor Swarm
6	Enchant An Item	Duo-Dimension	Mass Charm	Monster Summoning VII
7	Extension III	Limited Wish	Maze	Power Word, Kill
8	Geas	Mass Invisibility	Mind Blank	Prismatic Sphere
9	Glassee	Monster Summoning V	Monster Summoning VI	Shape Change
10	Globe Of Invulnerability	Mordenkainen's Sword	Otto's Irresistible Dance	Temporal Stasis
11	Guards And Wards	Phase Door	Permanency	Time Stop
12	Invisible Stalker	Power Word, Stun	Polymorph Any Object	Wish
13	Legend Lore	Reverse Gravity	Power Word, Blind	
14	Lower Water	Simulacrum	Serten's Spell Immunity	
15	Monster Summoning IV	Statue	Symbol	
16	Move Earth	Vanish	Trap The Soul	
17	Otiluke's Freezing Sphere			
18	Part Water			
19	Project Image			
20	Reincarnation			
21	Repulsion			
22	Spiritwrack			
23	Stone To Flesh			
24	Tenser's Transformation			

ILLUSIONISTS (Magic-Users)

Number	1st Level	2nd Level	3rd Level
1	Audible Glamer	Blindness	Continual Darkness
2	Change Self	Blur	Continual Light
3	Color Spray	Deafness	Dispel Illusion
4	Dancing Lights	Detect Magic	Fear
5	Darkness	Fog Cloud	Hallucinatory Terrain
6	Detect Illusion	Hypnotic Pattern	Illusionary Script
7	Detect Invisibility	Improved Phantasmal Force	Invisibility 10' Radius
8	Gaze Reflection	Invisibility	Non-detection
9	Hypnotism	Magic Mouth	Paralyzation
10	Light	Mirror Image	Rope Trick
11	Phantasmal Force	Misdirection	Spectral Force
12	Wall Of Fog	Ventriloquism	Suggestion

Number	4th Level	5th Level	6th Level	7th Level
1	Confusion	Chaos	Conjure Animals	Alter Reality
2	Dispel Exhaustion	Demi-Shadow Monsters	Demi-Shadow Magic	Astral Spell
3	Emotion	Major Creation	Mass Suggestion	Prismatic Spray
4	Improved Invisibility	Maze	Permanent Illusion	Prismatic Wall
5	Massmorph	Projected Image	Programmed Illusion	Vision
6	Minor Creation	Shadow Door	Shades	First Level Magic-User Spells
7	Phantasmal Killer	Shadow Magic	True Sight	
8	Shadow Monsters	Summon Shadow	Veil	

Other Swords & Sorcery, Fantasy, and Science Fiction Titles from TSR

THE DUNGEONS & DRAGONS® GAME FAMILY:
BASIC DUNGEONS & DRAGONS®, **COMPLETE BASIC GAME SET.** Everything needed to begin playing D& D®: Basic Game Book, Polyhedra Dice Set, and Introductory Module "In Search of the Unknown" — especially designed for beginning players and Dungeon Masters. All in a beautifully illustrated full color game box

BASIC DUNGEONS & DRAGONS®, **basic game book** only

INTRODUCTORY MODULE B1, **"In Search of the Unknown"** only

ADVANCED DUNGEONS & DRAGONS®, **MONSTER MANUAL.** Over 350 descriptions of monsters, from Aerial Servant to Zombie, illustrated

ADVANCED DUNGEONS & DRAGONS® , **PLAYERS HANDBOOK.** Complete information on characters, levels, equipment, spells, and more

ADVANCED DUNGEONS & DRAGONS®, **DUNGEON MASTERS GUIDE.** A compilation of tables, lists, and information designed especially for the Dungeon Master

ADVENTURE MODULES FOR ADVANCED DUNGEONS & DRAGONS®
—DUNGEON MODULE G1, **Steading of the Hill Giant Chief**
—DUNGEON MODULE G2, **Glacial Rift of the Frost Giant Jarl**
—DUNGEON MODULE G3, **Hall of the Fire Giant King**
—DUNGEON MODULE D1, **Descent Into the Depths of the Earth**
—DUNGEON MODULE D2, **Shrine of the Kuo-Toa**
—DUNGEON MODULE D3, **Vault of the Drow**
—DUNGEON MODULE S1, **The Tomb of Horrors**

DUNGEONS & DRAGONS® PLAYING AIDS
—DUNGEON GEOMORPHS
  Set One, **Basic Dungeon**
  Set Two, **Caves & Caverns**
  Set Three, **Lower Dungeon**
—OUTDOOR GEOMORPHS
  Set One, **Walled City**
—MONSTER & TREASURE ASSORTMENTS
  Set One, **Levels One-Three**
  Set Two, **Levels Four-Six**
  Set Three, **Levels Seven-Nine**

DUNGEONS & DRAGONS® CHARACTER RECORDS — A pad of 23+ record sheets covering every essential fact regarding your D & D® character

DUNGEONS & DRAGONS®, **Gods, Demi-Gods & Heroes.** The deities of myth and mythos compiled for incorporation in the D & D® campaign

Original **DUNGEONS & DRAGONS®** *Collector's Editions*
  —DUNGEONS & DRAGONS®, three booklets, boxed
  —SUPPLEMENTS
  I. GREYHAWK
  II. BLACKMOOR
  III. ELDRITCH WIZARDRY

SWORDS & SPELLS — DUNGEONS & DRAGONS® miniature wargame rules for 1:10/1:1 scale

THE DRAGON — The only professional magazine of swords & sorcery, fantasy, and science fiction gaming and related fiction   Single Issue
                    13-Issue Subscription (U.S. & North America)
                              (Overseas)

For a complete listing of DUNGEONS & DRAGONS® miniature figures, send two first class stamps.

DUNGEON! — The boardgame of fantastic Dungeon Adventuring for 1-12 players, boxed

GAMMA WORLD — Science Fantasy Role Playing Game, set upon a strange future world where nuclear disaster has altered the form of life to the forbidding and terrible. Includes rulebook, game map, and polyhedra dice set — all in a beautifully illustrated full color box

CHAINMAIL — Rules for Medieval Miniatures (plus Fantasy)

WARLOCKS & WARRIORS — Introductory level fantasy boardgame for 2-6 players age 8 years and up

METAMORPHOSIS ALPHA — Game of science fiction adventures on a lost starship

STAR PROBE — Complete boardgame of adventure, exploration, and conflict in space: for 1 to 8 or more players, this game system will be expanded by several additional booklets in the near future.

STAR EMPIRES — The 2nd part of the STAR PROBE game system which allows play to progress to the governing of interstellar empires and conducting fleet combat; game includes the map from STAR PROBE.

ACCESSORIES
  Polyhedra Dice
  Percentile Dice
  Small Hex Sheet Pads

If your favorite hobby, book, toy, or department store does not have what you want, you may order from us direct. **ALL MAIL ORDERS MUST INCLUDE $1.00 FOR POSTAGE AND HANDLING, REGARDLESS OF HOW MANY OR HOW FEW ITEMS ARE ORDERED.** For a complete listing of the entire line of TSR games and rules, send $2.00 for our catalog.

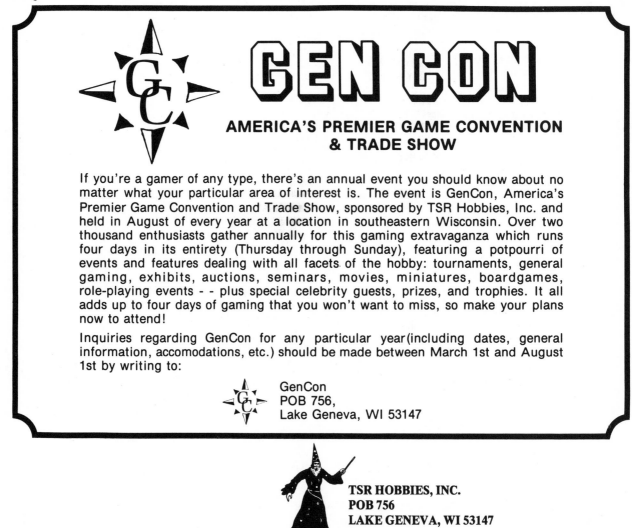

GEN CON

AMERICA'S PREMIER GAME CONVENTION & TRADE SHOW

If you're a gamer of any type, there's an annual event you should know about no matter what your particular area of interest is. The event is GenCon, America's Premier Game Convention and Trade Show, sponsored by TSR Hobbies, Inc. and held in August of every year at a location in southeastern Wisconsin. Over two thousand enthusiasts gather annually for this gaming extravaganza which runs four days in its entirety (Thursday through Sunday), featuring a potpourri of events and features dealing with all facets of the hobby: tournaments, general gaming, exhibits, auctions, seminars, movies, miniatures, boardgames, role-playing events - - plus special celebrity guests, prizes, and trophies. It all adds up to four days of gaming that you won't want to miss, so make your plans now to attend!

Inquiries regarding GenCon for any particular year(including dates, general information, accomodations, etc.) should be made between March 1st and August 1st by writing to:

GenCon
POB 756,
Lake Geneva, WI 53147

TSR HOBBIES, INC.
POB 756
LAKE GENEVA, WI 53147